VISUAL QUICKSTART GUIDE

ADOBE GOLIVE 6

FOR MACINTOSH AND WINDOWS

Shelly Brisbin

 Peachpit Press

Visual QuickStart Guide
Adobe GoLive 6 for Macintosh and Windows
Shelly Brisbin

Peachpit Press
1249 Eighth Street
Berkeley, CA 94710
510/524-2178
800/283-9444
510/524-2221 (fax)
Find us on the World Wide Web at: http://www.peachpit.com
Peachpit Press is a division of Addison Wesley Longman

Copyright © 2002 by Shelly Brisbin

Editor: Whitney Walker
Production Coordinator: Lisa Brazieal
Copyeditor: Kate McKinley
Tech editors: Tonya Engst, Jeep Hauser
Compositor: Christi Payne
Indexer: Emily Glossbrenner, FireCrystal Communications
Cover Design: The Visual Group

ISBN 0-321-11222-9

9 8 7 6 5 4 3 2 1

Printed and bound in the United States of America

Dedication

For the finest bunch of friends a cranky writer could ever have:

Kate, Phyllis, Teresa, and Dawn

Acknowledgements

Here's to Whitney Walker, my Peachpit editor, for stage-managing this project. Thanks also go to Lisa Brazieal, Christi Payne, Kate McKinley, and Emily Glossbrenner—the great production and copyediting team at Peachpit Press. Technical editor Tonya Engst made sure that everything I wrote was true, and Jeep Hauser applied a fine-tooth comb to Chapter 18, "The Workgroup Server." The fabulous Kate Hayes took about half of the screen shots in this book and helped out with Windows consistency checking, too.

I was fortunate to have the help of three great contributing writers. Thanks to Steven Shmerler who revised (and renamed) Chapter 9, "Floating Boxes and Positioning." Steven is a Web site consultant, designer, and developer in Los Angeles, who runs Sasnet Design (www.sasnet.com). Richard McLean documented an astonishing number of new actions in Chapter 19, "Using Actions." Richard is a Web developer (www.designeffect.com) and artist (www.byrichard.com) from Newcastle, Australia. Clifford VanMeter, Director of Web Services for Playbox Media (www.playboxmedia.com), helped out with a major update of Chapter 20, "Animation and QuickTime." Thanks to fellow GoLive guru Deborah Shadovitz for introducing me to these guys.

I couldn't have put the book together so quickly without the support of John Kranz, Erik Cottrell, Diana Hollander, and the rest of the Adobe team. The same goes for the gang of GoLive geniuses on the beta list.

My agent, Debbie McKenna of Moore Literary Agency, always knows where my next meal is coming from, and that's a good thing.

As always, warm and fuzzy thanks go to my husband, Frank Feuerbacher, a super-groovy guy.

TABLE OF CONTENTS

INTRODUCTION

Welcome to *Adobe GoLive 6 for Macintosh and Windows: Visual QuickStart Guide*. This book is intended to help you get the most from Adobe GoLive and to acquaint you with building Web pages generally.

Even if you've used Web authoring tools before, you'll probably find that GoLive is a new experience: It takes a comprehensive approach to page design and site management that isn't available elsewhere.

But I'm not here to sell GoLive to you. You probably already own a copy or are considering making it a part of your Web-publishing arsenal. Whatever the case, my goal is to give you the information you'll need to make the most of the software and a convenient reference as you learn how to work with it.

Who Should Read This Book

This book is an introduction to GoLive. I cover most features of the software in enough detail to allow you to design Web pages and build Web sites quickly and easily. I've designed the book so that you can easily leave it open on your desk as you work in GoLive, following along with the step-by-step tasks.

It is not intended as a comprehensive guide to GoLive, however. Advanced Web authors, particularly those who use animation, scripting, and dynamic development tools will find this book a useful introduction, but may want to consult other resources for complete coverage of these topics.

For some readers, this book will serve as an introduction to Web authoring, as well as a GoLive tutorial. Though I don't spend a great deal of time explaining the basics of HTML or the Web, new Web authors need not fear. The step-by-step approach of this book and the visual orientation of GoLive's tools make it possible to design increasingly complex pages without knowledge of HTML.

If you've created Web pages before, dive right in. You won't be bored, even in the early chapters. Though they're introductory, the first few chapters relate specifically to GoLive, so they'll be useful to you as you learn the conventions of both the software and the book.

Whatever your level of Web authoring experience, use this book to jumpstart your adventure with GoLive. You'll be designing cool Web pages and complete sites before you know it.

How This Book Is Organized

Chapters 1 and 2 introduce you to GoLive's interface and basic tools. You'll learn how Adobe organizes tools, what they're called, and how to begin using them. Chapters 3 through 8 introduce you to basic page-building techniques, including adding and formatting text, working with page layout, and adding images and links. In Chapters 9 through 14, you'll explore more advanced page-building topics, including the use of floating boxes, forms, frames, Cascading Style Sheets, HTML code, and multimedia.

Chapters 15 through 18 introduce GoLive's extensive site-management capabilities, moving Web publishing beyond merely linking a bunch of pages. You'll encounter the visual and logical tools GoLive gives you to organize and maintain a killer Web site, including Adobe's new Web Workgroup Server for collaborative development. For advanced and ambitious Web authors, Chapters 19 through 21 introduce GoLive actions—a scripting tool that uses JavaScript and Cascading Style Sheets to automate Web page activity and add special effects. You'll also learn about GoLive's animation and QuickTime authoring features and about dynamic content, GoLive's interface for developing data-driven Web sites.

Visual QuickStart conventions

The heart of the Visual QuickStart Guide format is taking a step-by-step approach to teaching GoLive's fundamentals. You'll find instructions and tutorials on all major and most minor GoLive features and functions. Along with each step-by-step example, you'll find screen shots that depict palettes, toolbars, menus, configuration windows, and Web pages as they are created and modified throughout the book.

✔ **Tip**

■ Each chapter contains tips that point out important tricks and suggestions for using GoLive better.

Mac or Windows?

GoLive is available for Macintosh OS 9.1 or later and OS X (Native and Classic mode), Windows 98, 2000, Me, and XP. The tools and interface for each platform are almost identical, though, so even if a particular screen shot represents a platform other than yours, I believe you'll be able to find your way around with no trouble. In those rare cases where a tool, window, or screen differs, I've included an example from each platform.

Windows and Macintosh computers use slightly different keyboard shortcuts and other interface conventions, and GoLive typically follows the rules set down by each operating system. When there's a difference, I've noted it within the text like this:

Press Command-Option-O (Mac) or Control-Alt-O (Windows).

What's New in GoLive 6

GoLive is a mature product. Version 6 looks a lot like version 5, which was the first edition of GoLive to sport the Adobe interface familiar to users of Photoshop, Illustrator, and other applications from the company. Still, there are some new, and many enhanced, features in the new version.

New operating systems

GoLive 6 adds support for Mac OS X and Windows XP, the newest operating systems from Apple and Microsoft. Both systems look very different from their predecessors (still supported by GoLive), but all versions behave pretty much the same way in practice. Throughout this book, I've used screen shots from the Mac OS X, Windows 2000, and Mac OS 9 versions of GoLive.

Authoring tools

GoLive 6 gives you new tools for simultaneously working with code and graphical views of a page. You can split the Document window to see both the HTML and graphical versions of the page, and you can view the current HTML tag, even when you're working in the Layout Editor, with the Markup Tree bar. You can find and fix problems with HTML code, or just zoom in on specific types of code using the Highlight palette. I describe these features in Chapter 12, "Working with Code." GoLive 6 also has enhanced table-building (Chapter 7, "Working with Tables") and Cascading Style Sheet management (Chapter 13, "Working with Style Sheets").

Another new authoring option is the ability to create versions of a Web page for WML-compatible wireless devices.

Adobe Web Workgroup Server

The new Adobe Web Workgroup Server is not a GoLive component at all, but a separate, free tool that allows Web authors to collaborate on the development of GoLive sites. It's a Web server and WebDAV server that stores and manages GoLive sites. Each developer with access to the server can download a copy of the shared GoLive site and work on it locally, checking out files, modifying them, and returning them to the server so that others can edit them. I cover all this and more in Chapter 18, "The Workgroup Server."

Dynamic content

Known as Dynamic Link in version 5, Dynamic Content is a GoLive module and a collection of tools that you can use to build data-driven Web sites. Where Dynamic Link supported only ASP scripting, dynamic content works with JSP and PHP, too. The package now includes Apache, PHP, and Tomcat Web servers, along with sample sites and databases that you can use to start dynamic sites for testing. You'll find a simple overview of this in Chapter 21, "Dynamic Content."

Site management

Site diagramming (formerly known as site design) features have been enhanced to make the diagrams easier to present in printed or electronic form during the development process. You can add labels and objects to diagrams and save them as PDF (Portable Document Format) files (Chapter 15, "Building Sites").

Images and rich media

Adobe continues to tighten the connection between GoLive and its image and media manipulation tools, Illustrator, Photoshop, and LiveMotion. Among other updates, GoLive now supports variable data, allowing authors to develop multiple versions of a graphic or banner (Chapter 4, "Working with Images"). The QuickTime editor has also been enhanced, and GoLive 6 adds a SMIL editor (Chapter 20, "Animation and QuickTime").

LEARNING YOUR WAY AROUND

1

When you open the Adobe GoLive application, you'll see that there's a lot happening on screen. The GoLive desktop is not simply a place to create Web pages—it's an environment, with professional tools and lots of different ways to look at the page or the entire Web site you're working on. Like other Adobe applications, GoLive uses a number of palette windows to provide access to tools and configuration options. The Document window, where you build your pages, provides several ways to look at the same document. There's a context-sensitive toolbar showing text formatting tools as you build the page, site management options for keeping large groups of pages under control, and more.

In this chapter, I'll give you a quick tour of GoLive, touching on the following:

◆ The GoLive workspace

◆ The Document window

◆ The toolbar

◆ The Objects and Color palettes

◆ The Inspector and View palettes

◆ Auxiliary palettes

◆ Site management tools

◆ The GoLive interface

◆ Getting help

The GoLive Workspace

The GoLive desktop, or *workspace*, as Adobe has dubbed it, consists of windows, palettes, toolbars, and menus that you can arrange in almost any configuration you like. You can save those custom configurations, or use the default workspace. I'll show you how to customize and save the look of the workspace a bit later in this chapter. For the moment, I'll introduce the major parts of the workspace and show you how GoLive lets you view the same information in multiple ways.

What do you want to work on?

When you launch GoLive for the first time, an introductory screen (**Figure 1.1**) gives you three choices: begin a new page, begin a new Web site, or open an existing file (this can be any file that GoLive can open).

You can disable this startup screen by clicking the check box at the bottom of the window. For now, click New Page to open a blank document. The GoLive workspace appears.

The first thing you'll notice in the workspace is the Document window—an empty window where you'll build your Web pages. The GoLive workspace also includes a number of palette windows containing tools you'll use to add objects to your pages and configure them. At the top of the screen is a context-sensitive toolbar. **Figure 1.2** shows the GoLive workspace as you see it when you first launch the Mac OS 9 version of the program. **Figure 1.3** shows the Windows 2000 workspace. We'll work our way around the workspace in this chapter.

✔ Tip

■ The figures shown here show all of the items you see in the workspace when you first launch GoLive. Depending on the size and resolution of your screen, items may be placed a bit differently on your monitor.

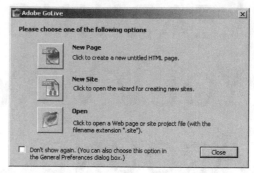

Figure 1.1 Launching GoLive displays an intro window where you can choose to begin a new file or Web site or to open an existing file.

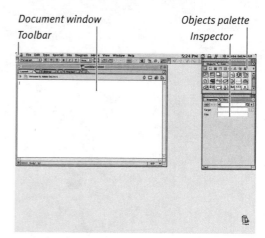

Figure 1.2 The workspace as it appears when you open the Mac OS 9 version of GoLive.

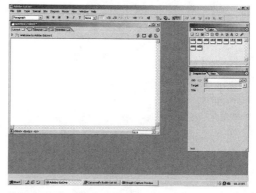

Figure 1.3 The Windows 2000 workspace resembles the Mac version.

Figure 1.4 Windows in GoLive are topped by tabs that display different things when clicked. The Document window (top), a palette window holding the Objects and Color palettes (middle), and Inspector/View window (bottom) are three examples.

Tabbed interface

If you think there are a lot of windows on the GoLive screen, I would agree with you. On the other hand, consider the alternative. Look at the top of any window on screen. Notice the labeled tabs below the title bar. Because GoLive windows are tabbed, Adobe can cram lots of tools and features into these windows, making them quickly available from the workspace. As you can see in **Figure 1.4**, some windows include two layers of tabs. The Inspector/View window, for example, may display a second layer of tabs with the Inspector tab selected.

The Document Window

The Document window is where you build and view the HTML pages you create in GoLive. Each tab in the Document window (six in the Mac OS, five in Windows) provides a different view of your page, giving you several working views of your page (called Editors), as well as preview options you can use to simulate the way the page will look in a Web browser. (For final page proofing, you should always use an actual Web browser—and preferably several different ones.)

Editors allow you to look at and work with the same Web page in four different ways. Use the tabs at the top of the Document window (**Figure 1.5**) to switch among the editors and preview windows for the current document.

Layout Editor

The Layout Editor gives you a more or less WYSIWYG (what you see is what you get) view of a Web page as you build it. You'll probably spend much of your time working in the Layout Editor.

When you launch GoLive and create a new page or open an existing one, it appears in the Layout Editor by default. To display the page in a different view, simply click a tab at the top of the Document window.

Frame Editor

Use the Frame Editor to examine and work on frames-based Web pages. Frames-based pages are actually composites of two or more HTML documents. The Frame Editor shows frames and icons for each file that makes up the frameset. The Frame Editor is empty if the document you're building does not use frames. You'll learn more about frames in Chapter 11, "Working with Frames."

Figure 1.5 Change the view by clicking a Document window tab.

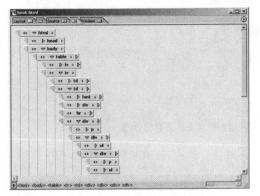

Figure 1.6 In the Outline Editor, you see the page as an HTML hierarchy.

Source Editor

The Source Editor displays the HTML code that makes up your page. If you know HTML, you can use the Source Editor to examine or edit your page. I'll have more to say about the Source Editor in Chapter 12, "Working with Code."

Outline Editor

The Outline Editor displays the HTML tags behind your Web page within a hierarchical structure that looks like an outline you might build in a word processing application (**Figure 1.6**). Use this view as a guide to your page's organization and to place new elements at the correct hierarchical location. I'll cover the Outline Editor in Chapter 12.

Layout Preview

In the Layout Preview, you can see an approximation of how the layout and objects you've created will look and behave when viewed in a Web browser. In many cases, the page will look very much the way it does in the Layout Editor. You should not count on the preview for accurate representations or advanced features, like JavaScript or animation. Always verify your work in one or more browsers before making your pages live.

Frame Preview

The Frame Preview (Mac OS only) assembles the frames that make up a frames-based Web page and displays the page as it will appear in a Web browser. There is no Frame Preview in the Windows version of GoLive. You will need to use a frames-capable browser to preview frames in Windows. Even if you have access to the Frame Preview, don't count on it for an accurate view of framed pages. Always preview framed pages in one or more Web browsers.

Other Document window tools

You can reach several other editing windows from the Document window. You can also split the window into two parts and simultaneously view a page's layout and source code (**Figure 1.7**). Finally, you can add tags to your document's head section.

Head section and page title

If you know anything about HTML, you know that every HTML document consists of two sections, the head and the body. The text and objects you see when you view a Web page are all part of the page's body and can be created in the main section of the GoLive Document window. The head section of an HTML document contains information about the page as a whole and can include instructions or scripts that tell a Web browser how to handle the page. To create and modify these elements in GoLive, use the Head area of the Document window. To view the head section, click the triangle

next to the page title at the top of the Layout Editor. Chapter 12 describes the head section.

The page title, which by default is "Welcome to Adobe GoLive 6," is next to the head section triangle. You can change the title by selecting the text and typing over it.

Advanced editors

The four buttons near the upper-right corner of the Document window take you to other windows where you can edit advanced content. The editors are

- ◆ JavaScript Editor
- ◆ DHTML Timeline Editor
- ◆ Content Source Editor
- ◆ CSS Editor

Clicking each of these buttons in the Document window opens a new window and gives you access to the tools for each advanced editor. I'll describe the use of these editors in later chapters of this book.

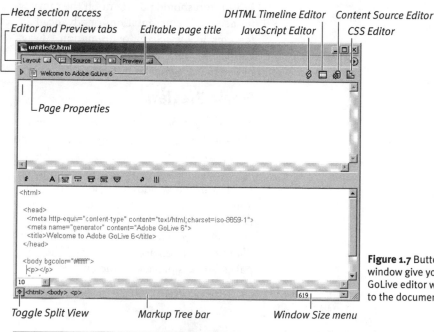

Head section access

Editor and Preview tabs   *Editable page title*   *DHTML Timeline Editor* *Content Source Editor*

JavaScript Editor   *CSS Editor*

Page Properties

Toggle Split View   *Markup Tree bar*   *Window Size menu*

Figure 1.7 Buttons in the Document window give you access to other GoLive editor windows as well as to the document's head section.

Split Source view

Though you can use the Source Editor to view and edit the HTML code for a Web page, it's often useful to see the layout and code at the same time. When you click the Toggle Split View button in the lower-left corner of the Document window, the window splits into two panes. The upper pane contains the editor you were working in when you clicked, and the lower pane contains the Source Editor. Changes you make in one pane are reflected in the other. Click the button again to restore your original view. You'll learn more about how to use this split view in Chapter 12.

Markup Tree bar

The Markup Tree bar, adjacent to the Toggle Split View button, gives you another way to view source code while using a graphical page view. When you click anywhere in the Document window, the Markup Tree bar displays the current tag and the HTML hierarchy that leads to it. Once again, consult Chapter 12 for details on using the Markup Tree bar.

Page size menu

Web page widths are most often expressed in pixels—a platform-neutral measurement used to build Web pages with a uniform width. To size the Document window for the page width you want, choose it from the Page Size pop-up in the lower right corner of the window. You can select one of the options provided or drag the window's lower-right corner to choose your own width. See Chapter 2, "Your First GoLive Project."

The Toolbar

Just like most modern office applications, GoLive's screen is topped by a toolbar. In the Layout Editor, the toolbar is primarily used to format text (**Figure 1.8**). You can choose a text format (head, paragraph, text, preformatted, and so on), and apply font size, alignment, indent, and more. You can also create or break HTML links and create lists in several formats.

The toolbar is context-sensitive. This means the toolbar changes to match what you're working on—some GoLive modes, including the Outline Editor and the site management interface, have their own toolbars. I'll explore each set of toolbar options as we move through this book. **Figure 1.9** shows the toolbar as it appears when you work in the GoLive site management interface.

Figure 1.8 The toolbar, as it appears in the Layout Editor and the Source Editor.

Figure 1.9 Here's another context-sensitive version of the toolbar—the one you see when using the site management interface. Using the toolbar in this context, you can add or delete pages from the site, change your view of the site, and change settings associated with your site, among other things.

Internet Explorer
Netscape Communicator™

Figure 1.10 Choose a browser from the Show in Browser menu on the toolbar. For browsers to appear there, you must set them up with the Edit command.

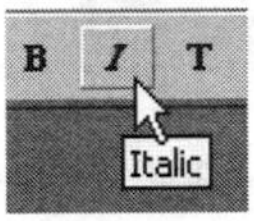

Figure 1.11 When you move the cursor over a toolbar item, a tool tip appears. This works whether the toolbar button is active or dimmed.

To use the toolbar:

1. With the Layout Editor open in the Document window, type some text.

2. Select the text.

3. Click an alignment or formatting item from the toolbar. The text changes accordingly.

✔ Tips

- The toolbar includes a button that will open the current document in a Web browser so you can see how your Web page will look to a visitor using that browser (**Figure 1.10**). To compare the look of your page in several browsers, add more browsers to the menu by choosing Edit from the Browser menu and then locating browsers you want to add. Click Find All to have GoLive search your computer for all installed browsers.

- To see what a toolbar button does, move the cursor over the button. A tool tip appears below the button (**Figure 1.11**).

The Workgroup toolbar

You can use GoLive to build Web pages and sites by yourself, or you can use it to collaborate with a group of developers and designers. The GoLive Workgroup Server software is included with the GoLive application and may be used within your organization. If you are part of a GoLive workgroup, you can use the Workgroup toolbar (located to the right of the main toolbar, by default) to connect with the server and check files in and out. If you aren't part of a workgroup, you can hide that toolbar by choosing Window > Workgroup Toolbar. Chapter 18, "The Workgroup Server," describes these features in detail.

THE TOOLBAR

The Objects Palette

Most of the tools you'll use to add objects to your Web pages can be found on the Objects palette (**Figure 1.12**). The Objects palette is actually composed of 11 separate sets of icons, each of which is accessible from the buttons at the top of the Objects palette. (In case you were wondering, sets is an Adobe term, and I will use it for the remainder of this book.)

To use an Objects palette icon, click the button for the set containing the object you want and drag and drop the icon into the Document window. In most cases, you can also double-click the icon. You use Objects palette icons to add layout grids, images, lines, Java applets, and tags that "iconically" specify most other HTML items. **Figure 1.13** shows an icon being dragged from the Objects palette into an empty Document window.

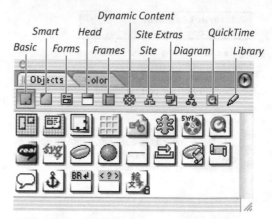

Figure 1.12 The Objects palette organizes icons into 11 sets. Each icon adds an object or some other piece of HTML to the current document when you drag or double-click the icon.

Figure 1.13 Use an Objects palette icon by dragging it from the palette into the Document window. In many cases, you can accomplish the same thing by double-clicking the icon.

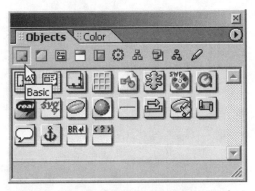

Figure 1.14 Find out what kinds of icons are stored under a button by moving the cursor over the button and looking at the tool tip.

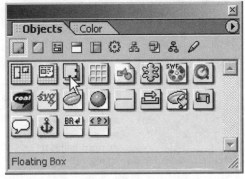

Figure 1.15 To find out the name of a palette icon, move the cursor over it and note its name in the lower-left corner of the Objects palette window.

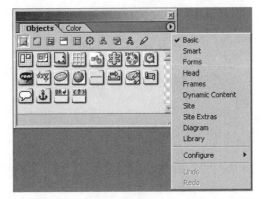

Figure 1.16 Use the menu in the upper-right corner of the Objects palette to view a specific set.

✔ Tips

- If you don't see the Objects palette when you launch GoLive, choose Window > Objects (or type Command-2 on the Mac and Control-2 in Windows) to display it.

- Objects palette set labels appear as tool tips when you move the cursor over the buttons (**Figure 1.14**). To see labels for individual icons, move your cursor over an icon and its name appears in the lower-left border of the palette (**Figure 1.15**).

- Like all other windows in GoLive, the Objects palette can be resized, either to view more icons, or to get it out of your way. Just drag the grow box in the lower-right corner of the palette to change its size. You can enlarge the palette to see all of its icons or make it smaller and scroll to see those that aren't visible.

- You can move between sets in the Objects palette by clicking the buttons or you can use the flyout menu in the upper-right corner of the Objects palette (**Figure 1.16**).

The Inspector

The Objects palette and the context-sensitive Inspector work together to give you control over the tools you use to build Web pages. In fact, they're the heart of the page-building interface. Once you've added an item (text, image, multimedia file, applet, or other object) to the page, you can configure its attributes in the Inspector. The Inspector window is empty until you select an object in GoLive, and its appearance and options change depending upon the object you choose.

To use the Inspector:

1. Drag an icon from the Objects palette into the Document window, or click an object that's already there.

2. Notice that the Inspector window is no longer empty, but contains buttons and fields. (If you don't see the Inspector, choose Window > Inspector.)

3. Click another object, or type some text in the Document window, and notice that the Inspector changes again to display other options.

As you can see in **Figure 1.17**, some Inspector windows have several sets of attributes, organized under tabs, but others don't. Click one of the tabs in the Image Inspector to view more options. **Figure 1.18** shows the Link tab for the Image Inspector.

✔ Tip

- If you need to change an object's attributes after you've placed it on a page, just click the object, and its Inspector returns.

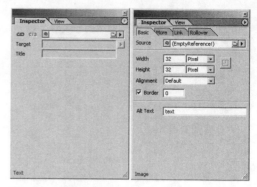

Figure 1.17 Here are the Text (left) and Image (right) Inspectors. You'll also use Inspectors to build forms, tables, multimedia files, and more.

Figure 1.18 Click the Link tab in the Inspector to set more attributes for an image.

Figure 1.19 The View palette lets you choose what items to show as you work on a GoLive document and how they should look.

Figure 1.20 When you're working on a site, the View palette gives you control over the appearance of the Site window.

The View palette: An inspector for pages and sites

See the tab labeled *View* adjacent to the Inspector tab in the Inspector window? The View palette is not really a part of the Inspector; it's another GoLive palette that just happens to share a window with the Inspector. In the View palette, you set options that tell GoLive what items to show and how to display a page or a site. Like the Inspector, the View palette is context-sensitive, changing based on what you're doing in GoLive. **Figure 1.19** shows the View palette as it appears when you're working on a GoLive document (a page). When you work with the GoLive site management interface, the View palette changes to give you control over what items are displayed in the text-based and graphical site views, and how they appear (**Figure 1.20**).

THE INSPECTOR

The Color Palette

The Color palette allows you to choose and add color to elements in your Web pages. You can color the background, text, links, table cells—almost any element GoLive offers. Just choose a color from the palette and drag it onto an object you want to color, or use the Color field in the Inspector to add color to an object. Learn more about using color in Chapter 5, "Working with Color."

The Color palette shares a window with the Objects palette. You can either open it with a click or a menu command, or activate it by using the Color field in an Inspector that supports color change.

Just like the Objects palette, the Color palette contains sets that organize its tools and color choices (**Figure 1.21**). Several sets (Grayscale, RGB, CMYK) represent the color types found in image manipulation applications such as Photoshop. Other sets (HSB, HSV, Palettes) allow you to choose colors from palettes that are optimized for viewing on a computer screen. Still other sets give you color options (Web Color and Web Name Colors) that match the Web color standard supported by all Web browsers that adhere to the standards set by the World Wide Web Consortium (known as "the W3C"). Finally, one set (Site Color) gives you a place to store custom colors that you have associated with a site you built in GoLive.

To open the Color palette:

◆ Choose Window > Color.

or

Click the Color tab in the window containing the Objects palette. The Color palette appears.

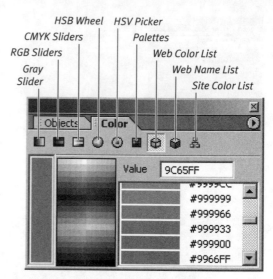

Figure 1.21 The nine sets of the Color palette.

Figure 1.22 Drag a color into the Color field to apply it to the selected object.

To add color to text:

1. With a document open and the Color palette visible, choose a color from one of the Color palette sets by clicking the set's button and then locating the color you want.

2. Click the Color palette's preview pane and drag onto the text you created. The text changes color.

To color an object or background:

1. Add an object such as a table, layout grid, or floating box to the Document window.

2. Open the Color palette and choose a color.

3. Drag the Color from the preview pane into the Color field of the Inspector (**Figure 1.22**).

Auxiliary Palettes

GoLive has a number of additional palettes that are sometimes available in the workspace and sometimes hidden, depending on the display choices you've made. Like the Inspector, these palettes give you access to configuration options for objects or items that are a part of your GoLive site. Each palette window includes two to four palettes.

The auxiliary palette windows that contain multiple palettes don't have names; they're simply windows containing several palettes, conveniently located on the GoLive workspace.

In addition, there are other palettes that are not grouped, and can be activated from the Window menu.

To open an auxiliary palette:

◆ Choose the palette from the Window menu.

or

Within the GoLive workspace, click the tab of the auxiliary palette you want to use.

✔ Tips

■ Auxiliary palettes are visible but not activated until you select objects or work in views that support them.

■ Previous versions of GoLive displayed auxiliary palettes by default. In GoLive 6, only the Inspector/View and Objects/Color palette windows appear when you choose Window > Workspace > Default Workspace. If you select several auxiliary palettes from the Window menu, however, they will arrange themselves neatly in the workspace, as shown in **Figure 1.23**.

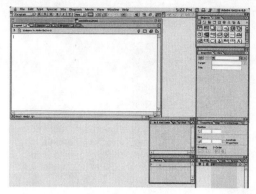

Figure 1.23 The workspace remains orderly, even with four auxiliary palette windows displayed.

Figure 1.24 Work with groups of objects in the Transform palette.

Figure 1.25 Align objects in all sorts of ways using the Align palette.

Figure 1.26 Add and work with pattern images in the Tracing Image palette.

Transform, Align, and Tracing Image palettes

The Transform and Align palettes share a window and often work together. Use the Transform palette to manage the position and size of objects, and combine them into groups (**Figure 1.24**). The Align palette lets you position objects relative to one another or to the Document window itself (**Figure 1.25**). Learn more about both palettes in Chapter 8, "Working with Layout Grids."

The Tracing Image palette, in the same window as Transform and Align, lets you control images that can be used as frameworks for page design—or as backgrounds for HTML pages (**Figure 1.26**). A tracing image functions as a pattern—you add it to a GoLive document before you place other objects, using the tracing image as a guide during layout. The Tracing Image palette gives you control over the opacity and location of the image. Chapter 4, "Working with Images," describes the use of the Tracing Image palette.

Floating Boxes, Table, and Actions palettes

Floating boxes and tables are HTML objects that help you position text, images, and other objects on the page. (You'll learn more about tables and floating boxes in Chapters 7 and 9, respectively). Actions (see Chapter 19) are prebuilt JavaScripts that allow you to add automated functions to your site.

Floating boxes, tables, and actions each have their own Inspectors, which become available when you create or select the item in question. The auxiliary palettes, however, give you further management options. In the Floating Boxes palette, you can manage multiple floating boxes, naming and positioning them relative to one another (**Figure 1.27**). The Table palette lets you manipulate the contents of table cells (by sorting the cells) and includes options for custom table formatting (**Figure 1.28**). The Table Inspector, on the other hand, assists you with building the table and its HTML attributes. What you do in the Table palette is much more specific to GoLive. While you do the customization in the Table Inspector, you can't really see what it looks like without the Table palette. Using the Actions palette, you can attach JavaScripts to objects you've already added to the page and configured. The Actions palette provides quick access to all of the actions included with GoLive (**Figure 1.29**).

✔ Tip

- The mild-mannered palette window I've described in this section is quite small when used to display floating box names. When you click the Table or Actions tab, the palette window gets larger—a feature unique to this group of GoLive palettes. Like all windows in GoLive, you can change the size of the palette further with the grow box in the lower-right corner of the window.

Figure 1.27 Use the Floating Boxes palette to view all of the floating boxes on a page. You can control their visibility and lock them in place.

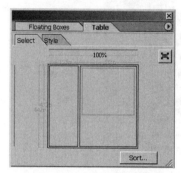

Figure 1.28 The Table palette shows the outline of the selected table. This one has been customized to form a framework for a complete Web page.

Figure 1.29 Set up actions to accompany HTML elements (such as images) in the Actions palette.

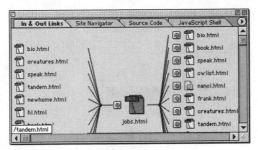

Figure 1.30 Use In & Out Links any time you want to see what the current file links to, and the condition of those links (if they are broken).

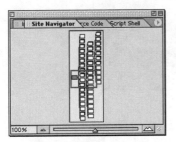

Figure 1.31 Drag the box to center the view of your Web site on the area inside the Site Navigator.

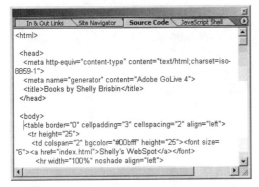

Figure 1.32 The Source Code palette gives you a view of the code for your page as you build it in the Document window.

In & Out Links, Site Navigator, Source Code, and JavaScript Shell palettes

The In & Out Links palette is very useful (**Figure 1.30**). Here you can view all of the items in your site that link to an open Web page, as well as links within that page. The Site Navigator palette is used when a graphical view of a GoLive site file is open and you need to move around the view (**Figure 1.31**). You'll read more about both these tabs in Chapter 16, "Viewing and Managing Sites."

The Source Code palette gives you a different view of the currently open document (**Figure 1.32**). You can build your page in the Layout Editor, and keep an eye on the code the program generates in the Source Code palette. Of course, you can use the Source Editor to view and edit code, but the Source Code palette offers the advantage of two simultaneous views, each in its own window. There will be more about the Source Code palette in Chapter 12.

The JavaScript Shell palette is used by developers to edit their own JavaScripts in GoLive.

The History palette

The History palette is like a super Undo command where you can back out of changes you've made to your page, one at a time (**Figure 1.33**). Say, for example, you're working on a table and make several changes to its size and contents. Then you realize that the change you made just before you added the new text to a cell should not have been made. Unlike the familiar Edit > Undo command, History lets you choose to undo changes in any order you like, just by selecting them. Just locate the change you want to undo in the History palette (they're called *states*) and select it. All of your recent actions except this single change are retained. Deleting a state removes that state and those that came after it. (States are added from the top down; that is, the oldest state is at the top of the list, the most recent one at the bottom.)

By default the History palette gives you 20 levels of undo. You can add more undos with the History Options command in the palette's flyout menu.

Highlight palette

Use the Highlight palette (**Figure 1.34**) to select code that you want to highlight. This palette is often used to check HTML syntax for errors. You can also have the Highlight palette color link warnings, particular HTML tag types, cascading style sheet code, and so forth. The choices you make in the Highlight palette are then highlighted in the Document window. Items that match your chosen highlights also appear in the window at the bottom of the Highlight palette.

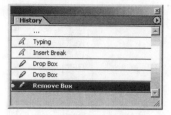

Figure 1.33 The History palette allows you to undo changes you've made as you work.

Figure 1.34 Use the Highlight palette to add color to certain types of code.

Figure 1.35 Apply predefined HTML formatting to text with the HTML Styles palette.

Figure 1.36 The CSS palette displays all CSS styles that are available in the current document.

HTML Styles palette

Like style sheets in a word processing or desktop publishing application, the HTML Styles palette (**Figure 1.35**) is a tool for creating and saving custom HTML formatting. You can apply GoLive's existing set of styles or add your own by first formatting text the way you want it and then saving a new HTML style.

HTML styles are not the same as cascading style sheets (CSS). CSS can be used to set style attributes for text, but they are not constrained by HTML formatting.

CSS palette

When you apply a cascading style sheet to a document, information about all of the styles included in the sheet is available from the CSS palette (**Figure 1.36**). Chapter 13 covers cascading style sheets in detail.

Site Management Tools

GoLive's interface for managing entire Web sites is one of its most useful features. By gathering elements of your Web site in an organized way, with a variety of tools for viewing, editing, and publishing your site, GoLive helps you keep track of even a very large site. GoLive includes tools that allow you to make global changes to the site, organize HTML and media files, and verify that all of your links work. You can also use its site management tools to view a map of your entire site, either as a collection of linked pages or as a group of links going to and from a single page. Finally, you can upload your site to a Web server using one of GoLive's publishing tools.

The Site window

The Site window displays the files and other elements that make up a GoLive Web site. Like the Macintosh Finder or Windows Explorer, the Site window displays files and folders that you can open or manipulate when making changes to the site's hierarchy. When you create a new site, GoLive creates a home page for it (called index.html), and a new Site window appears (**Figure 1.37**). You can drag files into the Site window to add them to your site, or you can create pages from scratch with GoLive.

Like the Document window, the Site window includes a number of tabs. The Site window tabs organize elements of your Web site. The Site window tabs are Files, External, Diagrams, Colors, Font Sets, and Library.

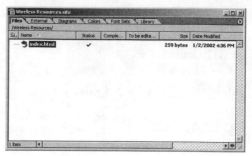

Figure 1.37 Here is a brand-new Site window, containing a home page (index.html).

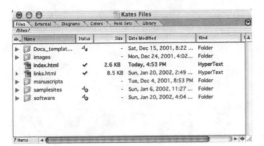

Figure 1.38 This Site window includes files and folders that are part of the site.

Figure 1.39 The secondary pane of the Site window includes four tabs: Extras, Errors, FTP, and WebDAV. The Extras tab, shown here, gives you access to objects you can use with your site, but that are not necessarily part of the site.

Each Site window tab shows different elements of your site. As you might expect, the Files tab displays your site's files—HTML, images, multimedia files, and the rest—and the External, Colors, and Font Sets tabs display remote URLs and email addresses, saved colors, and fonts, respectively. You can view prototype site designs in the Diagrams tab. The Library tab holds HTML snippets, called Library Items in GoLive. You can copy and reuse these snippets in your site's documents. **Figure 1.38** shows a site with the Files tab selected and a full complement of files.

✔ Tip

■ The Site window also contains several secondary tabs that give you a view of specialized site objects and allow you to set up access to your Web server. To view the secondary panes, click the button in the lower-right corner of the Site window. The secondary pane and its tabs appear in **Figure 1.39**. I'll discuss the secondary site pane in Chapter 16.

The Navigation view

Almost all Web sites consist of a hierarchical grouping of HTML pages and links to other Web sites. The Navigation view is designed to make it easier for you to visualize and work with your site in these terms. You can even use the Navigation view to organize your site before you design its individual pages.

To use the Navigation view:

1. Open a site file.

2. Choose Site > View > Navigation. The site's Navigation view appears.

   or

   Choose Navigation from the flyout menu of the Site window.

(continues on next page)

3. The first time you use the Navigation view, you'll see a single file—your home page. Click the plus sign below it to expand your view (**Figure 1.40**).

You can work with files while using the Navigation view (or the Site window, for that matter). Clicking a file once displays the File Inspector and highlights the file's relationship to others in the site. The File Inspector gives you creation and location information about the file, and lets you view a thumbnail version of it.

✔ Tip

■ Double-clicking a file in the Navigation view opens it. This applies to HTML and image files created in GoLive as well as to multimedia files you've added to your site. GoLive will hand off these "foreign" file types to the applications that created them, allowing you to edit the files.

Links view

While the Navigation view provides an overview of the relationship of the pages that make up your Web site, the Links view digs one step deeper, displaying the links associated with individual pages.

To display pages in the Links view:

1. With a site open, choose Site > View > Links.

or

Within the Navigation view, click the Links tab. The Links view appears.

2. Click the plus sign to the left of your home page to see files in your site that link to the page; click the right plus sign to see links from the home page to other files (**Figure 1.41**).

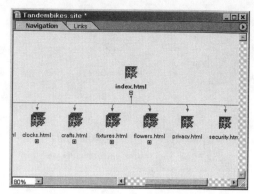

Figure 1.40 The Navigation view shows your site's contents as a hierarchy, with icons representing the files.

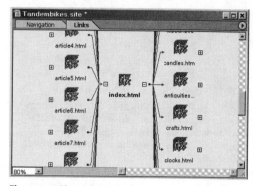

Figure 1.41 The Links view shows a page and all site links that go to and from that page.

✔ Tip

■ Both the Navigation and Links views include a menu for resizing your view of the site. To see more of the site, decrease the magnification using the menu in the lower-left corner of the Navigation/Links window.

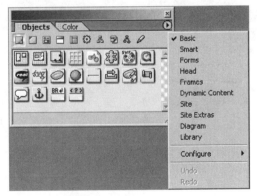

Figure 1.42 The Window menu includes commands that open all of GoLive's palettes. The dividers between the menu items tell you which palettes share a window.

Figure 1.43 Click the arrow in the upper-right corner of a window to view a menu. In some, you'll see a list of the tabs in the palette window. In others, you'll see commands that you can use with the currently selected palette.

Using the GoLive Interface

If you've used Adobe products such as Photoshop or Illustrator, many of the interface elements I've described in this chapter are probably familiar to you. Because GoLive was not originally created by Adobe, some things, like the draggable palette tools, are different, but others, like the tabbed interface, come right out of Adobe's standard playbook.

In this section, I'll show you how to make the best use of the interface for your needs. Things like window position and different ways of choosing the command you need make a great difference in your productivity and aren't the same for everyone who uses any piece of software.

Several ways to reach the same place

You can open any palette by clicking its tab at the top of its window, but there are several other ways to reach GoLive palettes.

- **Choose from the Window menu:** All of the palettes that are open when you launch GoLive, and all of the tabs within those windows, have corresponding commands on the Window menu (**Figure 1.42**).

- **Use the flyout menu within the host window:** If the window containing a palette you want to use is visible, choose that tab from the menu in the upper-right corner of the window, indicated by the right-pointing arrow (**Figure 1.43**). In some, like the Site window, this menu contains commands that open additional windows. In the Site window, use the menu to reach the Navigation and Links views, neither of which is open on screen otherwise.

(continues on next page)

USING THE GOLIVE INTERFACE

◆ **Use a contextual menu:** Control-click (Mac) or right-click (Windows) almost anywhere in GoLive and you will be rewarded with a menu (**Figure 1.44**). In many, you will find access to the Inspector or to auxiliary palettes on the menus. Since these palettes are context-sensitive, what you see depends on where you click (the Document window, within a table, in the Site window).

◆ **Select from the toolbar:** Like the menus I just described, the toolbar, which is always present at the top of the GoLive desktop, is context-sensitive. Sometimes the toolbar includes buttons that open GoLive windows.

Figure 1.44 Contextual menus differ depending on where you click within GoLive. Here, I clicked inside a table cell. This menu offers access to both cell options and text formatting commands.

✔ Tip

■ Use the Default Workspace command from the Window menu to return palettes to their default position in the GoLive workspace.

Managing the workspace

The array of palettes and windows available in the GoLive workspace can be somewhat daunting when screen real estate is limited or if you're new to the program. Experienced users find that they prefer a very specific arrangement of windows—not necessarily the one Adobe provides. When you discover just the right number and arrangement of windows you can save a workspace of your own.

Among the items you can customize to build the perfect workspace are

◆ The number of windows and palettes in the workspace

◆ Size and position of palette windows

◆ Palettes that share a window

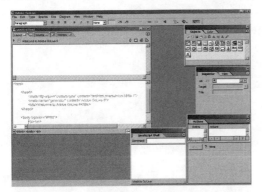

Figure 1.45 Add, remove, arrange, and organize palettes in any way that's comfortable for you. I've chosen palettes I'll need when working with scripts and actions.

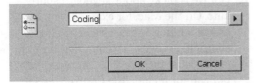

Figure 1.46 Name and save your new workspace. It will be available from the Window > Workspace menu.

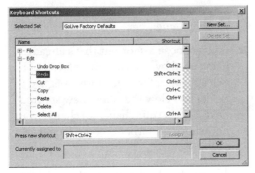

Figure 1.47 The Keyboard Shortcuts dialog lists GoLive's menus.

To save a custom workspace:

1. Arrange your GoLive workspace in any way that is convenient for you. I chose to display palettes I will need when writing code or applying Actions (**Figure 1.45**).

2. Choose Window > Workspace > Save Workspace.

3. Name the new workspace and click OK. I named my workspace Coding (**Figure 1.46**).

To use a workspace:

◆ Choose Window > Workspace > and the name of your new workspace. The palettes and windows take the positions they had when you first saved the workspace.

Using keyboard shortcuts

GoLive provides a number of keyboard shortcuts for frequently used commands, but you can also create your own. Logically enough, the Keyboard Shortcuts command (Edit > Keyboard Shortcuts) also has a keyboard shortcut—Option-Command-Shift-K (Mac) or Control-Alt-Shift-K (Windows).

The Keyboard Shortcuts dialog gives you access to all shortcuts that are currently mapped to GoLive menu options, as well as an option to create your own set (**Figure 1.47**). That set can add shortcuts to existing ones (not all menu items have shortcuts), or you can replace the existing GoLive shortcuts with ones you choose.

In the Keyboard Shortcuts window, you can choose a set of keyboard shortcuts from the Selected Set menu. Decide whether your new shortcut will be a new set of your own (highly recommended) or an addition to the GoLive Factory Defaults shortcuts already in place.

To assign a new keyboard shortcut:

1. Click the New Set button to begin your own group of shortcuts.

2. Name your new set in the New Set dialog. From the "Copy from" menu, choose whether to base your set of shortcuts on GoLive Factory Defaults or the GoLive 5 set.

3. Click OK to return to the Keyboard Shortcuts dialog.

4. From the list of GoLive menus, identify the one containing the command you want to add a shortcut for and open it by clicking the triangle (Mac) or plus sign (Windows) next to the menu name. If the command you want is in a submenu, open that as well.

5. Select the item for which you want to add a shortcut.

6. Click in the "Press new shortcut" field and type the shortcut. It must be a combination of a modifier key or keys (Shift, Option, or Command on the Mac; Shift, Alt, or Control on Windows) and a letter or number. The shortcut you've chosen appears in the field.

7. Click Assign to confirm your choice.

8. When you're finished adding shortcuts, click OK to close the window.

✔ Tips

- GoLive is picky about keyboard shortcuts. On the Mac, for example, you can't assign a function key as a keyboard shortcut, and any key combination you create must include the Command key, but cannot include the Control key. On Windows systems, you can't use Alt in a keyboard shortcut unless you also include the Shift key. Experiment with shortcuts until you find one that you like and will remember.

- If you choose a shortcut that's already being used by GoLive, that information will appear in the "Currently assigned to" field, just below the "Press new shortcut" field. This is your chance to change your new shortcut, rather than replacing an existing one.

- To change an existing shortcut, select a menu item, click in the shortcut field, and type the new shortcut. When you click Replace, the old shortcut is replaced.

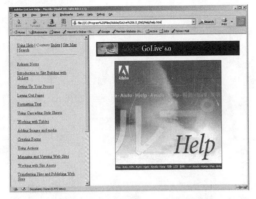

Figure 1.48 Choose a help option from GoLive's Help menu.

Figure 1.49 GoLive Help has hyperlinked information about most GoLive features and a search engine to help you find it.

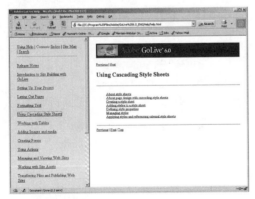

Figure 1.50 Click a topic to display available subtopics.

Getting Help

There are a number of ways to get help in GoLive. The most obvious place to start is the Help menu (**Figure 1.48**). Adobe has included a lot of documentation with the GoLive package. You can get to it directly from GoLive, or you can read or print an Adobe Acrobat version of the user's guide.

To view GoLive Help:

1. Choose Help > GoLive Help. Your Web browser opens and displays an HTML page containing links to Adobe documentation (**Figure 1.49**). The information in these documents is stored on your hard disk, so GoLive doesn't need to connect to the Internet to load these help files.

2. Click a topic on the left side of the HTML page. Subtopics appear on the right (**Figure 1.50**).

3. Click the Search link to look for specific information.

The PDF user's guide

The GoLive CD contains a PDF version of the printed user's guide that is included with the software. The electronic version is not installed on your hard disk with GoLive. It's located at the root level of the CD. The Acrobat file is called User Guide.pdf. If you have Acrobat Reader, double click to launch the guide. If you don't have Acrobat, you can install it from the GoLive CD.

Online resources

The GoLive Help menu includes commands that take you directly to Adobe Web resources. They include downloadable software updates, tips, forums for GoLive users, and opportunities to buy stuff. You can also register GoLive from the Help menu. Explore the Support, Downloadables, and Adobe Online links to learn more.

YOUR FIRST GOLIVE PROJECT

2

Now that you've had a walking tour of GoLive's interface and important features, it's time to begin a Web page and a Web site. In this chapter, I'll show you the practical side of the tools introduced in Chapter 1. But I'll keep things simple, leaving the exploration of the full power of GoLive for subsequent chapters.

In this chapter, I'll cover

◆ Starting a GoLive site

◆ Opening and creating files

◆ Saving and adding files

◆ Introducing Point & Shoot

Setting Up a Site

If you've ever taken a class in Web site building or read a book on the subject, you've learned that the key to building a Web site is advance planning: having a goal and taking steps to reach it, rather than simply diving in and filling in the details later. Whether you take this advice to mean that you should plan every page in your site or simply think in terms of the site as a whole before you begin making pages, it's a good idea to set up a GoLive site, even before you create your first HTML page. When I talk about a GoLive site, I mean a group of elements (HTML files, images, and other file types) that form a Web site, are managed as a unit, and are saved under the umbrella of a site file and folder structure that keeps track of everything.

If you think getting organized is a bit of a pain when there's creative work to be done, there are practical reasons to start by creating a site. For one thing, file and link management, a key feature of GoLive's site management interface, is a whole lot easier when you've built a site and added files to it as you create or acquire them. Using GoLive to manage a site is a great way to keep track of things locally, and to ensure that your link relationships are correct when you upload your HTML files to a Web server.

Web sites the GoLive way

The GoLive site file contains pointers to all of the elements of your site. It does not contain the actual HTML pages and other files; it simply keeps them organized.

I'll introduce you to GoLive's site management tools by showing you how to set up a simple site. (For a more in-depth look at sites, see Chapter 15, "Building Sites.") You can create GoLive Web sites from scratch, import files belonging to an existing Web site into a new GoLive site file, or use a template to begin the site. In this section we'll start a site from scratch.

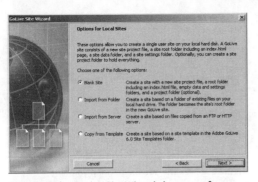

Figure 2.1 The GoLive Site Wizard shows you four ways to begin a new site.

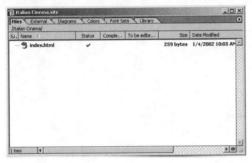

Figure 2.2 After you start a blank site, the Site window opens, listing the new site's home page, `index.html`.

To create a new site:

1. Choose File > New Site. The GoLive Site Wizard appears and will walk you through the site-creation process.

2. Click the Single User button to indicate that this site will not be shared using an Adobe workgroup server. Then click Next.

3. Choose the way you want to create your site. GoLive gives you four options for beginning a site (**Figure 2.1**). Choose Blank Site, and click Next.

4. Name the site. The name will be applied to the site file and its folders. It won't be used when the site is uploaded to a Web server.

5. To enclose the site file and all of its sub-folders in a folder with the site's name, leave the Create Project Folder check box selected and click Next.

6. Click Browse to choose a location on your hard drive for the site folder. Select the location and click Finish. The Site window opens (**Figure 2.2**).

GoLive automatically created an empty home page called `index.html` when you started the site. If you already have a home page that you wish to use with this site, you can replace `index.html` with that file. Otherwise, edit `index.html` from within the Site window.

SETTING UP A SITE

To replace the blank home page:

1. Quit GoLive.

2. In the Finder (Mac) or Windows Explorer (Windows), locate and open the site folder you just created. Notice that, depending on how your preferences are set, the site folder may contain three folders and two files—the site file and a backup site file.

3. Inside the site folder, open the New Site folder (if New Site is the name you gave your site). The index.html file is stored here.

4. On your hard drive, locate the home page file you want to use instead of index.html. If your file isn't currently named index.html, rename it.

5. Copy the file into the New Site folder, replacing the index.html file already there.

6. Open your site by double-clicking the site file in the root folder of your site (**Figure 2.3**). As before, index.html appears in the Site window.

7. Double-click the index.html file. Your home page opens in the Layout Editor.

✔ Tip

■ If you have created a Web page in an application other than GoLive, you can use the dragging technique to bring the page into a GoLive site. If you need to add a large number of files, or a complete site, however, the best method is to use GoLive's Import from Folder option to create the site, or the Import Files to Site feature to add items to an existing site. Both of these options are explained in Chapter 15.

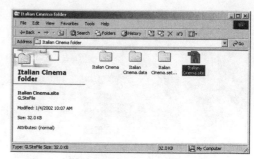

Figure 2.3 Click the site file to open your site.

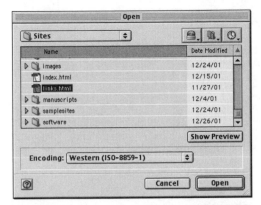

Figure 2.4 The Open dialog box (this one is Mac OS 9's) shows available files and directories.

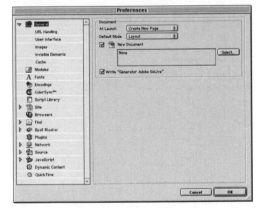

Figure 2.5 In Windows environments, the "Files of type" menu (in the Open dialog box) gives you the option of viewing only certain types of files. Choose one or view all file types GoLive can open by default.

Opening and Creating Files

Documents you create in GoLive can be viewed in any Web browser and served by any Web server. That's because, unlike files created by word processing, database, or spreadsheet applications, GoLive files are plain old text files—HTML files, to be precise. You can work on a file in GoLive and immediately open it in a local browser or upload it to a Web server for viewing over the Internet.

By the same token, you can open and edit HTML files created by other applications in GoLive. If you have an existing Web page, for example, and want to use GoLive to edit it, just open the file in GoLive.

To open a file in GoLive:

1. Launch GoLive by double-clicking it, or by choosing it from the Start menu (Windows).

2. Choose File > Open. The Open dialog box appears (**Figure 2.4**).

3. Navigate to a file on your hard disk and choose Open. The file opens in the GoLive Document window.

You can now edit the file, just as if you had created it in GoLive in the first place.

✔ Tip

- In Windows, by default, the Open dialog box displays all files in the current directory that GoLive can open. That includes any plain text file, whether it's a Web page, a script, a GoLive site file, or other files that are readable as text. You can choose to see only HTML files, GoLive site files, or a range of others by choosing an option from the "Files of type" menu (**Figure 2.5**).

OPENING AND CREATING FILES

Setting GoLive launch preferences

You can change the way GoLive behaves when you launch the application. As I described in Chapter 1, GoLive asks whether you want to open a new document, a new site, or an existing document. You can choose to skip the Intro dialog box in the future by checking the "Don't show again" check box at the bottom. You can also use the Preferences window to make other choices about how GoLive behaves on launch.

To change launch preferences:

1. Choose Edit > Preferences. The Preferences dialog box opens (**Figure 2.6**).

2. In the General Preferences section (selected by default), choose an option from the At Launch menu (**Figure 2.7**). This tells GoLive whether to open a new document, show the Intro dialog box, or open the application without opening the Intro dialog box or a new document.

3. Select an option from the Default Mode menu if you want GoLive to use a mode other than the Layout Editor as the default when opening documents.

4. If you would like to use a document as a template for all new documents that you open, click the New Document check box and then click the Select button to locate a file you want to use.

Creating a new file

Most of the files you create in GoLive will be HTML files—Web pages. However, you can also create scripts, site files, QuickTime movies, and style sheet documents. We'll learn about these in later chapters. For now, we'll concentrate on HTML files—creating a new one in GoLive and building a simple Web page.

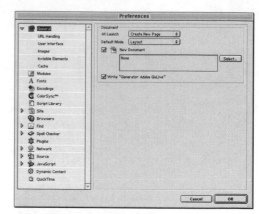

Figure 2.6 Change the way GoLive launches in the General Preferences window.

Figure 2.7 To launch a blank document, the Intro dialog box, or no document at all, choose an item from the At Launch menu.

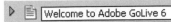

Figure 2.8 Click the page title in the Document window to activate it. Then type a new title over the selected text.

To create a new HTML page in GoLive:

1. Open the GoLive site you created earlier in this chapter. (This step is not essential to creating a new HTML file, but it's a good idea if the page you're building will be part of a site.)

2. Choose File > New, or type Command-N (Mac) or Control-N (Windows). An empty document opens in the Document window.

This is a good time to define a few basic parameters and settings for your Web page before you begin adding text and graphics.

To give your page a title:

1. Click anywhere within the title "Welcome to Adobe GoLive 6" at the top of the Document window, to the right of the Page icon (**Figure 2.8**).

2. Type a title for your page. In Mac, the text you type will overwrite the original title. In Windows, select the original text and then begin typing to replace it. The title you type will appear at the top of a browser window when the page is viewed and will also appear in a Web browser's bookmark list. The title should indicate what your Web page is about in clear, concise terms.

✔ Tip

- Your page's title is not the same as the name you give it when you save the file. The file name (`page.html`, for example) identifies this page to other sites and pages that link to it, but the title is merely a way to refer to the page in the browser title bar and on bookmark lists.

Sizing your page

Because Web pages are viewed on a wide variety of computer monitors, some small, some large, it's usually a good idea to develop your pages so that they will appear somewhat consistently under the wide range of possible viewing conditions. The easiest way to do this is to be sure that the window size you work with in GoLive's Layout Editor is narrow enough to be used on a 14-inch monitor without requiring the viewer to scroll left or right.

GoLive lets you change a window's dimensions by dragging the grow box at the bottom-right corner of the Document window (in the Layout Editor), but that's not an efficient way to ensure that every page you build has the same horizontal dimensions. The Window Resolution pop-up menu lets you choose a pixel width that's compatible with a 14- or 17-inch monitor, for example.

The window width you choose is only a guide as you build pages. To control the actual width a page occupies when displayed in a browser window, make sure that objects on the page conform to a precise pixel measurement or set options that enable your page to fill a browser window, regardless of its size. This applies mainly to pages that use tables, floating boxes, or frames to define the margins of the page (see Chapters 7, 9, and 11).

To choose a window width:

◆ Click the Window Resolution pop-up menu in the bottom-right corner of the Document window (**Figure 2.9**) and choose an appropriate page width (in pixels) for your page. GoLive includes sizes that support 14- and 17-inch monitors, and some smaller page sizes as well. The 580 (14-inch monitor) and 720 (17-inch monitor) options are probably safer choices, since most current computer monitors are at least 14 inches. GoLive resizes the main window.

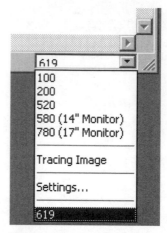

Figure 2.9 Choose a size from the Window Resolution pop-up menu.

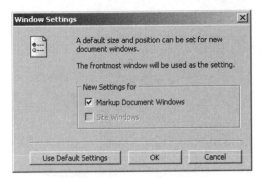

Figure 2.10 Choose the default page size in the Window Settings dialog box.

Figure 2.11 Click the Page icon to set options for the current document.

Figure 2.12 Set options for the current document in the Page Inspector.

To choose a default window width for all documents:

1. Choose the window size you want to use for all pages you work with, either by choosing an option from the Width Resolution pop-up menu or by dragging the grow box to the size you want.

2. From the Page Size pop-up menu, choose Settings. The Window Settings dialog box opens (**Figure 2.10**).

3. Be sure that Markup Document Windows is checked and click OK to confirm your new settings. Each new document you open will have the horizontal and vertical dimensions you've chosen.

4. To return to GoLive's default settings, click the Use Default Settings button in the Window Settings dialog box.

Setting page options

When you open a new GoLive document, you see an empty, colorless window. You can change that by setting background, margin, and text properties for the page before you begin to add text and objects.

To set a background color:

1. In the Document window, click the Page icon located below the Editor tabs (**Figure 2.11**). The Page Inspector appears (**Figure 2.12**). (If the Inspector window is not open, double-click the Page icon to view the Page Inspector.)

2. To choose a background color for the page, click the Color field in the Background section of the Page Inspector.

(continues on next page)

✔ Tip

■ Window Settings can also be used to choose a different view for the Document window. If you want to see the Source Editor, Outline Editor, or other Document window tab rather than the Layout Editor when you open a file, choose that tab before you open the Window Settings dialog box.

OPENING AND CREATING FILES

3. Select a color from the palette. (For details on using the Color palette, see Chapter 5, "Working with Color.")

4. When you click in the Color palette's preview pane to apply color, the Color field in the Inspector changes to match. The Document window's color changes, too (**Figure 2.13**).

To add a background image:

1. In the Page Inspector, click the Image check box in the Background section.

2. Click the Browse button, to the right of the Image field (it looks like a folder). A file navigation box appears.

3. Navigate to the image you want to use as a background for your page and click Open. You'll see the image in the main window, and visitors to your Web page will see the image behind the page's other elements.

✔ Tips

■ If you choose a small image for your page's background, the image will repeat across and down the page, as shown in **Figure 2.14**. This arrangement would probably not be the best background for a page with text, especially if the text is fairly small in size. Choose a larger, less busy background for pages that include lots of text.

■ If you choose both a background color and a background image, the image will be shown unless the user's browser does not support background images, in which case the color appears behind the page content.

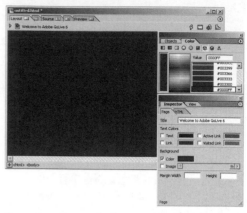

Figure 2.13 Choose a background color using the Page Inspector and the Color palette.

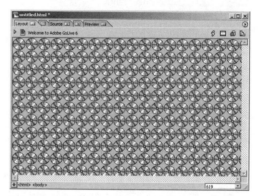

Figure 2.14 This busy page background consists of repeated images of a single compact disc.

OPENING AND CREATING FILES

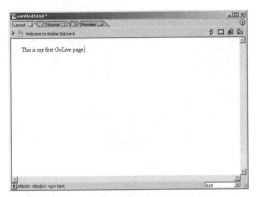

Figure 2.15 This document's margins have been set to 20 pixels high and 30 pixels wide. Notice that the horizontal margins affect both sides of the page.

To choose colors for text and links:

1. In the Text Colors section of the Page Inspector, click a color field for the item whose color you want to specify. Your choices are Text, Active Link, Link, and Visited Link.

2. When the Color palette appears, choose a color. The new color appears in the color field. When you add text and create links on this page, they will be the color you chose.

✔ Tip

■ If you decide to use custom colors for text, links, or background, use GoLive's Preview view or a Web browser to check the colors you've chosen, especially if you're using more than one kind of background or custom color.

To set page margins:

1. In the Page Inspector, enter a pixel value in the Margin Width and Height fields.

2. Type some text in the Document window. Notice that the text does not begin in the upper-left corner, but at the margin you set. **Figure 2.15** shows a page whose Height margin is 20 pixels and Width margin is 30.

Saving and Adding Files

After you've added a few items to your new Web page, it's a good idea to save it. Saving files in GoLive is pretty much like saving them in other applications you have used.

To save a Web page:

◆ Choose File > Save (Command-S on a Mac and Control-S on Windows) and navigate to the folder where you want to store your new page.

When you choose Save, GoLive presents the default file name `untitled.html`. Though you should change it to something more appropriate, be sure not to remove the `.html` extension, and don't add spaces or slashes (/) within the file name. HTML files must follow this naming convention to be recognized by servers as Web pages. Even if you're using a Mac, where file name extensions usually aren't important, keep the `.html` extension.

To save a file within a site:

1. Be sure that a GoLive site is open.

2. Create a new file by choosing File > New Page. Edit the file by adding text and objects and choosing page options.

3. Choose File > Save.

4. Name the file.

5. In the Save dialog box, navigate to the folder containing your site's HTML files. The quickest way to do this is with the Site Folder pop-up menu at the bottom of the Save dialog box. In **Figure 2.16**, the site's root folder is `Wireless Resources`.

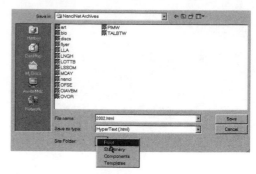

Figure 2.16 To save a file to the root level of this site, open the `Wireless Resources` folder within the main site folder, which is also called `Wireless Resources`. To get there, I chose Root folder from the Site Folder pop-up menu.

✔ Tips

■ If you're working within a GoLive Web site, be sure to save your file to the folder that contains the rest of the HTML files that are part of your site.

■ If your Web server is not a Macintosh, you should ensure that your file names will work with the operating system of your Web server. In the Preferences dialog box, open the Site section and, in Filename Constraints, choose the appropriate operating system from the Selected Constraints pop-up menu. (Ask your Web server administrator if you aren't certain of the operating system.)

Adding files to a site

It's a simple matter to add files created outside the GoLive site structure or built by others to your site.

To add existing files to a site:

1. Be sure that a site file is open and the Site window is open.

2. On your hard drive, locate the file you want to add to the site. It can be an HTML file, an image, or a multimedia file.

3. Drag the file or files from a Finder window (Mac) or Windows Explorer (Windows) into the Site window. The file is copied to the site folder and its links are checked for errors. It appears in the Site window.

To add a file by copying:

1. This only works in Windows. On the desktop, select and right-click a file you wish to add to the site.

2. Choose Copy from the menu.

3. Switch to GoLive and view the Files tab of the Site window.

4. Right-click the Files tab and choose Paste. The file is added.

Chapter 15 has more to say about adding files to existing sites.

SAVING AND ADDING FILES

Introducing Point & Shoot

The Point & Shoot feature brings everything you've learned in this chapter together. With Point & Shoot, you can quickly link HTML files, images, and multimedia files on your site to the Web page you're building. Point & Shoot lets you establish a link between an item in the Document window (a word or phrase, an image, or a multimedia file, for example), by dragging from the item's Inspector to the corresponding file or URL in the Site window.

Figure 2.17 Arrange the Document window and Site window so that you can see parts of both.

In Chapter 1, I introduced you to the Objects palette, which contains icons you use to add objects to GoLive documents. The Image icon is among the most often used of these. By dragging the icon to the Document window, you indicate that you want to add an image to the page. But you need to tell GoLive which image to add.

For our Point & Shoot introduction, I'll show you how to choose an image. (Though as you'll learn in Chapter 4, "Working with Images," you can specify the image to add in a number of ways.)

To use Point & Shoot to add an image:

1. Open a site containing HTML files and image files.

2. Open a GoLive document by double-clicking its icon in the Site window.

3. Arrange the document and the Site window for the current site so both are visible on screen. You only need to be able to see the icons and file names of items in the Site window (**Figure 2.17**).

4. Drag the Image icon from Basic set of the Objects palette into the Document window. The Image Inspector appears.

INTRODUCING POINT & SHOOT

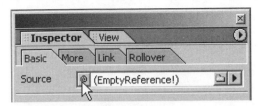

Figure 2.18 Use the Fetch URL button to Point & Shoot, or link to an image stored within a GoLive site. All Inspectors that allow you to browse to files on your hard disk also have a Point & Shoot task.

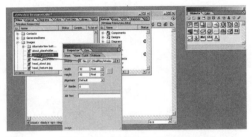

Figure 2.19 Click the Fetch URL button and drag the mouse into the Site window. A line follows the path you draw.

5. Click and hold the Fetch URL button in the Image Inspector. It's located immediately to the left of the Source field (**Figure 2.18**).

6. Drag from the Fetch URL button to the Site window. A line appears as you drag (**Figure 2.19**).

7. When the cursor is over an image file that you want to link to and the image file is highlighted, let go of the mouse button. The image appears in the Document window and the image path appears in the Source field of the Inspector, just as if you had used the Browse button to locate the file on your hard drive.

✔ Tips

- If you want to Point & Shoot to an image or other item that is stored in a subfolder of the Site window, drag to the Site window and over the folder's icon. The folder will open to reveal the files inside. Then you can finish the link by pointing to the file and letting go of the mouse button.

- In this example, I showed you how to Point & Shoot to an image. You can also Point & Shoot in any Inspector window that contains a way to link the selected item to a file or URL.

WORKING WITH TEXT

Adding text is just about the easiest task there is for a Web page developer. But formatting text so it looks the way you want it to and getting it to appear at precisely the right location on the page require a bit more thought. You must add HTML tags to the text to tell browsers what typeface, size, and style you want the text to have, and you'll need more HTML tags to ensure that the text is placed properly.

Adobe GoLive's text-handling features are a familiar combination of word-processing and page-layout tools that graphically build the HTML you need. You can create text in GoLive or copy it from elsewhere. From there, you can edit, format, position, search, spell check, and manipulate text and text blocks to polish your Web pages.

In this chapter, I'll cover

- Entering text

- Formatting text

- Formatting text blocks

- Spell checking

- Finding and replacing text

Entering Text

You can add text to a GoLive document in several ways. You also have a choice of views in which to add your text. Most of the time you'll use the Layout Editor, either by typing directly into the Document window or by copying or importing into a document. You can also use other views to add or edit text—more on that in Chapter 12, "Working with Code."

To type text directly into a document:

1. Open a new or existing GoLive document.

2. If necessary, click the Layout tab at the top of the window to make sure that the Layout Editor appears in the Document window.

3. Type some text in the Document window.

Editing text

You can edit text in GoLive just as you would in most other applications. Select text, then cut, copy, or paste it. Use your cursor (arrow) keys to move around the document, adding or deleting text as needed. Later in this chapter, you'll learn how to check your spelling and use GoLive's Find & Replace tool to locate and change text when you need to.

You can also paste text into GoLive from another application, though the text will not retain formatting from the native application. GoLive will attempt to encode special characters such as ampersands so they will appear properly in a Web browser.

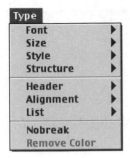

Figure 3.1 Use the Type menu's commands to format selected text.

Figure 3.2 With text selected in the Layout Editor, control-clicking (Mac) or right-clicking (Windows) reveals a contextual menu with text formatting and other commands. If you use the menu when no text is selected, you'll see an abbreviated version.

Formatting Text

Text on a Web page, like text that appears in print or onscreen in a word processor, can come in all styles and sizes, but it is affected by many factors, such as different browsers, browser versions, preferences, and platforms. To format text for the Web, you must apply HTML tags to it. Though GoLive insulates you from the need to know these tags, you do need to know something about the formatting features HTML supports and how to get around the limitations imposed by the Web. You apply text formatting in much the same way you would in a word-processing application or page-layout program. GoLive's text formatting tools are available from the Type menu (**Figure 3.1**) and the contextual menu (**Figure 3.2**), and many are repeated on the toolbar (**Figure 3.3**).

In this section, I'll show you options for changing text size, weight (bold, italic, and so on), color, and typeface. Because we're working with HTML rather than traditional typography tools, there are special and sometimes confusing rules for formatting text You can see the encoding in the Source Editor (more on this in Chapter 12).

Figure 3.3 The toolbar includes most of the same options found on the Type menu.

Changing text size

In traditional (print) typography, the size of text on a page is expressed in *points*. There are 72 points in an inch. Most body text is 10 to 12 points, for example, and a heading might be anywhere from 14 to 36 points, or even larger. In HTML, text size is not usually expressed in points, unless you are working with Cascading Style Sheets (described in Chapter 13, "Working with Style Sheets"). In plain old HTML, the size of text on the page is expressed in relation to the size of baseline text on the page. The actual size of the baseline is determined by the browser used to view it and the text size settings that have been set. Though this means that your text will not appear exactly the same way in all browsers, the size relative to the baseline will be fairly constant.

To add a bit of confusion to the mix, there's another kind of relative text sizing in HTML. The size of text on the Web is expressed using either the *absolute* or *relative* scale. The absolute scale provides for text sizes from 1 to 7, with 3 being the baseline. Setting text to 5 displays it at a size somewhat larger than the baseline, while 1 is smaller. **Figure 3.4** shows text sizes from 1 to 7. The relative scale works the same way, but is applied differently. Instead of an absolute number (3, 4, 5, and so on), a relative text size is expressed as −2, −1, +1, +2 and so on. The numbers on this scale are relative to the baseline. There's not much difference in appearance between absolute and relative text sizes unless browser font size preferences have been changed, in which case, the differences between font sizes on the relative scale will remain apparent, while text that was sized using the absolute scale will not grow or shrink relative to the baseline.

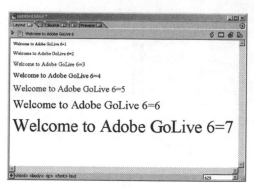

Figure 3.4 Text in this window is from 1 to 7 on the absolute scale.

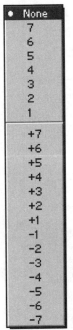

Figure 3.5 You can use the Size pull-down menu to select absolute or relative font sizes.

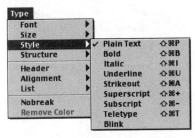

Figure 3.6 The Style submenu of the Type menu contains text styles.

To change the size of text:

1. Select some text in the Layout Editor.

2. From the toolbar, select the Size menu (**Figure 3.5**).

   or

   Choose Type > Size.

   or

   Control-click (Mac) or right-click (Windows) and choose Size.

3. Select an absolute size from the top portion of the menu or a relative size from the lower portion. The size of the selected text changes.

Text display styles

HTML specifies two types of display styles: *text styles* and *structure styles*. Text styles, such as bold and italic, always look the same, regardless of the Web browser being used to view the page. Structure styles, such as strong and emphasis, take their visual marching orders from the user's Web browser. In general, newer browsers do a better job of displaying structurally styled text than do older ones.

Only three text styles—bold, italic, and teletype—are available from the toolbar. All of the text styles appear in the Style submenu of the Type menu (**Figure 3.6**) and under Style in the contextual menu. These are the rest of the text styles:

- Plain text

- Underline

- Strikeout

- Superscript

- Subscript

- Blink

(continues on next page)

FORMATTING TEXT

Structural styles appear in the Structure submenu of the Type menu and in the lower portion of the contextual menu's Style submenu. **Figure 3.7** shows the Structure submenu.

Because the look of text formatted with a structural style can vary depending on the viewer's browser, it's particularly important to take a look at the page using several browsers, preferably on both the Mac and Windows platforms. **Figure 3.8** compares the look of structural styles in three popular browsers—two Macintosh and one Windows.

✔ Tips

■ Text styles and structural styles should not be confused with Cascading Style Sheets (CSS), which I'll discuss more fully in Chapter 13. Style sheets allow you to specify fonts, type sizes, and other text attributes much the way you do in non-Web applications. To view them, though, a user must have a style sheet–capable browser. Netscape and Microsoft browser versions 4.0 and later support style sheets, though later versions have more complete support.

■ Blink is a Netscape-only tag. GoLive cannot display blinking text in either the Layout Editor or Layout Preview. If you want to see a Web page's text flash, you'll need to preview it in a Netscape browser. But think twice before you make text blink. The blink tag is universally reviled by Webmasters and users alike.

■ Blink will be dimmed in the Style menu unless you change the DOCTYPE code (which tells GoLive and Web browsers how to identify the document) from the default HTML setting to None or to another setting that supports the blink tag. Use the flyout menu in the upper right corner of the Document window to change the DOCTYPE. For more on DOCTYPES, see Chapter 12.

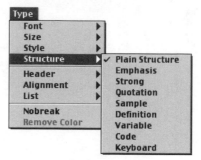

Figure 3.7 The Structure submenu of the Type menu contains structural styles.

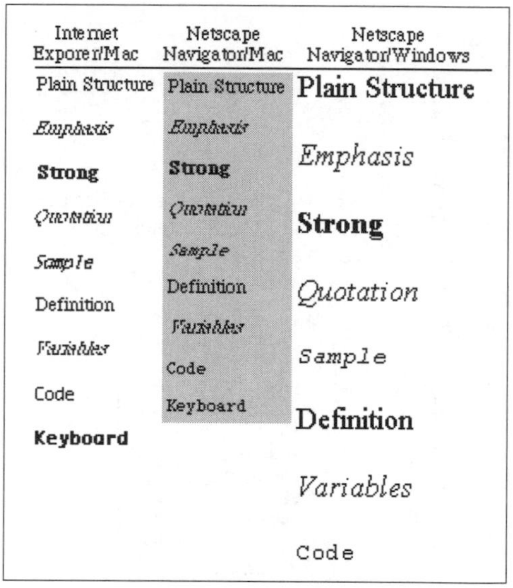

Figure 3.8 Here are structural styles, as displayed in three different browsers. Note that besides slight differences in type size and display attributes, browsers render vertical spacing differently.

Fonts

You can specify typefaces (commonly called fonts) in GoLive, but there are some HTML-specific barriers that limit your options some-what and require that you observe a few special rules.

Like type sizes (described earlier in this chapter), typefaces displayed by a user's browser are subject to the behavior of that browser. If you don't specify a typeface when you build a Web page, the user's browser will provide one. If you do want to use a specific typeface, there is still no guarantee that the user's browser will display it if that typeface is not installed. HTML and GoLive allow you to specify several typefaces for a single text element: a default typeface and as many backup fonts as you like. When a user's browser displays an HTML page, it tries to use the specified default typeface and then the backup fonts in turn, looking for one that is available on the user's system. You can specify font relationships in GoLive with font sets, described in the next section.

To use a font:

1. Select some text in the Document window.

2. Choose a font from the Font submenu of the Type menu, or use the contextual menu. The font is applied to the selected text.

✔ Tip

■ You can apply a font to any text block—a word, a sentence, or a paragraph, for example. When you do, GoLive applies a font tag to just the text you select. If you have already applied a font to a larger block of text containing the text you selected, the font for the smaller block overrides the font that you previously applied, but only for selected text.

Font sets

With font sets, you can easily manage the groups of font choices that browsers display on your Web page. If, for example, you create a font set that includes Arial, Helvetica, and Geneva, and then select Arial in GoLive to produce a page, users who don't have Arial installed will see the text in Helvetica or Geneva, depending on the fonts installed on their systems.

GoLive allows you to build two types of font sets: Default (also known as global) and Page. The Default font set includes fonts that will be used with all GoLive pages you create, unless you override the default on a specific page or text selection. Page fonts are used only on the GoLive document for which you create them.

To edit a font set:

1. With a page open in the Document window, choose Type > Font > Edit Font Sets. The Font Sets Editor appears.

2. If necessary, click the triangle (Mac) or plus sign (Windows) next to the page's name to display a list of current font sets (**Figure 3.9**). Page fonts apply only to the current document.

3. Choose a font from the pull-down menu at the bottom of the window, or type the name of a font you want to use in the field next to it.

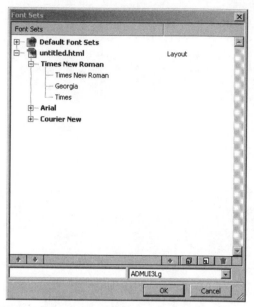

Figure 3.9 Page fonts appear in the Font Sets Editor. If you haven't made changes to page sets, they will be identical to the Default Font Sets in the editor.

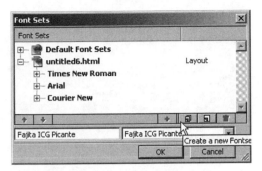

Figure 3.10 Add a new font set with the Create a new Fontset button.

4. Click the Create a new Fontset button (**Figure 3.10**). A new font set, named for the font you selected, appears under the page fonts heading.

5. To add more fonts, click the Add a New Fontname button, then type in or choose a font.

6. When you're finished adding fonts, click OK to close the Font Sets Editor. You'll be reminded that the changes you've made can't be undone.

Font sets you've created (named for the first font in the set) appear in the Font submenu of the Type menu, as long as the current document is open.

This procedure applies to creating global font sets, too. Click the Default Font Sets item and then add new sets and fonts that can be used with all of your GoLive documents.

✔ Tip

■ If you added a font to a set by typing its name into the Font Sets Editor, GoLive adds that name to the source code for your page (Page fonts) or globally (Default), regardless of whether that font exists on your system, or even whether you've ever used it. If you apply that font to text in GoLive, the font will be used on a system where that font is installed. You can also see the font name by clicking the Source tab and taking a look at the HTML code surrounding the text to which you applied the font.

Setting font preferences

Though the choices you make won't affect the look of your pages in a user's browser, GoLive allows you to set the fonts that you see in the Layout Editor when no other fonts have been specified.

To set font preferences:

1. Choose Edit > Preferences. The Preferences dialog box appears.

2. Click the Fonts label on the left side of the dialog box (**Figure 3.11**).

3. Click one of the items under the Western label to select it.

4. Choose a font and a size from the menus at the bottom of the dialog box.

✔ Tip

■ These preferences affect text in the Layout Editor. To change the fonts in the Source Editor, open the Source section of the Preferences window and click Fonts. You can change the font, size, and style here.

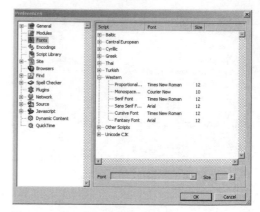

Figure 3.11 Use the Preferences dialog box to choose display fonts in GoLive.

Text color

As you saw in Chapter 2, "Your First GoLive Project," you can choose color for the text and links on a page in the Page Inspector. To apply color to text, add a color from the Color palette.

To color a block of text:

1. Select some text in the Document window.

2. Choose a color from the Color palette. (Click the Color tab above the Objects palette if the Color palette isn't visible.) For more about creating or choosing colors, see Chapter 5, "Working with Color."

3. Click in the Color palette's Preview pane and drag to the text you selected in the Document window. The text changes color.

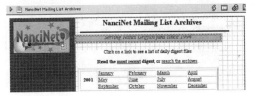

Figure 3.12 Align text using the Left, Center, and Right buttons on the toolbar.

Figure 3.13 Text is aligned relative to the dimensions of the layout text box. Note: If you're not using a layout text box on a layout grid, the text is aligned relative to the width of the user's browser.

Formatting Text Blocks

Up to this point, all of the text-formatting options I've described have been intended to format text characters. Now let's concentrate on text formatting that changes the way a block of text looks on the page: how it is indented, its relationship to other text blocks, and so on.

First, we'll look at general formatting options for all blocks of text. Next, we'll move on to paragraphs, headings, lists, and alternative ways to arrange and organize text blocks.

Text alignment

You can align text to the left, center, or right margins. Alignment applies to an entire block of text (paragraph, heading, or other block followed by a line break), even if you select only a portion of the block or simply click within the block.

To align text:

1. Click in a text block.

2. Choose the Left, Center, or Right button from the toolbar (**Figure 3.12**).

   or

   Choose Type > Alignment and make a choice.

   or

   Choose Alignment from the contextual menu.

✔ **Tip**

■ If you center text in a layout text box as shown in **Figure 3.13**, your text will not be centered on the page, but within the box itself. You'll have to center the layout text box on the page to achieve text centered relative to the layout grid. If you want to center text over a portion of the Web page, first center the layout text box relative to the grid using GoLive's object alignment tools. You can read more about these tools in Chapter 8, "Working with Layout Grids." Similar rules apply to floating boxes, covered in Chapter 9, "Floating Boxes and Positioning."

Indenting text

You can indent blocks of text from the margin using an HTML tag called *blockquote*. Blockquote indents text from both sides of the page. You can use it multiple times to create a deeper indent.

To indent text:

1. Click some text in the Document window. You don't need to select it.

2. Choose Type > Alignment > Increase Block Indent (**Figure 3.14**). Text is indented from the left and right margins.

3. Repeat Step 2 to increase the indent.

✔ Tip

■ You can remove or decrease text indents with the Decrease Block Indent command.

Paragraphs and line breaks

Text blocks, like everything else on a Web page, are defined by HTML tags. Paragraph tags set off most body text. You can also use a line break or a heading to set off a block of text from other blocks on the page.

You don't have to do anything special to create paragraphs in GoLive. When you type text into the Document window, GoLive generates an opening and closing paragraph tag by default. If you press Enter, GoLive creates a new paragraph. A blank line separates HTML paragraphs. If you want a new text block without a blank line between blocks, use a line break. You can also use a line break to control the way text interacts with adjacent elements such as images.

To create a line break:

1. Place your cursor where you want the line break to appear.

2. Press Shift/Enter. A line break character appears (**Figure 3.15**).

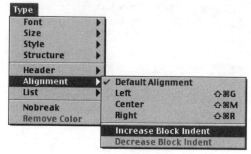

Figure 3.14 You can use the Type menu's Alignment submenu to change alignment and text indents.

This text is set off by paragraph marks.

The mark after this line of text indicates a line break.↵

Figure 3.15 When you type Shift/Enter the line break character appears in the Document window.

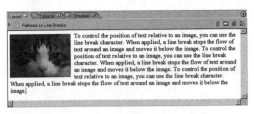

Figure 3.16 The image is aligned to the left of a continuous block of text.

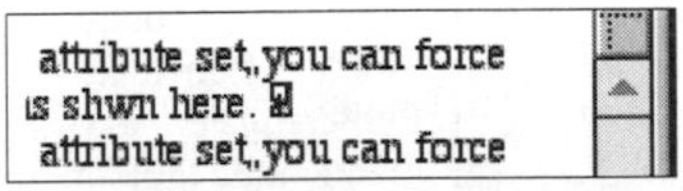

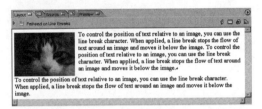

Figure 3.17 A line break character appears when you type Shift/Enter. Select the character to use the Line Break Inspector.

Figure 3.18 When you select the line break character and click the Clear check box in the Line Break Inspector, the flow of text stops until it is clear of any images that are adjacent to the text.

To use a line break to stop text wrap:

1. Add some text and an image to a document.

2. Click the image to select it and choose Left from the Alignment menu in the Inspector. Text wraps to the right of the image as shown in **Figure 3.16**.

3. Create a line break within the block of text by pressing Shift/Enter.

4. Select the line break character (**Figure 3.17**) to display the Line Break Inspector.

5. Click the Clear check box. The adjacent menu becomes active.

   Notice that the All option is selected and that the text below the line break in the Document window now falls below the image (**Figure 3.18**). The line break's Clear attribute stops text from flowing until it is clear of all images. If you choose the Left or Right attribute from the Clear pop-up menu in the Line Break Inspector, text will not wrap to images on the left or right of the text, respectively, following a line break.

✔ Tip

■ You can gain still greater control over the way lines break and the distance between text blocks with Cascading Style Sheets. I'll cover CSS fully in Chapter 13.

FORMATTING TEXT BLOCKS

Headings

HTML provides for six levels of headings that you can use to call attention to and organize text on the page. HTML headings are larger and bolder than standard Web page text. Unlike paragraph tags, headings change the size and weight of the text they surround. Heading 1 is the largest heading choice; heading 6 is the smallest.

To create a heading:

1. Type or select some text in the Document window.

2. From the toolbar, choose Header 1 from the Paragraph Format pull-down menu (**Figure 3.19**).

    or

    Choose Type > Paragraph Format > Heading 1

    or

    Choose Header > Heading 1 from the contextual menu. The text is now larger and bold.

Note that if you apply heading formatting to text within a paragraph, GoLive applies the format to the entire paragraph.

Addresses and Preformatted text

The Address and Preformatted formats are found in the toolbar's Paragraph Format menu. The Address style is usually used to identify the owner/copyright holder/author of the Web page and is traditionally located at the bottom of a Web page (**Figure 3.20**). You can't change the appearance of the Address style.

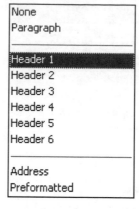

Figure 3.19 Choose Header 1 from the Paragraph Format menu in the toolbar.

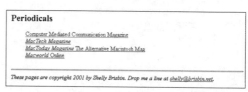

Figure 3.20 An example of the Address style.

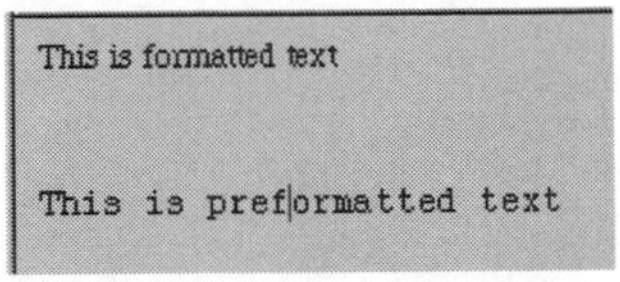

This is formatted text

This is preformatted text

Figure 3.21
Preformatted text looks like this.

Text that is preformatted does not use the HTML tags that give Web page text a typeset look. Instead, using the Preformatted style displays text in a fixed-width font. GoLive displays preformatted text using the Courier font (**Figure 3.21**). Web browsers display preformatted text in whatever fixed-width font is specified in the browser. Preformatted text is most often used to display code or to differentiate certain passages from the rest of the text on the page.

The Address and Preformatted commands are in the Paragraph pull-down menu of the toolbar and the Paragraph Format submenu of the Type menu.

Lists

An HTML list organizes a group of lines of text on the page by indenting them. Each line is usually preceded by a number or a bullet. The list begins and ends with a list tag and each line has its own tag.

HTML lists come in two varieties: numbered and unnumbered. Numbered lists are more precisely referred to as ordered lists—you can use numbers or letters to order the items on the list. Unnumbered lists, too, come in several varieties, with bullets, circles, or squares denoting each item.

You'll find list-creation commands in the List submenu of the Type menu and in the contextual menu. Both list types—numbered and unnumbered—also appear on the toolbar.

To create a new list:

1. Type the items for your list into the Document window. Press Enter after each item.

2. Select all of the lines in the list.

(continues on next page)

FORMATTING TEXT BLOCKS

3. Choose a list format from the List submenu of the Type menu (**Figure 3.22**)

or

Choose a list type from the contextual menu's List submenu. The Arabic numeral style is shown in **Figure 3.23**.

4. With the list still selected, choose a different list format and notice how the appearance of the text changes. **Figure 3.24** shows a bulleted list.

To format a list as you type:

1. Place your cursor where you want the list to begin.

2. Choose a list format from the menu.

3. Type the first list item and then Enter.

4. Type the rest of the list items in the same way.

5. To complete the list, toggle the menu command or toolbar button you used to start the list.

Changing list indents

Lists are indented relative to other body text. You can change the list indent to build a nested list or simply to control the position of the list.

To change the indent of a list:

1. Select a list.

2. To add a greater indent to the list, click the Increase List Level button on the toolbar (**Figure 3.25**), or use the same command on the List submenu.

3. To move the indent back one level, choose Decrease List Level.

✔ Tip

■ If you remove indenting completely, GoLive removes all list formatting and inserts paragraph tags for each line.

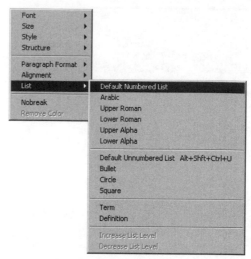

Figure 3.22 You can choose from several list types in the List submenu of the Type menu.

Figure 3.23 To format a list that looks like this, choose Arabic from the List submenu.

Figure 3.24 Change to a bulleted list to get this look.

Figure 3.25 The toolbar includes four buttons for managing the display of lists.

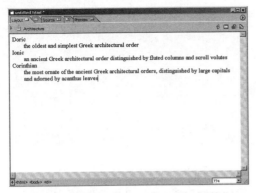

Figure 3.26 A definition list consists of flush left lines and indented list items.

Definition lists

As the name implies, you can use a definition list to display a glossary of terms and their definitions. As shown in **Figure 3.26,** a definition list consists of lines of text that are flush with the page margin and indented lines that use list formatting.

To create a definition list:

1. Type a line of text. Leave your cursor on the line you just typed.

2. Choose Type > List > Term.

3. Press Enter.

4. Choose Type > List > Definition. The new line is now indented from the Term line.

5. Type some text and press Enter again. Another indented line appears, allowing you to add another definition.

6. To create another term, press Enter and choose Type > List > Term.

Though the definition list format looks a lot like a paragraph with a list below it, they are different. For one thing, a paragraph always has a blank line after it, but the term/definition arrangement does not add an unused line.

Spell Checking

GoLive's built-in spelling checker can locate spelling errors in a single page or throughout your site. You can use one of several English or non-English dictionaries or add your own words to a Personal Dictionary. To use a non-English dictionary, select it when you install GoLive for the first time or run the installer again later to add the dictionary.

To check spelling:

1. Open a GoLive document and make sure that you're working in the Layout Editor.

2. Choose Edit > Check Spelling. The Check Spelling dialog box appears (**Figure 3.27**).

3. If you would like to use a dictionary other than the default U.S. English dictionary, choose it from the Language pull-down menu. The dictionary must have been installed with GoLive.

4. Click Start.

5. The spelling checker locates words that it does not recognize, whether they're misspelled or simply not included in the dictionary.

6. To correct a spelling mistake, click one of the suggestions offered (**Figure 3.28**), then click the Change button. If you don't see a suggestion you like, type a new spelling for the word in the field provided.

   You can also tell the spelling checker to simply Ignore a word that it doesn't know. Ignore All passes over all occurrences of the word.

7. If the spelling checker has pointed out a word that is not misspelled and should be added to your personal dictionary, click the Learn button.

8. To delete a flagged word, click the Delete button.

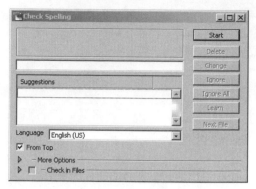

Figure 3.27 The Check Spelling dialog box lets you choose from several dictionaries.

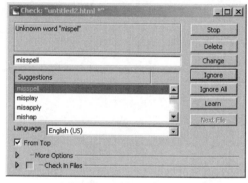

Figure 3.28 When the spelling checker questions a word, you can choose the correct spelling from the list presented in the lower pane.

✔ Tips

- While you have the Check Spelling dialog box open, GoLive highlights questionable words in the Document window. You may need to move the dialog box in order to see the highlighting. That's what I did in **Figure 3.29**.

- If you're working in the HTML Source or HTML Outline Editor, the spelling checker ignores the HTML code that surrounds your text when performing its check.

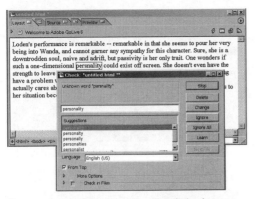

Figure 3.29 Move the Check Spelling dialog box out of the way to see where a misspelled word appears in your document.

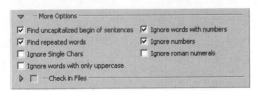

Figure 3.30 From the More Options panel of the Check Spelling dialog box, you can customize your check to ignore certain words and look for common typing errors.

Figure 3.31 Choose the open site in the Files from menu in the Check Spelling dialog box to check the spelling throughout your entire site.

To customize the spelling checker:

1. With the Check Spelling dialog box open, click the More Options triangle at the bottom of the window (**Figure 3.30**). A list of options appears.

2. Check or uncheck options to customize the way GoLive checks your spelling.

To check spelling in multiple files:

1. With the Check Spelling window open, click the Check in Files triangle.

2. Click Add Files.

3. Locate files whose spelling you want to check and click Add.

4. When you're finished, click Done. The files you've added appear in the Check in Files pane of the Check Spelling window. You can now begin the check.

To check an entire site's spelling:

1. Open a GoLive site file and be sure that the Site window is visible.

2. Click on a file in the Site window.

3. The Check Spelling dialog box appears. Click the in Files triangle at the bottom of the Check Spelling window.

4. Choose your site's name from the Files from menu (**Figure 3.31**).

5. Click Start to begin checking your site's spelling. When the checker has finished with the first file, it opens the next file (alphabetically) in your site and begins checking.

✔ Tip

- When you click Ignore All or Learn, your instructions are carried throughout the current checking session, including all of the files in your site.

Find and Replace Text

You can search one document or a whole site with GoLive's Find and Replace features. You can search text (including Web page content and HTML code) for characters, words, or phrases. Find and Replace work in the Layout, Source, and Outline Editors.

✔ Tip

■ GoLive allows you to locate and replace items within a single file (locally), a site (globally), or within a group of files you select. You can also search within site reports, which I cover in Chapter 16, "Viewing and Managing Sites." You can look for text or code or search with powerful regular expressions (commonly called "grep") that use wildcards, then use the Replace feature on whatever you find. The Element feature, which allows you to search for HTML tags and other code, is covered in Chapter 12.

Finding text locally

You can search for and replace text contained in one or more files using the Find command.

To find text in a file:

1. Open a GoLive document and make sure that you are in the Layout, Source, or Outline Editor.

2. Choose Edit > Find, or type Command-F (Mac) or Control-F (Windows). The Find dialog box appears.

3. Type a word that can be found within the current document. **Figure 3.32** shows the Find dialog box ready to search.

4. Click Find.

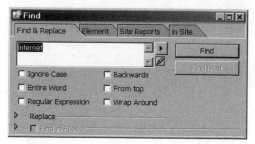

Figure 3.32 Enter text to search for in the Find dialog box.

nd and receive e-mail, participate in newsgroups, and access Internet
a connection to the Internet. This connection might be through an Internet
or through a network.

Figure 3.33 Text matching your search request is highlighted in the Document window.

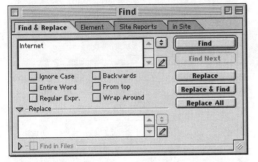

Figure 3.34 Open the Replace field by clicking the triangle in the Find dialog box.

5. When GoLive finds an instance of the word you've searched for, it highlights the word in the Document window (**Figure 3.33**). Click Find Next to look for another instance of the word.

To replace text locally:

1. Use the Find dialog box to search for text.

2. If it isn't already visible, open the Replace field by clicking on the triangle near the bottom of the window (**Figure 3.34**).

3. Type some text to replace whatever you're going to find.

4. Click Find. Notice that you have the option to replace the text individually (Replace) or to automatically find and replace all occurrences within your document (Replace All). If you would rather make the decision to replace text case by case, simply click the Find & Replace button to replace the current instance and then locate another occurrence of your text in one step.

✔ Tip

■ When you use Find & Replace to change text in the Source or Outline Editor, you may inadvertently destroy links if they contain the text you are replacing, because the Replace command does not distinguish between text that is part of a URL and text that is part of the body of the document.

Search options

The Find dialog box includes several check boxes that allow you to modify your search (**Figure 3.35**).

- ◆ Ignore Case searches only for text without regard to its capitalization.

- ◆ Entire Word limits your search to results that match the spacing of the word you type. For example, if you search for "go" with Entire Word checked, you won't find occurrences of the word "GoLive".

- ◆ Regular Expression tells GoLive to activate wildcard searching using regular expressions.

- ◆ Backwards searches before the current insertion point.

- ◆ From top starts the search at the beginning of the document.

- ◆ Wrap Around starts a search at the current location, continues to the end of the document, and starts again at the beginning.

Searching multiple files

Searching for text in several files works very much the same way as searching the currently open document.

To search multiple files:

1. Click the Find in Files triangle (**Figure 3.36**). Don't worry if the Find in Files label is dimmed. You can still open that section of the window.

2. Click Add Files and navigate to a file you want in the upper pane.

3. Click Add. The file's name appears in the lower pane (**Figure 3.37**).

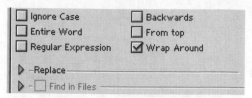

Figure 3.35 Choose one of these options to narrow or organize your search.

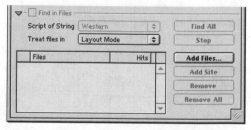

Figure 3.36 Click the Find in Files triangle to open this part of the dialog box and search in multiple files.

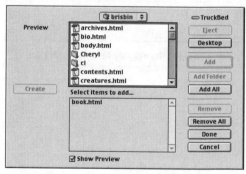

Figure 3.37 When you click Add Files, GoLive presents a file browser window where you can choose files to include in the search. Select one, click Add, and it will appear in the lower pane of the dialog box.

Figure 3.38 When you add files to a search in the Windows version of GoLive, choose HTML Files only, because GoLive can't search non-HTML files, even though it will let you add them to a search.

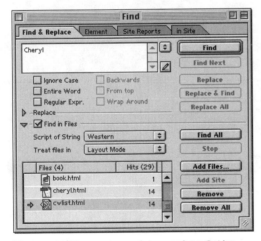

Figure 3.39 When your search is complete, GoLive shows the number of occurrences in each document in the Find dialog box.

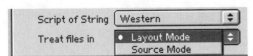

Figure 3.40 Search the contents (including tags and URLs) of the Source view by choosing Source Mode from the Treat files in menu.

4. Repeat Step 3 to add more files.

5. When you're finished, click Done. The files you've added appear in the Files field of the Find dialog box.

6. Use the Find & Replace commands as described above. When GoLive finds an occurrence of the text you're searching for, it opens the file, unless it's already open.

✔ Tips

■ In the Windows version of GoLive, you can add any file to a multifile search list while you're browsing your hard drive. But only HTML files will show up in the Files list in the Find dialog box. Make sure that HTML is selected in the "Files of type" pull-down menu (**Figure 3.38**). GoLive's Mac version simply won't let you add incompatible files to a search.

■ When GoLive searches multiple files, the Find dialog box displays the number of matches in the Files field (**Figure 3.39**). View the document with text matching your search by double-clicking its name in the Files field.

Searching HTML source code

When HTML files with results that match your search criteria open, they do so in the Layout Editor. In a multifile search, you can choose to have GoLive look at URLs and tags, and open files with matches in the Source Editor. To do so, in the Find dialog box choose Source Mode from the Treat files in pull-down menu (**Figure 3.40**).

✔ Tip

■ You'll find much more powerful code-searching tools under the Element tab in the Find dialog box, which I discuss in Chapter 12.

Working with Images

Images bring Web pages to life. They may be pictures that accompany text, buttons, or navigation elements. They may even be animated.

Unlike text that exists as part of a Web page, images are external files that are connected to a Web page by special HTML tags. HTML and GoLive allow you to specify a number of image attributes that change the appearance of pictures or alter their relationship with surrounding elements.

GoLive includes a number of features that make it easier to integrate image building in other Adobe applications, such as Photoshop, Illustrator, and Live Motion.

In this chapter, I'll cover

- Using images on the Web

- Adding images

- Setting image attributes

- Creating image maps

- Smart Objects and Save for Web

- Using layered Photoshop images

- Importing tracing images

Using Images on the Web

Adding an image to a Web page is remarkably easy. Basically, you create a link between the page and a graphics file, and the picture appears on your Web page. But there are a few rules that make that straightforward process a bit more complicated. In other words, you need to know a little about image formats and loading characteristics before you go dropping images into your Web pages.

Web image formats

The two most common image types, or formats, on the Web are GIF (Graphic Interchange Format) and JPEG (Joint Photographic Experts Group). GIF and JPEG account for almost all of the still images on the Web. All browsers support both formats. You can also use the newer PNG (Portable Network Graphics) format, which is supported by current versions of Internet Explorer and some versions of Netscape Navigator. PNG, like GIF, supports 256 colors, but compresses them without the patented compression method used by GIF. Trouble is, PNG is not as universally supported as GIF, so it isn't used a great deal. Other file formats, such as QuickTime and PDF (portable document format), are viewed with Web browser plug-ins. I'll discuss them more fully in Chapter 14, "Working with Rich Media." In this chapter, I'll describe how to add and use static GIF and JPEG images in your Web pages. All the rules apply to both formats.

GoLive can import images that are not HTML-friendly and can convert these graphics files for the Web when you drag them onto a GoLive document. For more about working with foreign file formats and image-editing applications, see "Smart Objects and Save For Web," later in this chapter.

Image loading characteristics

Images make your Web page look great, but they also cause the page to load more slowly. That's usually a handicap you can deal with by planning your use of images carefully. You can control the download time of images by choosing the format that's both the most compact and appropriate for the task at hand. In this case, compact has more than one meaning. Both JPEG and GIF images are compressed, but you can shave even more download time by saving any GIFs or JPEGs at the lowest number of colors that will still preserve the integrity of the image. You'll need to make these adjustments in your image-editing software and evaluate the tradeoff between image size and quality by taking a careful look at your images.

GoLive gives you some help in creating images that are compact: You can use the Lossy slider in the Image Inspector (described more fully in "Adding Images," later in this chapter) to establish just the right balance between compression and color. You can also use the Image Inspector to *interlace* a GIF image. An interlaced image loads gradually as a Web page loads, increasing in resolution as it does, so that when the page is fully loaded, the GIF is at its best quality. This option doesn't make your images any smaller, but it is a way to give your visitors something to look at while a complex page loads.

You can also keep images compact by using smaller ones—smaller in terms of width and height, that is. There are two ways to size an image destined for the Web: Size the image in a graphics program like Photoshop before you add it to a Web page, or use GoLive (or any Web page authoring tool) to adjust the size attributes of the image. I recommend you use the first method, determining approximately what size your image should be before you begin working in GoLive.

You'll have more flexibility in dealing with images in their native applications. In this chapter, I'll show you how to use GoLive to size images, but doing so will not decrease graphic download time, because whatever measurement the image attribute shows, a Web browser still must download a full-size image.

Finally, using one image rather than several can save on download time for your site's visitors. Each individual graphic requires a separate request to the Web server, and a separate, though usually quick, download. If you want to create a navigation element or a large graphic that looks as if it's composed of several images, try building an image map— a single image that contains several sections indicated by clickable hot spots. I'll explain how to create image maps later in this chapter (see "Creating Clickable Image Maps").

Figure 4.1 The Image icon appears on the Basic tab of the Objects palette.

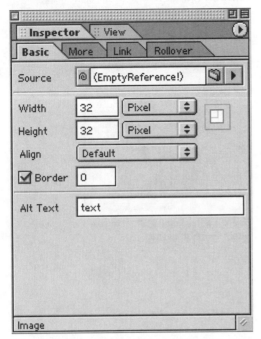

Figure 4.2 When you add an image to a page, the Image Inspector's Basic tab is displayed.

Adding Images

You can bring images into a GoLive document using the Image icon from the Objects palette, or you can drag an image file from your hard drive into the Document window. If you're working in a GoLive site, you can drag an image from the Site window to the Document window. If you use the Image icon to add an image, you'll need to use the Inspector to help you locate the image you want to use.

GoLive will display Web-friendly image files and can also import other formats (see "Importing Images"), but the process for adding the picture to the page remains the same.

Wrangling images

When you add an image to a document, GoLive builds a URL for it based on the image's location within your site or on your hard drive. It's essential, then, that images be stored with the rest of your Web files or, better yet, within a GoLive site. If for some reason you aren't working within a GoLive site, I recommend that you at least create a folder for all of your images within the folder that contains your HTML files, and add your image files to it before you begin adding the images to your pages. Consider this a pitch for GoLive's site management tools, which make it easy to get all of your files organized and to update links to images automatically if necessary.

To add an image to a document:

1. With the Layout Editor visible, drag the Image icon (**Figure 4.1**) from the Objects palette into the Document window.

   or

   Double-click the Image icon. An image placeholder appears in the Document window and the Image Inspector (**Figure 4.2**) opens.

(continues on next page)

2. In the Inspector, click the Browse button (the icon that looks like a folder, next to the Source field, and shown in **Figure 4.3**) and locate an image file.

or

If you're working in a GoLive site, Point & Shoot by clicking the Fetch URL button to the left of the Source field and drag to the Site window. Let go of the mouse button when it's over the image file you want (**Figure 4.4**).

✔ Tip

■ If the image is stored in a closed folder within the site window, drag the cursor over the folder to open it.

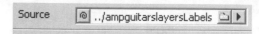

Figure 4.3 Click the Browse button in the Image Inspector to locate an image on your hard drive.

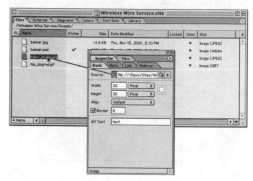

Figure 4.4 Use Point & Shoot to select an image within your GoLive site.

Setting Image Attributes

Images on Web pages can have a variety of attributes that specify their size, alignment, and arrangement on the page. In most cases, you'll configure images in the Image Inspector.

Sizing images

The HTML image tag includes optional attributes that specify the dimensions of an image. Though it's optional in HTML, GoLive always adds the width and height attributes to the page's code when you place an image.

GoLive gives you the ability to resize an image with the Inspector or by dragging the handles within the Document window, but I advise against both options. Resizing an image on an HTML page does not actually change the image's dimensions, but instructs the browser to render the image differently. That takes time and decreases the accuracy of the image's display on the page. If you add an image to a page and decide that it needs resizing, use an image-editing application to do it, then place the new version in GoLive. Image resizing in GoLive can be useful, however, if you're designing a prototype of a new page and simply want to see how changing the image's size affects your design.

Let's take a look at GoLive's resizing tools. The Image Inspector provides three measurement systems for resizing an image.

◆ Pixel: the image's size in pixels

◆ Percent: the image's size as a percentage of the size of the original image

◆ Image: automatically sets the width or height measurement to that of the original

Pixel is the default measuring system. To use the Percent or Image option, make the appropriate choice from the Width or Height pop-up menu.

To resize an image with the Inspector:

1. Select an image in the Document window.

2. Change the unit of measurement in the Height pop-up menu to Image.

3. Type a number in pixels in the Width box with the Pixel option still selected (**Figure 4.5**).

4. Press Tab to apply the change. The image is resized proportionally.

✔ Tips

- You can use the Width and Height fields to choose measurements manually, but unless you do the math, the two dimensions are likely to have a skewed aspect ratio and the image will look distorted.

- You can also resize an image in the Document window by dragging one of the handles on each side and corner of the image. To resize an image proportionally, hold down the Shift key as you drag the handle in the lower-right corner of the image in the Document window. Note that if you have changed the measurement in the Inspector's Height pop-up menu to Image, as previously described, you won't be able to resize with the handles.

When you resize an image, a resize warning icon appears in the lower-left corner of the image (**Figure 4.6**).

To return a resized image to its original dimensions, click the Set to Original Size button next to the Width and Height fields (**Figure 4.7**) in the Image Inspector. You must choose Pixel from the Height and Width pop-up menus for this to work.

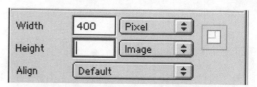

Figure 4.5 Choose Image as the unit of measure for one dimension. Then, for the other dimension, change the Pixel value.

Figure 4.6 The resize warning icon in the lower-right corner tells you that the image has been resized.

Figure 4.7 Click the Set to Original Size button in the Image Inspector to return an image to its original size.

Figure 4.8 Choose an image alignment option from the Image Inspector's Alignment pop-up menu.

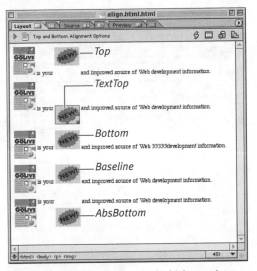

Figure 4.9 Top aligns the icon to the highest point on the line. TextTop aligns the icon to the upper-most element of the text. Bottom aligns the image to the bottom of the text. Baseline aligns the image to the baseline of the adjacent text. AbsBottom aligns the bottom of the icon to the bottom of the largest item on the line—the book cover.

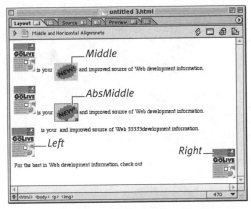

Figure 4.10 Middle relates the middle of the icon to the text baseline. AbsMiddle aligns the middle to the largest item on the line. The Left and Right alignment options align the book covers to the left and right of the page.

Aligning images

In HTML parlance, aligning an image means aligning it with adjacent text. It's not necessary to align an image with text unless you want the text and image to move together. In other words, if you want text to wrap around an image or to maintain a certain position relative to the image, you need to align the image. If you're using a layout grid, table, or floating box, you'll need to insert the image into the layout text box containing the text you want the image aligned with. Image alignment also works (and is almost essential) if you're designing pages without a layout grid.

You can align images vertically or horizontally, in one of several ways. It's simple enough to apply an alignment to an image, but it's trickier to know just which alignment to choose, because many of the choices have similar properties.

To align an image with adjacent text:

1. Add an image to the area where the text will be (Document window, layout grid, table cell or floating box).

2. Type some text; a sentence should do.

3. Click the image to select it.

4. In the Inspector, choose an alignment from the Alignment pop-up menu (**Figure 4.8**). **Figures 4.9** and **4.10** show the effect of aligning images with text, using the nine available options.

Alternative text

Some Web browsers, such as Lynx, do not support images. In addition, visually impaired users often turn off image display in their browsers because they have difficulty navigating graphical Web pages, especially if they use screen-reading software to speak the contents of Web pages. To accommodate these circumstances, you can add an alternative (alt) text attribute—just a word or two. Text-only Web browsers and browsers with graphics support turned off display alternative text where the image would otherwise be.

To add alternative text to an image:

1. Click the image to select it.

2. If necessary, open the Image Inspector, and then type a one- or two-word description of the image in the Alt Text field.

Low-source images

You can give your site's visitors something to look at while large image files load by adding a low-resolution version of the image to your page. This image is displayed while the higher-quality image is downloaded to the visitor's computer. GoLive can generate a low-source image for you, or you can create it yourself.

To add a low-source image:

1. Select an image in the Document window and click the Image Inspector's More tab.

2. Click the Generate button. GoLive creates a low-resolution version of the image you're working with and stores it in the folder with your original image (**Figure 4.11**). The file name appears next to the Low check box. It's the same as the source image file name, with *ls* inserted just before the file extension, as in *mydogls.gif.*

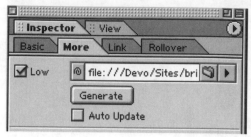

Figure 4.11 When you generate a low-resolution version of an image, GoLive stores it along with the original image.

If you would rather create your own low-resolution image, use Photoshop, Graphic-Converter, DeBabelizer, or the image manipulation program of your choice to save a low-resolution version of your original image.

To use your own low-res image:

1. Give the low-resolution image a name similar to that of the original (for example, *imagels.gif*) and store it in the same folder as the original.

2. In GoLive, add the higher-quality version of the image to your layout.

3. In the More tab of the Image Inspector, click the Low check box.

4. Click the Browse button next to the check box and locate the low-res image.

   or

   Point & Shoot to the low-res image.

Spacing and borders

You can give an image some breathing room with the HSpace (horizontal space) and VSpace (vertical space) attributes, which move adjacent text and objects away from the image by the number of pixels you specify. Or you can create a black border around an image for emphasis, in which case, the distance between the image and other items on the page is filled with color on all four sides.

Enter a pixel value in the HSpace or VSpace field to create space around the image. Unlike a border, which is visible, the space options simply leave an empty area around the image.

To add space around an image:

1. With the image selected, click the More tab in the Image Inspector.

2. Type pixel measurements in the HSpace and VSpace fields of the Inspector (**Figure 4.12**).

3. Press Tab to confirm your change. The box around the image expands to show the space you have added (**Figure 4.13**).

To add a border to an image:

1. Select an image. Notice that the Border check box is checked in the Image Inspector.

2. In the Border field, type the size (in pixels) for the border. A border appears around the image (**Figure 4.14**).

3. If you uncheck the Border check box, the border disappears.

Figure 4.12 Add space around an image with the HSpace and VSpace fields in the Inspector.

Figure 4.13 With horizontal and vertical space around an image, a border appears in the Layout Editor and adjacent text moves over.

Figure 4.14 This image has a 12-pixel border.

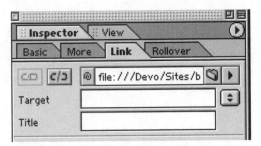

Figure 4.15 The Link tab of the Image Inspector lets you set an image as a link to another Web page.

Using an image as a link

Just as you can link one Web page to another with a text hyperlink, you can make an image into a link. This is useful when your design includes buttons or other image-based navigation and when you want to link a thumbnail version of an image to a larger one.

To link from an image:

1. Select an image you want to be a link and click the Link tab in the Image Inspector.

2. Click the Link button. The fields become active (**Figure 4.15**).

3. Use the Browse button or Point & Shoot to the page or URL you want to link to.
   or
   Type a URL in the Link field.

✔ Tips

- You can also link from an image by Control-clicking (Mac) or right-clicking (Windows) the image in the Document window and choosing New Link. You can then add the Link in the Inspector.

- The Inspector's Link tab includes fields for setting a Target for your image link. Basically, the Target option allows you to choose where the link will open—usually a new frame or a new window. I'll have more to say about targets in Chapter 6, "Working with Links," and Chapter 11, "Working with Frames."

Creating Image Maps

We've seen that you can use an image not only as decoration for your page, but also as a link to another location on the Web. Actually, you can include several links within a single image. That arrangement is called a *clickable image map,* and the locations your site's visitors will click are called *hot spots.* Some site designers use image maps to add hot spots to navigation bars or provide more information from large graphics such as maps or diagrams. A picture of a car, for example, might include hot spots on the tires, doors, and hood, indicating that the viewer can get more information about these parts of the car by clicking on the appropriate hot spot. A world map could include hot spots for each region, leading to a page for that region's sales office.

You can invoke image maps in two ways. The first is from the Web server, using a CGI (Common Gateway Interface) application to support the image map. The second, simpler, way is to create *client-side* image maps, which are configured entirely within your Web pages. When you use a client-side image map, neither you as the page designer nor a visitor clicking on an image map needs to have any interaction with the Web server beyond the usual downloading of HTML files and images. Client-side maps, as you can imagine, are easier to work with. GoLive allows you to create client-side maps. Server-side image maps are outside the scope of this book.

There are two steps to creating a client-side image map: setting up the map and linking hot spots.

Figure 4.16 Click the Use Map check box to activate the Name field in the Image Inspector.

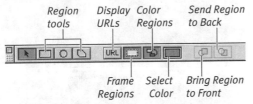

Figure 4.17 Clicking the Use Map check box in the Image Inspector also activates the Image Map toolbar.

Figure 4.18 Image map tools appear in the contextual menu.

To set up a clickable image map:

1. Choose an image from which you will create an image map. The image should be large enough to accommodate several hot spots and should include distinct sections that lend themselves to the image-map treatment.

2. Add the image to a GoLive document.

3. Make any needed changes to the image's attributes.

4. In the Inspector, click the More tab and then the Use Map check box.

   or

   Control-click (Mac) or right-click (Windows) and choose Set Map. The Name field is activated in the Inspector, and a default map name is supplied (**Figure 4.16**).

5. You can change the map name by typing over the default name in the Name field. Use a single word or other string of characters that appeals to you.

The Image Map toolbar contains the tools you need to create and modify image map hot spots (**Figure 4.17**). To create hot spots, you use the tools to draw them on the image. You can also use the contextual menu to access the tools (**Figure 4.18**).

To create hot spots:

1. Select the image map in the Document window.

2. From the toolbar, choose the region tool (rectangle, circle, or polygon) that best matches the hot spot shape you want to create.

   or

   Control-click (Mac) or right-click (Windows) and choose one of these options from the contextual menu.

   (continues on next page)

3. Draw the hot spot on your image. Handles appear at the sides and corners (**Figure 4.19**) so that you can adjust the size of the hot spot if necessary. When you add or select a hot spot, the Map Area Inspector appears.

4. With the hot spot selected, type a URL for it in the Inspector's URL field (**Figure 4.20**) or use Browse or Point & Shoot to locate a local file or URL.

5. Repeat Steps 1–4 for each hot spot you want to create.

Viewing hot spots as you work

GoLive includes tools that allow you to deal more easily with hot spots as you work with them. You can add a border or a linked URL, or even choose a color for the region so that it stands out from the rest of the image. The Color and URL buttons are also toggles that allow you to display or hide a hot spot's color or URL. These enhancements are for your convenience, and don't appear on the finished area map.

To control the display of hot spots:

1. Turn off region framing by clicking the Frame Regions button on the toolbar. Click it again to see the hot spot borders, as shown in **Figure 4.21**.

2. Customize your hot spot color by clicking the Select Color button. The Color palette appears, allowing you to choose a new color.

Figure 4.19 The amp has a rectangular hot spot drawn on it.

Figure 4.20 Configure the hot spot's link in the Map Area Inspector.

Figure 4.21 Use the Frame Regions button to show or hide a border around the hot spot.

✔ Tip

- It can be tricky to select an image when it includes hot spots. To select a previously created hot spot, click the arrow button on the Image Map toolbar and then, when the cursor is an arrow, click over the hot spot. Clicking when the hand is visible (when you move the mouse over the edge of the image) selects the image, not the hot spot. Use the Bring Region to Front or Send Region to Back buttons to work with hot spots that overlap one another.

Smart Objects and Save For Web

Smart objects allow you to bring Photoshop, Illustrator, or LiveMotion files in a variety of formats into GoLive pages. GoLive creates a Web-safe version of the image and maintains a link between the Web-safe version and the original. When you make changes to the original image in its native application, GoLive updates the Web-safe version of the image.

The Smart Object feature also recognizes Photoshop, Illustrator, and LiveMotion variables. Setting a variable allows you to use multiple versions of a source file in GoLive, giving you the ability to choose the one that looks best when saved for the Web.

You can add Smart Objects from the Site window or by placing a Smart Object icon in a document. You'll find Photoshop and Illustrator icons on the Smart set of the Objects palette, along with a Smart Generic icon for importing other supported formats, including PDF and EPS. The GoLive installer adds a LiveMotion icon if it finds the application on your hard drive.

To import a smart image, just add the appropriate smart icon (not the Image icon from the Basic tab) or drag the image from the Site window into the Document window, with the Layout Editor visible. Either way, GoLive's Save For Web tool opens and displays options for optimizing a Web-friendly version of the image from the imported file.

✔ Tip

- Because smart objects consist of both a source and a Web-safe file, it's particularly important to work within a GoLive site when using them. The site hierarchy even has a place for smart source files, and the site interface's link management features help you to find and repair broken links when they occur. Copy your original file to your site folder's `site.data/SmartObjects` folder. When you add the image to a GoLive page and save it for the Web, store it in the site hierarchy (visible in the site window) so that it can be properly linked and uploaded to your Web server.

To add a smart object:

1. With a document open in the Layout Editor, drag a Photoshop, Illustrator, LiveMotion, or other supported image to the Document window.

   or

   Click the Smart set of the Objects palette and double-click the Smart Photoshop, Smart Illustrator, Smart LiveMotion, or Smart Generic icon (**Figure 4.22**).

   or

   Control-click (Mac) or right-click (Windows) in the Layout Editor, and choose, for example, Insert Object > Smart > Smart Photoshop (**Figure 4.23**). A Smart Object placeholder appears in the Layout Editor and the Smart Image Inspector opens (**Figure 4.24**).

2. If you added the image with a Smart Object icon, click the Browse button or Point & Shoot from the Source field to the image you want to import.

Figure 4.22 Smart Object icons appear on the Smart set of the Objects palette. LiveMotion is not installed on this computer, so there is no Smart Object icon for that application.

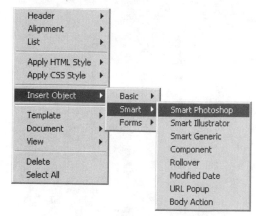

Figure 4.23 Add a Smart Object from the contextual menu.

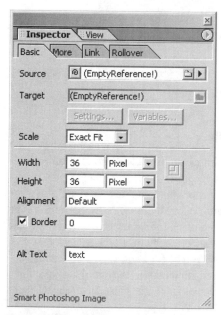

Figure 4.24 The Smart Image Inspector lets you choose image attributes and smart object–specific settings.

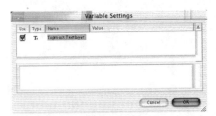

Figure 4.25 If a smart image contains variables, this dialog box appears before Save For Web. Click the Use check box to bring the variable into GoLive. This variable is a Photoshop text layer.

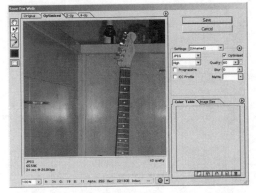

Figure 4.26 The Save For Web window shows the image you're working on and the tools you can use to optimize it for the Web.

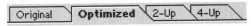

Figure 4.27 View the original and a Web-optimized version of the image.

Figure 4.28 The dialog box should open to your site's root folder. Save the Web image here or in a folder with other images.

3. If you choose a source image containing variables, GoLive displays the Variable Settings dialog box (**Figure 4.25**). Choose the variables you want to import by clicking the Use check box next to each.

4. Click OK. GoLive either opens Save For Web (**Figure 4.26**) or opens the source file in its native application.

To optimize an image in Save For Web:

1. Click the Optimized tab or the 2-Up tab at the top of the window (**Figure 4.27**) so that you can see the image change as you work with it. If you click the 4-Up tab, you can work with four versions of the image (including the original).

2. If you like the optimized image, click OK to save it.

3. Choose a location for the Web-safe image in the dialog box that opens. You should store the image within your site hierarchy as shown in **Figure 4.28**.

✔ Tips

■ Once you've created a smart object, you can open the original file in its native application by double-clicking the Web image in the Layout Editor. When you edit the file in Photoshop, LiveMotion, or Illustrator, the Web-safe version is updated.

■ When you import a Photoshop file that contains multiple layers, the Web-friendly version of the file becomes a "flat" file, containing no layers. You can, however, import Photoshop layers individually (see "Adding Layered Photoshop Images" later in this chapter).

A tour of Save For Web

Save For Web optimizes images based on its best guess about what settings will work with your image. You can accept these or make changes to them in the Save For Web window. You can also save sets of image settings for future use.

You can customize a variety of options—different ones for each format. You can also choose one of the preconfigured groups of settings that are commonly associated with the GIF, JPEG, PNG, and WBMP formats.

Choosing Save For Web settings

Each of the file formats in Save For Web has its own set of options. You can change one or more and save the set to build your own group, but GoLive is usually pretty good at guessing the best file format for displaying an image on the Web. For example, photographic images should be saved as JPEGs because JPEG handles a greater range of colors than does the GIF format. And as I mentioned early in this chapter, though the PNG format is fully supported by GoLive, it is not universally supported by browsers and is not usually the best choice.

To choose a different file format in Save For Web:

1. Either import a new smart object or select one and click the Settings button in the Smart Image Inspector. The Save For Web window opens, showing GoLive's choices of optimum settings for your image.

2. To view both the original image and an optimized version, click the 2-Up tab at the top of the window.

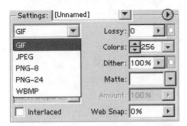

Figure 4.29 Choose a different Save For Web format if you wish.

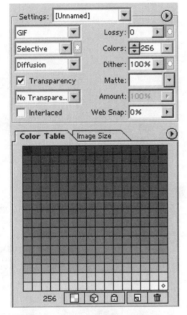

Figure 4.30 GIF options include number of colors, transparency, and dithering.

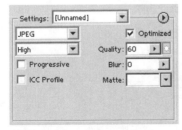

Figure 4.31 The JPEG format does not offer options for choosing color, but does allow you to specify the quality of the image relative to its file size.

3. To choose a different image format, select it from the Format menu, immediately below the Settings label (**Figure 4.29**). The options for customizing the image's quality and color characteristics change when you select a new format. **Figure 4.30** shows GIF options. JPEG options appear in **Figure 4.31**.

To choose GIF optimization settings:

1. With GIF selected in the Save For Web format menu, enter a percentage value in the Lossy field or click the arrow next to the field to compress the image more. Using more compression reduces file size, but can result in degradation of your image. Be sure to examine the image carefully if you use the Lossy setting, and strike a balance between compression and quality that you're comfortable with.

2. Choose a color reduction algorithm from the pull-down menu (just below the Format menu) if you want to use a palette other than the standard Web palette for this image.

3. Choose a maximum number of colors to use in this image. Fewer colors means a smaller file size.

4. Choose a dithering option from the Dither menu and a dithering percentage to indicate how the browser should deal with 24-bit color images that are displayed on 8-bit computer monitors.

5. Click the Transparency check box to maintain existing transparency within the image.

6. To avoid "halos" around your image, choose a Matte color (the color to which transparent pixels are changed) that matches the background color of your page.

(continues on next page)

7. Click the Interlaced check box to load a GIF image in a series of consecutive stages, with the first hint of the image displaying in the browser almost immediately.

8. Use the Web Snap field to convert colors within the image to the closest Web-safe color. GoLive will locate and use the Web-safe colors nearest to the colors in the image.

To chose JPEG optimization settings:

1. With JPEG selected in the Save For Web Format menu, click the Optimized check box to "streamline" the file, decreasing its file size.

2. Choose an option from the Quality menu, or use the Quality field to choose an option that displays the JPEG image. Higher Quality settings display more color, but cause the file to be larger in size.

3. Click the Progressive check box to cause the image to load in stages in a browser. This option is somewhat like the Interlaced GIF option described earlier.

4. Enter a Blur value to smooth images with sharp angles or edges.

PNG-6 settings are identical to those for the GIF format. PNG-24 has Transparency and Matte settings, and WBMP files can be dithered.

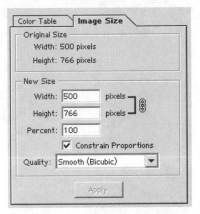

Figure 4.32 Use the Image Size tab to resize the Web-formatted image in the Save For Web dialog box. Doing so does not affect the HTML for the page, only the size of the image file.

Sizing a Save For Web image

The Image Size tab is the same, regardless of the file format you're using (**Figure 4.32**). Because you're creating a new file rather than resizing one in HTML, my admonition earlier in the chapter about resizing images in GoLive does not apply here. You can resize the image as you see fit. Remember that this action has no impact on the source file for your smart object.

When you enter a pixel value in the Width field, the Height field is changed proportionally, unless you uncheck the Constrain Proportions check box.

Adding Layered Photoshop Images

Savvy Photoshop users use layers to make complex, visually stunning layouts. Layered Photoshop images can be directly imported into GoLive, either as described earlier, by "flattening" the contents of the layers into a single GIF or JPEG document when a smart object is imported, or by preserving the layers as individual elements. The layers are imported into GoLive as floating boxes that can be stacked on top of one another. Using layered images will bulk up your layout with multiple image files, but the flexibility and quality are often worth the few extra seconds of download time for your site's visitors.

Note that Photoshop layers imported individually are not smart objects. Editing the original file doesn't affect the files you create in Save For Web.

To import Photoshop layers:

1. With a document open in the Layout Editor, choose File > Import > Photoshop as Floating Boxes.

2. In the dialog box, locate a Photoshop file containing layers.

3. Select a folder (or make a new one) that will contain the Photoshop layer files. You should store this folder within your site folder, preferably within an existing Images folder.

4. The Save For Web window opens, displaying the first layer of the Photoshop document. Adjust the settings if you need to and click Save.

5. Click OK. The next layer appears in the Save For Web window.

6. Configure it, click OK, and repeat the procedure for each layer in the document.

Figure 4.33 This group of floating boxes was created when a Photoshop image with four layers was imported into GoLive.

Once the image has been assembled, its components appear within floating boxes in the GoLive document (**Figure 4.33**). The boxes can be manipulated and reorganized using techniques described in Chapter 9, "Floating Boxes and Positioning." The original layer numbers appear in the floating boxes.

✔ Tip

■ When you create layers in Photoshop or, at the very least, when you import the layered image into GoLive, be sure to name the layers so that you can easily tell which is which. This will help enormously when you begin to rearrange floating boxes or change their stacking order. In Photoshop, you can name layers in the Layers palette. Use the Floating Box palette in GoLive.

ADDING LAYERED PHOTOSHOP IMAGES

Importing Tracing Images

Tracing images have two main uses. They can bring a mock-up created in a program such as Photoshop into GoLive for actual page building, and they can be used as a background—a graphic element, usually lighter in opacity, above which all the other elements of a page sit.

GoLive supports the following import formats for tracing images:

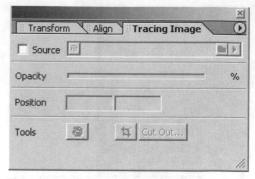

Figure 4.34 Open the Tracing Image palette by choosing Window > Tracing image.

◆ PSD (only RGB 8-bit images)

◆ JPEG

◆ GIF

◆ PNG

◆ BMP (Windows)

◆ TARGA

◆ PCX

◆ PICT (Mac)

◆ PIXAR

◆ TIFF

◆ Amiga IFF

✔ Tip

■ Photoshop file colors are automatically changed to Web-safe colors.

To add a tracing image to a page:

1. Choose Window > Tracing Image. The Tracing Image palette opens (**Figure 4.34**).

2. Click the Source check box to activate the adjacent field.

3. Browse or Point & Shoot to the file you wish to use as a tracing image. The image is imported into your page.

4. You can now adjust the opacity of the image with the Opacity slider in the Tracing Image palette. The less opaque the image, the easier it will be to see other objects placed over it.

5. Click the hand tool in the Tracing Image palette and drag the image to change its position on the page.

or

Use the Position fields to choose where the tracing image will begin in relation to the upper-left corner of the page.

If you use a tracing image to develop a layout, you may want to remove portions of it as you fill in the elements of the design, or you may want to use a portion of the tracing image as part of the final page. You can do this by converting a portion of the tracing image into a floating box. Just like importing Photoshop layers, this process creates a Web-safe image that is located in a floating box, allowing you to manipulate, move, or delete the box as needed.

To cut out a portion of a tracing image:

1. Click the Cut Out tool in the Tracing Image palette.

2. In the Document window, draw a rectangle on the section of the image you want to convert to a floating box.

3. Click the Cut Out button in the Tracing Image palette.

4. Double-click the rectangle in the Document window. Save For Web opens, displaying the section you cut from the tracing image.

5. Select the portion you want to save as a floating box and choose Web-safe options.

6. Click Save to create the new image and store it with your site's other image files. The cut-out portion of the tracing image now appears as a floating box in your document, allowing you to move or modify it separately from the tracing image.

✔ Tip

■ The Image Move and Cut Out tools in the Tracing Image palette can be toggled on and off by clicking.

WORKING WITH COLOR

Placing color on a Web page is easy. Making the right choices, so that the colors you choose work, presents some challenges.

People view Web pages on different computers that employ different color-handling conventions. Thankfully, there is a Web color standard that makes it possible for all color-capable browsers and computers to display the same colors. This "Web-safe" color standard employs a chromatic lowest common denominator, so many colors available on some systems (notably the Macintosh) are not part of the Web-safe color set.

Whatever development platform you use, it's important to use Web-safe colors. This will prevent "dithering," the process whereby a computer fakes a color by the splotchy imposition of one color over another.

GoLive gives you the ability not only to add color—Web-safe or not—to text and objects, but also to associate colors with a site, helping you maintain consistency throughout your project. You'll learn about site colors in Chapter 15, "Building Sites."

In this chapter, I'll cover

◆ Color choices in GoLive

◆ Adding color to pages and objects

◆ Color matching

GoLive Color Schemes

In GoLive, all color comes from the Color palette, which shares a window with the Objects palette. Just click the Color tab or choose Window > Color. The buttons on the Color palette (**Figure 5.1**) provide nine different methods of defining color, or "color spaces" in graphic designer parlance. They are, from left to right:

Figure 5.1 The Color palette contains nine ways to choose color. Only one, Web Color List, contains colors that will appear predictably across all platforms.

◆ Gray Slider defines up to 256 levels of gray. The lower the value, the closer the "color" is to black.

◆ RGB Sliders are how your computer monitor assembles colors from its red, green, and blue light sources. Values here are represented on slider bars for each base color, which can be mixed in near-infinite combinations.

◆ CMYK Sliders are the color model most used in the printing industry. Pigmented "process" inks of cyan, yellow, magenta, and black are mixed for four-color printing. Actually, you're seeing an RGB representation of the CMYK color space on your computer screen. The CMYK set contains millions of colors that are not Web-safe, but are useful when you're trying to match a printed color.

◆ HSB Wheel has a circle in which the RGB color space is defined in hue (base color) and saturation (color density). Pick a color point inside the circle, then use the Brightness slider to modify its level of brightness.

◆ HSV Picker is based on the Windows color model. The set's controls are a combination of RGB percentages moderated by Hue, Saturation, and Value controls.

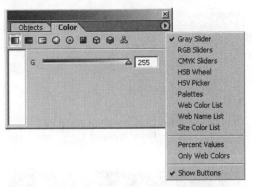

Figure 5.2 The Color palette has a handy flyout menu for selecting the right color scheme.

- Palettes contains the 256-color system palette. In its pull-down menu, you'll find arbitrary palettes of 16 colors, 16 levels of gray, and the 34 colors reserved by Windows for its desktop, as well as a Custom palette for making up to 36 colors, so that your site uses a consistent group of colors.

- Web Color List is the most useful group of colors because these colors can be displayed in all browsers on all computer platforms. Colors in this palette appear on the left side of the palette, with their hexadecimal code equivalents on the right. Confusing? Maybe so, but to the rescue comes...

- Web Name List displays colors with some rather odd but memorable names and hexadecimal values. Web Name Colors are not necessarily Web-safe colors, as some of these colors will dither when displayed on some systems.

- Site Color List contains a visual list of all the colors used on a loaded site. This button is very useful for maintaining color consistency in a growing site.

There are very few colors visible to the human eye that are not contained somewhere in the color gamuts of the Color palette. However, for universal and most predictable results, use the 216-color Web Color List.

✔ Tip

- You can identify any of the nine color sets by moving your cursor over it to view tool tips, or you can use the flyout menu in the upper-right corner of the palette (**Figure 5.2**).

GoLive Color Schemes

Applying Color

To apply color to an object or text in GoLive, first choose a color in the Color palette, then, with the object selected, drag the color to the appropriate Color field in the Inspector. As an example, I'll show you how to apply a background color to a page.

To apply background color to a page:

1. With a document open, click the Page icon (**Figure 5.3**) in the upper-left corner of the page, just above the Document window.

2. Under the Background heading in the Inspector, make sure Color is checked.

3. Open the Color palette (click the Color tab in the Objects palette or choose Window > Color).

4. Select the Web Color List button.

5. Choose a pleasing color. You can use the eyedropper cursor to select a color on the left or scroll through the list on the right side of the window. When you click to select a color, your choice appears in the color preview pane on the left side of the Color palette (Win) and/or as a selection with a hexadecimal name to the right (Mac) (**Figure 5.4**). (The color itself is not selected in the Mac OS version.)

6. Click and hold the mouse button in the preview pane of the Color palette.

7. Drag the cursor out of the preview pane. The cursor becomes a small square outline. You are now carrying a color swatch.

8. Drag the swatch onto the Background Color field in the Inspector (**Figure 5.5**).

   or

   Drag the swatch onto the Page icon in the Document window. The selected color fills the Color box in the Inspector and fills the Document window.

Figure 5.3 Click the Page icon in the Document window to view the Page Inspector.

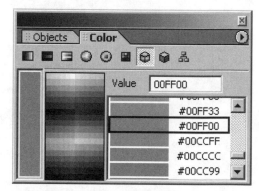

Figure 5.4 Choose a color from the Web List, and it appears in the preview pane on the left, while its hexadecimal value shows on the right.

Figure 5.5 Drag the color over to the Inspector and drop it on the Background Color field.

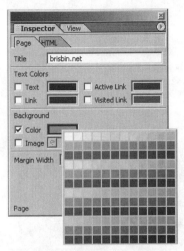

Figure 5.6 Drop a selected color onto the toolbar's Text Color field to change the text color at the insertion point. Selected text can also be colored using this method.

Figure 5.7 Control-click (Control-right-click in Windows) any Color field to choose a Web-safe color.

Applying color to objects

Adding color to a page element (a block of text, a table, a floating box, or some other object), is as simple as choosing the color and dragging it to the object in the Document window or to the Color field in the object's Inspector. To color text, select the text, then drag the color over the selection or onto the Text Color field on the toolbar (**Figure 5.6**). This also works to change the existing color of an element.

✔ Tip

■ You can quickly choose a Web-safe color by Control-clicking (Mac) or Control-right-clicking (Windows) on any Color field (in an Inspector or on the toolbar) and choosing a color from the swatches that appear (**Figure 5.7**). These are the same swatches that appear on the Web Color List of the Color palette. You'll see the hexadecimal number that corresponds to the color you select. If you would like to see the color's name, too, use Control-Option-click (Mac) or Control-Alt-right-click (Windows) in the Color field.

Maintaining Web safety with other color palettes

If you have a background in print publishing, or even if you're a Photoshop veteran, you may be more familiar with CMYK, RGB, and other color formats than you are with Web color. In which case, you might decide to create colors using a palette other than the Web-safe one. When you choose a color from one of these other color spaces, you can see its equivalent in any other space by clicking a different button in the Color palette. This is especially helpful when you click the Web Color List or Web Name List, where you'll see either an exact match to the color you've created or the nearest Web-safe equivalent.

Using the Color Palette to Match Colors

From time to time you may want to change the color of a Web page object to match a color that appears elsewhere on your site—or you may simply like a color that appears in an image you have on hand. The Color palette's eyedropper cursor will sample colors from any object or graphic in a GoLive document and give you an exact match in RGB or the closest Web-safe match available.

To match an existing color:

1. Open the document containing the graphic or other object whose color you want to use.

2. In the Color palette, choose Palettes or Web Color List. Your graphic may have colors that are not Web-safe, but GoLive will locate the nearest match from the Web Color List.

3. Place your cursor over a color swatch. The cursor becomes an eyedropper (**Figure 5.8**).

4. Click and drag the eyedropper over the color you want to sample in the Document window (**Figure 5.9**) and release the mouse button. The eyedropper samples the color and displays the nearest Web-safe color in the preview pane of the Color palette. You can now drag that "borrowed" color to an Inspector's Color field or to any object that accepts color directly.

✔ Tip

■ As you drag the eyedropper over the document containing the color you want to match, notice that the Color palette's preview pane changes as you go. Keep an eye on the pane until you see just the color you want to match. This is especially helpful if you're taking color from a complex image.

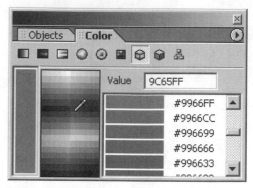

Figure 5.8 Clicking and dragging the mouse over the displayed colors changes the cursor into an eyedropper, which you can use to sample colors.

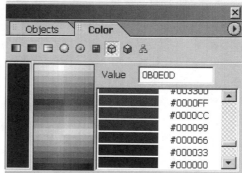

Figure 5.9 Drag the eyedropper pointer to the area that contains the color you wish to sample and release the mouse button. The color appears in the preview pane of the Color palette, ready for use.

WORKING WITH LINKS

Hyperlinks are as essential to the World Wide Web as phone numbers and email are to telecommunication. Links between Web pages make it possible for people to jump instantly (surf) from place to place on the Internet.

Using links effectively is also an integral part of building a useful Web site. You include links on your site to provide points of reference (in the form of navigation bars and tables of contents) and to allow visitors to move from one page to the next.

GoLive provides several ways to create and maintain links. In this chapter, I describe how to create both text and image links. Chapters 4 ("Working with Images") and 14 ("Working with Rich Media") focus on linking with images and to multimedia files respectively. The process of creating these different kinds of links is quite similar, however.

In this chapter, I'll cover

◆ How links work

◆ Creating links

◆ Editing links

◆ Named anchors

◆ Using targets

◆ Link warnings

How Links Work

An HTML link is a pointer from a Web page to another item on the Internet. Links can be indicated using text (often blue and underlined) or images. When you link from a Web page to another Internet item, you must set up two aspects of the link: the text or image that marks the link's beginning and the URL (Uniform Resource Locator) that gives the address of the link's destination. When a Web site visitor clicks a link's beginning, the Web browser uses the link's URL to display, download, or connect to the desired item.

Links can point to other pages within your site, to a remote Web site, or to non-Web resources, such as FTP servers, newsgroups, and email addresses.

Anatomy of a URL

URLs contain all the information needed to turn a link into a means of transportation from one page to another. Most URLs have the same basic structure (see **Table 6.1**):

`Protocol://server.domain/page.html`

Absolute and relative links

Links to remote locations always appear in the URL format described above. These are *absolute* links. URLs that point to items within the same Web site as the referring page may be absolute (with full URLs), or they may be *relative*, specifying only the portion of the URL that's needed, in relation to the page where the link originates.

Table 6.1

URL Anatomy	
ELEMENT	**DESCRIPTION**
Protocol	The type of link. Links to Web pages use http, while FTP links begin with ftp. Email addresses use mailto.
Server	Most Web URLs include www here, though some don't use it. A server may have another name that identifies the specific server, or there may be no server name in the URL at all. Non-Web URLs may include a server name, too, but they're not required.
Domain	The name of the site (often a version of the company's or organization's name) followed by the domain type, such as .com, .org, .gov, .edu, and net.
Page	The name of the individual page to which the URL points. In most cases, entering a URL without a specified page takes you to the site's home page. When you connect to a URL with no page specified, you may see the page name index.html in your browser. If the link leads to a subsidiary page within a site, the page's name will appear, preceded by a slash (/) and followed by an extension (usually .htm or .html). Links to pages stored within directories include the directory name (/directory/page.html).

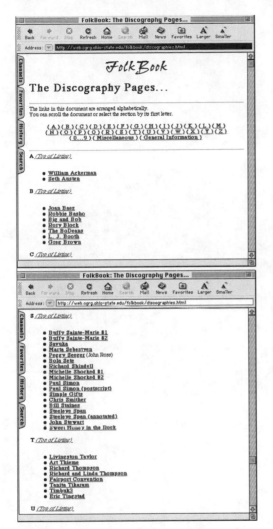

Figure 6.1 Each letter in the alphabet at the top of the FolkBook Artists' Page links to a lettered anchor farther down the page.

For example, a relative URL from your home page to a product catalog page within your site might be `/catalog.html`, or even `/products/catalog.html`, if the file resides within the products directory of your site. The full URL is not needed because Web servers know to look in relation to the current Web page for requested items. Relative URLs can point to any object within the same site, whether it's in the same directory or in a directory that is above or below the source file.

You can also create links that point to locations on the same page as the link; these links are called *anchors* and are used to make it easier to navigate through long documents (**Figure 6.1**).

Using relative links is simpler than typing long absolute URLs, and it also makes things go a lot more smoothly when you need to add or change links within your site, or when you move your site from one server to another. For instance, you might move a site from an internal staging or production server to a live public server; or from one Web hosting provider to another. By default, the links you create in GoLive will all be relative, unless you specifically choose to use absolute links. To do so, you'll need to select the "Make new links absolute" option in URL Handling Preferences in the General section of the Preferences window.

Creating Links

GoLive link tools are everywhere: in every Inspector, on the toolbar, on the contextual menu. You can link to and from just about anything, at any time, while working in GoLive.

When you link to a remote URL, whether it's a Web site, an email address, an FTP server, or some other resource that is not part of your site, you'll use the full URL, as described in the previous section. If you want to link to a file stored on your hard disk, be sure that the item you link to (HTML file, image, or multimedia file) is located within the folder that contains your GoLive site files. If you aren't using GoLive's site management tools to store and maintain your site, be sure that both the file you link from and the file you link to are stored in the same relative location they'll be in when you upload them to a Web server. In other words, build your hierarchy of files and folders before you begin making links with GoLive. If you ignore this step and move files or change file or folder names after you have made links, the links will not work because the URLs you created will be incorrect.

✔ Tip

- The best way to improve your chances of avoiding broken links is to build your Web site with GoLive's site management tools, as described in Chapter 15, "Building Sites." Besides helping you maintain a good site hierarchy, the site management interface will let you know if a link somehow becomes broken.

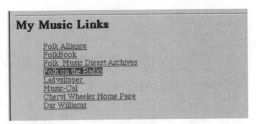

Figure 6.2 Text links should be short, but descriptive.

Figure 6.3 Use the toolbar's New Link button to create a link.

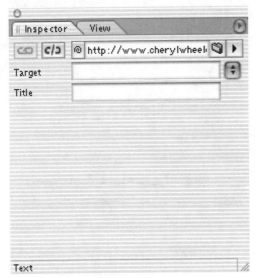

Figure 6.4 Enter your link's URL in the Link field of the Text Inspector.

To link text to a remote URL:

1. In the Layout Editor, select some text (a single word or a short phrase) or an object that you would like to link to a remote resource (**Figure 6.2**). The Text Inspector opens.

2. Click the New Link button on the toolbar (**Figure 6.3**).

   or

   Press Command-L (Mac) or Control-L (Windows).

   or

   Control-click (Mac) or right-click (Windows) and choose New Link from the contextual menu. The link fields in the Text Inspector become active (**Figure 6.4**).

3. Type a complete URL in the URL field. Be sure that the URL includes the correct protocol and syntax, such as http:// or ftp://.

4. Optionally, you can type a title for the link in the Title field. Some browsers can display a link title when you move the mouse over the link.

5. Choose a window location for the link in the Target field, if you wish. For more information on using targets, see Chapter 11, "Working with Frames." Targets are primarily used to direct links within frames-based pages or sites.

CREATING LINKS

To link to a local file:

1. In the Document window, select some text that you would like to link to another file on your hard drive.

2. Create a new link using one of the methods described in the previous set of steps.

3. In the Inspector, click the Browse button and locate the file you want to link to. The relative URL appears in the Text Inspector (**Figure 6.5**) and the linked text is underlined in the Document window.

✔ Tip

- When you link to a file stored on your hard disk, the URL will appear in the Inspector in the format: `file://drive/folder/page.html`. Don't be concerned until you save the current file. The actual URL that appears in the GoLive pages you upload to a Web server does not contain this local path information, but the proper relative URL. The relative URL will work as long as you do not change the relationship between a document and an item you've linked it to. You can use this method to link to files that are part of a local Web site, whether you use GoLive to manage the site or not, as long as the directories and file locations are set up exactly as they will appear when you upload your site to a Web server.

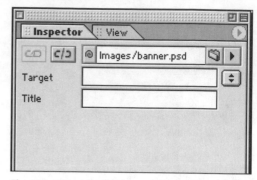

Figure 6.5 When you've chosen a file to link to, the relative URL appears in the Text Inspector's URL field.

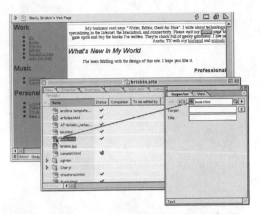

Figure 6.6 Select a link, and then click the Fetch URL button in the Inspector to Point & Shoot, establishing a link to an item in the Site window.

Linking to GoLive site items

In the next few step-by-step examples, I'll describe how to create links between a Web page and items that are part of a GoLive Web site. Site files can store pointers to HTML files, images, scripts, components, and even external resources—Web bookmarks and email addresses, for example. Provided the files to which you are linking are within the site hierarchy, your links will always be valid. GoLive monitors changes you make and updates links automatically.

To link text to a file with Point & Shoot:

1. Open a site file.

2. Open a document by double-clicking its icon in the Site window. Arrange the two windows onscreen so that you can see at least part of the Site window behind the Document window.

3. If the file you want to link to is not already part of your site, add it by dragging it into the Site window before proceeding to Step 4.

4. In the Document window, select some text or an object that you would like to link.

5. Click the Fetch URL button in the Inspector.

6. Drag the cursor from the Inspector into the Site window. A line appears as you drag (**Figure 6.6**). If the Site window is hidden by other windows, it will be brought to the front as you drag over it.

7. Stop dragging when your cursor is over the file you want to link to, and release the mouse button to finish the link. You can verify that the link is complete in the Text Inspector.

✔ Tip

■ In Windows and in Mac OS 9, dragging the Point & Shoot line creates a straight line from your starting point (in the Inspector, in this case) to its destination. In Mac OS X, pointing and dragging diagonally creates a series of horizontal and/or vertical lines that resemble stairs.

Creating links to URLs

GoLive sites can manage not only HTML files and images, but also bookmarks that contain URLs for remote resources. You can store the remote resources your site points to within the site file, and then Point & Shoot your way to them whenever you need to add a link.

You can link to an email address with Point & Shoot if the address is stored within your site file. To learn how to add email addresses to a site file, see Chapter 15. You can also type email links directly into the URL field of the Inspector, using the format `mailto:user@domain.com`. When an email link is clicked, the user's browser opens an email application, if the user's system is configured to do so.

To link to a stored URL:

1. Open a site file.

2. Open the document that you want to link from by double-clicking it in the Files tab of the Site window.

3. In the Site window, click the External tab to display external resources that you have stored there.

4. In the Document window, select the text or object that you want to link.

5. Command-click (Mac) or Control-click (Windows) the selection and drag the resulting line to the Site window.

6. Stop dragging when your cursor is over the item you want to link and release the mouse button.

7. Verify that the link is complete in the Link field of the Text Inspector.

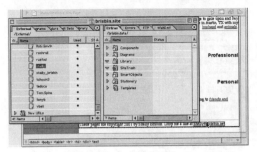

Figure 6.7 Drag a URL from the External tab of the Site window to the selected text in the Document window to create a link.

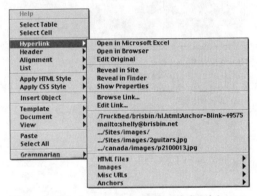

Figure 6.8 When you choose Apply Link (Mac) from the contextual menu, you have quick access to the resources within your site.

Figure 6.9 The Inspector duplicates the Apply Link (Mac) contextual menu. Choose or edit a link from the flyout menu next to the field that contains the link.

✔ Tips

■ You can also make a link by dragging and dropping a URL from the External tab of Site window to the selected text (**Figure 6.7**).

■ Here's a shortcut for making a link from a document to a file or URL, for those who like to work with menus. Use the contextual menu's Apply Link (Mac) or Hyperlink (Windows) command to quickly locate HTML files, images, URLs, or anchors within your site. Submenus show these items, as well as links you have made recently (**Figure 6.8**).

■ The list of site resources and recent links is also available in the Inspector. Click the flyout menu next to the Source or URL field (**Figure 6.9**) and choose a link.

CREATING LINKS

Linking open documents

You can use the GoLive Page icon to create links between open documents, whether or not they are part of a GoLive site.

To create a link with the Page icon:

1. In the Document window, select some text or an object that you would like to link.

2. Open another document.

3. Position the new document on screen so that you can see the portion of the first document that contains the selected text or object.

4. Drag the Page icon (at the top of the new document's window) onto the selected text or object in your destination document (**Figure 6.10**). The link is complete.

✔ Tip

■ You can use the Page icon method whether you're working within a site or just constructing individual pages. If you're working within a site, you may prefer using Point & Shoot.

Figure 6.10 Select text you want to link to another GoLive document, and then drag that document's Page icon over the text.

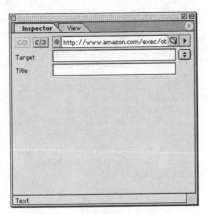

Figure 6.11 Select the URL in the Inspector and type the new URL over it.

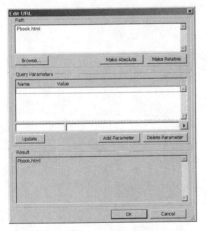

Figure 6.12 The Edit URL dialog box.

Figure 6.13 The Result pane of the Edit URL dialog box shows your updated link.

Editing Links

Once you've created links, you may need to change them. A remote URL may change, or you might rename a directory or update an email address. In any case, you can edit links in the URL field of any Inspector in which they appear or with Point & Shoot.

To edit a link in the Inspector:

1. Open the file containing the link you want to change. Make sure you're in the Layout Editor.

2. Click the link. The Inspector displays the link's URL and other information.

3. Type the new absolute (full) URL or relative URL in the URL field of the Inspector (**Figure 6.11**).

   or

   Point & Shoot from the Inspector to the new linked item in your site.

To change links with the Edit URL dialog box:

1. Click the text or object whose link you want to change.

2. In the Inspector, choose Edit from the flyout menu. The Edit URL dialog box opens (**Figure 6.12**).

3. Make changes to the existing link by typing in the Path field. You can also browse to a new file, change the link from relative to absolute, or add database query information to the link. Changes you make to the link appear in the Result area at the bottom of the dialog box (**Figure 6.13**).

(continues on next page)

✔ Tip

- Not all Inspectors use the same label for the field where you enter a link, though they all place the link-entry field in the same location. In the Text Inspector, for example, the field has no label. In the Image Inspector, the field is called Source. Plug-in Inspectors use the term File (**Figure 6.14**). Whichever Inspector you're working with, the field you want to edit is the one that links the object in the Document window to a URL.

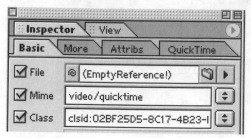

Figure 6.14 To link to a plug-in file, be sure the File check box is checked, and then add a link in the adjacent field in the Plug-in Inspector.

To edit a link within a site:

1. Open your GoLive site.

2. Open the file containing the link you want to change.

3. If you are linking to an external URL or an email address, click the External tab in the Site window. Otherwise, proceed to Step 4.

4. In the Document window, Command-click (Mac) or Alt-click (Windows) on the link and Point & Shoot to the new item in the Site window.

✔ Tip

- You can use GoLive's site management tools to update all occurrences of a link within your site (see Chapter 16, "Viewing and Managing Sites"). The Site window's error icons also let you know which pages contain broken links.

To delete a link:

1. In the Document window, select the linked text.

2. Click the Remove Link button on the toolbar. The link is deleted.

    or

    Click the Remove Link button in the Inspector.

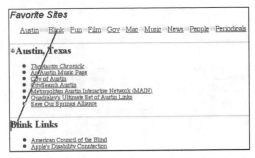

Figure 6.15 Command-click (Mac) or Alt-click (Windows) the item you want to link, and drag to the location where you want the anchor to appear.

⚓**Blink Links**

Figure 6.16 When the anchor is complete, the Anchor icon appears next to the anchored text in the Document window.

Linking to Anchors on a Page

Anchors are a special kind of link. Rather than linking one page to another, named anchors are used to navigate within a single page—linking a list of headings at the top of a page to subsequent sections of the document, for example, or linking to a location in the middle of a different page. Clicking on an anchor link scrolls the browser to the appropriate point on the page or opens another page in the middle, displaying the specified anchor point.

You can begin by creating links, then making named anchors to go with them, or you can set up the anchors first. The first method works better if you're creating a single link that connects to a single anchor. The second method works better if you plan to create several links that point to a single anchor point, or if you are designing a navigation scheme or table of contents that goes with an existing document.

To create a named anchor on the current page:

1. With a document open in the Layout Editor, select the text or object to link from.

2. Command-click (Mac) or Alt-click (Windows) the text or object and drag the resulting line through the document until you reach the point where you would like the anchor to appear (**Figure 6.15**).

3. Release the mouse button; an Anchor icon appears (**Figure 6.16**).

4. Click the Anchor icon to activate the Anchor Inspector. You can then change the unique anchor name if you wish.

✔ Tips

■ Anchors work best when they appear at the left margin of a text block.

■ As always, it's a good idea to check your work by previewing it. Open your page in a Web browser; then click the link you've created to see whether it properly connects to the anchor.

To create anchors before linking them:

1. With a document open, drag the Anchor icon (**Figure 6.17**) from the Basic set of the Objects palette to the Document window. An Anchor icon appears where you release the mouse button, and the Anchor Inspector becomes active (**Figure 6.18**).

2. In the Name field, type a unique, one-word name for the anchor.

3. Locate some text or an object (in the current document or in any other document that is part of your site) that you would like to link to one of the anchors you just created.

4. Select the text or object and Point & Shoot to the anchor you created. The link is now complete.

When a Web page visitor clicks on the new link, the Web browser responds by displaying the page holding the anchor, at the location of the anchor.

To move an anchor:

◆ In the Document window, click the Anchor icon and drag it to its new location on the page. Any links you've created will now point to the new location.

To delete an anchor:

1. Click an Anchor icon to select it.

2. Press the Delete key to remove the anchor. Now you need to remove links to the anchor you've just deleted.

3. Locate a link that leads to the anchor and select it.

4. Click the Remove Link button in the toolbar.

   or

   Click the Remove Link button in the Inspector. The link is removed.

Figure 6.17 The Anchor icon is available on the Basic set of the Objects palette.

Figure 6.18 The Anchor Inspector becomes active when you drag the Anchor icon to the Document window.

✔ Tips

■ You can create as many links to a single anchor as you like, from any number of documents. Just Point & Shoot from each link to the anchor.

■ It's important that you delete the anchor before you break the link. Even if you select a link and click the Remove Link button in the Inspector, the link stays intact if there's an anchor in place.

Figure 6.19 To target a link, choose an option from the Target menu in the Text Inspector.

Links and Targets

When a site visitor clicks a link, the resulting new page usually opens in the same browser window, replacing the previous page. Sometimes, however, you might want a link to open in a new window or in a frame. Opening a new window for a link preserves the previous window onscreen (especially useful if you're linking from your site to someone else's), and opening a link in a frame allows you to link to a remote site without the user leaving your site. The link attribute that allows you to choose where a link should open is called a *target*.

There are four kinds of target attributes:

◆ _top

◆ _blank

◆ _parent

◆ _self

Specifying a _top target replaces the browser window's (or frame's) current contents with the contents of the browser window with the linked page. A _blank target opens the link in a new window. The _parent and _self links are used in frames-based Web pages. I'll describe their use in Chapter 11.

To apply a target to a link:

1. Create a link using any of the methods described in this chapter.

2. In the Text Inspector, choose a target type from the Target pull-down menu (**Figure 6.19**).

Finding Broken Links

GoLive can locate broken links at both the site and page level. Link warnings can be used to locate broken links on an open page. The warnings highlight broken links in red (or a color you choose) in the Document window. I'll cover dealing with broken site links in Chapter 16.

Figure 6.20 Activate link warnings by clicking the Link Warnings button in the Highlight palette.

To view link warnings:

1. With a document open, choose Window > Highlight and click the Link Warnings button (**Figure 6.20**) in the Select tab of the Highlight palette.

   or

   Click the Link Warnings button on the toolbar. Any broken links in your document will be highlighted.

2. To turn link warnings off, click the Link Warnings button again.

To change the color of link warnings:

1. In the Highlight palette, click the Colors tab.

2. Click the Link Warnings Color field to bring up the Color palette.

3. You can also change the opacity by moving the Opacity slider next to the Color field.

4. When you're finished, return to the Select tab of the Highlight palette and activate Link Warnings if they aren't already visible. Your warnings now use the new color you selected.

✔ Tip

- GoLive will display link warnings for images and multimedia files as well as text. When an image or media file link is broken, you'll see a red (or whatever color you chose) border around the image box. Of course, you'll also notice that the image itself is missing, since its link is no longer in place.

Working with Tables

7

HTML tables are among the most useful Web page design tools available. You can use them to display information in rows and columns or to build multicolumn layouts in which the grid pattern isn't visible, and you can easily put text blocks and objects just where you want them. Tables are the first of the three major GoLive layout tools I'll cover. Layout grids and floating boxes are described in the next two chapters.

Table building is among the best reasons to use a WYSIWYG Web-authoring tool like GoLive. It's a whole lot easier to build and edit tables using a graphical interface than it is to write the HTML code in a text editor.

In this chapter, I'll cover

◆ Table basics

◆ Changing table dimensions

◆ Setting table attributes

◆ Adding and removing cells

◆ Adding table content

◆ Nesting tables

◆ Using table styles

◆ Converting tables to grids

Table Basics

Tables are a versatile HTML feature that you can use to create grid-like page elements such as calendars, spreadsheets, and other items that use columns and rows. Tables are also an important design tool because they allow you to "fake" multicolumn layouts in HTML. GoLive employs this fakery to create layout grids (covered in Chapter 8, "Working with Layout Grids").

You can use layout grids to create the appearance of snaking text columns or simulate frames, but conventional HTML tables allow you to create and manage a large number of columns and rows simultaneously.

Table tools

A table in GoLive is just another object—there's a Table icon on the Objects palette and an Inspector window where you specify the size, shape, color, and other attributes of a table, as well as how many rows and cells it has. In addition, GoLive provides the Table palette, a window that shows a graphical representation of the table as you work. This is especially helpful when you're working with large tables or tables that are actually contained within other tables—*nested*, in HTML-speak. You'll also use the Table palette to view GoLive's table templates, called table styles. I'll describe the palette and its uses later in this chapter, but notice as you add and edit tables that the Table palette provides an updated view of the cells as you work (**Figure 7.1**). To view the Table palette, choose Window > Table.

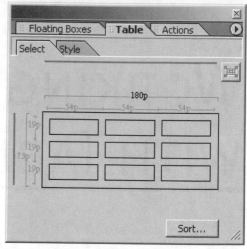

Figure 7.1 Here, the Table palette displays a three-by-three table.

Figure 7.2 The Table icon.

Figure 7.3 Dragging the Table icon into the Document window creates a three-by-three table.

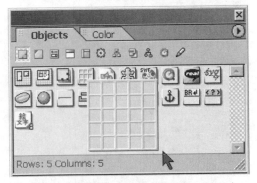

Figure 7.4 Hold the Command key (Mac) or Control key (Windows) and click and drag from the Table icon to create a table with the number of rows and columns you want.

Adding a table

Adding a table to a GoLive document is just like adding any other object.

To create a table:

1. With a document open, double-click or drag the Table icon (**Figure 7.2**) from the Basic set of the Objects palette to the Document window. By default, a three-cell-by-three-cell table appears in the Document window (**Figure 7.3**).

   or

   Press and hold the Command key (Mac) or the Control key (Windows) and click the Table icon in the Objects palette. Drag downward and to the right to create a table with the number of rows and columns you want (**Figure 7.4**). Then, release the key (but not the mouse button) and immediately drag the custom table object to the Document window.

2. Type 4 in the Rows field of the Inspector and press Tab. The table expands downward to add a new row.

3. Type 5 in the Columns field and press Tab. The table expands to the right, adding two columns.

TABLE BASICS

123

Selecting tables

In order to work with a table or a table cell, column, or row, you must first select it in the Document window. That sounds simple enough, but if your layout is complex it can become tricky. Even if you're only trying to make changes to a row, column, or cell rather than the whole table, selecting the part you want to work with can sometimes be a challenge. In this section, I'll show you how to easily select tables, rows, columns, and cells. You may want to refer back to this section as you move through the chapter.

To select a table:

◆ Place your cursor at the top or left border of the table. The cursor will change into an arrow with a box (**Figure 7.5**), called the Table Selector Pointer. Click the border to open the Table Inspector.

or

Click within a table cell and choose Select Table from the contextual menu. The Table Inspector (**Figure 7.6**) appears. If you see the Cell tab, rather than the Table tab, reselect the table or click the Table tab.

To select a row:

1. Move the cursor to the left border of a table. It changes to a right-facing arrow (**Figure 7.7**).

2. Click to select the row. Each cell in the selected row contains a bold outline.

3. To add more rows to the selection, drag upward or downward.

or

To select nonadjacent rows, Shift-click each one.

Figure 7.5 The Table Selector Pointer allows you to select a table.

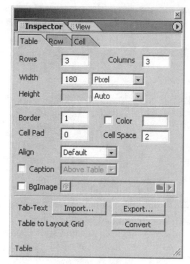

Figure 7.6 The Table tab of the Table Inspector offers measurement options.

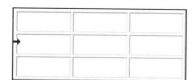

Figure 7.7 Move the cursor to the left border of the table to get the Row Selector Pointer.

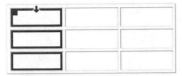

Figure 7.8 Select a column by clicking on the table's top border when the arrow cursor is visible.

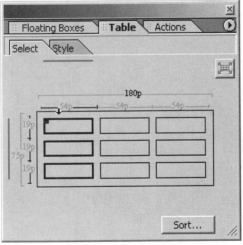

Figure 7.9 Move the cursor to the lower or right border of a cell and click to select the cell.

Figure 7.10 To select a column in the Table palette, first select the table, then click its top border.

To select a column:

1. Move your cursor to the top of the table column you want to select. It changes to a down-facing arrow.

2. Click to select the column (**Figure 7.8**).

3. To select multiple columns, drag from the initial selection, or Shift-click each column.

To select a cell:

1. In the Document window, move the cursor to the bottom or right border of a cell. The cursor becomes an arrow (**Figure 7.9**).

2. Click to select the cell.

3. To add cells to the selection, Shift-click them or drag from the selected cell.

✔ Tips

- Selecting a cell in the Table palette doesn't require quite as much care. Just click anywhere in the cell to select it.

- If you prefer, you can use the contextual menu to select a cell by clicking in the cell and choosing Select Cell.

- You can also select a table row or a column by clicking the border of the table in the Table palette (**Figure 7.10**).

- To deselect a row or column while others are still selected, Shift-click in the Document window or the Table palette.

TABLE BASICS

Setting Table and Cell Dimensions

Tables can be resized with the mouse or the Inspector. You can change the size of the table as a whole or resize individual rows and columns. Dragging is easier, but it's a less precise way to size the table and its cells. On the other hand, using the Inspector sometimes requires two steps—setting the measurement scheme to pixels and then entering a value.

To resize a table by dragging:

1. Move the cursor to the right or bottom edge of a table. The cursor changes to a two-ended arrow (**Figure 7.11**).

   or

   If you have changed the measurement unit for the table from Pixel to Percent in the Inspector, hold the Option key (Mac) or Alt key (Windows) to get the arrow cursor, and drag the table.

2. Drag to enlarge or shrink the table. All of the cells change size in proportion, and the value you change by dragging the table border (height or width) is converted into pixels in the Inspector.

✔ Tip

■ By default, the Inspector displays the width of a table in pixels, but the height is set to Auto. The first time you drag the table's border to resize it vertically, you will need to hold the Option key (Mac) or Alt key (Windows) as you drag, or change the Height measurement to Pixels in the Inspector first. When you drag, the Height measurement changes from Auto to Pixel and allows you to edit the table height from the Inspector, or without holding the modifier key as you resize by dragging.

Figure 7.11 The cursor becomes a two-ended arrow when you move it over the right or bottom border of the table.

To resize a column by dragging:

1. Place your cursor on the right border of an interior cell. Hold down the Option key (Mac) or Alt key (Windows). The cursor changes to a two-ended arrow.

2. Drag the column border to the left to shrink the column or to the right to expand the column. Unlike resizing a table, resizing columns does not affect adjacent columns, although it does change the table width.

To resize a row by dragging:

1. Place the cursor on the lower border of the row. Hold down the Option key (Mac) or Alt key (Windows). The cursor changes to a two-ended arrow.

2. Drag the border down to expand the row or up to shrink it. Unlike resizing a table, resizing a row does not affect adjacent rows. It does change the height of the table itself, however.

✔ Tip

■ Though you can select the table and its cells in the Table palette, you can't use the palette to resize them by dragging.

SETTING TABLE AND CELL DIMENSIONS

Resizing with the Inspector

I mentioned earlier that the most precise way to change the size of a table or its cells is to use the Inspector. Besides simply specifying an exact number of pixels for each item's size, you can also choose to express the dimensions as a percentage of the enclosing container (the page or page element in which the current table is nested), or use the Auto option to tell browsers to draw the table cells to fit the text or objects inside them.

To resize a table with the Inspector:

1. Select a table.

2. In the Table Inspector, choose a measurement type in the Width and Height pop-up menus.

3. Type the number of pixels or a percentage in the Width and Height fields. The table's dimensions change accordingly.

To resize a row or column:

1. Select a cell in the row or column you want to change. The Table Inspector appears with the Cell tab selected.

2. In the Inspector, choose Pixel or Percent in the Width (column) or Height (row) pop-up menu (**Figure 7.12**).

✔ Tip

■ Because table cells are dependent upon the rows and columns of which they are a part, you can't resize them individually. You can, however, stretch a table cell across multiple columns or down multiple rows. This is called *spanning* (see "Row and column spanning" on page 131).

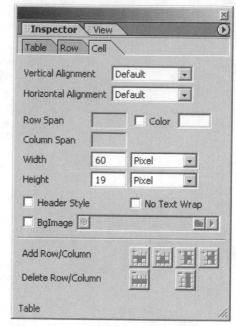

Figure 7.12 To resize a column or row in the Inspector, choose a measurement type from the Width or Height pop-up menu and type the measurement in the adjacent field.

Mailing List Archives				
2001	January	February	March	April
	May	June	July	August
	September	October	November	December
2000	January	February	March	April
	May	June	July	August
	September	October	November	December
1999	January	February	March	April
	May	June	July	August
	September	October	November	December
1998	January	February	March	April
	May	June	July	August
	September	October	November	December

Figure 7.13 This table has a 10-pixel outer border.

Mailing List Archives				
2001	January	February	March	April
	May	June	July	August
	September	October	November	December
2000	January	February	March	April
	May	June	July	August
	September	October	November	December
1999	January	February	March	April
	May	June	July	August
	September	October	November	December
1998	January	February	March	April
	May	June	July	August
	September	October	November	December

Figure 7.14 Adding cell padding increases the space between a table cell's edge and its contents.

Setting Table Attributes

You can change the appearance of tables, rows, columns, or individual cells using many of the same attributes that apply to other objects, including color, spacing, border, and alignment.

To change the appearance of a table:

1. Select a table by clicking on the top or left border.

2. In the Table tab of the Inspector, type a value (in pixels) in the Border field. **Figure 7.13** shows a table with a 10-pixel outer border.

3. Click the Color field and choose a background color for the table from the Color palette.

4. Type 2 in the Cell Pad field to create extra space between the cell edge and cell contents. **Figure 7.14** shows the table we've been working on, with two pixels of padding in each cell.

5. Enter a different value to change cell spacing. The Cell Space field controls the amount of space between cells. By default, cells are spaced two pixels apart.

6. Choose an option from the Alignment menu to place the table relative to the page or object (table, floating box, or layout grid) containing it. You can align the table to the left, center, or right margin or leave it unaligned.

7. To add a background image, click the BgImage check box and Browse or Point & Shoot to an image within your site.

To change the appearance of a row:

1. Select one or more rows in a table.

2. In the Table Inspector, choose the Row tab (**Figure 7.15**).

3. Choose an alignment for the row content from the Vertical Alignment pop-up menu. You can align the content to the top, middle, or bottom of the cells.

4. Choose an alignment for the row content from the Horizontal Alignment pop-up menu. You can align text to the left, right, or center of the cells.

5. To choose a height for the selected row, select Pixel or Percent from the Height pop-up menu and type a value in the field. Leave Auto selected to allow the row to grow or shrink with its contents.

6. Click the Color field and select a color from the Color palette.

To change the appearance of a column or cell:

1. Select a column or cell. The Cell tab of the Table Inspector appears (**Figure 7.16**). If you select a column, options for adding and deleting rows and columns are dimmed. If you select a cell, they are active.

2. Choose vertical and horizontal alignment options.

3. Click the Color field and choose a color for selection.

4. Click the No Text Wrap check box if you want to keep column text on a single line. This option increases the width of the column as text is added.

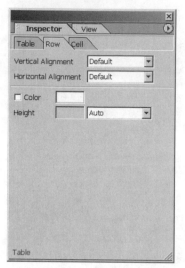

Figure 7.15 The Row tab of the Table Inspector offers alignment options.

✔ Tip

■ If you are creating a table that will contain an empty cell—one not filled with text or another object—insert a nonbreaking space in the cell. If you don't do this, Web browsers are unlikely to display any background color or borders you have applied to the empty cell. To add a nonbreaking space, place the insertion point within the cell and type Option-spacebar (Mac) or Shift-spacebar (Windows). To add non-breaking spaces to several cells, select them and Control-click (Mac) or right-click (Windows) and choose Insert Nonbreaking Spaces from the contextual menu. You can remove a nonbreaking space by choosing that option from the contextual menu. You can see where GoLive inserted a non breaking space by scanning the Source code for the   entity. Interestingly, you can't use the keyboard shortcut to add a nonbreaking space in the Source Editor.

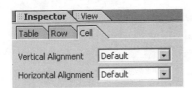

Figure 7.16 The Cell tab of the Table Inspector appears when you select a cell or column.

	January	February	March	April
2001	May	June	July	August
	September	October	November	December
	January	February	March	April
2000	May	June	July	August
	September	October	November	December
	January	February	March	April
1999	May	June	July	August
	September	October	November	December
	January	February	March	April
1998	May	June	July	August
	September	October	November	December

Figure 7.17 The cells in the leftmost column in this table have row spans of 3.

Mailing List Archives				
2001	January	February	March	April
	May	June	July	August
	September	October	November	December
2000	January	February	Marh	April
	May	June	July	August
	September	October	November	December
1999	January	February	March	April
	May	June	July	August
	September	October	November	December
1998	January	February	March	April
	May	June	July	August
	September	October	November	December
1997	January	February	March	April
	May	June	July	August
	September	October	November	December
1996	January	February	March	April
	May	June	July	August
	September	October	November	December
1995	January	February	March	April
	May	June	July	August
	September	October	November	December
1994				December

Figure 7.18 The top cell of the table spans five columns.

Row and column spanning

It is often helpful to include a table cell that spans multiple columns or rows. For example, you might span two columns with a header that describes both. In **Figure 7.17**, I've created a table that uses row spanning to associate a year heading with three rows that contain links for each month.

To span columns:

1. Select a table cell.

2. In the Cell tab of the Table Inspector, type a number of cells in the Column Span field. The cell expands right across the number of columns you've selected. **Figure 7.18** shows a table cell that spans five columns.

To span rows:

1. Select a cell.

2. In the Cell tab of the Inspector, enter a number of cells in the Row Span field. The selected cell expands down to span the number of rows selected.

SETTING TABLE ATTRIBUTES

Headers and captions

In addition to customizing the overall appearance of a table using familiar attributes like color and alignment, HTML also specifies a pair of table-specific tag types: captions and headers.

A caption spans the entire width of the table, and is meant as a place to provide a description of the table contents. By default, caption text is centered over the table, but you can format the text in any way you like. A caption can also consist of as many lines of text as you like.

To add a caption:

1. Select a table.

2. In the Table tab of the Inspector, click the Caption check box.

3. Use the pop-up menu to place the caption above or below the table.

4. Type your caption text in the caption element created above or below the table. The table shown in **Figure 7.19** has a caption above it.

5. To remove a caption, uncheck the Caption check box.

Not to be confused with text headings or the head section of a document, a table header is another cell style. Applying the header style centers text in the selected cell and makes it bold. As the name implies, it's most often used to create a heading for rows or columns.

To create header cells:

1. Select a cell or cells.

2. In the Cell tab of the Table Inspector, click the Header Style check box. Text in the selected cells becomes bold and is horizontally centered (**Figure 7.20**).

Read the <u>most recent</u> digest, or <u>search the archives</u>

2001	January	February	March	April
	May	June	July	August
	September	October	November	December

Figure 7.19 This table has a caption above it.

2001	January	February	March
	May	June	July
	September	October	November
2000	January	February	March
	May	June	July
	September	October	November
1999	January	February	March
	May	June	July
	September	October	November

Figure 7.20 The leftmost cells in this table are header cells.

✔ Tip

■ A caption looks much like a table cell with centered text that spans the full width of the table. You can achieve the same effect by selecting a the left-hand cell in the bottom or top row of a table and typing a column span (in the Cell tab of the Table Inspector) that equals the total number of columns in the table.

Figure 7.21 Add a row or column with the top four buttons in the Cell tab of the Table Inspector. The two buttons below delete rows and columns.

Figure 7.22 Select a table cell and Control-click (Mac) or right-click (Windows) to see a context-sensitive menu where you can add or remove rows and columns.

Adding and Removing Cells

Once you have created a table, you can add new rows or columns.

To add a row or column:

1. Select a table cell that is adjacent to the position your new row or column will occupy.

2. In the Cell tab of the Table Inspector, click one of the Add Row or Add Column buttons (**Figure 7.21**).

   or

   Control-click (Mac) or right-click (Windows) and select Insert Column Left, Insert Column Right, Insert Row Above, or Insert Row Below from the contextual menu (**Figure 7.22**). A new row or column appears by the selected cell.

✔ Tips

■ To add a new row to the bottom of a table, place the insertion point in the cell at the lower-right corner of the table. Then press Tab.

■ The easiest way to add rows or columns in bulk, and without regard to where in the table they appear, is to edit the Rows and Columns fields in the Table tab of the Table Inspector.

The process of removing table rows and columns mirrors the process for adding them. You can use the Delete Row/Column buttons in the Cell tab of the Table Inspector. Or, with a cell selected, choose Delete Column or Delete Row from the contextual menu (Control-click on the Mac and right-click in Windows).

Adding Content to a Table

HTML tables can include any element you can put on a Web page, including text, images, and multimedia objects. You can type directly into the table. Use the Objects palette to add objects, or drag and drop items into a table from the desktop.

To add text:

1. Click in a table cell to place the insertion point there.

2. Type the text.

3. Press Tab. The insertion point moves to the next cell in the row. Tabbing from the last cell in a row moves the insertion point to the first cell in the next row.

✔ Tips

■ When you type text into a default table cell and the text exceeds the visible boundaries of the cell, the cell grows to accommodate the text. So if you're typing the contents of your table from scratch, you should type and format the text before you finish sizing the table cells.

■ When you add an image to a table (either by drag-and-drop or using the Image Inspector to place the image), the default table cell grows to accommodate the image. If you resize the image, the cell's size changes too, though not in direct proportion to the image.

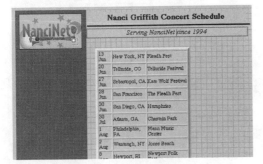

Figure 7.23 To import a tab-delimited text file, select a table and click Import in the Table Inspector.

Figure 7.24 When you import a tab-delimited file into a GoLive table, you may need to adjust the table's dimensions to display the data correctly.

Importing table content

You can also add content to a table by importing the contents of a text file into your GoLive document. The fields (which will become table cells) in your file must be separated by tabs, commas, spaces, or semi-colons, and each record (row) must include a carriage return at the end. You can create such files by saving spreadsheet data in tab-delimited format.

To import table content:

1. Create a new table or select an existing table. If you choose an existing table, imported text will be added to existing cells.

2. In the Table tab of the Table Inspector, click the Import button (**Figure 7.23**).

3. Locate a tab-delimited file on your hard drive and choose the delimiter used in the file from the Column Separator pop-up menu. When you click Open, the file's contents appear in the table (**Figure 7.24**).

4. Resize the table, and its rows and columns, so that the data fits correctly on the page.

Sorting table content

You can sort the contents of table rows and columns in much the same way you can in a spreadsheet program. This is useful if you want to change the order of table data without retyping it. You can sort a table by row or column, in ascending or descending order, using multiple criteria.

To sort the contents of a table:

1. Create or select a table containing cells you want to sort.

2. Open the Table palette by choosing Window > Table.

✔ Tip

■ There's no need to add empty table cells before importing text. GoLive will add the necessary cells when you import the text file.

(continues on next page)

ADDING CONTENT TO A TABLE

3. In the Select tab, select the table or the portion of the table you want to sort by clicking on the table cells that appear there. If you want to sort rows in the table, you must select the column containing the row cells you want to sort. If you are sorting table columns, select all of the affected rows (**Figure 7.25**).

4. Click the Sort button.

5. In the Sort Table dialog box (**Figure 7.26**), from the Sort pop-up menu, first choose whether to sort by rows or columns. The choice you make determines the content of the three sort criteria menus.

6. If you have chosen Rows from the Sort menu, the criterion menus will contain items for each column in the table. Conversely, choose Columns to see choices for each row in the menus.

7. From the Sort by pop-up menu, choose a row or column to sort by. Rows are listed by number from top to bottom and columns from left to right.

8. If you want to sort in descending order rather than ascending order, choose that option from the adjacent menu.

9. Repeat Steps 7 and 8 if you have more rows or columns to sort.

10. Choose whether to sort the entire table or only the selected portion. The default is Sort Selection Only.

11. Click OK to sort the table.

✔ Tip

■ You can also sort the table by selecting it in the Document window and choosing Sort Table from the contextual menu.

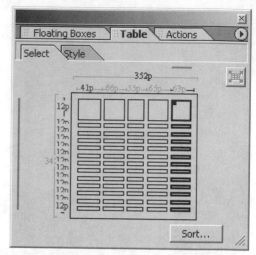

Figure 7.25 Select the portion of the table you want to sort in the Table palette.

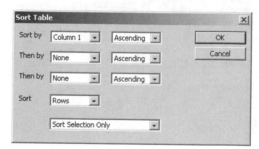

Figure 7.26 Use the Sort Table dialog box to choose sorting criteria.

Figure 7.27 This three-cell table creates a structure for the page. The cell on the left has a row span of 2. The nested table will be added to the lower-right cell—the cell containing the main content of the page.

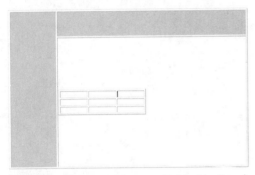

Figure 7.28 When you add a second table, it is aligned in its parent cell, by default, to the left horizontally and the center vertically.

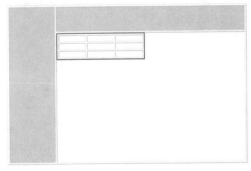

Figure 7.29 To align the new table to the top of the parent cell, choose the appropriate option in the Cell tab of the Table Inspector.

Nesting Tables

It's often useful to create multiple tables on a page: one serving as a container for all or part of the page, with a second table, *within* the first, providing a modular structure for a smaller section of the page, perhaps a site-navigation scheme. Such an embedded table is also an effective way to structure tabular information like a calendar or spreadsheet. Placing a table within another table is called *nesting* tables. You can nest as many tables as you like, but it's best to use as few as you can to keep your page simple. Nested tables can add to page download and display time, and make it a bit of a challenge to manage and edit a group of tables. First, I'll show you how to nest tables, and then I'll describe some ways of working with them.

To nest a table:

1. Add a table to a GoLive document. Format the table to provide a structure for your page, or a part of it. **Figure 7.27** shows a large table that divides the page into three sections.

2. Drag the Table icon from the Objects palette into the cell where you wish to nest the new table. The new table appears, centered vertically in the table cell (**Figure 7.28**).

3. Select the parent cell—the one containing the new table.

4. In the Cell tab of the Table Inspector, choose Top from the Vertical Alignment pop-up menu. The second table now appears in the upper-left corner of the cell (**Figure 7.29**).

5. Select the second table (the one you just added) and configure it, using the Table Inspector. Add or delete rows and columns as needed and then add the table's content.

(continues on next page)

NESTING TABLES

✔ Tips

- Selecting a cell within a nested table can be difficult, because it requires a steady hand to get the cursor just where you want it. To select a cell in a nested table, click it and then press Control-Enter. Press Control-Enter again to select the entire nested table. One more press of these keys selects the cell in which the nested table lies. One more? You've selected the parent table.

- You can use the Table palette to switch between nested tables. Select a nested table (also known as a *child* table). In the Table palette, press the Select button in the upper-right corner (**Figure 7.30**) to select the parent table. To return the selection to the child table, simply click it from within the Table palette.

- Using the HTML Outline Editor view is another way to get your bearings when using nested tables. Click the Outline Editor tab in the Document window and look for the <table> tags that indicate the tables that are part of your page. You can select the table you want by clicking on one of these tags. From there, you can configure or edit it in the Outline Editor, or you can switch back to the Layout Editor and work in the Table Inspector or Table palette.

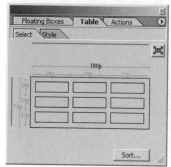

Figure 7.30 The Table palette shows the child table and lets you select the parent.

Figure 7.31 Choose a table style from the Style pop-up menu in the Table palette.

Read the most recent digest, or search the archives				
	January	**February**	**March**	**April**
2001	May	June	July	August
	September	October	November	December
	January	February	March	April
2000	May	June	July	August
	September	October	November	December
	January	February	March	April
1999	May	June	July	August
	September	October	November	December
	January	February	March	April
1998	May	June	July	August
	September	October	November	December

Figure 7.32 When you apply a style to a table, it is reflected in the Table palette and on the table.

Read the most recent digest, or search the archives				
	January	February	March	April
2001	May	June	July	August
	September	October	November	December
	January	February	March	April
2000	May	June	July	August
	September	October	November	December
	January	February	March	April
1999	May	June	July	August
	September	October	November	December
	January	February	March	April
1998	May	June	July	August
	September	October	November	December

Figure 7.33 Here's a table using the Just the Facts style.

Figure 7.34 Click the New Style button to save your own table style.

Using Table Styles

Just as many applications include templates that allow you to quickly add a particular look to a word processing document or spreadsheet, GoLive provides a selection of predefined table styles that come complete with color, border, and other attributes.

To use a table style:

1. Add a new table to a document.

2. Choose Window > Table to open the Table palette.

3. Click the Style tab.

4. From the Style pop-up menu (**Figure 7.31**), choose a table style. I chose Seventies.

5. Click the Apply button. The table changes to reflect the new style (**Figure 7.32**).

To change a table style:

1. Be sure that the table is selected and choose a new style from the Style pop-up menu in the Style tab of the Table palette.

2. Click the Apply button. The table's appearance changes (**Figure 7.33**).

3. To remove a style, click the Clear button in the Style tab of the Table palette.

To create your own table style:

1. Set up a table. Customize it any way you like, as described earlier in this chapter.

2. Save your work.

3. In the Table palette, click the Style tab, then click the New Style button, which is located at the bottom of the Style tab (**Figure 7.34**).

4. Give your custom table style a name and click the OK button The name of your style appears in the Style pop-up menu and is now available for use with any table.

Converting Tables to Layout Grids

GoLive allows you to break tables out into text frames within a layout grid. This feature lets you redesign a page by moving its tabular content around freely.

To convert a table to a layout grid:

1. Select a table.

2. In the Table tab of the Inspector, click the Convert button.

   or

   Control-click (Mac) or right-click (Windows) and choose Convert to Layout Grid from the contextual menu.

The table is replaced onscreen by a layout grid. Each former cell that held text is now a text box (**Figure 7.35**).

Read the most recent digest, or search the archives			
January	February	March	April
2001 May	June	July	August
September	October	November	December
January	February	March	April
2000 May	June	July	August
September	October	November	December
January	February	March	April
1999 May	June	July	August
September	October	November	December
January	February	March	April
1998 May	June	July	August
September	October	November	December

Figure 7.35 When you convert the table, the cell grid disappears and its text-containing cells are replaced by text boxes. Notice that the text boxes take up more room than do the table cells.

WORKING
WITH LAYOUT GRIDS

Today's Web page designers have access to a variety of tools that are not as limiting as early HTML and can help them build pages and lay them out. Three HTML layout options in particular—tables, frames, and layers (called "floating boxes" in GoLive)—offer the Web designer more options than ever.

GoLive takes this "evolution" one step further with a unique feature—the layout grid. In fact, a layout grid is an HTML table that includes proprietary layout tags invented by GoLive's developers. In practice, grids are often used to build mockups or to simulate the positioning options available with floating boxes. Like graph paper or a drawing program with a grid that can be used to "snap" objects into place, GoLive's layout grid feature provides a guide for arranging objects on a page.

In this chapter, I'll cover

◆ Layout grid basics

◆ Adding text to a layout grid

◆ Objects on a grid

Meet the Layout Grid

With single-pixel accuracy, GoLive's unique layout grid is helpful for designers looking to control their layouts. Text, images, and other objects can be easily placed, arranged, and aligned using the grid.

Grids can be customized so objects snap to their lines, painlessly aligning elements with respect to the grid and to each other. Grids can be sized to fit any page or any portion of a page. They can also be placed on top of and adjacent to each other, though you can only place two grids side-by-side, and it's best to position them vertically, rather than side-by-side, to keep the tables simpler.

Grids are not always the right solution, and you will want to read Chapter 7 ("Working with Tables"), Chapter 9 ("Floating Boxes and Positioning"), and Chapter 11 ("Working with Frames"), before you decide which layout options are best for your pages.

To add a layout grid:

◆ Drag or double-click the Layout Grid icon (**Figure 8.1**) from the Basic set of the Objects palette onto the Document window. A square layout grid appears (**Figure 8.2**).

By default, the grid is a 16-cell-by-16-cell square, 201 pixels on each side. You can change its overall dimensions, and the number of cells, using the Layout Grid Inspector.

To change the grid's density:

1. Click the grid to display the Layout Grid Inspector (**Figure 8.3**). In the Inspector, you can resize the grid, change the distance between the horizontal and vertical gridlines, and make other changes.

Figure 8.1 Double-click or drag the Layout Grid icon into the Document window.

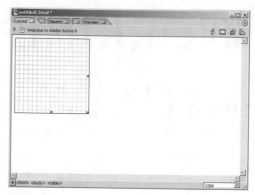

Figure 8.2 A grid appears at the first available space in the Document window. Note the three handles on the grid, used for dragging and sizing.

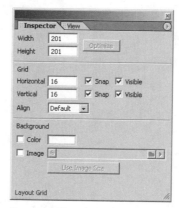

Figure 8.3 The Layout Grid Inspector controls size, position, behavior, and color of the grid.

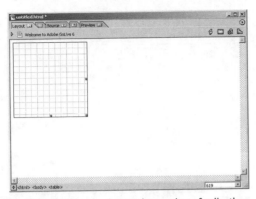

Figure 8.4 When you change the number of cells, the grid's dimensions remain unchanged, but the grid's density changes.

2. Click in the Horizontal field under the Grid heading. The Horizontal field controls the cell width. Type 12, to replace the default value of 16.

3. Press Tab. The Vertical field is now selected. Notice that the vertical gridlines are now closer together.

4. Change the cell height by typing 12 in the Vertical field, and press Tab to finish the grid (**Figure 8.4**).

Closer grid spacing can be useful if you want to place a number of objects close together on a grid. Likewise, adding space between gridlines keeps objects farther apart on the page.

✔ Tips

■ By default, both the Horizontal and Vertical Snap check boxes are selected in the Layout Grid Inspector. With Snap turned on, objects you drag onto a layout grid automatically snap to the nearest gridlines.

■ Turning off the Visible check boxes hides the grid from view but doesn't prevent it from snapping objects into place if the Snap option is on. Because the grid will not be visible on the finished page, hiding the grid temporarily can make previewing pages in the Layout Editor a bit easier.

■ Grids can be optimized so that they're just large enough to contain the elements placed upon them. Clicking on the Optimize button in the Inspector will eliminate the empty area of a grid. Optimize only works when the grid contains objects and excess space.

■ You resize grids by dragging their handles or by entering new pixel values in the Width and Height fields in the Inspector. Grids cannot, however, be repositioned on the page, because the code underlying the grid is an HTML table, which makes the grid subject to the same positioning limitations that affect tables.

Positioning a layout grid

You can use a single layout grid to cover a complete Web page, or you can use a grid in combination with tables or floating boxes. A single, page-wide grid forms a consistent background for the entire document and is usually a good choice if your Web page contains lots of items that are positioned or aligned relative to each another. If your page design is modular, with common sections such as a navigation bar or logo section, a grid for each section is an option—but one that should be used carefully, making sure that each element (text boxes, for example) lines up exactly into rows and columns on the grid. (Using snap to grid can help with alignment.) This will minimize the number of extra cells and columns that are generated, thus streamlining your code. In the following example, two grids accommodate a modular layout.

To size a layout grid:

1. If you intend to fill the page with the layout grid, resize the page first, using the grow box, or the Window Resolution menu, both in the lower right corner of the Document window.

2. Drag the lower right handle of the grid down to the corner of the window (**Figure 8.5**) to once again fill the page with the grid.

    or

    Resize the grid by typing a number that matches the value in the Window Resolution menu in the Inspector's Width field (**Figure 8.6**). Now, the grid matches the pixel width of the window.

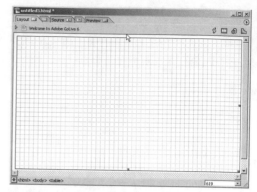

Figure 8.5 Drag the grid's handle to the bottom-right corner of the Document window.

Figure 8.6 Change the grid's width in the Layout Grid Inspector.

✔ Tip

■ As you drag to resize the grid, the width and height measurements in the Inspector change, reflecting the grid's new size in pixels. While "eyeballing" may work when dragging a layout grid, you can always enter the precise size of the grid in the Inspector's Width and Height fields.

Figure 8.7 When you add a background image to the layout grid, the portion of the image that fits in the grid will be visible.

Setting layout grid options

You can align a layout grid horizontally, and choose either a background color or an image to appear behind the grid.

Choose an option from the Align pop-up menu in the Inspector to place the grid on the left, center, or right margin of the page.

Choosing a background color for a layout grid is as simple as selecting a color from the Color palette and dragging it into the Inspector's Color field. To open the Color palette quickly, try clicking the Color field in the Layout Grid Inspector.

To add a background image to a grid:

1. With a layout grid selected, click the Image check box in the Inspector. The Image field becomes active.

2. Browse or Point & Shoot to locate an image. The image you've chosen appears behind the grid. If the image is smaller than the grid, it will be tiled. If it's bigger than the grid, you'll see only a portion of the image (**Figure 8.7**).

3. Resize the grid if you want to see more of the image.

   or

   Click Use Image Size in the Inspector to resize the grid to the same dimensions as your image. This works whether the image is displayed in full or is tiled when you add it to the layout, but not if the image is larger than the layout grid.

✔ Tip

■ If you would rather size the image for the grid, note the size you want, open the image in a graphics application, and resize it before adding it to a GoLive grid.

Adding Text to a Grid

Text on a layout grid must be contained in a text box. The box may overlap one or more cells in the grid. You can make it as large as you like, either by typing directly into it or dragging its handles.

The text box allows you to place text fairly precisely on the page, without regard for the page's margins. Without the grid or some other layout mechanism, such as a table, text on a Web page either appears at the margin, or next to an object that's on the margin.

To add a text box to a grid

1. In a document containing a layout grid, drag the Layout Text Box icon (**Figure 8.8**) from the Basic set of the Objects palette. A text box appears on the grid (**Figure 8.9**).

2. Drag the handle at the lower-right corner of the text box to the right, so that you can see what you're about to type.

3. Click within the text box and type some text. (You can also add text by pasting or dragging from another document).

✔ Tips

■ If you type or paste text into a text box without enlarging it first, GoLive expands the box vertically (but not horizontally) as you type. You can resize the box after you enter text, but it's easier to give the text some room first, resizing more as necessary later.

■ To resize a text box, first click the box edge to display the resizing handles. Then, click and drag a handle. (The cursor looks like a double-ended arrow when it is directly over a handle.) To move a text box, place the cursor on the border, but not on a handle. The cursor changes into a hand; then, click and drag the box to a new location.

Figure 8.8 The Layout Text Box icon is on the Basic set of the Objects palette.

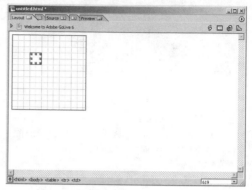

Figure 8.9 When you drag the Layout Text Box icon onto a layout grid, a small text box appears on the grid.

Figure 8.10 The Layout Text Box Inspector lets you change the background and alignment of a text box.

Figure 8.11 The plus sign indicates that this Layout Text Box contains more text than displayed.

Once you've added text to a text box, you can format it just as you would any other text block in GoLive. See Chapter 3, "Working with Text," for more information about formatting text in GoLive.

You can also add objects to a text box—an image, for example. The relationship between the text in the box and any object you add is the same as it would be on a page with no layout grid. Any alignment options you choose, for example, apply to the items in the box and nothing else.

Setting text box attributes

You can customize the background, alignment, and overflow behavior of a text box. Select the text box by clicking its edge (be sure the handles are visible) to activate the Layout Text Box Inspector (**Figure 8.10**) (double-click the box edge to open the Inspector window if it is closed). You add a background color or image to a layout text box just as you did for the layout grid itself. (See "Setting layout grid options.")

Choosing a horizontal alignment option changes the alignment of the contents inside the layout text box with respect to the box edges. You can add text to a layout text box by typing, pasting, or dragging. When you paste in text from another file, or even from another portion of your GoLive document, the text box expands to display all of the text you have added. You can keep the text box size constant by clicking the Allow Content Overflow check box in the Layout Text Box Inspector before you drag or paste text. The text box shows a plus sign in the lower right corner when you add more text than it can display (**Figure 8.11**).

ADDING TEXT TO A GRID

Objects on a Grid

You can add multiple objects to a layout grid and work with them singly or as a group. Once objects are placed on the grid (unlike when they are placed in the Document window without a grid), they can be moved freely, as long as they stay on the grid. Just drag the object from one position on the grid to another. If the Snap check boxes in the Layout Grid Inspector are activated, objects you drag will snap to the nearest gridline.

✔ Tip

■ You can move an object on a grid with your keyboard's arrow keys. If Snap is selected in the Inspector, the object will move one grid square at a time, up or down, left or right. Holding down the Control and Alt keys (Windows) or the Option key (Mac) while using the arrow keys will move the object one pixel at a time. Additionally, the toolbar shows the position of the object in pixels relative to the upper-left corner—0,0 on the x and y axes—of the page (**Figure 8.12**).

Figure 8.12 The Layout Grid toolbar shows the distance (in pixels) of a selected object from the left and top margins of the page.

Figure 8.14 Choose an alignment option from the Align palette. You align objects relative to the grid with the Align to Parent buttons.

Object management tools

We'll now work with three GoLive tools: the Layout toolbar, the Align palette, and the Transform palette. Some of their features overlap, but each will help you align and group objects and gain more control over layout grids.

The Layout Grid toolbar (see **Figure 8.13** below) replaces the Formatting toolbar at the top of the screen when you select an object on a layout grid. You can use it to view an object's position relative to the grid, to align an object with the grid, and to group multiple objects.

All of the alignment tools on the Layout Grid toolbar also appear on the Align palette, along with some additional tools (**Figure 8.14**). To reach the Align palette, choose Window > Align. Using the palette, you can align objects with the grid, but you can also align them with one another or distribute them around the grid.

Aligning and distributing objects

Objects on a layout grid can be aligned with the grid or one another. You can also evenly distribute space between objects, using the objects' horizontal or vertical axes.

To align an object on a grid

1. Add an image to a layout grid.

2. With the image selected, click one of the alignment buttons in the toolbar or on the Align palette to place the image relative to the grid. Notice that only the Align to Parent buttons—and not all of these—are available on the Align palette.

OBJECTS ON A GRID

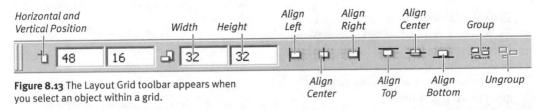

Horizontal and Vertical Position   Width   Height   Align Left   Align Right   Align Center   Group

Figure 8.13 The Layout Grid toolbar appears when you select an object within a grid.

Align Center   Align Top   Align Bottom   Ungroup

To align objects with one another

1. Open a new document and fill the entire page with a layout grid.

2. Add three objects anywhere on the page.

3. Shift-click all of the objects to select them (**Figure 8.15**).

4. Open the Align palette (**Figure 8.16**). With multiple objects on the grid, options for aligning and distributing objects relative to one another become active. (If some are inactive, it's because GoLive can't perform their actions given the current arrangement of selected objects.)

5. Under Align Objects, click Top align (this option lines up all objects with the topmost object), Center align (which vertically aligns them to the center object), or Bottom align (which aligns them with the bottom of the lowest object). The objects in **Figure 8.17** are center aligned.

To distribute objects on a grid

1. Select at least three objects on a layout grid.

2. In the Align palette, click the Use Spacing check box under the Distribute Objects label, and enter the number of pixels by which to separate objects.

3. Click one of the Distribute Objects buttons. The first three distribute objects relative to their vertical axes (left, center, right). Buttons in the second group distribute objects relative to their horizontal axes (top, center, bottom)

✔ Tip

- Use the Distribute Spacing buttons to make the amount of white space between the selected objects equal, horizontally or vertically. Choose the number of pixels by activating the Use Spacing check box and entering a value.

Objects on a Grid

Figure 8.15 Three images are placed on the grid. All three are selected.

Figure 8.16 The Align palette gives you options for aligning objects with the grid (Align to Parent) and relative to one another (Align Objects).

Figure 8.17 These objects are center aligned to each other.

Figure 8.18 You can control an object's position and size with the Transform palette.

Figure 8.19 Click the left-hand button to group selected objects.

Positioning and grouping objects

Earlier, I showed you the toolbar fields that identify an object's coordinates on the layout grid. You can use these fields or the Transform palette to position an object at the pixel level.

GoLive also allows you to group several objects, making it possible to move and manipulate them together.

To position an object on a grid

1. Create a large, blank layout grid.

2. Add an object to the grid.

3. Open the Transform palette by choosing Window > Transform, or clicking the Transform tab in the window containing the Align palette you used in the previous section.

4. In the Transform palette (**Figure 8.18**), change the pixel measurements in the two Position fields.

   or

   Change the pixel measurements in the leftmost pair of fields on the toolbar.

5. Press Tab. The object moves to the new horizontal and vertical pixel position you've chosen.

To group objects

1. In a layout grid containing at least two objects, Shift-click to select several objects and align or distribute them as you like.

2. Click the left-hand button under the Grouping label of the Transform palette (**Figure 8.19**).

   or

(continues on next page)

OBJECTS ON A GRID

Click the Group button on the toolbar. The objects' individual selection handles disappear and the newly grouped object is now surrounded by a single border (**Figure 8.20**). If you drag a grouped object, all the elements move together.

3. When you create a group, the Layout Grid Inspector changes to the Group Inspector (**Figure 8.21**). Use the padlock icon (Mac) or the check box (Windows) to lock the group so that its elements cannot be accidentally ungrouped.

4. To break up a group, click the right-hand button under the Grouping label of the Transform palette.

Figure 8.20 Grouped objects are contained within a single border, and you can move them as one object.

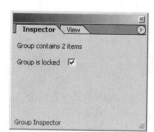

Figure 8.21 The Group Inspector lets you know how many items are in a group. You can unlock a group by clicking the check box (Windows) or the padlock (Mac).

Tables vs. Grids: Which Is Better?

Both ordinary tables and GoLive layout grids are, in fact, HTML tables.

Layout grids are useful tools for Web page designers, who can use them to position objects with pixel-level accuracy. This makes it possible to choose the exact location in the layout where an object will appear—though you shouldn't expect that level of accuracy when a page is actually viewed in a specific browser. Objects you drag around a layout grid can snap to the grid, allowing you to arrange them along the horizontal and vertical gridlines. Layout grids are also easy to build and change as you work with them.

Despite their flexibility as a way to build pages in GoLive, grids do make it even more necessary than usual for you to check your page design in several browsers as you build it, to make sure that objects on a grid appear where they should, especially in relation to one another.

In some cases, a layout grid is not the right choice. Use a table instead if you are building a design containing content whose size varies by browser, such as text, which is rendered at a substantially larger size by Windows browsers than by Mac browsers. This is also true of HTML form elements (see Chapter 10, "Working with Forms"). In a similar vein, stick to a table if you want to align text with an image, since you can keep the two in a single cell and thus maintain their relationship.

If you decide to use layout grids, keep them simple. Don't load up a single grid with lots of objects (if you have 20 objects or more, chances are that the grid is too complicated) and use multiple grids if you need to build a more complex layout. Make sure that your grids are arranged vertically, not side-by-side. This keeps both grids simpler, since a grid that appears to the right of another grid must include extra code for needed columns.

FLOATING BOXES AND POSITIONING

With GoLive, you can position text, graphics, and rich media content on your Web pages in several ways: basic HTML, tables, layout grids, or Cascading Style Sheets (CSS) and floating boxes. Each method can be used independently or in combination, giving you an amazing array of creative layout options.

Floating boxes let you control the precise position, movement, and visibility of any content you place inside. Unlike tables or layout grids, floating boxes function independently of each other and of the Web page on which they're placed—giving you new functions for your text, images, and layouts. If you don't care about the size of your files, you can add as many floating boxes to a page as you like.

In this chapter, I'll cover

- ◆ Floating box basics
- ◆ Floating box tools
- ◆ Working with floating boxes
- ◆ Working with positioning

Floating Box Basics

Historically, with the exception of displaying a background image underneath your content, HTML layout has mostly been two-dimensional. Floating boxes, however, function in three dimensions and can be placed side-by-side or stacked over one another (layered). Floating boxes are invisible to Web site visitors, but the content they contain is not. When you layer floating boxes, the content can overlap or float over the content on the underlying page (**Figure 9.1**). As you might imagine, breaking into the third dimension was a major advance in Web authoring. If you're familiar with layers in Adobe Photoshop, you have some insight into the creative potential that floating boxes offer.

In addition to stacking, you can animate floating boxes to move independently around the page and to show or hide the content they contain. Combined with actions, a floating box's movement and visibility can be triggered by any number of events, such as a mouseover—rolling your mouse over a navigation bar link to reveal a drop-down submenu of links.

✔ Tip

- If you are familiar with Web design, you may already know about *layers*, which were introduced by Netscape (4.0) to use Dynamic HTML (DHTML) to animate and display Web content. *Floating boxes* are Adobe's brand of DHTML layerings and use a combination of Cascading Style Sheets (CSS) and JavaScript, rather than the original Netscape <LAYER> tags.

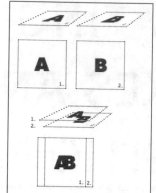

Figure 9.1 Floating boxes are independent and can overlap in 3D.

The pros and cons of floating boxes

Floating boxes can be precisely positioned anywhere on a page. The text and images they hold can be overlapped, hidden, displayed, or animated to move around the page. Text inside a floating box can also be formatted independently of any text not in the same box. Finally, floating boxes are platform-independent, client-side applications that do not require a browser plug-in and can be updated dynamically without making additional calls to the server.

Unfortunately, floating boxes must be used with caution. Although they're primarily based on the standard HTML <div> tag, some Web browser versions below 4.0 do not support floating boxes. So in some pre-4.0 browsers, instead of overlapping in 3D, your content will be repositioned to display in 2D, which will dramatically, if not drastically, alter the look of your page.

FLOATING BOX BASICS

Floating Box Tools

Similar to a table with its border set to 0, floating boxes are invisible to your Web site visitors, but are visible in GoLive's Layout Editor. The content they contain is, of course, visible in both the Layout Editor and version 4.0 and higher browsers.

There are several ways to add a floating box to your page. You can use the Objects palette, or the contextual menu from either the Layout Editor or the Floating Boxes palette.

To add a floating box:

◆ Drag the floating box icon (**Figure 9.2**) from the Objects palette into an open GoLive document.

or

Control-click (Mac) or right-click (Windows) in the Layout Editor and select Insert Object > Basic > Floating Box from the contextual menu (**Figure 9.3**).

or

Control-click (Mac) or right-click (Windows) in the Floating Boxes palette and select New FloatBox from the contextual menu **(Figure 9.4)**.

or

Click the New Floating Box button on the lower-right corner of the Floating Box palette to place a new floating box on the page (**Figure 9.5**).

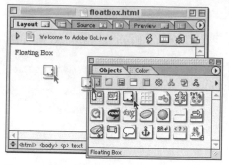

Figure 9.2 Floating box icons are located on the Basic set of the Objects palette.

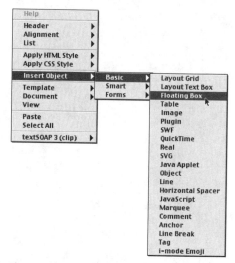

Figure 9.3 You can insert a floating box from the Layout Editor's contextual menu.

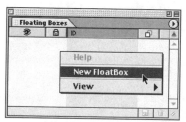

Figure 9.4 The Floating Boxes palette contextual menu.

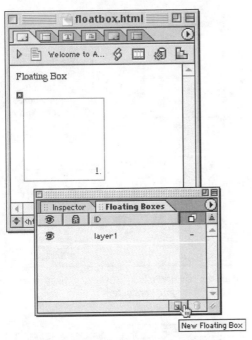

After you complete any of these creation methods, an empty floating box appears on the page (**Figure 9.6**) with the default name layer1. The box's number, which is used to identify its *stacking order* (its depth, relative to other floating boxes on the page), also appears in the lower-right corner. A tiny yellow placeholder box appears at the upper-left corner of the Layout Editor, indicating the presence of a floating box.

Palettes, windows, and Inspectors

There are several interfaces you can use to format and position floating boxes: the Floating Box Inspector, the Floating Boxes palette, Floating Box Grid Settings, CSS Editor, and the CSS Style Inspector. You may use some or all of them depending upon the complexity of your pages.

The Floating Box Inspector (**Figure 9.7**) is your primary tool for defining box attributes. To open the Floating Box Inspector, select a floating box on your page, go to the Window menu, and select the Inspector or use the keyboard shortcut Command + 1 (Mac) or Control + 1 (Windows).

Figure 9.5 Click the New Floating Box button in the lower-right corner to place a new floating box on the page.

Figure 9.6 The floating box placeholder has a number, identifying it for layer ordering.

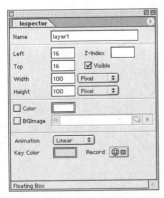

Figure 9.7 The Floating Box Inspector is the primary tool for defining floating box attributes.

The Floating Boxes palette (**Figure 9.8**) lists all floating boxes on your page. Use this to select boxes, toggle visibility, and lock editing.

Floating Box Grid Settings (**Figure 9.9**) control the grid parameters that GoLive uses to position floating boxes on the page. You can access the Grid Settings from the flyout menu in the upper-right corner of the Floating Boxes palette (**Figure 9.10**).

The CSS Editor lists all the floating boxes on your page. To edit a box's attributes, select it from the CSS Editor. You can then edit the box's position attributes in the Position set of the CSS Style Inspector.

To access the CSS Editor, select it from the View menu, click the Open CSS Editor button at the right edge of the title bar above the Layout Editor, or use the keyboard shortcuts (Option + Command + C in Mac or Alt + Shift + Control in Windows).

The CSS Style Inspector contains all the parameters for your style sheets. The Position set contains all the CSS positioning parameters for your floating box. Alternatively, you can access these parameters in the Floating Boxes palette.

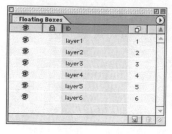

Figure 9.8 The Floating Boxes palette lists all floating boxes on your Web page.

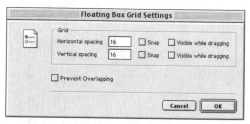

Figure 9.9 Use the Floating Box Grid Settings to set and control the grid parameters.

Figure 9.10 You access the Grid Settings via the flyout out menu of the Floating Boxes palette.

Figure 9.11 Click the edge of a floating box (when the cursor is a hand) to select it or move it around the Layout Editor.

Working with Floating Boxes

When you use one of the previously described methods for adding a floating box, an empty floating box appears on the page (see **Figure 9.5**) with the default name *layer1*. The box's number, which appears in the lower-right corner, is used to identify its stacking order. A tiny yellow placeholder box appears at the upper left of the Layout Editor indicating the presence of a floating box.

To configure a floating box:

1. Slide the cursor around the edge of the floating box until it changes from an I-beam to a hand **(Figure 9.11)**.

2. With the hand cursor, drag the box to another position. Unlike other objects such as images, text, tables, and grids, you can freely drag and position a floating box to anywhere on the page in the Layout Editor.

3. With the *layer1* floating box selected, change the size of the box by dragging any one of the eight blue handles on the sides or corners of the box.

To change a floating box's attributes:

1. Select the floating box by clicking on one of the box's borders. If the Inspector is already open, it will change to the Floating Box Inspector. If not, select the Inspector from the Window menu or use the keyboard shortcut Command + 4 (Mac) or Control + 4 (Windows).

2. If you'll be using more than one floating box on your page, it's a good idea to change the default name to a descriptive one in the Name field of the Inspector.

(continues on next page)

WORKING WITH FLOATING BOXES

3. Enter pixel values in the Left and Top fields of the Floating Box Inspector to position the box from the top left corner of the page.

4. Set the Width and Height of the box in pixels or percent, or choose Auto.

5. Enter a value in the z-index field to set the stacking order of this box when you have multiple floating boxes. A higher z-index will place the floating box higher in the stacking order. For example, a floating box with a z-index of 4 will overlap ones with z-indexes 3, 2, and 1.

6. The Visible check box toggles visibility of your floating box. With the box checked, your floating box and its contents are visible in the Layout Editor and the Web browser.

7. Set the background color for your box using the Color field of the Floating Box Inspector. Click the Color field and choose a color as you normally would for any object (whenever possible, use the 216 Web-safe color palette), by clicking the Web Color List set in the Color palette or using the keyboard shortcut Command + 3 (Mac) or Control + 3 (Windows).

8. To set an image for your box's background, check the BGImage check box, and then Point & Shoot or Browse to the image you want to use.

9. To lock settings chosen in the Inspector, switch to the Floating Boxes palette and then click the lock column next to the layer's name (a small padlock tops the lock column.)

Adding content to a floating box

If you know how to add content to a page in the Layout Editor, then you already know how to add content to a floating box. You can use any method you'd normally use in the Layout Editor, including the Objects palette, typing directly in the box, and pasting content from somewhere else. You can even place tables within a floating box, which are often used for pull-down submenus.

To add content to your floating box:

1. Place your cursor inside the floating box, and type some text.

2. Format the text either as you normally would or using the CSS Style Editor.

3. To add an image to a floating box, drag the Image icon from the Objects palette into your floating box and then Point & Shoot or Browse to the image you want to use. When working with images, don't forget to name the ALT tag in the Image Inspector.

   or

   Drag an image file directly from the File tab of the Site window into the box.

✔ Tip

■ If you do need to place a table in a floating box, you can minimize certain table-related problems within a floating box by setting the box's z-index to a value greater than zero in the Floating Box Inspector, and setting the table's width to Auto in the Table Inspector.

WORKING WITH FLOATING BOXES

Working with Positioning

As I mentioned earlier, floating boxes are completely independent objects and will not affect the layout or position of any other content (text, images, or other objects) on the page. The rest of your layout will flow as formatted, regardless of any floating boxes above it. **Figure 9.12** shows a typical full page of text flowing normally across and down the page, unaffected by the images above, which are contained inside floating boxes. For comparison, **Figure 9.13** demonstrates how the same images affect the text layout when they're removed from the floating boxes and placed directly on the page.

Although floating boxes don't affect the layout of underlying content, they do affect display. In **Figure 9.14**, the images in floating boxes 1 and 2 obscure the underlying text. Floating box 3 has a transparent background so that the text appears to overlap the underlying page text. That can be an interesting design option, though in this example it still doesn't let us read the underlying text clearly. Look at how adding a black background in box 4 or leaving the background transparent in box 5 can achieve different layout effects.

Aligning floating boxes

Use the Align palette to position floating boxes relative to one another. (Open it by selecting Window > Align.)

* **Align to Parent** is used to align one floating box in relation to the page, similar to how the alignment buttons in the toolbar work.

* **Align Objects** is used with two or more boxes to align them in relation to each other.

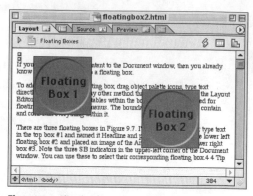

Figure 9.12 Floating boxes are independent containers that allow you to overlap and layer your content.

Figure 9.13 This is how image content would look without floating boxes.

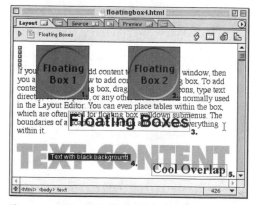

Figure 9.14 Floating boxes can obscure underlying content visibility or be used for effective design layering.

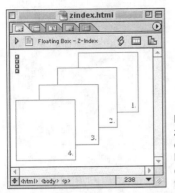

Figure 9.15 The z-index value is displayed in the lower-right corner of the floating box.

Figure 9.16 The higher the floating box's z-index, the closer it is to the top of the stack. Use the Floating Box Inspector to change the default z-index.

◆ **Distribute Objects** allows you to define a specific distance (in pixels) between your boxes. Check the Use Spacing box, then enter the pixel value you want between the boxes you've selected.

◆ **Distribute Spacing** is similar to Distribute Objects and allows you to define the space between objects.

Layering floating boxes

Whether you call it floating, layering, or stacking, floating boxes can be positioned over or under one another to create very exciting visual effects not possible in standard HTML.

The CSS attribute for a box's stacked position is its z-index. Each floating box brought onto the page is assigned a z-index value, which is displayed in the lower-right corner of the box (**Figure 9.15**). The higher the floating box's z-index, the closer it is to the top of the stack. You can change the z-index in the Floating Box Inspector (**Figure 9.16**).

Managing multiple floating boxes

If you use floating boxes to organize a page and don't need to overlap them, manipulating each floating box is fairly easy. You can position a floating box by dragging it or by assigning position values in the Floating Box Inspector or the Floating Boxes palette.

You can use the Floating Boxes palette to view the list of available boxes on your page. The Floating Boxes palette lets you

◆ Temporarily set visibility (hide/show)

◆ Temporarily lock floating boxes

◆ Edit the ID names

◆ Change the layer order

◆ Convert to Layout Grid

◆ Change the Floating Box Grid Settings

To reorder layers:

1. Add three floating boxes to a document

2. Click one of the floating boxes in the Layout Editor to select it.

3. The default layer order is based on the order in which a box was created as indicated by the number in the lower right corner. In the Floating Box Inspector, changing the z-index changes the default order. A z-index of 2 will stack over a z-index of 1.

4. Choose Window > Floating Boxes. The Floating Boxes palette opens (**Figure 9.17**).

5. Click the fourth column of a floating box to define or change the z-index.

✔ Tip

■ You can use the Floating Boxes palette to temporarily control the visibility of any box by clicking the Eye icon in the first column. This will turn on a floating box in order to view or work on its contents without changing the box's visibility source code. Use the Floating Box Inspector to make actual changes to a box's visibility.

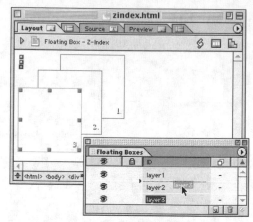

Figure 9.17 You can also change layer hierarchy by dragging within the Floating Boxes palette.

Figure 9.18 Launch the Floating Box Grid Settings window from the flyout menu in the upper-right corner of the Floating Boxes palette.

The Floating Box Grid

You can use the Floating Box Grid to position floating boxes on the page. Unlike the standard Layout Grid, the Floating Box Grid is only visible while you're dragging a floating box in the Layout Editor. You can set the gridlines as close or far apart as you like, and set floating boxes to snap to the grid as you drag.

To set floating box grid options:

1. Go to the flyout menu in the upper-right corner of the Floating Boxes palette and choose Floating Box Grid Settings (**Figure 9.18**).

2. In the Horizontal spacing and Vertical spacing boxes, enter the number of pixels you want between each of the gridlines.

3. Select the Snap check boxes that correspond to how you want your floating boxes to snap to the nearest gridlines. (For instance, if you want boxes to always jump to the nearest vertical line when you drag them, select the Snap check box that goes with vertical spacing.)

4. Click the "Visible while dragging" check boxes if you want to see the grid as you move a floating box.

5. Click the Prevent Overlapping check box to keep floating boxes from being stacked.

✔ Tip

■ All of the transform and alignment techniques you learned in Chapter 8, "Working with Layout Grids," can be used to align and distribute floating boxes.

Working with Forms

Forms add interactivity to your Web pages. Guest books, search engines, and product ordering systems are just a few of the applications that use forms. Basically, a form is a Web page component that allows a user to send information to the owner of the page via the Web server. A form can contain one or more elements that allow user input. Web servers accept the input and return information or confirmation to the user, depending on how the server software is programmed to respond.

To use forms with your Web site, your Web server (run by your company or an ISP) must have server-side scripts installed that support the forms you create. Before you design any forms, be sure that you'll be able to use them with your server. Find out whether you have scripting access to your server, either through an ISP or your corporate IS manager. If you are building a site using GoLive's Dynamic Content tools (see Chapter 21, "Dynamic Content"), gather the information you need to connect your forms to the dynamic site.

In this chapter, I'll cover

- ◆ How forms work
- ◆ Creating and configuring forms
- ◆ Adding form elements
- ◆ HTML 4.0 form elements and features

How Forms Work

Web forms are a lot like other HTML page elements: You build them in the GoLive Layout Editor, choose formatting attributes, and create links to remote resources. But unlike images, hyperlinks, QuickTime movies, or text, form elements are dependent on the Web server and other "behind the scenes" technology.

What differentiates forms is how they work behind the scenes. When a user enters text in a form, clicks a check box, and hits the Submit button, the form's work is done. From that point on, the Web server takes over.

A Web server must be running a CGI (Common Gateway Interface) application or other script designed to process the information Web site visitors submit. CGI applications are often written in Perl, C, or other languages. (Other server-side data-processing languages include Microsoft's ASP, Sun's JSP, and PHP.) Once the contents of a form arrive at the server, the script processes the information, sometimes transferring it to a database, sometimes querying the database for information that will be returned to the Web site visitor. If, for example, the site visitor uses a form to query a search engine, the query will be forwarded to the database by a server-side script. The database sends the search result to the server, which sends it back to the user's browser through a script. The script may also be responsible for combining the search results with static HTML to build a search results page. That page is then delivered to the browser. When you create a form page in GoLive, you have two tasks: designing the form so that it looks and functions the way you want it to and creating the "hooks" that allow your form to work with a Web server and scripts. Those hooks are loosely analogous to URLs that link one page to another. With the hooks in place, a server can accept data from, and return data to, a site visitor's Web browser.

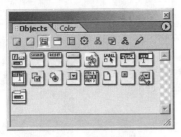

Figure 10.1 Here the Objects palette displays the Forms set.

Creating Forms

Forms have their own set on the Objects palette (**Figure 10.1**), where you'll find icons for each kind of form object.

Before you begin dragging form icons from the GoLive Form set onto your page, take some time to design the form you want to build, preferably on paper. Choose the fields and labels you want to use and draw the page as you would like it to appear on the Web, positioning and aligning form objects so that they're easy for your visitors to locate and use.

When you're ready to begin building the page, you'll probably discover that positioning form elements, even with a design for the page in hand, is a tricky proposition. The easiest way to build form-based pages is to use either tables or floating boxes (covered in Chapters 7 and 9, respectively) as containers for form elements. You can add a table to the form container and use table cells to align form objects with other objects and with their labels, for example.

To build a form, you first add the Form object to your document (creating a form container) and then add individual form elements to it. All form elements must be located within the Form object on your page. The Form object does not provide layout structure for the page: Its job is to give you a visual indication of the boundaries of the <FORM> and </FORM> tags.

To create a form:

1. Open the Forms set of the Objects palette by clicking its icon or choosing Forms from the palette's flyout menu.

2. Drag the Form icon (**Figure 10.2**) into the Document window. GoLive creates a form box, indicated by a frame and a small F.

3. Add a table to the Form container (**Figure 10.3**) by dragging the Table icon from the Basic set of the Objects palette.

4. Set up the table to accommodate your form's design.

5. Place the Form object in the upper-left corner of the area where your form will be. If the form is located in a table cell, select the cell and align the contents of the cell to the top, left of the cell, using the alignment options in the Table Inspector's Cell tab. That will move the form object to the upper-left corner of the cell.

The Form Inspector allows you to configure your new form. In order for the form to work, you must connect it to a CGI script on your Web server and provide the server with other information about how to work with the data that will be transferred from the form.

To configure a form:

1. Click the Form box to make the Form Inspector active (**Figure 10.4**).

2. Type a unique name for the form in the Name field.

3. In the Action field, Browse, Point & Shoot, or type the URL of the script that will process data entered in the form. You will need to get this information from your Webmaster or from your Internet service provider.

Figure 10.2 Begin a form by adding the Form icon to a document.

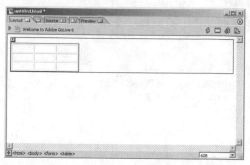

Figure 10.3 The Form object encloses all items that are part of your form. Adding a table to the container allows you to lay out the form's fields efficiently.

Figure 10.4 Use the Form Inspector to set up the interaction between the form and the script.

4. To specify the target window for your form's output, choose a target in the Target field. By default, the form's results will appear in the current browser window, replacing the form. You don't need to specify a target unless you're using frames on your page or have some other reason to send output to another window.

5. Choose an option from the Encode pop-up menu. Applications/x-www-form-unencoded tells the browser to send form data using the ASCII character set. (Leaving the Encode menu set to default is the same as choosing this option.) The other option, multipart/form-data, effectively encapsulates the form data by supplying a beginning and end-point for data sent.

6. From the Method pop-up menu, choose Post or Get to specify the way the form's output will be delivered to the server. Post is usually the better choice.

The Post method separates form data (such as a search query) from other information sent from browser to Web server. Get, on the other hand, appends the form data to the request that is sent to the server. Post is preferable, since Get requests are submitted as cumbersome URLs that can expose passwords or other sensitive information onscreen or in a browser's history file. In addition, Get submissions are limited to 256 characters.

You've just linked your form to the Web server, making it possible for the form to send and receive information. You've also set up a container for all the elements that will become part of your form. In order for your form to be useful, you now need to add fields, buttons, and other elements with which your Web page visitors can interact.

✔ Tips

■ The quickest way to specify actions for your forms is to set each action you use as an external item within your site. You can then Point & Shoot from the Form Inspector to the External tab to reach the script you need.

■ Many Web designers will never write a CGI application or other script, though they should understand how CGIs work and, specifically, the demands of the CGI that will be used to process form data. To learn more about CGI programming, check out *Perl and CGI for the World Wide Web: Visual QuickStart Guide* by Elizabeth Castro.

Adding Form Elements

Think of the Form object you just created as a container; it encloses the rest of the items that make up your Web page form and includes instructions (the Method and Action attributes) that indicate how the form's input and output should be handled. Every element of the form must fall between the <FORM> and </FORM> HTML tags, which control all items within the form. You'll see these tags only if you examine your page in the Outline Editor or Source Editor. When you add form elements in the Layout Editor, they should be added to the area bounded by the Form object.

✔ Tip

■ The Form element Inspectors shown in the next few sections include a section labeled Focus. I'll describe how to use Focus later in this chapter. For now, I'll concentrate on options related to the specific form elements.

Text and Password fields

Text fields allow users to enter a single line of text into a form. Text fields can contain names, addresses, search engine queries, or just about anything else that can be expressed in a single line of text. If you need to accommodate multiple lines of text, use the Text Area field, described in the next section. The Password field element is identical to the Text field except that it supports password entry, which conceals text as it is entered.

To create a Text or Password field:

1. With a Form object in place and configured as discussed earlier in this chapter, drag the Text Field icon (**Figure 10.5**) from the Forms set of the Objects palette into the form area. The Form Text Field Inspector appears (**Figure 10.6**).

Figure 10.5 Here are the Text Field and Password Field icons (left), and a Text field as it appears in the Layout Editor.

Figure 10.6 Configure a Text field in the Form Text Field Inspector.

2. Type a name in the Name field.

3. If you want the field to contain default text (such as "Type Your Search Request Here"), enter it in the Value field. If not, leave the field blank.

4. In the Visible field, enter the number of characters you want to be visible to the user. The field may actually contain more characters. The field's visible contents will scroll horizontally as a user types beyond the number you've chosen to make visible.

5. Enter a larger number in the Max field if you want to give the user more room to type but don't want the entire field to be visible.

6. Leave the "Is Password Field" box unchecked unless you're creating a Password field.

✔ Tips

- When you choose a name for your field or other form element, keep in mind that the field names are used by the Web server's scripts . Your field names should exactly match the field names of your database or text file and should provide logical clues to the field's purpose.

- You create a Password field using exactly the same procedure you used to make the Text field. When you drag the Password Field icon into the Document window, the Inspector selects "Is Password Field." Simply adding a Password field to a form does not password-protect the page, however. Password fields require a connection to a server script.

When you're designing forms, you can choose whether to provide a description for its fields. To give each form element (such as a Text field) a description, you'll need to provide a location for it (text frame, table cell, or floating box) and leave room on the page for the description. , You can (and should) use the Name and Value fields found in most form elements to label the fields internally.

You can resize a Text field by dragging the field's handle. As you drag, the value in the Inspector's Visible field changes.

Text Area fields

A Text field contains a single line of text, but a Text Area field allows you to provide multiple lines in which a user can enter information. You can use text areas to provide visitors a place to submit comments about your site, for example.

To create a Text Area field:

1. Drag the Text Area icon into the form (**Figure 10.7**). The Form Text Area Inspector appears (**Figure 10.8**).

2. Name the text area.

3. If you want to change the default size of the text area, increase or decrease the values in the Columns and Rows fields or drag the text area's handles.

4. Use the Wrap pop-up menu to tell the form whether or not to wrap the text at the end of each line—usually a good idea. Unless you choose a wrap option, text in the field will continue past the field's boundary.

Check boxes and radio buttons

Adding a set of check boxes or radio buttons to your form provides a way for site visitors to choose from a number of options. Radio buttons allow visitors to choose a single option among several. Check boxes allow the visitor to pick one or more items from a group.

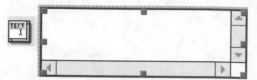

Figure 10.7 Here are the Text Area icon (left) and a text area, or multi-line text field.

Figure 10.8 Set dimensions for the field in the Form Text Area Inspector.

Figure 10.9 Set up a group of check boxes with the Check Box icon (left) and a check box.

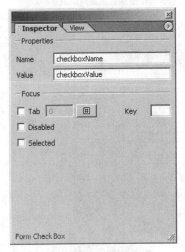

Figure 10.10 Control behavior of check boxes in the Form Check Box Inspector.

Figure 10.11 You configure radio buttons as a group. Here are the Radio Button icon (left) and three radio buttons.

Figure 10.12 Name the group of buttons in the Form Radio Button Inspector.

To create a check box:

1. Drag the Check Box icon into the form in the Document window. A check box appears (**Figure 10.9**).

2. In the Form Check Box Inspector (**Figure 10.10**), type a name for the box.

3. In the Value field, enter the information that should be passed to the Web server when a user submits a form in which the check box is selected.

4. If you want the box checked by default, click the Selected check box.

5. Create additional check boxes by selecting the first one and typing Command-D (Mac) or Control-D (Windows). Be sure to select and configure each check box in the Inspector.

To create a set of radio buttons:

1. Drag several radio buttons (**Figure 10.11**) into the form.

2. Instead of a single name for each button, the Form Radio Button Inspector (**Figure 10.12**) asks for a group name to represent all the radio buttons in this part of the form. Type a group name in the Group field.

3. Type a value for this particular radio button in the Value field. The value is transmitted to the Web server if the user selects the corresponding radio button.

4. Repeat Steps 2 and 3 for each button you created, entering the same group name that applies to all of them in the Group field. Once you've created a group, you can choose that group's name from the pop-up menu associated with the Group field.

ADDING FORM ELEMENTS

175

Submit and Reset buttons

The Submit and Reset buttons are an important final step to making your forms truly interactive. After filling out a form, the user clicks the Submit button to send the information off to the server. A Reset button clears the form, which is useful if the site visitor decides to erase all the data entered and start over.

To create a Submit or Reset button:

1. Drag a Submit Button icon (**Figure 10.13**) to the form in the Document window.

2. Type a name for the button in the Input Button Inspector (**Figure 10.14**).

3. If you want the button text to say something other than "Submit Query," click the Label check box and type your new label. It will appear within the button.

Because you used the Submit Button icon, GoLive has chosen Submit as your button's type (at the top of the Input Button Inspector). Leave it unchanged.

✔ Tip

■ You create a Reset button using the same procedure you used to make the Submit button. When you drag the Reset Button icon onto the main window, the Inspector selects Reset rather than Submit as the button type.

Popups and list boxes

You can display a list of choices within your form using a pop-up menu or a list box. They perform the same basic function but look a bit different. Pop-up menus allow the user to make a single choice from a list of options, while list boxes can support multiple choices.

Figure 10.13 The Submit and Reset Button icons (left) create nearly identical buttons. At right are the buttons they create.

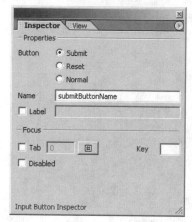

Figure 10.14 The Input Button Inspector configures Submit and Reset buttons.

✔ Tips

■ Popups and list boxes can be used like radio buttons and check boxes, but they're much easier to configure. They also take up less space on the page—a design bonus or drawback, depending on the look you're trying to achieve.

■ A form pop-up menu looks just like a Macintosh pop-up menu. (Windows users call them drop-down menus.) Only a rectangle containing a downward-pointing triangle is visible until you click it to pull down the menu. List boxes, on the other hand, display more of their contents on the Web page. Simply clicking an item in the list box selects it.

■ Configuring these two form elements is similar.

Figure 10.15 Add a pop-up menu to the form with the Popup icon (left). Size and position a pop-up menu element within the form (right).

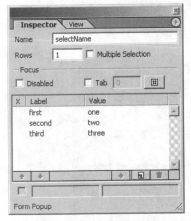

Figure 10.16 Add items to the pop-up menu in the Form Popup Inspector.

To create a pop-up menu:

1. Add the Popup icon (**Figure 10.15**) into the form.

2. Name the menu in the Form Popup Inspector (**Figure 10.16**).

3. If you want site visitors to see more than one menu item, enter the number of items to be displayed in the Rows box.

   Note that making multiple rows visible makes your pop-up menu identical to a list box. The same goes for the Multiple Selection check box, which lets users select more than one item from the menu.

4. By default, the Inspector shows the labels and values for three menu items. You can modify them, add items, or delete items here. To modify an item, select it.

5. Change the Labels and Values to the names you want to appear in your menu by selecting them and then editing the fields at the bottom of the Inspector.

6. To indicate the default menu item, click the check box to the left of the Label name at the bottom of the Inspector.

7. To add new items to your menu, click the New Item button and type the new item's label and value in the appropriate fields.

✔ Tip

■ With a pop-up menu item selected in the Inspector, you can create another by clicking the Duplicate button. This is handy if you have several pop-up items with similar names and values. Just select the duplicate you created and edit its information.

ADDING FORM ELEMENTS

To create a list box:

1. Add a List Box (**Figure 10.17**) into the form.

2. In the Form List Box Inspector, give the list box a name (**Figure 10.18**).

3. Because the whole idea of a list box is to view several options, use the Rows box to enter the number of items you want to be visible on the list. You can display as many list box items as you like, but more than five or six may occupy more vertical space on the page than you want.

4. Click "Multiple Selection" if you want to permit the user to select several options from the list.

5. Follow Steps 4–7 of the "Pop-up menu" section above to finish your list box.

✔ Tips

- List boxes have scroll bars, allowing you to display some rows and make others available by scrolling. Choose the number of rows you think will both look best on the page and also display the items you think will be most popular, saving site visitors the extra mouse movement of scrolling down the entire list.

- You can change the number of visible rows either by using the Inspector or by dragging the handle on the list box.

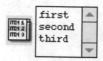

Figure 10.17 Use the List Box icon (left) to let visitors select one or more items from a list (right).

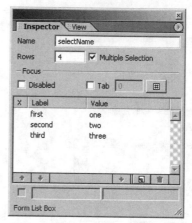

Figure 10.18 Add list items in the Form List Box Inspector.

Figure 10.19 An Input Image form item is almost identical to an ordinary image.

Figure 10.20 The Is Form check box must be checked before typing in the Name field.

Input Image

The Input Image element allows you to substitute an image for the Submit or Reset button. Configuring it is almost identical to setting up an image that would appear anywhere on a page.

To create an input image:

1. Add a Form Input Image (**Figure 10.19**) into the form. An image placeholder appears.

2. Browse or Point & Shoot to locate the image you want to use.

3. Use the Inspector to configure the image's attributes, as described in Chapter 4, "Working with Images."

4. In the More tab of the Form Input Image Inspector, type a name for the input image in the Name field, next to the Is Form check box, which should be checked (**Figure 10.20**).

✔ Tip

■ You can turn a previously placed image into a button by clicking the Is Form check box in the More tab of the Image Inspector. Optionally, you can name the image, as a part of the form, in the Name field to the right of the Is Form check box.

ADDING FORM ELEMENTS

Elements that interact with the server

Several HTML elements are very useful in maintaining communication with the Web server, enhancing security, and allowing users to upload files to your site. Configuring these elements requires very specific information about your scripts and Web server, so though I'll describe them here, I'll leave the details to you and your Webmaster, who can tell you the values that should be entered in the Inspectors for each of these items.

- Hidden elements are not a visible part of a form. Instead of holding information entered by a form user, hidden elements store information that has already been collected. For example, if your Web site includes one form that asks for a user's name and address, and a second form where the user can place an order, a hidden field can link the information on the two forms by providing the user's name and address to the second form.

- Key generators insert an encryption key into the transaction between Web site visitor and Web site owner. Keys can be used when forms contain financial or personal information. When a site visitor submits a form, the Web server sends a dialog box to the visitor, asking the visitor to accept or decline the key so that the transaction can be completed. The key generator tag is an outdated method of managing encrypted transactions.

- The File Browser element lets you open a window to the FTP directory on your Web site. Using a File Browser, site visitors can access and download files, provided they've been granted private access (with a username and password) or public access (known as *anonymous FTP*).

Figure 10.21 Use the Button icon to add a button that's not a Submit or Reset button.

Figure 10.22 The text in this button has been styled using HTML text formatting.

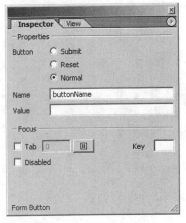

Figure 10.23 The Button element uses the same Inspector you used to configure Submit and Reset buttons.

HTML 4.0 Form Elements

The latest version of the HTML specification includes several new form tags and a couple of features that can help users navigate your forms. The catch is that your Web site's visitors must use a 4.0 (or later) browser to view and use the new tags and features. In addition, some of these tags are only supported by one of the major browsers (Netscape Navigator or Internet Explorer).

Button

An HTML 4.0 button is similar to the Submit and Reset buttons I described earlier in this chapter, except that you can customize its appearance and function with the Text Inspector.

To create a button:

1. Add a button (**Figure 10.21**) object into the form.

2. Move your cursor over the button until it changes from a box containing an arrow to an I-beam and click. You can now edit text just as you would any other text in your document. You can even apply formatting from the toolbar or from the Type menu. The button in **Figure 10.22** includes text formatted as a heading and italicized.

3. Click the border of the button to select the entire button. The Form Button Inspector becomes active (**Figure 10.23**).

4. In the Inspector, enter a name and value for the button.

Label

It seems like a fairly simple matter to create a text label for a form element such as a radio button or check box. HTML 4.0's Label form element is a nifty way of linking a label with a button or a box, because clicking on the label activates the button or box, much as clicking on a label in the Inspector activates the button or box associated with it. In other words, an HTML 4.0 label belongs to and is part of the form element it describes.

To create a label:

1. Add or select a check box, radio button, or any other form element you would like to label. Be sure to configure your form elements before creating a label.

2. Add the Label icon (**Figure 10.24**) to your form.

3. Double-click the label in the Document window to select the text, and type the label.

4. Select the label by clicking on its border.

5. Position the Label icon near the item you want to connect it to.

6. Command-click (Mac) or Alt-click (Windows) the label (not the text inside it) and click and drag to the box, button, or other element you want to link to. The Form Label Inspector becomes active (**Figure 10.25**), and it now displays an ID number in the Reference field that connects your label to the form element

   or

   Point & Shoot from the Form Label Inspector to the field to which you want to connect the label.

 Figure 10.24 Drag the Label icon to the item it will label.

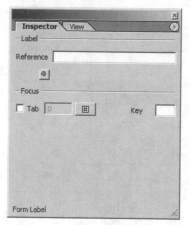

Figure 10.25 This is how the Form Label Inspector appears when the label has been associated with a form field.

✔ Tip

■ Just like with an HTML 4.0 button tag, you can format label text when the text (not the label) is selected. Formatting the text ensures that your labels are consistent with the look and feel of your page. Use the formatting commands on the toolbar or in the Type menu.

Figure 10.26 Begin a group of files with the Fieldset icon.

Figure 10.27 Set up a fieldset in the Form Fieldset Inspector.

Grouping elements with Fieldset and legend

The Fieldset element provides a physical grouping for other form elements. You can work with and move around a group of buttons, check boxes, or radio buttons as one once they've been added to a Fieldset. The Legend option allows you to label the group.

To create a Fieldset and legend:

1. Add the Fieldset icon (**Figure 10.26**) to the form. A Fieldset appears in the Document window, with the word *Legend* at the top.

2. In the Form Fieldset Inspector (**Figure 10.27**), choose an alignment for the Fieldset legend or uncheck the Use Legend box to disable this feature altogether.

3. If you plan to use a legend, click the word *Legend* in the Document window and replace it with the title of your choice.

4. Drag a table (either one you've worked on already or a new one) into the Fieldset box you just created. The Fieldset box expands to hold the table.

5. Drag some radio buttons or other form elements into the Fieldset box and table. Add labels to the table to complete the Fieldset.

✔ Tip

- Fieldsets are only supported by Internet Explorer 4.0 and above.

HTML 4.0 FORM ELEMENTS

HTML 4.0 form features

You may have noticed several items under the Focus label of many form element Inspector windows. These items specify the HTML 4.0–specific features I'll cover in this section.

The HTML 4.0 form features supported in GoLive are

◆ Tabbing chains

◆ Access keys

◆ Read-only elements

◆ Disabled elements

Tabbing chains

Filling out a long online form is much easier if you can move from one field to the next using the Tab key. GoLive and HTML 4.0 give you a way to create and control the order in which users move from field to field. It's called a *tabbing chain*.

The following form elements support tabbing chains:

◆ Text and Password fields

◆ Text areas

◆ Submit and Reset buttons

◆ Check boxes and radio buttons

◆ Pop-up menus and list boxes

◆ Labels

To create a tabbing chain:

1. Open a document that contains form fields that require the user to make text entries, such as a Text or Text Area field.

Figure 10.28 When you start tabulator indexing, yellow boxes containing question marks appear within each form field.

Figure 10.29 To set the tab order, click each box in turn to give the field a number. Here, the user will type name and address information and then be moved to the email field.

Figure 10.30 Click the Tab check box and enter a number to establish the order in which visitors will tab through the fields in the form.

2. Choose Special > Start Tabulator Indexing. Small yellow boxes with question marks appear next to the indexable fields in your form (**Figure 10.28**).

3. Click the boxes in the order you want them tabbed. The question marks change to numbers (**Figure 10.29**).

4. Choose Special > Stop Tabulator Indexing. When visitors type text into your form's fields and press Tab, their cursors will move to subsequent fields in the order you've specified here.

5. Test your tabbing chain in a browser by clicking in the first field of the chain and pressing Tab to move to subsequent fields.

✔ Tip

■ You may have noticed a check box and a field labeled Tab in the Inspector of form elements that support tabbing chains (**Figure 10.30**). You can activate or change the tab order of fields within your forms in this Inspector field.

Access keys

Defining an access key within a form element allows the user to activate the element or field by typing a specific keyboard shortcut.

The following form elements support access keys:

◆ Text and Password fields

◆ Text areas

◆ Submit and Reset buttons

◆ Check boxes and radio buttons

◆ Labels

◆ Legends

To create an access key:

1. Select a supported form element in the Document window.

2. In the Inspector, type an alphanumeric character in the Key field.

3. Test your new key in a browser that supports access keys, such as Internet Explorer for Windows. To activate a key, type Command-accesskey (Mac) or Alt-accesskey (Windows).

✔ Tips

■ It's a good idea to include some sort of label or other visual cue on the page, so that your visitors will know that the form field includes an access key.

■ Many possible access keys are already used by browsers. A browser key will override access keys you create if they are identical.

Read-only elements

You can use read-only elements to prevent visitors from editing the contents of a form field. If, for example, you want to limit the visitor to submitting a predefined text string, you could create a field that includes it.

The following form elements support read-only elements:

◆ Text and Password fields

◆ Text areas

◆ Submit and Reset buttons

◆ Check boxes and radio buttons

◆ Pop-up menus and list boxes

To create a read-only element:

1. Select the element you want to make read-only in your document.

2. In the Inspector, add text that you would like to appear in the field.

3. Click the "Read-only" check box.

Disabled elements

You can disable any form element. While it may seem silly to create an element only to disable it, you can use a GoLive action or a JavaScript to bring disabled elements to life conditionally—the item will be disabled unless it is activated by some event. You could, for example, create two versions of the same form page for use in a sales transaction. If a customer makes a purchase from your site and checks a Gift Wrap check box on the order form, a second form could include paper style and color options. If on the other hand, the customer doesn't click Gift Wrap when placing the order, a second version of the order confirmation form appears, identical to the first, but without gift wrap options displayed. Those elements are disabled form elements, rendered unavailable by a JavaScript when the customer chooses whether or not to have the package gift wrapped.

To disable a form element:

1. Choose the form element to disable.

2. Write a JavaScript (or choose a GoLive action) to enable the element conditionally. For more information about GoLive actions, see Chapter 19, "Using Actions."

3. Select the element in the Document window.

4. In the Inspector, click the Disabled check box. The element will be disabled by default.

HTML 4.0 FORM ELEMENTS

WORKING WITH FRAMES

Think of a framed page as multipaned window to your Web site. Instead of a single, scrollable page full of text and images, a framed page displays two or more pages within the same browser window. Usually, framed pages (*framesets,* in HTML-speak) contain a main pane and one or more smaller panes. A pane may include scroll bars that permit you to move through it independent of the other elements on the page. Some frames, used for navigation menus or logos, remain stationary in the browser as you click through other pages within the frameset.

Many Web designers use frames to hold navigation elements. For instance, a frame can display a sitewide table of contents alongside each individual page. Other sites use frames to force visitors to view advertisements or other banner images.

In this chapter, I'll cover

- How frames work
- Creating frames
- Adding content to frames
- Adding frames and framesets
- Adding noframes content

How Frames Work

Most Web pages consist of a single HTML file. Frames-based Web pages, on the other hand, actually display several HTML documents at once, each in its own pane of the browser window. **Figures 11.1a** and **11.1b** show a couple of design options available using frames.

To use frames, you'll need to create and link several files into a frameset. In this example, I'll show you how to create a frameset like the one in Figure 11.1b containing two frames, one for navigation and the other for content. We'll create three files:

◆ A frameset document

◆ A navigation document

◆ A body document

The frameset document doesn't include text or images, just the HTML code needed to describe how the frames that are a part of the frameset should be displayed in the browser window.

The file I'm calling the navigation document contains a table of contents (including links) of pages within the Web site. The body document is a placeholder for content (and the HTML code used to describe it) that will appear in the main pane of the browser window. When you click a link in the navigation pane, the resulting page will appear in the body section of the browser window.

You can add advertising banners, text, images, or other items using additional frame documents. Like basic navigation and content frames, you specify the frame size and appearance within the frameset document.

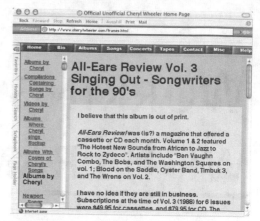

Figure 11.1a A Web site run by a fan of singer/songwriter Cheryl Wheeler uses navigation frames on the left and top of the page, with a third frame containing the body of the page.

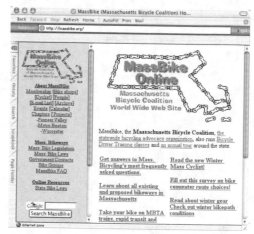

Figure 11.1b The Massachusetts Bikeway Resources page uses two frames: a table of contents on the left and a main frame containing individual links.

Frame caveats

Frames were not a full-fledged part of the HTML standard at the outset. Netscape Communications introduced frame tags as an extension to HTML. At this writing, only Netscape browsers (Navigator and Communicator) and Microsoft Internet Explorer support frames. Although browser software from Netscape and Microsoft dominates the marketplace, Webmasters who use frames run the risk of creating pages that users of other browsers cannot view. The solution for some is to create both frame and no-frame versions of their Web sites.

Even when site visitors use browsers that support them, frames can be problematic for Web site visitors. Although frames make it possible to look at more of your site at once, they also limit the user's ability to use the mouse and cursor to move freely. For example, if you're used to using the Page Down key to scroll through a Web page, you'll find that impossible to do in some framed pages unless you first click in the frame you want to navigate.

Frames also decrease the amount of visible screen space available to display Web site content. Navigation-related frames leave less room for showing content. However, the same is true of other highly structured site design methods that use tables to create navigation elements fixed to the side or top of the browser window. The challenge is to leave as much space as possible in the main frame while retaining readability within smaller frames.

HOW FRAMES WORK

Creating Frames

Once you've decided which portions of your Web site belong in frames, you can create a page with a frameset. Framesets specify the way a group of frames on the page will look and interact.

All the tools you need to create and customize frames-based pages can be found in the Frames set of the Objects palette (**Figure 11.2**).

To create a frameset document:

1. Open a new GoLive document.

2. Switch from the Layout Editor to the Frame Editor by clicking the Frame Editor tab in the Document window. The Frame Editor appears (**Figure 11.3**).

3. Choose the Frames set from the Objects palette.

4. Drag a Frameset icon (all but the upper, leftmost icon are framesets) from the palette into the Document window.

   The two-pane configuration I chose as an example is displayed in **Figure 11.4**. The Frame Set Inspector (**Figure 11.5**) opens.

✔ Tip

- For a description of each available frame-set, move your cursor over its icon in the Frames set of the Objects palette, without clicking the mouse button. A description of the frameset appears at the bottom of the palette (**Figure 11.6**).

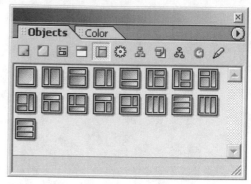

Figure 11.2 The Objects palette's Frames set contains tools you can use to create a variety of framesets.

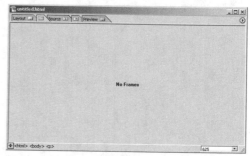

Figure 11.3 The Frame Editor displays the structure of a frameset page. It's blank when no frames are present.

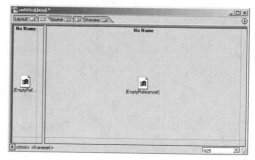

Figure 11.4 Here's a simple frameset, displayed in the Frame Editor.

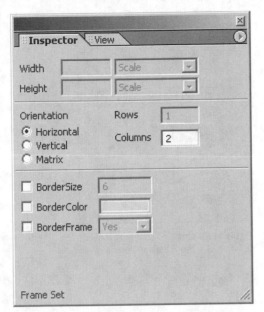

Figure 11.5 The Frame Set Inspector sets all preferences for frames within a frameset. To set options for individual frames, click within them and use the Frame Inspector.

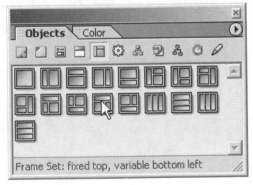

Figure 11.6 Move the cursor across a Frameset icon to see a description of the frameset's layout.

Figure 11.7 When you attempt to resize a frame, be sure that your cursor is positioned on the border between frames, rather than within one of them.

Configuring framesets

Options you choose in the Frame Set Inspector apply to all frames within the frameset. You can change the set's orientation, specify the thickness of the border, the border color, and whether there should be a border frame. You can also tell GoLive whether or not to preview frames within the Frame Editor. When you work with individual frames within the set, you'll have other configuration options.

To arrange frames by dragging:

1. Shift-click and hold the mouse button inside the leftmost frame on your page and drag to the right. When the frame you've selected reaches the other frame onscreen, the two change places.

2. Press Shift while dragging the frame to the left to return it to its original position.

To resize frames by dragging:

◆ By default, the smaller frame in this example, sometimes called a sidebar, is very narrow. To widen it, click and drag the border of the frame to the right (**Figure 11.7**). I'll need the extra space, because I'm going to use the frame as a table of contents for a Web site, as you'll see in the next set of steps.

To arrange frames in the Inspector:

1. Click within the left-hand frame. The Frame Inspector becomes active (**Figure 11.8**).

2. If you wish, choose Pixels or Percent from the Width and Height pop-up menus and enter a number in the adjacent field. To have the frame sized automatically when a visitor views the page (based on the contents of the frame and the browser and operating system being used) choose Scale. Scale tells the browser to use all available space not assigned to other elements for the frame.

3. Type a name for the frame in the Name field. The name describes the frame and is also used with the target attribute, described later in this section. The name should consist of alphanumeric characters only and should not include any spaces. I'll call the leftmost frame Nav.

4. In the Scrolling pop-up menu, choose Yes or No to determine whether your navigation frame will have scroll bars, or leave Auto selected to allow the browser to add bars only when the content is long enough to warrant them. In this example, I'll turn off scrolling because the table of contents won't be long enough to require scrolling. Leaving off the scroll bars also conserves valuable screen real estate.

5. Select the Resize Frame check box if you want users to be able to resize the frame in their browser windows. Although this option gives users more flexibility to customize the look of the frameset , you may want to leave it unchecked to maintain the exact size of a frame in order to properly display a logo, image, or other object.

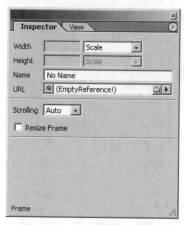

Figure 11.8 Name and configure individual frames in the Frame Inspector.

6. Repeat Steps 1–5 for each frame in the frameset. The second, larger frame in my set will be called Body.

7. Save your frameset document. Because this example Web site uses only one frameset, I'll name the file `frameset.html`. Remember that this document won't contain any content, just instructions for the display of framed pages.

I named the page `frameset.html` so that it would be obvious which document we were working with. Chances are, though, that you'll want to use a different name (`index.html` or `home.html`, for example) if your new, framed look will display the home page of your site. Since the frameset document will contain instructions telling the browser which pages to display, using the frameset document as your home page has the effect of sending your visitors to the frame pages that contain your site's contents.

✔ Tip

■ Some Webmasters avoid this naming issue (as well as problems caused for people whose Web browsers don't support frames) by offering framed and non-framed versions of their home pages and sites. To do this, create a page that offers that choice, name it `index.html`, and let site visitors click the version of their choice. In that case, you can name your frameset document anything you like and can link to it from your index page.

Linking Content to Frames

With your framework in place (pun intended), it's time to dress up those window panes with some content. Although frames can simply provide windows to individual Web pages, they are much more powerful when used as a navigation aid for your entire site. The example frame structure I'm using in this chapter does that. The navigation frame appears at all times when you view the site and offers a list of available pages, while the larger frame (I'll call it the body frame) displays the page that site visitors see when they choose a link from the navigation frame.

To add a body page to your frameset:

1. Begin a new document.

   or

   Locate a GoLive document you want to appear by default in the body frame of your frameset.

2. In the Layout Editor, Click the title field (labeled "Welcome to Adobe GoLive" by default) and change the title to "Body." This step is not essential, but now is a convenient time to change the page's title.

3. If you began with a new document, add text and/or objects to the page to complete it.

4. Save your document as body.html.

5. Open the frameset.html document you created in the preceding section. Switch to the Frame Editor.

6. Click in the larger of the two frames (on the right) to select it.

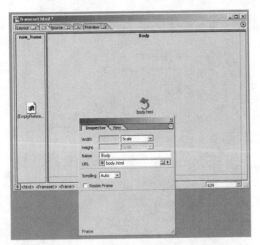

Figure 11.9 With the URL field Frame fields filled in, the question mark in the body frame changes to a page icon .

Figure 11.10 The nav.html page will appear as a navigation frame on each page of my Web site. I narrowed the window so that it would be easier to work with.

✔ Tip

- If you'd rather use the mouse than the keyboard, you can resize the frame by dragging its border.

7. Browse or Point & Shoot from the Frame Inspector and locate the file you want to appear in the body frame by default. This is probably your home page. (I added body.html.)

    or

    Drag a file from the Site window into the body frame.

8. With the body frame selected, configure it in the Frame Inspector. Be sure to name the frame Body. **Figure 11.9** shows the Frame Inspector for the body frame and the frame itself.

The navigation frame contains a fixed, unresizable HTML page, usually including links that activate content in the body frame. You can also add text, graphics, or any other object you'd like to appear in the navigation frame.

When you're designing your navigation frame, remember that it will probably be quite narrow. Limit your text elements to headings and listings, and keep logos and graphics small. Of course, you can make your navigation frame as wide as you like, but you'll be sacrificing valuable body-frame screen space with every expansion of the navigation frame.

To add a navigation frame:

1. Open a new GoLive document.

    or

    Choose a document you want to use as the navigation frame.

2. Title your document Nav and save it as nav.html.

3. Type the text for your frame. **Figure 11.10** shows my navigation page. I included headings and listings, including links to individual pages.

Your next task is to create hyperlinks that connect the listed items to the body frame. Although connecting frames is similar to creating links or anchors for a normal page, it comes with one added wrinkle: the target.

Targets tell the Web browser where a link should be displayed: in a new window, at the top of a page, or, in this case, in a frame that is part of the current frameset.

To create targeted links:

1. Open nav.html. Be sure that frameset.html is also open.

2. In nav.html, select some text and link it to the file within your site that should appear in the body frame when a visitor clicks the link in the navigation pane.

3. Connect the new link to the main frame (body) of your frameset (frameset.html) by filling in the Target field of the Text Inspector (**Figure 11.11**). Because this is the first frame link you've created, you need to type the name Body in the Target field.

4. Save the nav.html document.

5. Bring frameset.html to the front.

6. On a Mac, choose the Frame Preview tab in the Document window. You should see the navigation document in the left frame and an empty pane on the right (**Figure 11.12**).

   or

   In Windows, open frameset.html in a Web browser to preview the navigation frame.

7. In your browser or in the Mac Frame Preview, click the link you just created in the navigation frame. The page you've linked appears in the body frame (**Figure 11.13**).

8. Repeat Steps 2 and 3 for each navigation link. Each link should target the body frame.

Figure 11.11 In the Inspector, enter the name of the target frame in the Target field, where the Web browser displays the resulting page.

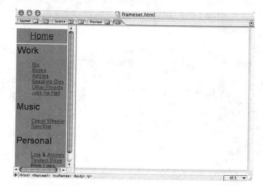

Figure 11.12 With the nav.html file linked to frameset.html, you can preview the navigation bar in Frame Preview mode.

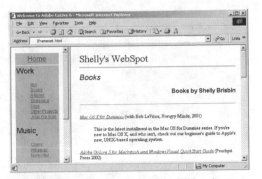

Figure 11.13 In Frame Preview mode, clicking the properly configured link in the navigation frame displays the requested page in the body frame.

LINKING CONTENT TO FRAMES

✔ Tip

■ When you choose targets in the Text Inspector, use the pop-up menu. Once you create the link to the body frame, you'll notice that the Target menu now includes the choice Body. Naming the frame "Body" in an earlier step added this item to the menu. This shortcut does not work, however, unless the frameset document (frameset.html) is open.

Does the navigation frame look right to you in Frame Preview mode or in your Web browser? Do the line breaks occur where they should? If not, you can adjust the navigation frame's width in the Frame Editor.

To tweak the navigation frame (Mac):

1. Open frameset.html and choose the Frame Editor.

2. Click the navigation frame.

3. In the Frame Inspector, click the Preview Frame button so that nav.html appears in the navigation frame.

4. Repeat steps 2 and 3 for the body frame, choosing one of the pages within your site that will occupy the body frame as an example.

5. To adjust the width of the navigation frame, drag the border to the left or right and note the impact the movement has on line breaks and available space within the body frame.

6. For that extra measure of accuracy, click the Frame Preview tab in the Document window and verify the look of your frames.

Adding Frames and Framesets

The Objects palette provides a wide variety of frameset configurations to choose from. You can also modify existing framesets by adding new frames, one at a time. You can even use multiple framesets on the same page, creating nested framesets, though it's not a good idea to include more than two framesets or a large number of individual frames per page. Because more framesets create denser code and add even more variability than usual to the way different browsers display frames, be extremely careful with nested framesets.

Frame orientation

Every frameset has an orientation—horizontal, vertical, or matrix. The two-frame set we've been building in this chapter is a horizontal set, containing two columns. Changing the set to Vertical in the Frameset Inspector would give it two rows, so the frameset would look like **Figure 11.14**.

You can add single frames to a frameset with the Frame icon from the Objects palette, but only horizontal ones. If you add a frame to a vertical frameset, GoLive creates a new, horizontal frameset for it. To include frames with two different orientations on a page you must either nest framesets, each with its own orientation, or use a matrix frameset. I'll describe these layouts next.

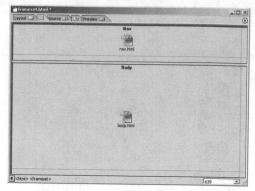

Figure 11.14 Change the orientation of `frameset.html` to Vertical to rearrange its frames.

Figure 11.15 Add a single frame to your frameset with the Frame icon.

To add a horizontal frame:

1. Open the `frameset.html` document you've been working with and switch to the Frame Editor.

2. Drag the Frame icon (**Figure 11.15**) from the upper left corner of the Frame set in the Objects palette to the Document window, dropping it into the body frame. A new horizontal frame appears.

3. Click in the new frame to select it. Now you can resize it in the Frame Inspector.

✔ Tip

- You can move the frame you just added by Shift-clicking and dragging the frame over a frame whose place you would like the new frame to take.

Matrix framesets

Unlike horizontal and vertical framesets, the matrix orientation gives the frameset attributes for both columns and rows. You can use it to include a grid of frames in a single frameset. In that way, a matrix frameset is like an HTML table, though considerably less useful since you don't have the same degree of flexibility in cell manipulation. The easiest way to set up a matrix of frames is to convert an existing frameset to a matrix.

To create a matrix frameset:

1. Add a frameset to a new document.

2. Select the frameset by clicking a frame's borders.

3. In the Frame Set Inspector, change the orientation to Matrix. You may not notice any difference in the appearance of the frameset.

4. Change the number of rows or columns in the frameset from 1 to 2. The frames shrink and reveal empty space in the Frame Editor. I've chosen two columns in the frameset.html file we've been working on (**Figure 11.16**).

5. Drag the Frame icon into the empty space in the frameset. In our example, GoLive adds the new frame to the upper portion of the frameset and moves the body frame to the lower-left corner. This occurs because all newly added frames are horizontal frames.

6. To return the body frame to the upper part of the frameset, Shift-click and drag the body frame over the new frame to cause the two to exchange places (**Figure 11.17**).

7. Drag another frame into the remaining empty space in the Frame Editor to complete the matrix.

✔ Tip

■ Matrix frames are a part of the HTML standard, but they are cumbersome to work with and usually not the best way to build groups of frames with different orientations. If your design calls for multi-dimensional frames—two horizontal content frames and a vertical banner frame, for example—consider using a second frameset to add the horizontal frame, as described in the next section.

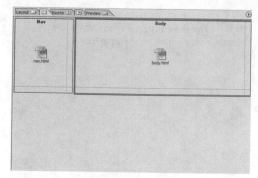

Figure 11.16 Adding a second column to a matrix frameset creates empty space in the Frame Editor.

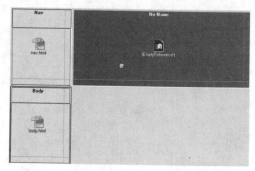

Figure 11.17 Rearrange frames by Shift-clicking as you drag one frame over another.

Nested framesets

If you want to add a group of frames to an existing frames-based page, or if you need to add one or more frames with a different orientation than the current frameset, drag another frameset from the Objects palette to the Document window. Or, if the existing frameset has a vertical orientation, drag a single frame as described in "To add a horizontal frame" to create a new, horizontal frameset.

Each frameset on a page operates as a separate entity, meaning that the attributes you set for one frameset do not apply to other sets on the same page. Like other nested tags, nested framesets reside completely within another frameset.

✔ Tips

- The easiest way to create a framed page with multiple framesets is to choose one from the Frame set of the Objects palette. You'll find several there.

- If you want to manipulate frames on a page with multiple framesets, be aware that you can't move a frame from one frameset to another. You can only rearrange frames within their own framesets. You can, however, resize individual frames or change the orientation of an entire frameset, as described on page 193.

Adding Noframes Content

Early versions of Netscape Navigator and Microsoft Internet Explorer don't support frames, and neither do text-only browsers like Lynx. Some modern browsers give users the option of disabling frames. Using the <noframes> tag, you can design your pages so that browsers that don't support frames will display a frameless version. The <noframes> tag encloses HTML that is displayed when a non-frames browser accesses the page. You can create a frameless version of the page or a message directing the user to a non-frames version of your site or to a frames-capable browser.

GoLive places the <noframes> tag in every frameset document, making it relatively easy for you to add or paste frameless content into the Source Editor or Layout Editor. If you use the Source Editor, all HTML and content you add between the opening and closing <noframes> tags will appear both in the Layout Editor and in browsers that don't support frames or where frames have been disabled. Unlike content that will appear within frames, non-frame content can be added to the frameset document, letting you specify a single URL for both a framed and a frameless home page. To build unframed pages deeper in the hierarchy of your site, link to them from the <noframes> portion of your frameset document.

To add a noframes element:

1. Create a frameset document.

2. Switch from the Frame Editor to the Layout Editor.

3. Create a page for visitors whose browsers don't use frames (**Figure 11.18**). The content you create appears within the <noframes> tag. The HTML source code for this page appears in **Figure 11.19**.

Figure 11.18 Here's a simple page that greets visitors whose browsers do not use frames. The HTML resides within the frameset document, which is called index.html.

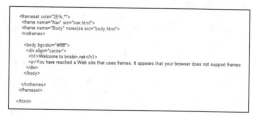

Figure 11.19 The code for the greeting page resides inside the <noframes> tags.

✔ Tips

- If you would rather not include your complete home page in the frameset document, you can simply include a short message within your frameset document that redirects visitors whose browsers don't support frames (automatically or through a link) to a non-frames version of your site.

- On the Macintosh, you can preview the page in Layout Preview mode (click the Preview tab in the Document window).

WORKING
WITH CODE

GoLive allows you to design pages and sites without getting your hands dirty or having to learn or edit HTML code. But as appealing as visual page design is, there are times when it's necessary to work directly with HTML.

GoLive includes two HTML editing views in the Document window: the Source Editor, which displays raw code, and the Outline Editor, which presents HTML in a hierarchical, organized fashion. The Source Code palette, Markup Tree, and Visual Tag Editor also provide access to Web page code.

In this chapter, you'll also learn about Head elements that affect an entire page rather than a single text block or object. You can work with and add your own HTML tags in Web Settings, a tool that helps you and GoLive keep up with the ever-changing HTML standard.

In this chapter, I'll cover

◆ Working with the Source Editor

◆ Using source code and visual tools together

◆ Working with the Outline Editor

◆ Head elements

◆ Using Web Settings

The Source Editor

The Source Editor provides an unvarnished view of the code and content that make up a Web page. You can use it to check your code for errors, make adjustments and tweaks to it, or view your page in ways not available in the Layout Editor.

The Source Editor is a text editor that lets you see and edit all of the tags, attributes, paths, and text that form the HTML page. **Figure 12.1** shows a Web page in the Source Editor. You can type directly into the Source Editor, move around with the cursor, and cut and paste code and content. Like other GoLive editors, the Source Editor supports drag-and-drop editing and allows you to use palette icons to add tags.

To view a document in the Source Editor:

1. Open a GoLive document.

2. Click the Source tab (**Figure 12.2**) to switch to the Source Editor. The view changes to show the HTML code underlying the page.

   or

   Click the button (**Figure 12.3**) in the lower-left corner of the Document window (it's called the Toggle Split View in Windows and Show/Hide Split Source on the Mac). The Document window splits to display the Source Editor in the lower pane. I'll describe using the Source Editor along with other views later this chapter.

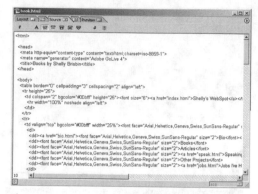

Figure 12.1 Here is a document as it appears in the Source Editor.

Figure 12.2 Switch to the Source Editor by clicking the Source tab in the Document window.

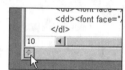

Figure 12.3 Click the Toggle Split View button to display source code in the lower portion of the Document window.

```
<html>

  <head>
    <meta http-equiv="content-type" content="text/html;charset=ISO-8859-1">
    <meta name="generator" content="Adobe GoLive 6">
    <title>Wireless Resources</title>
  </head>

  <body bgcolor="#ffffff">
    <div align="center">
      <h1>Welcome to the Wireless Resource Site</h1>
    </div>
    <p>Here you will find information and links for users of 802.11-based LANs. </p>
  </body>

</html>
```

Figure 12.4 Here is a basic Web page in the Source Editor.

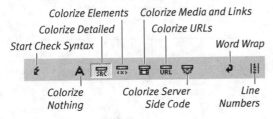

Figure 12.5 The Source Editor toolbar provides access to formatting and syntax highlighting options.

Exploring the Source Editor

Even before you add content to a GoLive document, the Source Editor contains HTML that establishes the framework for a new Web page. Each block of text or object you add to the page, regardless of the editing view you use, adds HTML, all of which appears in the Source Editor. **Figure 12.4** shows a basic Web page with only two lines of text. The tags here represent the HTML hierarchy, as well as minimal formatting for the text.

Text items within < > brackets (and colored differently than the page's content) are HTML tags and attributes. By default, tags are indented according to their placement within the HTML hierarchy. Those indents are included to remind you where you are on the page. You can change the way the Source Editor displays HTML with Source Preferences, discussed later in this chapter.

You can type text or tags into the Source Editor, and you can format text as you would in the Layout Editor, selecting it and using menus or the toolbar. You can add objects to your document by dragging palette icons or the objects themselves (from the Site window or a folder on your hard drive) into the Source Editor.

In addition to the standard Formatting toolbar, the Source Editor has its own inline toolbar for setting source view–specific options. Most of these options control the way the editor highlights tags and attributes on the page. One of the Source Editor's most important uses is locating specific code, either to correct errors or to edit your code.

The toolbar (**Figure 12.5**) gives you quick access to syntax highlighting and other options, and allows you add line numbers, and apply word wrap to your view.

Editing code and content

You can add or change content or tags in the Source Editor.

To format text:

1. In a document containing text, switch to the Source Editor.

2. Select the text that you want to format, excluding any tags that surround it.

3. Use the Formatting toolbar or the Type menu to choose formatting options. **Figure 12.6** shows selected text that has been italicized.

✔ Tips

■ Format an entire paragraph by triple-clicking to select it. Then choose a formatting tool to add tags.

■ When you type more than a line's worth of text in the Source Editor, GoLive does not wrap text to the next line as it does in the Layout Editor. You can wrap text automatically in the Source Editor by clicking the Word Wrap button on the Source Editor toolbar (**Figure 12.7**).

To add an image:

1. With the Source Editor visible in the Document window, drag an Image icon from the Objects palette to the location in your document where you want the image to appear.

2. Configure the image by typing its attributes or by switching to the Layout Editor and completing the configuration in the Image Inspector.

Figure 12.6 Select text in the Source Editor and apply text formatting.

 Figure 12.7 Click the Word Wrap button to toggle word wrap in the Source Editor.

```
<html>

  <head>
    <meta http-equiv="content-type" content="text/html;charset=ISO-8859-1">
    <meta name="generator" content="Adobe GoLive 6">
    <title>Wireless Resources</title>
  </head>

  <body bgcolor="#ffffff">
    <div align="center">
      <h1>Welcome to the Wireless Resource Site</h1>
    </div>
    <p>Here you will find information and links for users of 802.11-based LANs.</p>
    <img src="(EmptyReference!)" height="32" width="32">
  </body>

</html>
```

Figure 12.8 The image tag and its attributes appear when you drag the Image icon into the Document window.

✔ Tips

■ Dragging an object to exactly the right location in the Source Editor can be tricky. You'll have to be careful to place the new tag in the right location, relative to other tags on the page. If you drag to the wrong location, don't deselect the tag. Just move the tag by dragging it to the correct location while the tag is still selected.

■ If you drag an image file from your hard disk or the Site window to the Source Editor (**Figure 12.8**), GoLive creates a link to the image, not a placeholder for the image itself. Since that's probably not what you want, use the method previously described to add an image.

Figure 12.9 Customize the appearance of source code in the Source Preferences dialog box.

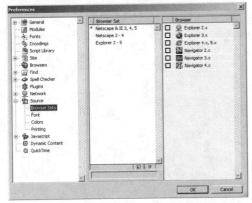

Figure 12.10 Choose a new browser set if you want to ensure that your HTML conforms to the browsers in that set.

Setting source preferences

GoLive gives you a variety of viewing options for the Source Editor that make it easier to locate and work with specific tags, content, or other code. You can change the color, font, printing behavior, and other options in the Preferences dialog box.

To set Source Editor preferences:

1. Choose Edit > Preferences. The Preferences dialog box appears.

2. Click the Source icon on the left side of the dialog box (**Figure 12.9**).

3. In the General Source Preferences window, choose options that control the default way you view and work with text and tabs in the Source Editor. Choose whether tags will appear in bold, the size of indents, and so forth. The changes you make are reflected in the sample pane at the bottom of the dialog box.

Browser sets specify how the Source Editor deals with tags associated with a particular browser, when checking tag syntax.

To choose browser sets:

1. In the Preferences dialog box, click the triangle (Mac) or plus sign (Windows) next to the Source icon.

2. Click the Browser Sets label (**Figure 12.10**). Choose a new browser if you want GoLive's syntax checker to match your tags with additional browsers.

3. When you click a browser name in the Browser Set list, GoLive checks the appropriate boxes in the Browser list.

4. You can add a custom set by clicking the New Set button (at the bottom of the Browser Set list), naming the new browser set, and checking off browsers that it should include.

To set font preferences:

1. Click the Font label under the Source icon.

2. Select a typeface, size, and style for text within the Source Editor. This typeface is used only in the Source Editor, not in other GoLive views. You can see how your changes will look below the font options.

To set color preferences:

1. Click the Colors label under the Source icon (**Figure 12.11**).

2. Choose the Code Coloring option for how you want code displayed by default in the Source Editor.

3. If you want to further customize the color display, click individual color fields and use the Color Picker to choose a new color.

To set printing preferences:

1. If you intend to print your Source Editor pages, click the Printing label under the Source icon.

2. Click printer-specific settings to activate its options.

3. Click the Code Coloring check box to print highlighted code according to the options you set under Colors.

4. Click the "Use special font for printing" check box to activate the printing font option if you would like to use a different font than you use to display the page onscreen.

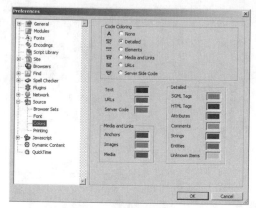

Figure 12.11 Source Color preferences let you color text and tags in the Source Editor.

Figure 12.12
Choose a doctype for a page from the flyout menu in the Document window.

Checking syntax

Whether you're working in the Source Editor or one of GoLive's other editors, it's possible to make mistakes, either by coding incorrectly, dragging items to the wrong place, or failing to properly set up tags and attributes. GoLive's syntax-checking feature allows you not only to look for obvious problems, but also to verify that your code is compatible with specific versions of HTML and other Web standards.

Once you've chosen the syntax you want to apply to your document, the syntax checker flags bad code so that you can correct it.

Syntax and the Web Settings database

GoLive stores the specifications for HTML (and variants advanced by browser vendors) and other Document Type Definitions (also called *DTDs* or *doctypes*) in the Web Settings database. You can choose a document's doctype when you create the page, identifying the page as one that conforms to the rules of the chosen DTD. When you check syntax, you first choose the DTD to check against. You can also use Web Settings to add custom DTDs, and the syntax checker will verify compliance with these, if you wish. If you have previously assigned a doctype for the page, the syntax checker will select that doctype in the "Comply with" list.

To add a doctype to an existing page:

1. Open the document in the Layout Editor.

2. From the flyout menu on the right edge of the Document window's tab bar, choose DocType > HTML 4 Strict or any other available option (**Figure 12.12**).

3. Switch to the Source Editor and notice the new Comment tab containing the doctype at the beginning of the document.

✔ Tip

■ Some GoLive documents acquire doctypes when you create them. If you begin an HTML, XML, or other file by choosing File > New Special, rather than File > New Page, the proper doctype is added to the new document.

To check syntax:

1. With a document open in any editor, choose Edit > Check Syntax.

   or

   Click the Start Check Syntax button on the Source Editor toolbar (**Figure 12.13**). The Syntax Check dialog box opens (**Figure 12.14**).

2. In the upper pane of the Syntax Check dialog box, choose a DTD from the "Comply with" list or accept the one that is already selected. Or, to look only for tags that are not complete, choose "Well-formedness only."

3. In the lower pane, choose any additional elements you want to allow in the document. These may be items that you've customized in the Web Settings database or elements specific to a particular Web browser.

4. Leave the Warnings and Errors check boxes selected to view syntax mistakes (errors) and attributes with invalid values (warnings).

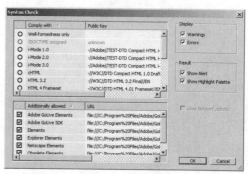

Figure 12.13 Click the Start Check Syntax button on the Source Editor toolbar to check for tagging errors in your document.

Figure 12.14 Choose an item from the "Comply with" list in the upper pane of the Syntax Check dialog box and select any special elements you've customized in the lower pane.

Figure 12.15 The Highlight palette lists syntax errors.

5. Leave Show Alert checked to see a dialog box that lists the number of errors found. Show Highlight Palette displays the found errors in the Highlight palette.

6. Click OK. GoLive presents a dialog box noting the number of errors found. Click OK. GoLive highlights syntax errors in the Document window and opens the Highlight palette (**Figure 12.15**).

To correct syntax errors:

1. Locate a highlighted error in the Layout, Source, Frame, or Outline Editor.

2. If you're unsure why the error was highlighted, use the description of the error in the Highlight palette to help you diagnose the problem.

3. Correct the error in one of GoLive's visual editors, if you wish, or switch to the Source Editor to get a look at the code.

4. Check syntax again to verify that the error has been corrected.

THE SOURCE EDITOR

Using Source Code and Visual Tools Together

GoLive provides several ways for you to work simultaneously with source code and visual editors. These options are handy for people who want to learn about source code by comparing the graphical page to the code that creates it; for those who like to work graphically, but need to tweak the underlying code on occasion; or for source code experts who want to check their work in a graphical editor.

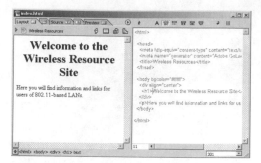

Figure 12.16 Option-click (Mac) or Alt-click (Windows) the Toggle Split View button to display the Source Editor on the right.

These are GoLive's tools for simultaneous text and visual tagging:

◆ Toggle Split View

◆ The Source Code palette

◆ The Markup Tree bar

◆ The Visual Tag Editor

Splitting your view

As I described earlier in this chapter, you can work in the Layout Editor together with the Source Editor by clicking the button in the lower-left corner of the Document window (called the Show/Hide Split Source on the Mac, and Toggle Split View in Windows). The result is a split window, containing both editors. When you click in one of the panes and edit your work, your view in the other pane changes accordingly.

✔ Tip

■ You can view the Source Editor on the right, rather than below the Layout Editor, by pressing Option (Mac) or Alt (Windows) as you click the Toggle Split View button. **Figure 12.16** shows the result.

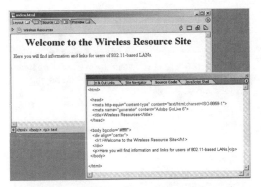

Figure 12.17 Position the Source Code palette so that you can see it and the Document window on your screen.

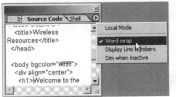

Figure 12.18 Choose Word wrap from the Source Code palette flyout menu.

The Source Code palette

The Source Code palette displays HTML source while you work in a visual editor. Unlike the split-window arrangement, the Source Code palette does not share the Document window.

To use the Source Code palette:

1. With a document open in the Layout Editor, choose Window > Source Code. The Source Code palette appears, displaying the current page (**Figure 12.17**).

2. Resize and arrange the palette so that you can see both it and the Document window.

3. Make changes in the Document window and notice the corresponding changes in the Source Code palette.

4. To enable word wrap, choose Word wrap from the Source Code palette flyout menu (**Figure 12.18**). You can also choose to show line numbers or dim the palette when it's not in use.

✔ Tip

■ Check syntax from the Source Code palette by choosing that option from the palette's contextual menu.

The Markup Tree bar

The Markup Tree bar focuses in on a tag or group of tags, letting you select it and understand how it fits into the larger HTML hierarchy. The tree is especially helpful if your page includes nested tables, floating boxes with lots of objects, or any other dense combination of difficult-to-isolate tags. To edit a tag, simply select it or its parent in the Markup Tree bar and work with it in the Document window editor of your choice.

To locate a tag with the Markup Tree bar:

1. In the Layout Editor, Source Editor, Frame Editor, or Outline Editor, click within the document. Notice that the tags displayed in the Markup Tree bar (below the horizontal scroll bar in the Document window, as shown in **Figure 12.19**) change.

2. Click a tag in the Markup Tree bar (**Figure 12.20**). The tag or the content enclosed by the tag is highlighted in the Document window.

The Visual Tag Editor

The Visual Tag Editor is not a full-scale editor, but a source-centric tool that provides a quick way to add source code.

To use the Visual Tag Editor:

1. Click in the Document window where you would like to add a new tag.

2. Choose Special > Visual Tag Editor.

3. In the Visual Tag Editor, type the tag you want to add (the cursor is already located between brackets) or select a tag from the list by double-clicking it (**Figure 12.21**). The Visual Tag Editor displays your chosen tag, as well as the HTML hierarchy above the current cursor location. It's the same information as in the Markup Tree bar.

4. To add the new tag, click OK.

Figure 12.19 The tags shown in the Markup Tree bar show the HTML hierarchy from the root of the page to the location you've selected.

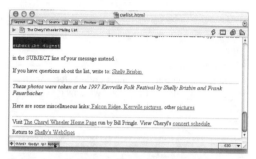

Figure 12.20 Select a tag from the Markup Tree bar with the contextual menu.

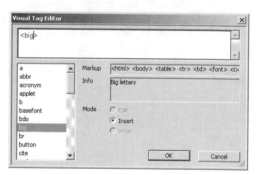

Figure 12.21 Type a tag name or double-click a tag in the list to select it.

✔ Tip

■ When you activate the Visual Tag Editor, GoLive displays a context-sensitive list of tags that you can add at the current cursor location. If you're not sure what a tag does, click it once and note the description in the Info field.

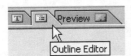

Figure 12.22 Click the Outline tab to view a page in the Outline Editor.

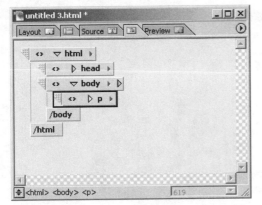

Figure 12.23 This is how a new document appears in the Outline Editor.

Using the Outline Editor

Think of the Outline Editor as a bridge between graphical Web page development and the dark recesses of HTML. Like the layout environment, the Outline Editor can display images and other objects, but it also provides a view of underlying HTML and Web-page hierarchy.

The Outline Editor displays a hierarchical version of your Web page with HTML tags around the text and graphic elements.

To view a document in the Outline Editor:

1. Open a GoLive document.

2. In the Document window, click the Outline Editor tab (**Figure 12.22**) to switch to the Outline Editor. The page's outline appears.

Anatomy of an outline

The outline that appears when you view a new GoLive document displays all the required elements of an HTML page. The HTML tags are arranged hierarchically, as they are in the Source Editor, but the hierarchy is more formal in the Outline Editor (**Figure 12.23**). Several required elements (html, head, and body) lead the hierarchy and, like most tags, must also be closed at the end of the document.

Boxes within the outline represent HTML tags. Tag attributes and Web-page content appear in subordinate (child) boxes within the outline. Tag lines also contain the structural and display attributes of HTML tags. These appear when you expand the outline. In addition to text, you can view images and other objects, just as you can in the Layout Editor.

Structural attributes

The Outline Editor uses three structural components:

◆ Boxes indicate HTML tags. These outline elements can contain content (objects and text) and/or tag attributes.

◆ Indents indicate an item's position within the HTML hierarchy. <p> (paragraph) tags appear under and to the right of the <body> tag, because paragraphs are contained within the body element. The same goes for <body> tags themselves, which are contained within the <html> tags.

◆ Vertical lines between tags indicate that the tags are paired open and close tags, as in <i> and </i>.

Outline Editor tools

The HTML tag entries shown in the Outline Editor also contain tools that let you manipulate the tag within the outline.

◆ The drag-and-drop handle moves a tag when you click and drag the handle through the outline.

◆ The collapse/expand triangle (located left of the tag name), when clicked, shows or hides content for a tag.

◆ The attributes triangle (located immediately to the right of the tag name) indicates a pop-up menu where you can choose attributes for the tag.

◆ The show/hide attributes triangle may appear on the far right of a tag. Open the triangle to view and configure attributes that are already associated with the tag.

◆ The HTML tag name is itself a tool. Command-clicking it (Mac) or Control-clicking (Windows) displays a pop-up menu of other HTML tags that you can replace it with if you choose.

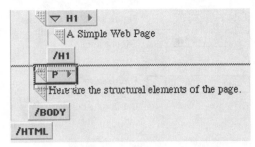

Figure 12.24 Move HTML tags with the drag-and-drop handle.

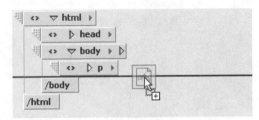

Figure 12.25 Drag an icon from the Objects palette into the Outline Editor to add a new tag.

- You can add any icon from the Basic or Forms set of the Objects palette to the Outline Editor, with one exception: You cannot add a layout text box. The layout text box is not actually an HTML tag but a GoLive layout convention.

Working with the Outline Editor

You can type and format text in the Outline Editor just as you would in the Layout and Source Editors. You can also add objects by dragging them or their corresponding icons into the Outline Editor. You can further rearrange tags by dragging them around within the Outline Editor.

To drag and drop within an outline:

1. In the Outline Editor, click and drag the drag-and-drop handle (to the left of an HTML tag) up or down. As you drag, a horizontal line and a box outline representing the item you're moving move up or down the screen (**Figure 12.24**).

2. Release the mouse button when you reach the tag's new location.

3. Click the Layout Editor or Layout Preview tab to examine the change you've made.

To add tags with a palette icon:

1. With the Outline Editor visible, select an icon from the Basic or Forms set of the Objects palette and drag it into the Document window. A horizontal line indicates where the tag is as you move the tool through the window (**Figure 12.25**).

2. Release the mouse button when you reach the desired location for your tag.

3. Click the rightmost, large triangle, adjacent to the tag. Empty tag attributes appear.

✔ Tips

- Unlike in the Layout Editor, dragging a palette icon to the Outline Editor does not display a context-sensitive Inspector for the tags you add or select. If you want to use the Inspector to configure a tag, return to the Layout Editor and click the object.

To add a tag with the Outline toolbar:

1. Click at the location in the outline where you want a new tag to appear.

2. From the toolbar, choose New Element (**Figure 12.26**). The empty tag appears in the Outline Editor (**Figure 12.27**).

3. Click within the new tag's box, but outside the tag's name, and then Command-click (Mac) or Control-click (Windows) directly on the tag name to view the Tag Type pop-up menu (**Figure 12.28**) and choose a tag from the list.

   or

   Replace the text that currently says "element" with the appropriate HTML (For example, the code for a floating box is div and the code for an image is img.)

4. Click the new tag's show/hide attributes triangle (to the far right of the tag's name) to view a list of attributes already associated with the tag you've created (**Figure 12.29**).

5. If you need to configure an attribute, click it and edit it as needed (**Figure 12.30**). If the value is a link, an arrow allows you to Browse or Point & Shoot to complete the link.

6. To add an additional attribute, click the choose attributes triangle (located immediately to the right of the tag) and choose an attribute. You can configure it via the show/hide attributes menu at the far right.

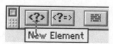

Figure 12.26 Choose New Element from the Outline Editor toolbar.

Figure 12.27 This is an undefined HTML tag in the Outline Editor.

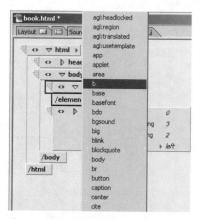

Figure 12.28 Command-click (Mac) or Control-click (Windows) to view the menu of available tag types.

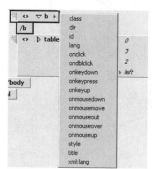

Figure 12.29 Click the show/hide attributes triangle to view tag attributes.

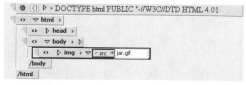

Figure 12.30 This img tag includes the SRC attribute and a value field where you can set a path to a specific image.

Figure 12.31 Choose New Text from the Outline toolbar.

Figure 12.32 Choose New Comment from the toolbar.

To add text to an outline:

1. In the Outline Editor, place the cursor where you want new text to appear or select the tag pair that encloses your text.

2. From the toolbar, choose New Text (**Figure 12.31**).

3. Type the text in the text box. When you preview your page, the text you typed will conform to the HTML tag surrounding it.

An HTML comment is a note to yourself or to someone else working on the Web page. It is only visible in the page's source and will not be seen by most Web site visitors.

To add an HTML comment:

1. Place your cursor where you would like to insert an HTML comment.

2. From the toolbar, choose New Comment (**Figure 12.32**). A blank text box appears in the outline.

3. Type the comment. In the Layout Editor, a comment is represented by a small icon. When you click it, the comment is visible in the Inspector. Within the Outline and Source Editors, comments appear in a different color than other text.

✔ Tips

- Using a palette icon to add a tag is also simpler than creating each attribute from scratch because the tool brings basic attributes along when you add it to an outline.

- On the other hand, some tags support browser-specific attributes. These are not available through the Inspector windows, but you will find them in the tag's attributes menu in the Outline Editor.

- You can also add comments with the Comment icon from the Objects palette.

- The Outline toolbar options described in this section are also available from a contextual menu. When you Control-click (Mac) or right-click (Windows) on an element in the Outline Editor, you'll see a menu that allows you to add new tags, attributes, text, and comments.

- If you're creating a tag that has lots of available attributes, such as an img tag, it may be easier to add the tag in the Layout Editor and use the Inspector to configure it.

Head Elements

HTML pages have two main parts: the body (enclosed in the <body> and </body> tags) and the head (enclosed in the <head> and </head> tags). All the text and graphics on the page appear between the body tags and can be edited in GoLive's Layout Editor. Tags in the head section, although they usually don't contain visible page elements, store lots of information about the page that visitors to your site can use when searching for your site. More importantly, head elements offer a means of controlling the loading characteristics, display, and other overall properties of Web pages. Head elements can vary the behavior of a page based on the user's browser, for example. Many head elements also contain scripts that execute when the page is loaded.

The most basic head tag is the <title> tag, which specifies the name of your page (for use in a Web browser's bookmarks list and search engine listings). You fill in the title tag when you replace the words "Welcome to Adobe GoLive" at the top of the Document window in the Layout Editor.

In this section, I'll describe the tags available in the Head set of the GoLive Objects palette and explain how to add and configure them.

Adding head elements

Like other HTML elements, head tags can be added from the Objects palette. There's a set just full of them, called the Head set (**Figure 12.33**). To add tags this way, you add icons to the head section of your page. If you prefer, you can tweak the head elements in the Outline or Source Editor, but—unless you like to type raw HTML—you'll want to create them in the Layout Editor and use the Inspector to set them up.

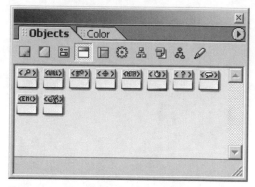

Figure 12.33 The Objects palette's Head set contains icons for each type of head element.

✔ Tip

■ Don't confuse head elements (which appear between the <head> and </head> tags above the Web page's body) with headings (which use the tags <h1>, <h2>, and so forth). Headings format text on the page, and appear within the <body> tags. GoLive makes this HTML distinction a bit of a challenge by referring in the toolbar to headings as *headers*—but they're really headings.

Figure 12.34 Click the triangle next to the page title to open the head section.

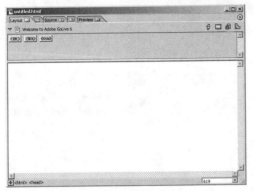

Figure 12.35 The head section is at the top of the Document window. New documents include icons relating to encoding, meta data, and page settings by default.

To add a head element to a document:

1. Open a document in the Layout Editor.

2. Click the Toggle Head Section triangle in the title bar of the Document window (**Figure 12.34**). The head section opens with three head tags already in place (**Figure 12.35**).

3. Double-click an icon in the Head set of the Objects palette. Its tag appears in the head section.

Default head elements

When you open a new GoLive document, it already contains three head tags. Icons representing them are visible in the head section of the Document window. Two of the head tags are meta items. They provide information about the page to visitors' browsers. I'll have more to say about meta tags later in this section.

◆ Encoding indicates the character set used on the page. By default, the character set is Western (ISO-8859-1). Though the tag is associated with the Encoding Inspector (where you can choose an encoding method for the page), it is, in fact, a meta tag.

◆ The meta name tag identifies the application that created the Web page. In this case, that's GoLive.

◆ The title tag shows the title of the page in the Source Editor. Clicking on the tag displays the Page Inspector. It contains global attributes such as color, background image, and margins.

You can change the attributes and values of any of these tags by selecting the tag in the head section and configuring it in the Inspector.

HEAD ELEMENTS

223

Base

The base tag allows you to specify a base URL for the current page, enabling resolution of relative links on the page. However, you don't have to use a base tag to do this. Most Web servers will correctly resolve relative URLs when the linked files are stored within the same site. On the other hand, relative links on a page that includes a base tag will work, even if the page has been separated from the rest of your site, perhaps by a visitor who saved the page to his or her hard drive.

To set up a base tag:

1. Add the Base icon (**Figure 12.36**) to the head section. The Base Inspector (**Figure 12.37**) appears.

2. Click the Base check box in the Inspector.

3. Browse, type, or Point & Shoot to set a base link—the one whose URL should be the base for all links from your page. In most cases, the base URL is simply your site's URL, as in http://www.yoursite.com.

4. Choose a target if you want to specify the window or frame in which all links from the page will be displayed by default.

Figure 12.36 Add a base tag with the base palette icon.

Figure 12.37 Choose a base URL in the Base Inspector.

Figure 12.38 Use a single Keywords palette icon to add one or more keywords to the head section.

Figure 12.39 Here is the Keywords Inspector, with a new keyword selected.

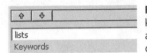

Figure 12.40 Select a keyword and click the arrow to move it up or down in the list.

Keywords

Use the Keywords icon to add a meta tag that sets keywords for your page. Web crawlers and search engines will use these keywords to categorize and add your page to their databases.

To set up a keywords item:

1. Add the Keywords icon (**Figure 12.38**) to the head section of a document.

2. Type a keyword and press Enter. The keyword appears in the upper field (**Figure 12.39**).

3. Repeat Step 2 for each keyword you want to add.

4. To remove a keyword, click it and then click the "Remove selected keywords" button.

✔ Tips

■ Here's another way to add a keyword. In the Layout Editor, select a word or phrase and choose Special > Add to Keywords. GoLive creates a meta tag for handling keywords (if one doesn't already exist) and adds the keyword. You can verify that the new keyword has been added by selecting the icon in the head section and having a look at the Inspector.

■ To change the order in which keywords appear in the list, select a keyword in the Inspector, and click the up or down arrow near the bottom of the Inspector (**Figure 12.40**) to move it.

Link

The link element establishes a relationship between the current page and another resource—a style sheet, font file, or other item that your page should reference before a browser loads it.

To set up a link tag:

1. Add the Link icon (**Figure 12.41**) to the head section.

2. In the Link Inspector (**Figure 12.42**), type, Browse, or Point & Shoot to a URL to which you want this page to refer.

3. Enter the related page's title in the Title field if you like.

4. If you're linking to an anchor, type it in the Name field.

5. Leave the URN and Methods fields blank unless you use these attributes. Most Web authors don't.

6. In the REL field, type the relationship of your page to the linked page that follows; for example, if the page you're working on is a subsidiary of the page to which you're linking.

7. Type the reverse relationship in the REV field.

Figure 12.41 The Link palette icon establishes a relationship between your page and another file.

Figure 12.42 Enter information about the related file in the Link Inspector.

Figure 12.43 You can choose a name or http-equivalent meta tag in the Meta Inspector.

Figure 12.44 The Meta Tag icon lets you provide information about the current page.

Figure 12.45 Choose a meta tag attribute in the Meta Inspector.

Meta

The meta tags provide a variety of ways to supply information about a page to visitors. There are two basic types of meta tags—name and http-equivalent (HTTP-Equiv). GoLive automatically includes a preconfigured name tag, containing meta information for file format, character set, and file creator (**Figure 12.43**).

The HTTP-Equiv tag provides header information to the Web server that can be used to modify the behavior of the page when it arrives in a Web browser. You can include as many meta tags as you want.

To set up a meta tag:

1. Add the Meta Tag icon (**Figure 12.44**) to the head section.

2. In the Meta Inspector (**Figure 12.45**), choose HTTP-Equivalent from the pop-up menu. HTTP-Equivalent values are used to pass information about the page from the Web server to the browser.

3. Type a name for the tag or choose from the menu to the right of the Name field (located just below the pop-up menu in the Meta Inspector).

4. In the Content field (the large text field at the bottom of the Inspector), type the meta tag content value that you want sent from the server to the browser.

HEAD ELEMENTS

Refresh

The refresh element updates a Web page at intervals you set. This tag is useful when you're creating pages with elements that change frequently (news items that are removed or updated regularly, for example) and want them to reload without user intervention.

To set up a refresh tag:

1. Add the Refresh icon (**Figure 12.46**) to the head section.

2. In the Refresh Inspector (**Figure 12.47**), choose the Delay interval in seconds.

3. Click the Target this Document radio button to apply the refresh rate to the page you're working with. Choose Target URL if you want the browser to replace your page with a new page. This is useful if you want to redirect users to a new URL when they type an outdated one into their browser.

4. If you choose Target URL, type, browse, or Point & Shoot to locate a URL.

IsIndex

The IsIndex element adds a search field to the Web page, allowing visitors to search a site by entering a text query. In most cases, it's more desirable to use a form (see Chapter 10, "Working with Forms") as an interface for site searching. Whether you use a form or an IsIndex element, you'll need to connect the page to a server-side script that actually performs the search. The IsIndex element is obsolete ("deprecated") in the HTML 4 and XHTML standards—you can achieve the same results much more easily with a form— but in the interest of completeness, here's how to configure IsIndex.

Figure 12.46 The Refresh icon.

Figure 12.47 Choose a refresh delay and a target in the Refresh Inspector.

Figure 12.48 The IsIndex icon.

Figure 12.49 Set up an IsIndex element with the IsIndex Inspector.

Figure 12.50 The Element icon allows you to add head elements that aren't included in the Head set of the Objects palette.

Figure 12.51 Configure the Element tag in the Element Inspector.

Figure 12.52 Click the New button in the Element Inspector to add an attribute.

To set up an IsIndex tag:

1. Add the IsIndex icon (**Figure 12.48**) to the head section.

2. In the IsIndex Inspector (**Figure 12.49**), type the text that you want to appear adjacent to the search field into the Prompt field.

Adding unknown head tags

As the HTML standard evolves, new tags become available to Web developers. You can add a head tag that is currently unknown to GoLive (whether it's one you made up or a new one from the W3C) using the Tag icon found in the Head set of the Objects palette.

To set up an unknown tag:

1. Add the Element icon (**Figure 12.50**) to the head section.

2. In the Tag Inspector (**Figure 12.51**), type a name for your new tag in the Element field.

3. Click the New button to add an attribute to the tag. This activates the Name and Value fields (**Figure 12.52**).

4. Type a name for the attribute.

5. Type a value for the attribute.

6. Repeat Steps 3–5 to add more attributes.

✔ Tip

■ The Element and Comment icons are the only ones in the Head set that you can use for either the head or body section of a document. When you double-click either one, it appears in the head section.

HEAD ELEMENTS

229

Comment

As I've mentioned, comment tags add a non-displaying comment to your Web page. Again, in the interest of thoroughness, I'll cover adding a comment from the Head set of the Objects palette.

To set up a comment tag:

1. Add the Comment icon (**Figure 12.53**) to the head section.

2. In the Comment Inspector (**Figure 12.54**), type the comment text.

✔ Tip

■ HTML comments do not appear in a visitor's browser, but anyone who views the source code of your page will be able to read your comments.

Script

The <script> tag adds JavaScript code to the head section, creating a script that is executed when a visitor opens the Web page. You can tag for JavaScripts that load when the page opens, but don't execute until the browser triggers them.

To set up a script tag

1. Add the Script icon (**Figure 12.55**) to the head section.

2. In the Head Script Inspector, type a name.

3. Choose a browser version from the Language pop-up menu. The corresponding JavaScript dialect appears in the field below (**Figure 12.56**).

4. Click the Source check box to activate the field, then Browse or Point & Shoot to locate a script.

5. To edit or create a script, click Edit. The JavaScript interface appears. (For more about JavaScript, see Chapter 14, "Working with Rich Media.")

Figure 12.53 You can use the Comment icon in the head or body section of a document.

Figure 12.54 Type a comment of any length in the Comment Inspector.

Figure 12.55 The Script icon.

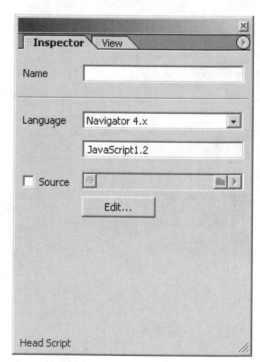

Figure 12.56 When you choose a browser version from the Language menu, the corresponding JavaScript dialect appears in the Head Script Inspector.

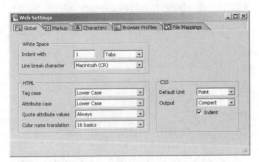

Figure 12.57 The Global tab lets you customize the look of HTML in the Source Editor, among other things.

Web Settings

All of the tags, characters, and styles GoLive provides for constructing your Web pages are stored in a database called Web Settings. When you choose a tag, GoLive uses Web Settings to specify its form and attributes. The software's syntax- and error-checking tools depend on the database to verify tags entered or edited by hand in the Source Editor. You can also use Web Settings to look up tags and attributes and to add new ones. As HTML and other languages of the Web evolve, new tags and attributes are likely to come into common use. With Web Settings, you can keep GoLive up to date.

Like many other GoLive tools, Web Settings appears as a tabbed window. The Web Settings window contents are organized under five tabs: Global, Markup, Characters, Browser Profiles, and File Mappings.

To open Web Settings

◆ Choose Edit > Web Settings. The Web Settings window appears.

Global settings

The Web Settings Global tab (**Figure 12.57**) is really an extension of the Source preferences described earlier in this chapter. Like those options, the Global items in Web Settings allow you to customize the appearance and behavior of your code. You can choose indent and line break options, as well as case and color naming preferences. Options in the Global tab include

◆ **Indent with**: By default, the Source Editor indents each element by one tab. You can change the unit to spaces and add more, if you like.

(continues on next page)

- **Line break character**: Windows, Unix, and Macintosh each generate line breaks differently. You can choose an option to match the platform of your Web server, but that's usually not necessary. By default, Web Settings uses the method favored by your Web development platform. If you plan to send files you are working on to another developer who uses a different platform, you can change the line break character for easier translation.

- **HTML formatting**: You can choose whether HTML tags and attributes appear in upper- or lowercase, or use initial capitalization. Other options allow you to choose whether numeric values are surrounded by quotation marks, and whether to convert hexadecimal numbers into color names.

- **CSS**: Choose a default unit of measure when working with Cascading Style Sheets (see Chapter 13, "Working with Style Sheets"), the type of code output to use, and whether to indent CSS code.

Markup tab

The Markup tab (**Figure 12.58**) is the heart of the Web Settings window because it contains all of the tags that GoLive (and the current markup language) recognizes and uses.

The Markup tab is divided into two types—Internal and Web. Internal markup includes GoLive proprietary items. These are the Web markup standards:

- **HTML (Hypertext Markup Language)**: HTML is the language of the Web, specifying the appearance and characteristics of most text and layout objects.

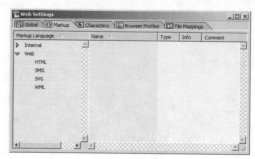

Figure 12.58 The Markup tab contains syntax for all of the markup languages supported by GoLive.

✔ Tip

- Unlike changes made in the Source section of the Preferences dialog box, changes made in the Global tag do not apply retroactively to HTML you've already created in GoLive documents. To apply Global tab changes to the active document, choose Edit > Rewrite Source Code and click OK in the resulting Alert box.

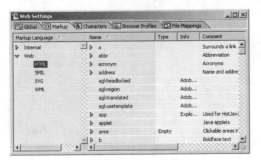

Figure 12.59 Click HTML to see tags and their attributes.

◆ **SMIL (Synchronized Multimedia Integration Language)**: Based on XML, SMIL (pronounced "smile") is a markup language that allows multimedia developers to divide multimedia content into small chunks, or *streams,* to keep file sizes and bandwidth requirements small. GoLive includes a SMIL editor.

◆ **SVG (Scalable Vector Graphics)**: This multimedia format provides another way to decrease the file size of Web graphics. SVG uses vectors, rather than pixels, to define an image by plotting its shape and the path it takes.

◆ **WML (Wireless Markup Language)**: In order to be viewed on wireless devices such as mobile phones, Web pages must be written in a markup language designed to work within the limitations of small amounts of screen real estate. WML is a leading language for the wireless environment.

Working with markup tags

Each of the markup languages included in the Web Settings database has its own set of tags and attributes, but you view and edit all of them in much the same way, using Web Settings.

In this section, I'll show you how to locate and work with markup tags. Because HTML is the most familiar markup language, I'll use its tags and attributes as examples. But the same steps apply to the other languages included in the Web Settings database.

To locate and edit a tag:

1. In the Markup tab of the Web Settings window, click the HTML category to display its contents (**Figure 12.59**).

(continues on next page)

✔ **Tip**

■ Though Web Settings allows you to view, change, or delete any tag in the database, you should be very careful not to alter standard tags in ways that will cause them not to work. If you want to modify a tag, duplicate it and work with the copy. You have been warned.

WEB SETTINGS

2. Locate a tag, such as h1, scrolling through the tag categories if necessary. Some tags contain other tags, which in turn contain attributes. Other tags simply list their own attributes

3. Click a tag. A Web Settings Element Inspector, with information specific to the tag you selected, becomes active (**Figure 12.60**).

Figure 12.60 Selecting a tag in the Markup tab brings up a Web Settings Element Inspector.

4. Note the Inspector settings for the tag you're working with. They tell you what the tag is (Name, Comment), how the tag appears (Structure), the amount of space used to format the tag (Content), and whether or not it needs an end tag to complete it.

5. Click the Output tab in the Inspector to set how much space will appear before and after the tag in the source code (**Figure 12.61**).

Figure 12.61 Look at the structure of the h1 tag in the Output tab of the Web Settings Element Inspector.

6. Click the Version tab to see a list of browsers that support the tag (**Figure 12.62**).

7. Return to the Web Settings window. Click the triangle for the tag you chose to display the tag's attributes and values. These are the same attributes you can edit in the Inspector when you add the tag to a document.

✔ Tip

- Take a look at the various options in the Inspector. Though the Structure, Content, and End Tag pop-ups can be changed, for example, it's almost always a bad idea to override the default options of existing tags. Web Settings stores tags and their configurations according to HTML standards, and altering a tag could cause serious problems if you're not sure you know what you're doing.

Figure 12.62 Click the Version tab to see which browser versions support a tag.

WEB SETTINGS

To add a new tag to the database:

1. In the Markup tab, click HTML.

2. Control-click (Mac) or right-click (Windows) in the right pane of the window. From the contextual menu, choose Add Element. A new tag called "element" appears in the tag list, and the Web Settings Element Inspector opens.

3. Name the tag in the Inspector. The tag's name is the actual text of the tag as it will appear in your HTML code.

4. Describe your new tag in the Comment field.

5. Configure the tag by choosing Structure and Content parameters from the pop-up menus in the Basic tab.

6. In the Output tab, make choices about the amount of space surrounding the tag.

7. Finally, in the Version tab, assign the tag to browsers that support it.

✔ Tip

■ Selecting a browser or HTML standard in the Version tab doesn't mean that your new tag will be supported by that version of HTML. It's just a reference. Before you use Web Settings to add new tags to your database, check an HTML reference book or Web site for detailed information about new tags, their attributes, and which browsers support them.

WEB SETTINGS

Tag attributes

You can add attributes to existing tags or to those you create. Attributes allow you to control features of a tag, such as its alignment, value, font, and so on.

To add an attribute:

1. Select a tag in the HTML category of the Markup tab.

2. Control-click (Mac) or right-click (Windows) and choose New Attribute from the menu. The tag expands and the Web Settings Attribute Inspector appears. Like the Web Settings Element Inspector, the Attribute Inspector provides fields for naming and describing the item (**Figure 12.63**).

3. Use the "Attribute is" pop-up menu to tell the database whether the attribute is optional or required.

4. Choose an option from the Value type pop-up menu.

5. Click the Version tab to identify browsers that support the attribute.

✔ Tip

- You can also choose a default condition for a tag attribute when nothing is specified. For instance, if you add an alignment attribute, you might choose to make the default alignment left. In the Web Settings Attribute Inspector, choose Fixed from the Attribute Is pop-up menu, then click the "Create this attribute" check box. Choose a value from the Value pop-up menu.

Figure 12.63 Create or edit tag attributes in the Attribute Inspector.

Figure 12.64 Configure a new enumeration in the Web Settings Enum Inspector.

Enumerations

Some tag attributes include a fixed set of values. An alignment attribute, for example, includes values to align the attribute to the left, right, or center. This group of values is called an *enumeration*.

To add or delete an enumeration:

1. In the HTML category of Markup tab, expand the triangle next to the <address> tag to expand it and then expand the tag's align attribute. Notice that the align attribute entry has a value of Enum in the Type column. This indicates that there are multiple values available. Each is called an enumeration by GoLive.

2. Control-click (Mac) or right-click (Windows) on the attribute and choose Add Enum from the menu. The Web Settings Enum Inspector appears (**Figure 12.64**).

3. Type a name for the enumeration in the Enum Name field.

4. In the Version tab, choose the browsers that support the tag of which the enumeration is an element.

5. Since this enumeration is only an example, select it and delete it by choosing Delete (Windows) or Clear (Mac) from the contextual menu.

The Characters tab

While the HTML language displays alphanumeric characters just as they are typed, a number of non-alphanumeric characters (all characters in the upper-ASCII character set, plus a few reserved characters—such as quotes and angle brackets—from the lower ASCII character set) require that you code them as entities in order to display properly in a browser. An entity begins with an ampersand (&), continues with a unique code, and ends with a semicolon (;), like this:

`M&auml;rz`

The "uml" is the special code for an *a* with an umlaut above it, as in *März*, the German word for March.

The Characters tab of the Web Settings window stores the HTML names of characters, a description of each character, and the code needed to display it on a Web page.

Special characters are stored under the Characters tab in three sections:

- **Basics** includes double quotation marks, ampersands, and the greater-than and less-than signs. These are the characters that HTML reserves from the lower ASCII character set. If you want them to appear in a Web page, you must specially code them so they are not interpreted as being part of an HTML tag.

- **Characters** includes accented letters and others that are not part of the lower ASCII character set.

- **General Punctuation** includes punctuation that is not part of the ASCII character set, such as special dashes and nonbreaking spaces.

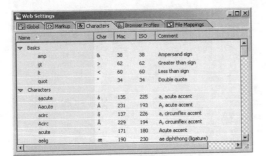

Figure 12.65 You can add or modify codes associated with characters in the Characters tab of the Web Settings window.

Figure 12.66 Configure a character in the Web Settings Entity Inspector.

To view a character:

1. Click the Characters tab (**Figure 12.65**).

2. Click quot in the Basics section. (Click the triangle to expand Basics, if it isn't open.) The Web Settings Entity Inspector (**Figure 12.66**) appears.

Items in the Characters tab are mostly useful as reference, helping you determine how to generate a particular character in HTML. The Inspector displays the name, code, and a comment about the character. In addition, you'll find the ISO and byte codes that identify the character within the HTML standard (the byte code is to the right of the labeled ISO code), and the Mac code that identifies the character to the Mac OS, if it is specific to the Mac. (The Mac code option is available in both the Macintosh and Windows versions of GoLive.) The Write option (unchecked in this example) can write the contents of the adjacent text box to the HTML code, instead of adding the name of the special character being defined. Finally, the lower field of the Inspector shows how the character looks when displayed in a browser.

To add a new character:

1. Decide in which section of the Character database your new character belongs and click the section heading.

2. Control-click (Mac) or right-click (Windows) on the heading and choose Add Entity from the contextual menu.

3. In the Web Settings Entity Inspector, type a name for the character in the Name field. The HTML code will be filled in automatically. It appears in the lower portion of the Inspector.

4. Type a description for the character in the Comment field.

(continues on next page)

WEB SETTINGS

5. Determine the correct ISO code, byte code, and (if applicable) Mac code for the character. Be sure you have this information before creating a new character. Without it, your character will not appear correctly in Web browsers.

6. Click the Version tab to specify browsers that support the character.

✔ Tip

- Like HTML tags, characters you add in the Web Settings window will not necessarily be supported. The character must have an ISO code and byte code, and browsers must support it.

Browser Profiles

Earlier in this chapter, I described the syntax checker and how you can use it to verify that your code is compatible with various browsers and standards. The information the syntax checker uses to verify support for browser types is stored in the Browser Profiles section of Web Settings (**Figure 12.67**).

The database of profile information is built with the information in the Markup section. The browsers that are checked in the Version tab of the Inspectors you see when you click on a tag in the Markup tab are cross-referenced in the Browser Profiles section. For example, if you expand Internet Explorer 5 Win to view tags it supports, you will see an entry for blockquote. Clicking blockquote in the HTML section of the Markup tab reveals that Internet Explorer 5 Win is one of the browsers that accepts that tag.

You can't edit tags in Browser Profiles. But you can view information about the browser in the Root Style Sheet Inspector. This can be helpful if you need information about an unfamiliar browser.

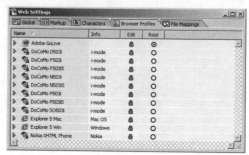

Figure 12.67 Browser Profiles contain the specifications for all Web browsers known to GoLive.

Figure 12.68 The Basic tab of a browser's Root Style Sheet Inspector displays basic information about the browser and shows the path to that browser's profile on your hard drive.

Figure 12.69 The Settings tab stores information about the browser's visual properties (DPI and gamma) and its use of HTML display elements.

To view a browser's root style sheet:

1. Click the DoCoMo N503i item. (DoCoMo is a division of Nippon, a maker of wireless phones, and the N503i is one model.) The Root Style Sheet Inspector opens (**Figure 12.68**).

2. Click the Settings tab of the Inspector. This tab (**Figure 12.69**) provides information about the browser's ability to use style sheets as well as its support for other HTML elements.

3. Click the Source tab for a listing of tags and how the browser displays them by default.

File Mappings tab

GoLive uses information stored in the File Mappings tab to open files that were created by applications other than GoLive. When you double-click an image or media file in the Document or Site window, GoLive opens it in the application that created it. The File Mappings tab (**Figure 12.70**) includes a large number of file types, but you can add new ones or change the configuration of existing ones.

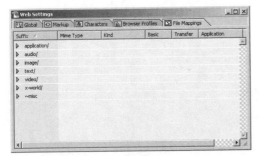

Figure 12.70 In the File Mappings tab, choose applications to use when opening foreign file types from within GoLive.

WORKING WITH STYLE SHEETS

You can do a variety of things with basic HTML tags. Unfortunately, though you can arrange objects and format text, you can't position text precisely, and you can't always format it exactly as you need to. If you're used to using styles in word processing and desktop publishing tools, HTML's limitations can be frustrating. Luckily, Cascading Style Sheets (CSS) pick up the formatting ball where HTML drops it, providing Web designers with styling power and flexibility.

GoLive includes support for Cascading Style Sheets Level 1 (CSS1), a method of separating formatting instructions from structure and content.

In this chapter, I'll cover

◆ How style sheets work

◆ Types of style sheets

◆ Creating style sheets

◆ Style types

◆ Adding properties

◆ Cascading and inheritance

◆ Using style sheets

How Style Sheets Work

Cascading Style Sheets consist of instructions, known as *rules*, on how to format HTML elements. These rules can redefine an HTML tag throughout a page, or they can alter a passage or block of text. There are lots of variations, which I'll describe throughout this chapter.

What style sheets are good for

Style sheets allow you to create and save sets of formatting instructions, which you can globally apply to individual elements (usually text), groups of elements, or whole pages, without having to recreate complex tags or run the risk of applying them inconsistently throughout your site. Once rules have been established, you can quickly apply styles with simplified tags that represent the formatting you have built.

Most importantly, style sheets provide some capabilities that are otherwise unavailable to Web authors. You can use them to specify the precise position of text on the page and to set measurements for margins and vertical and horizontal spacing, though not all browsers fully support style-sheet-based positioning.

Style sheets and their components have a specific hierarchy. Style sheets can be contained externally in a style sheet document to which pages refer and/or embedded in the head section of a page. Individual style rules can also appear inline with HTML tags.

Style sheet syntax

Rules within a style sheet specify formatting, and each rule is defined by its selectors, properties, and values.

A *selector* describes which HTML elements the style may format. *Properties* identify types of formatting in the style (for instance, font size, display, or positioning). Finally, each property has a *value* that gives specific formatting instructions, including relevant measurements.

Here's an example of correct style syntax:

```
Selector
{property:value;}
```

As you'll see later in this chapter, there are several types of style-sheet selectors. In the following example, the selector is the name of an HTML tag, <h1>:

```
H1 {font-
family:palatino;}
```

A single style may have multiple property:value pairs, like this:

```
H1 {font-family:palatino;
font-size:36pt;}
```

Of course, GoLive doesn't require you to type style-sheet code. You generate it using the tools described in the "Creating Style Sheets" section on pages 248–249.

Using CSS1 correctly

CSS1 is part of the HTML 4.0 specification issued by the W3C. But only Web browsers that support the CSS language will recognize and interpret style sheets properly. Even within CSS1, there are a few style elements that version 4.0 browsers either don't support at all or only partially support. This is because both Netscape and Microsoft have incomplete implementations of CSS1. As I proceed through this chapter, I'll note these inconsistencies, so that you can plan for them when constructing your own style sheets. You can learn more about the W3C's official CSS1 guidelines at www.w3.org/TR/REC-CSS1.

Types of Style Sheets

All types of style sheets support the same content-formatting options (properties) and most of the same selectors, but they differ in the way they connect to Web pages. *Internal* style sheets format the content of a single HTML document, whereas *external* style sheets can be used to change the appearance of a group of documents. Within each category are two methods for applying style sheets and styles to text.

Internal style sheets

There are two types of internal style sheets: *embedded* and *inline*. Each is actually contained within the HTML page it supports. An embedded style sheet is included in the document's head section within the `<style>` and `</style>` tags and uses the syntax described earlier to specify individual styles.

Inline styles are included in the body of an HTML document and apply formatting to specific tags only. In other words, if you create an inline style to change the color of an `<h2>` tag to blue, that style rule would appear as an attribute in the `<h2>` tag, and would apply only to that instance of the heading. By contrast, to make all `<h2>` headings in a document blue, you would add a rule to an embedded style sheet in the head section of the document.

Inline style sheets use *class* to apply formatting to the location of the HTML tag whose appearance you want to change.

✔ Tip

■ Earlier versions of GoLive referred to tag selectors as just that. In GoLive 5 and 6, tag selectors are chosen with commands that refer to "element styles." I'm not sure if the problem is linguistic (GoLive is developed in Germany) or typographical, but elements and tags are the same when it comes to using style sheets in GoLive.

External style sheets

You can use external style sheets to apply styles to one or more documents—even your whole Web site. External style sheets can be linked and imported.

Linked style sheets are the easiest to understand. All styles for a site can be stored in a single style sheet document, and you use the `<link>` tag to connect each site page to the style-sheet document.

An imported style sheet, like a linked one, is contained in a style-sheet document that you link to from an HTML document in which you want to use the styles. Within the HTML document, you add import instructions to the `<style>` tag with a link to the document containing styles. An advantage of imported styles is that, unlike linked styles, you can import a style or styles that can, in turn, import more styles. Imported styles are only supported by Internet Explorer at this writing.

✔ Tip

■ GoLive supports imported style sheets, in that it can display them in the style-sheet window and preview their results correctly, but you can't use GoLive tools to edit an imported style sheet. To change an imported style sheet, you need to use a text editor.

Creating Style Sheets

There are two ways to create a style sheet, and two ways each to apply internal and external ones. In this section, I'll describe how to generate both style sheets and styles. In the "Using Style Sheets" section starting on page 263, I'll explain how to connect internal and external style sheets to HTML documents. Also, later in this chapter, I'll show you how to configure each style-sheet property that specifies the appearance or position of items.

To create an internal style sheet:

1. In the Layout Editor, click the open CSS Editor button at the right edge of the title bar (**Figure 13.1**). A CSS Editor window for the current document appears (**Figure 13.2**).

2. Click the New Class Style button in the CSS Editor (**Figure 13.3**).

   or

   Control-click (Mac) or right-click (Windows) within the CSS Editor and choose New Class Style from the menu. A folder named Internal appears in the CSS Editor, and a style called .class is within the folder. You can also choose New Element Style or New ID Style from the contextual menu to create these kinds of style selectors, which you'll learn more about in the next section.

Figure 13.1 Click the Open CSS Editor button to open the CSS Editor for the current document.

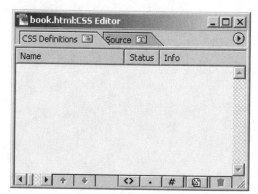

Figure 13.2 The empty CSS Editor bears the name of the document you're editing.

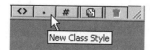

Figure 13.3 Click the New Class Style button to add a class to the style sheet.

Figure 13.4 The buttons in the CSS Style Inspector correspond to individual style properties.

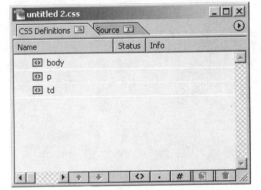

Figure 13.5 The CSS Editor window for an external style sheet includes body, paragraph, and table cell styles.

3. Name the style by clicking the mouse on the style name and typing.

or

With the new style selected, type a name in the Name field of the CSS Selector Inspector. The name must begin with a period and should be followed by a few characters describing the style, and the suffix *class* (e.g. `.subheadclass`) Do not use spaces or underscores in the style name.

4. Begin configuring the style in the CSS Style Inspector (**Figure 13.4**). Click the other buttons in the CSS Style Inspector to configure the style's properties. I'll walk you through configuring each property in the "Adding Properties" section, starting on page 253.

To create an external style sheet:

1. Choose File > New Special > Cascading Style Sheet. An untitled CSS window opens (**Figure 13.5**). It contains styles labeled body, p, and td.

2. You can edit the default rules in the style sheet or add new ones using the contextual menu or buttons at the lower right of the window, as described in the previous section.

3. Save the style sheet to your site's root folder. When you give the style sheet a name, be careful to retain the `.css` suffix so that the style sheet can be recognized.

CREATING STYLE SHEETS

Style Types

Style types tell the style sheet how an individual style relates to the style sheet and the documents it supports. GoLive recognizes three types of styles:

◆ HTML element styles

◆ Class styles

◆ ID styles

HTML element styles

Element styles apply style rules to their corresponding HTML tags within a document. Applying an element style tells GoLive (and your visitors' browsers) to "style" all occurrences of the tag according to your specifications. You can use element styles with internal and external CSS1 style sheets.

You might choose to create element styles if you have a highly formatted HTML document with lots of particular tags, like headings or lists. Using element styles, you can uniformly modify the appearance of a document. If you continue to work with the document in the Layout Editor, any HTML formatting you add will be converted to the element style in browsers that support style sheets.

To add an element style:

1. Open a new or existing style-sheet document for which you want to define an element style and then open the CSS Editor.

2. Type some text in the HTML document and format the text as a first-level heading, <h1>.

3. In the CSS Editor, click the New Element Style button (**Figure 13.6**).

   or

   Control-click (Mac) or right-click (Windows) and choose New Element Style from the contextual menu. The new tag appears in the CSS Editor.

Figure 13.6 Click the New Element Style button in the CSS Editor.

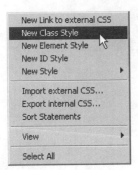

New Link to external CSS
New Class Style
New Element Style
New ID Style
New Style ▶
Import external CSS...
Export internal CSS...
Sort Statements
View ▶
Select All

Figure 13.7 Add a class by choosing New Class Style from the contextual menu.

4. Change the name of the style you've created to h1 by clicking the default name and typing over it.

5. Configure the new style's properties in the CSS Style Inspector. Notice that the text in your document changes as you specify style properties. All of the properties you set will apply to any occurrence of the <h1> tag in this document.

✔ Tip

■ To apply an element selector to a particular HTML tag, you must know the tag. If you're not familiar with specific HTML tags (for example, if you spend most of your time in the Layout Editor), switch to the Source Editor to find the syntax for the tag you want to style.

Class styles

Unlike element styles, which map to all instances of the tag(s) named in their selectors, class styles can be applied to different tags on a case-by-case basis. For instance, the element rule: h1 {color:red} will make every top-level heading red (unless it is overridden). By contrast, the class rule: .valentine {color:red} could be applied to any particular HTML element you like—perhaps only a few of your top-level headings but all of your blockquote paragraphs.

To create a class style:

1. With the CSS Editor open, click New Class Style.

   or

   Choose New Class Style from the contextual menu (**Figure 13.7**).

   (continues on next page)

2. Name the class, being careful to preserve the . leading character (that is, make certain that the first character is a period). You can use any name you like, because classes don't depend on or expect to see an HTML tag as the identifier within the style-sheet code.

3. Configure the class style using the property buttons of the CSS Style Inspector.

ID Styles

ID styles apply a chosen style to a single text block or element. ID selectors can be used only once within an HTML document, and are generally not used unless they play a role in a script.

To create an ID style:

1. In the CSS Editor, click New ID Style (**Figure 13.8**).

   or

   Choose New ID Style from the contextual menu.

2. Name the ID style. You can use any name you like, but it must be preceded by a number sign (#).

3. Configure the ID style with the property buttons in the CSS Style Inspector.

Figure 13.8 Choose New ID Style from the toolbar to add an ID.

Adding Properties

Throughout this chapter, I've referred to style-sheet *properties*. Properties are formats that change the appearance or position of text or objects. All style-sheet rules use the same set of properties.

Properties are truly the nuts and bolts of style sheets, because they add formatting capabilities that are otherwise unavailable to Web authors who use standard HTML. For example, using a property, you can specify that all level two (H2) headings should be 18 point Helvetica, with 36 points of leading—referred to as *line height* in CSS parlance—above the heading. Try doing that with basic HTML!

GoLive supports these seven categories of style-sheet properties:

- Font
- Text
- Margin
- Positioning
- Border
- Background
- List

In this section, I'll describe how to configure style-sheet properties. But first I need to explain a couple of unique configuration elements: measurements and color handling.

✔ Tips

- Just because you can create a property doesn't mean that it will work with all style-sheet-capable browsers. Unfortunately, browser vendors are inconsistent about the way they support properties. It's important that you test style-sheet-enhanced pages with all major browsers before making your pages live.

- If you don't choose an option in one of the property sets of the CSS Style Inspector, the style you create will not have that property associated with it. In other words, the default for all style properties is to do nothing.

Measurements

Style-sheet properties support a different measurement scheme than standard HTML. Although they do support the familiar pixel and percentage measurements, for example, you'll find that style sheets also accept measurements in picas, centimeters, inches, and others. The following units of measure are supported by style sheets:

Figure 13.9 Set the appearance of type in the Font properties set in the CSS Style Inspector.

♦ Absolute measurements: point, pica, millimeter (mm), centimeter (cm), and inch.

♦ Relative units: em, ex, and pixel. Em measures the item relative to the height (in points) of the current font. Ex measures text relative to the lowercase letter *x* in the current font. Pixels are relative to the resolution of the screen.

♦ Percent unit. Expresses styled text as a percentage of the default.

♦ Keyword units: ranging from XXSmall to XXLarge. Like standard HTML size tags, they measure text relative to the default size.

To set font properties:

1. Open the CSS Editor and create a style.

2. In the CSS Style Inspector, click the Font button (**Figure 13.9**).

3. Choose a font color (if you want to change it) from the pop-up menu, or drag a color from the Color palette.

4. Type a number in the Size field and choose a unit of measure from the pop-up menu.

5. Type a Line Height and choose units of measure from the pop-up menu. (Line Height is referred to as *leading* in the print publishing world.)

6. Choose Style and Decoration options for your font.

ADDING PROPERTIES

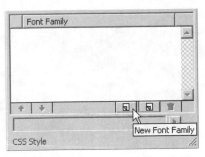

Figure 13.10 Click New Font Family to add an existing font set to the property.

Figure 13.11 Fonts you've added to this style appear in the Inspector.

Figure 13.12 Set the alignment position, and size (among other things) in the Text set of the CSS Style Inspector.

7. To change the font's weight, choose a number from 100 to 900 from the pop-up menu. Choosing Normal applies a weight of 400, while Bold equals a weight of 700. Font weights are absolute, but the Bolder and Lighter options are relative to the default or to any existing style from which this new style inherits properties.

8. To apply a font set that you created previously, pop up the New Font Family menu and choose a family (**Figure 13.10**). The fonts in the set you've chosen appear in the Font Family window (**Figure 13.11**).

9. To add an individual font, click the New Font button and choose a font from the pop-up menu below.

To set text properties:

1. Click the Text button in the CSS Style Inspector (**Figure 13.12**).

2. Enter Text Indent, Word Spacing, and Letter Spacing values. For each value, you can change the unit of measurement using the pop-up menu to the right of the field.

3. Choose an option from the Vertical Align pop-up menu; all choices are relative to the styled text's baseline.

4. Use the Font Variant menu to specify capitalization (for example, small caps) if you like. Leaving the pop-up menu unchanged has no effect on the capitalization of styled text.

5. Choose an option from the Transformation pop-up menu if you want styled text to always be capitalized, uppercase, or lowercase. Leaving the menu unchanged has no affect on capitalization.

6. Use the Alignment pop-up menu to align lines of text with respect to the margins of the page or the element (such as a table cell or floating box) that contains the text.

ADDING PROPERTIES

255

To set block properties:

1. Click the Block button in the CSS Style Inspector (**Figure 13.13**). The "box" created by applying block properties defines the area of the document controlled by the style you are creating—its margins.

    If you don't change block properties, the boundary is the text itself. If you do, there will be space between styled text and other elements of the page.

2. Choose margins for the block by entering values in the four Margin fields and choosing measurement units from their pop-up menus. You only need to choose margins for those boundaries you want to extend.

3. Add padding to create space between the styled element and the margin you've created.

4. You can use the Block options (horizontal and vertical) to define the width and height of the box. This is most useful when you need to include an image within the styled box.

✔ Tip

- To set the same margin and/or padding amount for all four sides of the box, enter a value in the "box" field.

Positioning properties

The options in the Position set control a text block's position, clipping behavior, order in a stack of layers, behavior if it overflows, and visibility. These settings are used in conjunction with floating boxes, also called layers, which allow you to place a box containing text and objects anywhere on the page, and even to animate the box. Chapter 9, "Floating Boxes and Positioning," describes how to create and use floating boxes. This set of steps will be more meaningful to you if you understand how floating boxes are used and stacked on a page.

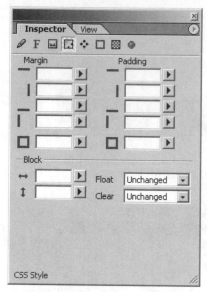

Figure 13.13 Set block properties to define a styled element's margins in the Block set of the CSS Style Inspector.

ADDING PROPERTIES

Figure 13.14 Position a styled element on the page with the Position set of the CSS Style Inspector.

To set positioning properties:

1. Click the Position button in the CSS Style Inspector (**Figure 13.14**).

2. From the Kind menu, select one of the following methods of positioning:
   - ◆ Absolute sets the position from the top-left corner of the page. Use pixels unless you have a compelling reason not to. The element will behave like a floating box.
   - ◆ Static allows the element to flow with the text.
   - ◆ Relative sets up a parent relationship with whatever container is holding the element, and positions it within that parent at x and y coordinates from the parent's upper-left corner.

3. Enter the dimensions of the element in the Width and Height fields.

4. Set the stacking order of the element with respect to other elements on the page in the z-index box. The higher the number, the higher the element will appear in the stack.

5. From the Clipping menu, select a method for dealing with text when the element overlaps adjacent elements:
   - ◆ Auto sets the area of the element within the clipping rectangle in relation to the outer edge of the element.
   - ◆ Inherit adopts the clipping method employed by the parent element.
   - ◆ Rect allows you to set the cropping dimensions (left, right, top, bottom, or auto) of the element contained within the clip rectangle.

(continues on next page)

ADDING PROPERTIES

6. Select a setting from the Overflow pop-up menu to set how browsers will display content that doesn't fit within the boundaries you defined for the element:

* Visible forces the content to display, even if it's outside the element box.

* Scroll adds a horizontal or vertical scroll bar to the element. The element's content is clipped (cannot be seen) and the extra (hidden) content can be seen by scrolling.

* Hidden hides overflowing content.

* Auto lets the browser sort things out. It may or may not add scroll bars.

7. From the Visibility pop-up menu, select a setting to determine whether the element will or will not be visible on the page.

* Inherit adopts the display settings of the parent element. By default, it is not inherited.

* Visible allows the element to be seen in the browser when the page is loaded.

* Hidden causes the element not to be visible when the page loads in a browser.

To set border properties:

1. Click the Border button in the CSS Style Inspector (**Figure 13.15**). Unlike the block properties discussed earlier, which create an invisible boundary around the element, border properties specify a visible border for the styled element. This border goes at the outer edge of the padding, inside the margin.

2. Choose left, right, top, and bottom border thickness by typing values and using the pop-up menus to choose units of measurement.

3. Choose colors for the borders from the Color palette or from the pop-up menus immediately to the right of each dimension's thickness field.

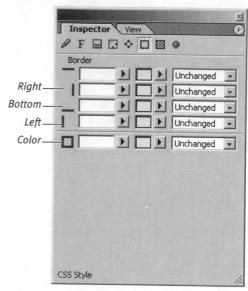

Figure 13.15 Create a border and choose its thickness in the Border set of the CSS Style Inspector.

Figure 13.16 Make the border uniform on all sides with the box options in the Border set of the CSS Style Inspector.

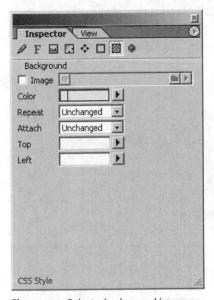

Figure 13.17 Select a background image or color and configure it in the Background set of the CSS Style Inspector.

4. Choose the type of border (solid, dotted, etc.) from the right-hand pop-up menus.

5. If you want a uniform border on all sides, use the box field and pop-up menus (**Figure 13.16**).

To set background properties:

1. Click the Background button in the CSS Style Inspector (**Figure 13.17**). Use these options to add a background color or image to the box that holds your styled element.

2. Click the Image checkbox, then Browse or Point & Shoot to locate a file you would like to use as a background image.

3. Choose a Repeat option to tile the background image within the box. Repeat x tiles the image horizontally; Repeat y tiles it vertically. Setting the option to Once means the background won't repeat.

4. Choose an Attach option to specify whether or not a background image should scroll as a visitor scrolls in the browser window.

5. Choose Top and Left measurements to position a background image in its box.

6. To choose a background color, select an option from the Color pop-up menu or click the Color field.

List properties

List properties extend the familiar HTML list tags to allow you to use custom markers, rather than the default bullet or dingbat specified in HTML. You can even choose an image as a list marker.

Not all style sheet-capable browsers support list properties. If you intend to use this property, preview your pages in as many browsers as possible.

(continues on next page)

ADDING PROPERTIES

To set list properties:

1. Click the List & Others button in the CSS Style Inspector (**Figure 13.18**).

2. Click the Image check box and locate an image to use as an alternative list-item marker.

3. From the Style pop-up menu, choose an HTML list style to use.

4. From the Position pop-up menu, choose Inside (to set the list-item marker inside the first line of text) or Outside (to set the list-item marker apart from the remaining lines of text, as it is in a regular HTML list).

Unsupported properties

You can add properties to style sheets that are not directly listed in the CSS Style Inspector: for example, if you want to use a style property that is supported by a new browser.

To add an unsupported property:

1. In the CSS Style Inspector, click the List & Others button.

2. Click the New Property button to add a property. The property-name and property-value fields are highlighted (**Figure 13.19**).

3. Type in the property's name and value, and press Enter to confirm.

Viewing selected properties

When you've configured all of the properties you want to use with a style, click the Basics button in the CSS Style Inspector. Your choices appear there (**Figure 13.20**).

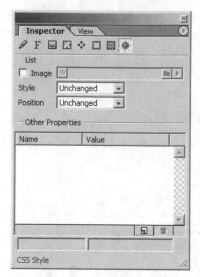

Figure 13.18 Choose your own list item markers in the List & Others set of the CSS Style Inspector.

Figure 13.19 Click New and type a name and value for the new property.

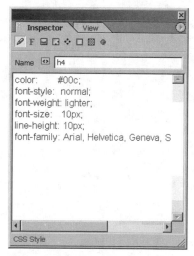

Figure 13.20 All style properties you specify in the CSS Style Inspector are described in the Basics set.

ADDING PROPERTIES

Cascading and Inheritance

As you've seen, style sheets can be implemented in a number of ways, to define the appearance or position of individual HTML elements or of all the elements on a page or pages. Before I describe applying style sheets in GoLive, you need to understand some of the rules that govern how style sheets work together and how they interact with HTML elements. A full discussion is beyond the scope of this book, but I'll give you the principles, which are especially useful if you plan to apply several style sheets to a single document or HTML element.

Since multiple style sheets and rules can be applied to a single HTML element, and since styled elements are displayed in browsers with a variety of visual characteristics—text size, and typeface, for example—it's important for a Web designer to understand how browsers sort out which styles take precedence in style hierarchies. That's where the *cascading* in Cascading Style Sheets comes in. Cascading sets the relative precedence of one style over another when several style sheets apply to the same HTML element. Cascading also tells the browser how to display styled content, based on the appearance precedence.

Style hierarchy

The more specific a style-sheet rule is—the more directly it impacts the HTML element in question—the more likely it will actually be applied, either along with or instead of a rule that is more general. So a style rule that applies to a particular tag will override a style that applies to all tags of that kind, including the tag in question. ID styles, which apply to a single HTML element, override class styles, which override tag styles.

Precedence

As I mentioned earlier, different browsers display styled content (and HTML content in general, for that matter) in different ways, depending on the platform (Mac, Windows, or Unix) and the maker of the browser (Microsoft, Netscape, or another developer). If a user changes the browser's display settings, those settings take precedence over the default settings defined by the browser maker. By the same token, style-sheet properties defined by a Web-page designer take precedence over the user's settings and the browser's default settings. This precedence gives the Web-page developer a measure of control over the look of content that uses style sheets.

Another factor is the distinction between kinds of style sheets. Those that are embedded in an HTML document have a higher precedence than external style sheets, and external style sheets that are linked to an HTML document take greater precedence the farther down the document their links appear. In other words, an external style sheet that is referenced at the top of the document has a lower precedence than one that appears after it. Finally, imported style sheets take precedence over linked external style sheets.

Inheritance

HTML is hierarchical. A <p> tag occurs within <body> tags, which occur within <html> tags, for example, and text-formatting tags also appear within other tags. If you add a <b> tag pair inside an <h2> tag pair that already includes a font attribute, all of the text within the <b> tag pair will also use the font specified in the <h2> tag. This is called *inheritance*, and it applies to style-sheet selectors as well as HTML tags and attributes.

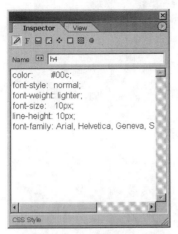

Figure 13.21 The CSS palette lists class styles available to the current selection.

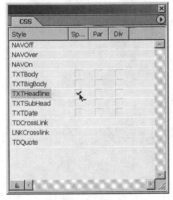

Figure 13.22 In the CSS palette, apply a class style to text by clicking in the column that indicates the kind of style you want.

Table 13.1

Style Type Definitions	
STYLE TYPE	**FUNCTION**
Span	Styles the selected text with a class that applies only to that span of text.
Par	Styles a full paragraph.
Div	Styles selected text and separates it from other elements on the page, allowing you to style it independently.
Area	Applies a class to the entire body section of the current HTML page.

Using Style Sheets

When I defined the two general types of style sheets (internal and external) and the four ways of applying them, I noted that *attaching* styles to one or more HTML documents differentiates the process of building style sheets in GoLive much more than *creating* them does. As promised, here's the scoop on adding the styles you've created to HTML pages.

First I'll explain how to apply internal style sheets, in the form of classes and IDs, and then move on to linking and importing external styles.

Applying classes

Unlike element styles, which apply automatically to all matching HTML tags in a document, classes—which apply to conditional instances of text—must be specifically connected to relevant text.

To apply a class style to text:

1. Create and configure an internal class style for a document by opening the document and then defining the style in the CSS Editor.

2. Choose Window > CSS. The CSS palette opens, displaying all styles that are available in the current document (**Figure 13.21**).

3. In the Document window, select the item you want to style (text, in this case).

4. In the CSS palette, choose the way you want to apply the style by clicking in the appropriate column next to the style you're working with (**Figure 13.22**). (See **Table 13.1** for style type definitions.) A checkmark appears beside the option you choose.

5. Click the Preview tab in the Document window to see how the styles you applied have changed the appearance of the text. For added verification, open the page you're working on in one or more Web browsers.

Applying IDs

Unlike most operations in GoLive, applying an ID style requires you to edit HTML code. You'll need to locate the text you want to style, modify the existing formatting slightly, and add the ID tag. Here we go!

To apply an ID style:

1. With an ID created and properties set, open the Source Editor.

2. Locate the item you want to format with an ID.

3. To apply an ID to all text enclosed within an HTML tag set, insert the ID selector within the starting tag, by adding ID=idname. Here are two examples:

   Original code

   ```
   <h2>One Day Sale!</h2>
   <p>All bicycles 50 percent off,
   today only.</p>
   ```

   With IDs added

   ```
   <h2 ID="salebanner">One Day Sale!</h2>

   <p ID="redandlarge">All bicycles
   50 percent off, today only.</p>
   ```

4. To apply an ID to only a portion of text that falls within tags, use the following syntax:

   ```
   <p>All bicycles <span
   ID="salebanner">50 percent</span>off,
   today only.</p>
   ```

5. Verify your work by returning to the Layout Editor or, better yet, checking out your new ID styles in a CSS-capable browser.

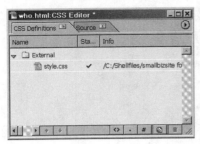

Figure 13.23 When an external style sheet is successfully linked to the current HTML document, a checkmark appears next to its label in the CSS Editor.

Referring to an external style sheet

Like an ordinary hyperlink, an external style sheet is referenced in an HTML page with links between the two documents.

To refer to an external style sheet:

1. Open a GoLive document to which you want to add external style sheet references.

2. Open the style sheet for this page by clicking the Open CSS Editor button in the upper-right corner of the Document window.

3. At the bottom of the CSS Editor, click the New Link to External CSS button.

   or

   Control-click (Mac) or right-click (Windows) and choose New Link to external CSS from the contextual menu. A new item appears in the window and the External Style Sheet Inspector opens.

4. In the Inspector, browse or Point & Shoot to locate a document containing styles you want to use in the current document.

   or

   With the Site window visible, locate the .css document within the Site window and drag it onto the Page icon at the top-left edge (near the page title) of the Document window.

   The CSS Editor now includes the name of the document, a checkmark indicating that the link is valid, and the URL (**Figure 13.23**). The document is updated automatically to reflect the newly linked style or styles.

   (continues on next page)

USING STYLE SHEETS

5. If the current document (as shown in the CSS Editor) includes or refers to multiple style sheets, use the up and down arrow buttons to move the current style sheet up or down in the cascading order.

6. To look at the external style sheet, click Open in the External Style Sheet Inspector.

Importing and exporting styles

You can add styles that are part of other documents or that are included in external style sheets by importing them.

To import an external style sheet into a document:

1. With an internal style sheet open in the CSS Editor (click the Style Sheet button), Control-click (Mac) or right-click (Windows) and choose Import external CSS from the contextual menu.

2. In the dialog box that appears, locate the external style sheet (with a .css extension) you want to import and click Open. The styles from the external style sheet are added to the current document's internal sheet (**Figure 13.24**).

3. Change the properties of the imported style sheet in the CSS Style Inspector.

To export an internal style sheet:

1. With an internal style sheet window open, Control-click (Mac) or right-click (Windows) and choose Export internal CSS from the contextual menu.

2. In the Save dialog box that appears, choose where you want to save the exported style sheet and name it (don't delete the .css extensions that GoLive has added to the default title).

3. Save the new .css file. It is now available for use as an external style sheet.

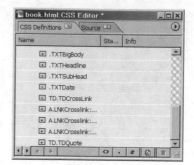

Figure 13.24 When you import styles from an external style sheet to an internal one, they're added to those that already appear in the CSS Editor.

✔ Tips

■ To duplicate a style, open the CSS Editor, select the style you want to copy, and then choose Duplicate Style from the contextual menu. Then rename and configure the new style. You can duplicate styles in both internal and external style sheets.

■ To delete a style, select it and choose Clear from the contextural menu.

WORKING WITH RICH MEDIA

You can add multimedia to your Web pages in much the same way you add GIF or JPEG images. Like images, some multimedia files are displayed inline—as part of the Web page. Others are displayed in their own windows.

Multimedia formats supported on the Web include QuickTime, Flash, Shockwave, Real-Media, and a number of other sound, video, animation, and publishing formats. GoLive can also display and execute Java applets, JavaScripts, and (on Windows machines) ActiveX controls, though not as reliably as browsers do. In order for site visitors to view multimedia files, their Web browsers must either directly support the files' format or have a compatible plug-in installed. A *plug-in* is software that is automatically activated when a multimedia file is called for and which can play or display the file.

In this chapter, I'll cover

◆ Setting up plug-ins

◆ Configuring existing JavaScripts

◆ Java applets

Setting Up Plug-ins

You add multimedia content by dragging palette icons into GoLive documents and then configuring attributes that control the way the plug-in content appears on a Web page. You can configure any multimedia type with the generic plug-in tool. GoLive supports custom attributes for four popular multimedia formats: QuickTime, SVG (scalable vector graphics), SWF (ShockWave Flash object), and RealMedia. Plug-in Inspectors associated with these media types include an extra tab with specialized options.

Like a Web browser, GoLive can play a media file inline if you've installed its plug-in software. GoLive can read the same plug-ins that browsers do. You can add and configure media content without installing plug-ins for GoLive, but you won't be able to preview your content from the Plug-in Inspector or inline within a GoLive document unless you install plug-ins.

To install plug-ins for GoLive:

1. Quit GoLive if it is running.

2. Locate browser plug-ins you want to use with GoLive. There are three sources of plug-ins:
   ◆ Your Web browser's plug-ins folder
   ◆ A folder on your hard drive containing multimedia player applications
   ◆ Web sites of plug-in vendors

3. Open the Adobe GoLive folder. If you used the default installation options, the Adobe GoLive folder is located in the Applications folder (Mac) or Program Files folder (Windows). Navigate to the Plug-ins folder.

4. Copy plug-in files into the GoLive Plug-ins folder.

5. Restart GoLive.

Figure 14.1 The Plug-in icon.

Figure 14.2 Choose a media file and a MIME type in the Basic tab of the Plug-in Inspector.

Figure 14.3 When you associate a MIME type with a plug-in placeholder, the image within the placeholder changes accordingly.

Figure 14.4 Choose a MIME type from the list.

Adding media content

The Objects palette includes a generic Plug-in icon and icons for SWF, QuickTime, Real and SVG. The Inspector for all plug-ins is the same, though there are a few items associated with particular formats. I'll show you how to add and configure a generic plug-in, then move on to options for specific file formats.

To add plug-in content to a document:

1. Add the Plug-in icon (**Figure 14.1**) from the Basic set of the Objects palette to the Document window.

   or

   Drag a media file into the Document window. The Plug-in Inspector appears (**Figure 14.2**).

2. If you added a placeholder, browse or Point & Shoot from the Inspector to a media file you want to add to the page. The plug-in placeholder in the Document window now shows the name of the media file (**Figure 14.3**).

To configure a plug-in file:

1. Select a plug-in placeholder in the Document window.

2. In the Plug-in Inspector, the Mime field may contain a MIME type, but the field is inactive. Click the Mime check box to activate the field.

3. If no MIME type is chosen, choose one from the pop-up menu (**Figure 14.4**). The MIME type identifies the media file to Web browsers, letting them know which application or plug-in to use when opening the file.

(continues on next page)

4. If you installed a plug-in for this file type in the GoLive Plug-ins folder, the Play button in the lower-left corner of the Plug-in Inspector is active (**Figure 14.5**). Click it to get a quick peak at (or listen to) your media file. This will also verify that you've selected the correct MIME type.

5. Resize the plug-in placeholder if you like by dragging one of its handles or by typing new values in the Inspector's Width and Height fields.

6. Align the plug-in placeholder with your Web page text using the Align pop-up menu. The same rules that govern the alignment of images with text apply when using plug-ins. For a full description of alignment options, see Chapter 4, "Working with Images."

7. From the HTML pop-up menu, choose the HTML tag that tells the browser how to play the file—with a browser plug-in <embed> or an application <object>. The safest setting is <object> <embed>, which supports both applications and plug-ins. Some media types use different playback methods for different operating systems.

8. Choosing <object> <embed> or <object> from the HTML menu activates the Class field (**Figure 14.6**). Change the default class using the pop-up menu, if necessary.

9. Click the More tab in the Plug-in Inspector (**Figure 14.7**).

Figure 14.5 Click the Play button to view a media file once you've chosen a MIME type.

Figure 14.6 GoLive assigns a class ID when you choose <object> or <object> <embed> from the HTML menu.

Figure 14.7 The More tab of the Plug-in Inspector includes extra media file configuration options.

10. Give the file a name in the Name field, if you wish. It's not essential.

11. To link the media file to a page or site containing instructions on how to install a needed browser plug-in, click the Page check box and type a URL for the instructions page. (You can also browse or Point & Shoot to a page or URL that is saved within your GoLive site.) The installation instructions will be presented only if the user's browser detects that the needed plug-in is not installed on the system.

12. If the media format you're working with requires a link to a code base (SVG and RealMedia do), click the Code check box and Browse or Point & Shoot to the code-base file.

13. Choose an option from the Palette pop-up menu to indicate whether the plug-in should appear in the foreground or background. Leaving the Default option selected places the plug-in in the background. The Palette option only changes the behavior of the plug-in in Windows browsers.

14. Use the HSpace and VSpace fields to set the distance (in pixels) between the plug-in and other content on the page.

15. Click the Is Hidden check box to cause the media file to play when the page it's on is loaded. This option is often used to play a sound when a visitor opens a page.

The Language of MIME

The MIME (Multipurpose Internet Mail Extensions) standard was developed as a means of including attachments with email messages. MIME-capable email clients can decode attachments using MIME-type information, regardless of the platform on which the file was created. MIME-enabled programs either display attachments within a message or save the attached file in a format that can be read by an application in the recipient's operating system.

On the Web, MIME performs a similar function, allowing a user's computer to associate files with a compatible application or plug-in.

To learn more about MIME, including media types associated with particular multimedia files, check out www.ac.uci.edu/indiv/ehood/MIME/MIME.html. You'll find information about media types in RFC 2046.

Plug-in attributes

Many plug-in formats have attributes that are not specified in the Plug-in Inspector. The third tab in the Plug-in Inspector, Attribs, shows attributes that control the display and behavior of the plug-in. You may see preconfigured attributes, as in **Figure 14.8**, or the window may contain no attributes. You can modify attributes or add new ones to a plug-in. Attribute information is usually available from the Web site of the company whose plug-in file you want to use.

Figure 14.8 Attributes associated with the plug-in format you're using appear in the Attribs tab of the Plug-in Inspector.

To add an attribute:

1. Click the Attribs tab in the Plug-in Inspector.

2. Click the New Attribute button (located at the bottom of the Inspector, on the right side).

3. Type autostart in the Attribute field and press Tab.

4. Type true in the Value field and press Enter. The attribute is complete and now appears in the upper portion of the window. The new autostart attribute tells a Web browser to play the content associated with this plug-in when the page is loaded.

5. Click the New button again.

6. Type loop in the Attributes field and type 3 in the Value field. Adding a loop attribute means that the file automatically plays again. I chose to play it only three times. If you had typed true instead of 3, the sound would play continuously.

✔ Tip

■ Microsoft's Internet Explorer browser supports a few IE-specific plug-in attributes. To learn about these, check out Microsoft's Developer Center at http://msdn.microsoft.com/ie/.

Figure 14.9 The QuickTime plug-in icon from the Objects palette.

Figure 14.10 When you add a movie placeholder, GoLive supplies the appropriate MIME and player information in the Plug-in Inspector.

Configuring specific plug-in types

You can add QuickTime, SVG, SWF, and RealMedia content with palette icons specific to each format.

The first three tabs of the Plug-in Inspector are the same for these media types as for the generic plug-ins we worked with in the previous section. Unless otherwise noted in this section, use the instructions in the previous section to configure the first three Inspector tabs. The fourth tab is specific to the plug-in you're using.

QuickTime

QuickTime is a video format invented by Apple, but compatible with Macintosh and Windows operating systems, using stand-alone applications and browser plug-ins. QuickTime files can be movies or links to video streams. They can include sound, too. You can add existing QuickTime movies to your Web pages or you can build them with GoLive's QuickTime Editor. See Chapter 20, "Animation and Multimedia Authoring," for details on how to use the QuickTime Editor.

To configure a QuickTime file:

1. Add the QuickTime icon (**Figure 14.9**) to a document. The Plug-in Inspector appears, with the File and Mime check boxes already checked. The Mime field says video/quicktime (**Figure 14.10**).

2. Browse or Point & Shoot to link to a QuickTime file, and resize or align the plug-in placeholder if you wish.

3. Click the More tab and then the Code check box if it's not already checked. The Code and Class fields are checked and include links to QuickTime instructions and code pages at Apple's Web site.

(continues on next page)

4. Click the QuickTime tab to configure items specific to QuickTime (**Figure 14.11**).

5. Click the Show Controller check box to include QuickTime controls with the movie when it plays. In the Layout Editor, the movie window expands a bit to make room for the control bar (**Figure 14.12**). In the Movie Viewer window, you'll see the movie and the controls. In the Layout Editor, you only see a slightly thicker lower border.

6. Click the BGColor check box, and choose a color if you want the movie to play over a colored background. (For details on selecting color, see Chapter 5, "Working with Color.")

7. Click the Cache check box to instruct the browser to cache the movie as the file is played.

8. Type a number from 0 (lowest) to 100 (highest) to set the volume of the movie's sound.

9. Leave the Autoplay check box selected if you want the movie to play automatically when the page is opened. Otherwise, uncheck the box.

10. In the Scale field, type a value (as a fraction of the movie file's current size) to shrink or enlarge the movie's play area. Leaving the field blank displays the movie at its original size. To see the movie at twice its default size, type 2 in the Scale field. To see it at half normal size, type .5.

11. Click the Loop check box to play the video continuously. If you choose to loop, checking the Palindrome option (which becomes available when you click Loop) will make the movie play forward, then backward, then repeat the process.

Figure 14.11 The QuickTime tab of the Plug-in Inspector includes QuickTime-specific options.

Figure 14.12 Here is a movie in the Layout Editor.

12. Click Play Every Frame to prevent the browser from dropping frames as the movie plays. Frames are dropped to improve playback speed, so forcing the browser to display every frame can slow down playback.

13. Click the Link check box, then type a URL, browse, or Point & Shoot to establish a link that is activated when the QuickTime file is clicked.

14. If you created a link in the previous step, you can choose a target page or frame from the Target pop-up menu.

Flattening QuickTime movies

In order for a QuickTime movie to play smoothly on the Web, it must be flattened—saved in a format that Web browsers can accept and that can play without dropping frames or appearing jerky. You can flatten movies before or after you've configured them within GoLive by using the QuickTime Editor.

To flatten a QuickTime movie:

1. Open a QuickTime movie in the Quick-Time Editor by choosing File > Open and locating the movie file.

or

Place a movie in a GoLive document and double-click it in the Layout Editor.

or

Click Open Movie in the QuickTime tab of the Plug-in Inspector and locate the file.

2. Choose Movie > Flatten Movie.

3. Save and close the movie file.

RealMedia

RealMedia refers to the audio and video formats from RealNetworks, known as RealAudio and RealVideo, respectively. Like QuickTime, they can be used to deliver pre-recorded content and streaming sound and images. They're often used to add sound clips to music sites and to provide streaming radio broadcasts.

To configure a RealMedia file:

1. Add the Real icon (**Figure 14.13**) to a document. The Plug-in Inspector appears with the File and Mime check boxes already checked. The Mime field is filled out (**Figure 14.14**).

2. Click the Real tab (**Figure 14.15**).

3. Click the Autostart check box to have playback begin when the page containing the media is loaded.

4. Leave No Labels unchecked if you want visitors to see the name of the audio file and other information when it is played.

5. From the Controls menu, choose which controls you want to appear in the page. You can make one selection. To add more controls, you must add another instance of the Real icon and choose the control you want in the Real tab. Fortunately, the default option provides most of the controls you're likely to want displayed. To view other options, choose one from the Controls menu and then click the Play button in the Plug-in Inspector.

6. In the Layout Editor, resize the Real plug-in placeholder horizontally to display the controls correctly. Use the Layout Preview to check your work. If you don't resize, the Real controls won't display properly. **Figure 14.16** shows a placeholder with default controls set.

Figure 14.13 The Real icon.

Figure 14.14 The Basic tab of the Plug-in Inspector looks like this when you add a RealMedia placeholder. If you've added the RealMedia plug-in to GoLive's Plug-ins folder, you'll see an entry in the Player field.

Figure 14.15 Configure RealMedia-specific options in the Real tab of the Plug-in Inspector.

Figure 14.16 Leaving Default selected in the Real tab of the Plug-in Inspector applies this set of controls to a Real file.

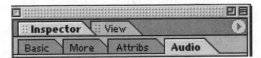

Figure 14.17 When you add an audio file to the Document window, the Plug-in Inspector displays the Audio tab.

Figure 14.18 Add audio attributes in the Plug-in Inspector's Audio tab.

✔ Tips

- The default controls for RealMedia plug-ins include Rewind, Play, Fast Forward, and Stop.

- Don't like the scrunched up controls in Figure 14.16? Just drag the handle in the plug-in placeholder to make it wider and not as tall.

- You'll find helpful hints on customizing the controls associated with your Real file in the SMIL Authoring Guide (page 25), located in the SMIL folder within the Adobe GoLive folder.

Other audio formats

Though GoLive doesn't include a palette icon for them, you can also configure WAV, AIFF, and other popular audio files for use on the Web. When you add a supported audio file to a page, GoLive adds the Audio tab to the Plug-in Inspector.

To set up audio files:

1. Add a Plug-in icon to a document.

2. Browse or Point & Shoot to add an audio file (WAV, for example). The Plug-in Inspector now includes the Audio tab (**Figure 14.17**).

3. Click the Mime check box to activate the pop-up menu. GoLive displays a MIME type it believes is compatible with the file you added.

4. Configure options in the Basic and More tabs of the Plug-in Inspector as described earlier in the section on configuring generic plug-ins.

5. Click the Audio tab of the Plug-in Inspector (**Figure 14.18**).

(continues on next page)

SETTING UP PLUG-INS

6. If you plan to call the audio file with a script (a JavaScript or GoLive action)—supported by Netscape browsers and the LiveAudio plug-in—click the Is Master-sound check box and give the audio file a name in the More tab.

7. Click Autostart to have the audio file play when the page is loaded.

8. To cause the sound to repeat automatically, click Loop, and enter the number of repeats in the adjacent field.

9. To specify start and stop times for the audio file, enter them in minutes and seconds in the Starttime and Stoptime fields.

10. Choose a volume level (from 0 to 100) for playback.

11. Choose how and whether to display a controller for the sound from the Controls menu. A controller, if you choose to display one, can include Start, Stop, and Pause buttons, as well as a volume control.

Flash (SWF)

Macromedia Flash is a versatile animation, video, and audio format that's often used to build interactive presentations, animations, and other nifty custom Web page components. Flash files use the extension .swf.

To configure a Flash file:

1. Add the SWF icon (**Figure 14.19**) from the Objects palette to a document. The Plug-in Inspector appears, with the File and Mime check boxes already checked. The Mime field is filled out with application/x-shockwave-flash (**Figure 14.20**).

2. Configure items in the Basic and More tabs of the Plug-in Inspector.

Figure 14.19 The SWF plug-in icon.

Figure 14.20 The Basic tab of the Plug-in Inspector looks like this when you add a Flash file.

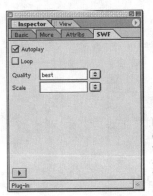

Figure 14.21 Choose options that control the behavior of a Flash movie in the SWF tab of the Plug-in Inspector.

3. Click the SWF tab (**Figure 14.21**).

4. Click Autoplay to have the Flash file begin playing when the page opens.

5. Click the Loop check box to play the file continuously.

6. From the Quality pop-up menu, choose a setting from Low to Best. The higher the quality setting, the better the movie will look, though it will play more slowly at higher settings.

7. Choose an option from the Scale menu to tell the browser how to deal with a difference between the size you've specified for the file and the size of the actual Flash movie. Default forces the movie to appear in the space you've provided for it and may add borders to maintain a proper aspect ratio. The No Border option retains the aspect ratio by cropping the movie if necessary. Choose Exact Fit to keep the movie in the space available and make no correction for aspect problems.

SVG

SVG is a language that describes vector graphics within XML. (XML is a language that allows Web developers to build custom tags.) SVG allows you to build scripted animation and add editable text labels to images, among other things. As of this writing, SVG has been recommended for review by the W3C, and chances are good that it will become a part of the Web specification.

SVG is a big deal in GoLive because Adobe has made a significant commitment to it. (For example, Adobe has included tools in its Illustrator drawing program that allow you to export Illustrator images in SVG format.)

To configure an SVG file:

1. Add the SVG icon (**Figure 14.22**) from the Objects palette to a document. The Plug-in Inspector becomes active, with SVG settings filled out in the Basic tab (**Figure 14.23**).

2. Choose other attributes in the Basic and More tabs of the Plug-in Inspector.

3. Click the SVG tab (**Figure 14.24**).

4. If you intend to use a compressed SVG file, click the Use Compressed SVG check box. You must store both the compressed and noncompressed versions of the file in the same folder and upload them both to your Web server.

Setting plug-in preferences

Most Web browsers that support plug-in playback allow you not only to use plug-ins but also to choose which file formats are read by each plug-in. Some of these choices are automatic. Besides movies, the QuickTime 5.0 plug-in (the current version at this writing) supports a variety of sound files that are listed in GoLive's Plug-ins Preferences dialog box. GoLive automatically associates a plug-in with each file format it knows about, and vice versa.

You can change these relationships if you would rather use different plug-ins to play files of a given format. You can also tell GoLive not to play the media files at all, if you choose.

Figure 14.22 The SVG plug-in icon.

Figure 14.23 The Basic tab of the Plug-in Inspector looks like this when you add an SVG file.

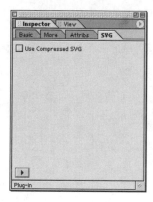

Figure 14.24 This check box on the SVG tab of the Plug-in Inspector indicates whether you intend to use a compressed SVG file or not.

Figure 14.25 The Plugins Preferences dialog box.

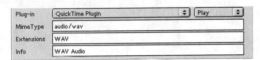

Figure 14.26 View or edit a media type by selecting it in the Plugins Preferences dialog box.

■ You can use the New button in the Plugins Preferences dialog box to create entries for new media formats, but that is usually not necessary. When you add a new plug-in to the Plug-ins folder and launch GoLive, the plug-in software registers the media formats it supports and displays them under Plugins Preferences.

■ The Plug-in pop-up menu in the Preferences window is a good way to remember which plug-ins support which formats. When you select a format and click the menu, only those plug-ins that support the format are available.

To change plug-in/media relationships:

1. Choose Edit > Preferences.

2. Click the Plugins label. Scroll the left pane in the Preferences dialog box to find it, if necessary. The Plugins Preferences panel (**Figure 14.25**) shows media formats, the plug-in used to play them (if they are installed in GoLive's Plug-ins directory), and the file extensions associated with each format.

3. Select a MIME type from the list. Editable fields become available in the lower portion of the window (**Figure 14.26**). You can edit the MIME type, plug-in, and extension; delete the selected item; or create a new one. If the media type you chose can be read by multiple installed plug-ins, the Plug-in menu will include several options.

4. Leave the Play/Don't Play menu alone so that files can play when you open a Web page that contains them.

✔ Tips

■ Like a Web browser, GoLive can use browser plug-ins to display files associated with them. To use a plug-in with GoLive, you need to store it in the Plug-ins folder. Install plug-ins as described earlier in this chapter. Note that you can't use an alias of a plug-in file. You must make a copy of it and drop it into GoLive's Plug-ins folder.

■ The QuickTime plug-in supports a large number of audio and video formats. You may be able to reduce the number of different plug-ins you use by selecting QuickTime whenever it's available.

JavaScript

Netscape created JavaScript as a scripting language to enhance Web pages. JavaScript can be used to give life to a Web page with moving banners, animation, and other decorative touches. JavaScript can also be used to give instructions to Java applets or link multiple applets together.

The most common and powerful use of JavaScript these days is the manipulation of HTML pages and elements with scripted behaviors. Scripts can create effects or invoke Dynamic HTML (DHTML) functions. For more on using actions built with JavaScript, see Chapter 19, "Using Actions."

Unlike Java, JavaScripts are composed of code that is part of your Web page or used by it. Java applets are actually programs that are downloaded to and run in a Web browser. GoLive's Script Editor allows you to write your own scripts and embed them within a document. You can also add existing scripts to a document using the JavaScript icon on the Objects palette. Finally, GoLive includes a Software Development Kit (SDK) that allows you to extend GoLive's functionality using JavaScript. You can use the SDK to build your own palettes and tools and other add-ons to the basic GoLive application.

In this section, I'll concentrate on adding existing JavaScripts to Web pages, and introduce the tools you use to build or edit your own. To learn to build your own scripts in GoLive or any other JavaScript-capable editor, check out one of the many good JavaScript resources available, both in print and online. Start with *JavaScript for the World Wide Web: Visual QuickStart Guide*, by Tom Negrino and Dori Smith. On the Web, there's Netscape's JavaScript documentation at http://developer.netscape.com/docs/manuals/javascript.html.

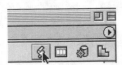

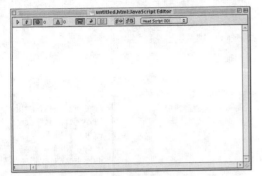

Figure 14.27 Click the Open JavaScript Editor button to open the JavaScript Editor.

Figure 14.28 Type or edit a head script in the JavaScript Editor.

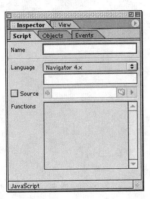

Figure 14.29 Name and configure your head script in the JavaScript Inspector.

Adding JavaScripts

JavaScripts can either appear in the head or body of a page. In most cases, they appear in the head section and are invoked when the page is loaded. The process for adding head and body scripts is slightly different.

To add a head script:

1. Open a document to which you want to add a head script.

2. In the upper right coner of the Layout Editor, click on the Open JavaScript Editor button (**Figure 14.27**). The Java-Script Editor opens.

3. Click the New Script Item button to acti-vate the window. GoLive names the file Head Script 001 (**Figure 14.28**). The JavaScript Inspector also appears.

4. Name the script in the JavaScript Inspector (**Figure 14.29**).

5. Use the Language pop-up menu to choose the browser version that you want to tar-get with your script. Generally speaking, newer browsers offer more features, but targeting them causes incompatibilities with older browsers. When you choose a language, GoLive fills in the correspon-ding JavaScript version.

6. To link to a script, click the Source check box and browse or Point & Shoot to the file. You can't edit a linked script in the JavaScript Editor.

✔ Tip

■ Once you've added a JavaScript to the head section of a document, you can return to it by opening the head section (click the triangle near the top of the Layout Editor) and double-clicking the Head Script item to view the Inspector.

JAVASCRIPT

To add a body script:

1. Add the JavaScript icon (**Figure 14.30**) from the Basic set of the Objects palette to a document. A JavaScript placeholder and the Body Script Inspector appear (**Figure 14.31**).

2. Name the script.

3. In the Language pop-up menu, choose a browser version for the script to target.

✔ Tip

■ To ensure the highest possible browser compatibility for your JavaScript, choose an older browser version from the Language pop-up menu. The tradeoff, of course, is that older browsers and script dialects don't include all of the features of newer offerings. For now, I recommend choosing Navigator 3.x (JavaScript 1.1) if you want to be conservative. Use Internet Explorer 5.x (JScript 5.0) to ensure support for all the latest JavaScript features.

Figure 14.30 The JavaScript icon.

Figure 14.31 Use the Body Script Inspector to link a JavaScript document and to indentify its JavaScript dialect.

Figure 14.32 The Java Applet icon.

Figure 14.33 Set up applets in the Java Applet Inspector.

Java Applets

JavaScripts and Java applets are not the same thing at all. JavaScripts are usually (but not always) fairly small pieces of code that are embedded in a Web page's HTML code. Java applets, on the other hand, are complete programs, written in the Java language, that are called by and may even appear within a Web page but are not part of that page. Java applets can be database interfaces, games, or any number of other applications. To write Java applets, you'll need Java development tools and enough knowledge of the Java language to create applets. You can connect existing applets to GoLive pages, specifying the appearance of the applet primarily within the applet itself. HTML (and GoLive) lets you specify basic size, spacing, and alignment options, but the rest is up to the applet developer. You can preview applets in GoLive because, like newer Web browsers, GoLive supports Java.

To add a Java applet to a document:

1. Drag the Java Applet icon (**Figure 14.32**) from the Basic set of the Objects palette to the Document window. The Java Applet Inspector appears (**Figure 14.33**).

2. Browse or Point & Shoot to locate a Java applet. The applet's location (Base) and Code appear in the Inspector.

3. Resize the applet by dragging the placeholder's handles in the Document window or typing dimensions in the Inspector's Width and Height fields (in pixels).

4. If the applet is not on a layout grid or if it is within a layout text box, you can add horizontal and vertical space between the applet and adjacent text with the HSpace and VSpace fields. Use the Align pop-up menu to align the applet with adjacent text.

(continues on next page)

JAVA APPLETS

5. Name the applet by typing a unique name (one that's not being used by any other applet on the page) in the Name field.

6. To add alternative text or HTML that will be displayed by browsers that support Java but whose Java option is disabled, click the Alt tab of the Java Applet Inspector (**Figure 14.34**).

7. Type new text in the Alt Text field.

8. If you want to display an HTML object when Java support is turned off in a browser, click the "Show alternative HTML" check box.

9. In the Document window, add HTML objects directly to the Java applet placeholder with palette icons, or type HTML directly into the placeholder.

Figure 14.34 Add HTML for users who have disabled Java support in their browsers.

✔ Tip

■ You can use GoLive to view the contents and action of a Java applet in two ways: Click the Play button in the Java Applet Inspector or view your document with Layout Preview. Of course, checking out your applet in multiple Web browsers is the best preview method.

To add Java parameters:

1. Select a Java applet in the Document window.

2. In the Java Applet Inspector, click the Params tab. Parameters are applet-specific attributes.

3. Click the New button to set up a new parameter.

4. Type the name of the parameter in the Param field when it appears. Press Tab.

5. Type a value for the parameter in the Value field. Press Enter to confirm your entry. The new parameter appears in the window above.

15

BUILDING SITES

A Web site is the sum of its parts: HTML pages, images, scripts, and multimedia files. Site management is a necessity for most modern Webmasters, who must juggle a large number of site elements and organize Web content so that users find it easy to navigate.

GoLive includes a full-fledged site-building and site-management interface that you can use to organize, plan, and manage the pages and other components of your site. You can also design a site before you build it or plan for and modify an existing site's elements and structure.

The first step is to design and build your site. After that, you can add items as you create or acquire them.

In this chapter, I'll cover

◆ Using site tools

◆ Creating sites

◆ Adding files and objects

◆ Working with site assets

◆ Fine-tuning preferences

◆ Using site templates

◆ Diagramming sites

Site-Building Tools

GoLive's site-building interface is built around the Site window, which gives you a view of everything that is part of your site. From the Site window, you can open files, monitor the condition of the site, and use the rest of GoLive's site-management tools. In this section, I'll give you an overview of the site-management tools. You'll use them to build sites in this chapter; to manage them in Chapter 16, "Viewing and Managing Sites;" and to publish them in Chapter 17, "Publishing Sites."

The Site window

The Site window is where the action is. You add, rearrange, and link the components of your site from here. Under the six tabs on its left side, you store files, external URLs, site diagrams, colors, font sets, and custom items (**Figure 15.1**). On the right are four tabs that assist you in managing your site and connecting to remote servers. (If the right side is closed, you can open it by clicking the Show/Hide button at the lower right of the Site window.)

The Site window looks and works much like the Mac Finder or Windows Explorer/Browser. You can view and sort files and folders and move items between folders within the site. You can even drag items between the Site and the Finder or Windows Explorer.

Site-related sets in the Objects palette

The Site set (**Figure 15.2**) contains icons that you can use to add elements to a site by dragging into the Site window. You can add new pages, colors, URLs, fonts, and other items to a GoLive site from the palette.

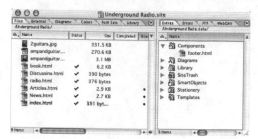

Figure 15.1 The Site window displays files and folders that make up a GoLive site.

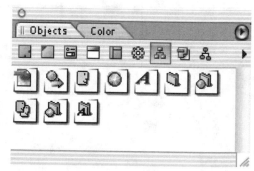

Figure 15.2 The Site set of the Objects palette includes icons for adding pages and other items to a site.

GoLive site assets, including components, stationery files, page templates, and library objects (or *snippets*), are stored in the site hierarchy. You'll find them in folders within the Site window. You can also reach individual site objects in the Site Extras set of the Objects palette. That's handy when you want to add a snippet, for example, by double-clicking it with a document open. Site objects are automatically added to the Site Extras tab when you save them with a GoLive site.

Site diagramming allows you to plan and build a prototype of all or part of your site before you create actual pages. The Diagram set features objects that you can drag into the diagrams you create, just as you add objects to a page from the Basic set.

Site toolbar

With a GoLive site open, the context-sensitive toolbar contains site-management items (**Figure 15.3**). You can create new folders, update a site's links, check and change preferences, and locate files.

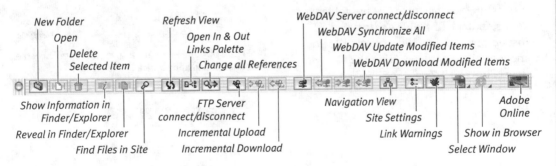

Figure 15.3 The toolbar contains site-management tools when a GoLive site is open.

Site Settings and Preferences

You can edit site-specific parameters within the Site Settings dialog box (choose Site > Settings to open it). Most of the options relate to publishing your site on a remote Web server (**Figure 15.4**). The options under Site in the Preferences dialog box (**Figure 15.5**) have more to do with the way you build and manage sites. They apply to all of the sites that you work with in GoLive, but if you want to override them for a specific site, you can do so in the Site Settings dialog box.

Inspector and View

Each site object has its own Inspector that allows you to configure and view options for that object (**Figure 15.6**). These properties are specific to the item's relationship with the site—for example, in the case of a Web page, you can't use the File Inspector to align or resize images on the page, but you can use it to choose whether its HTML file should be uploaded to the Web and to look at a thumbnail view of the page, among other things. Other site objects—folders, colors, fonts, URLs—have associated Inspectors, too. The View palette lets you show or hide columns within the Site window (**Figure 15.7**).

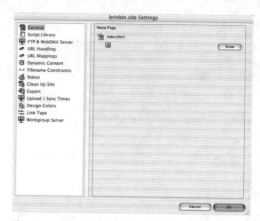

Figure 15.4 The Site Settings dialog box contains settings for uploading and mapping your site.

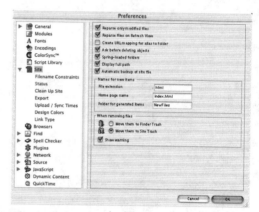

Figure 15.5 Site Preferences give you control over the behavior and appearance of site elements.

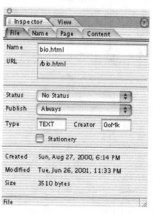

Figure 15.6 Configure the characteristics of individual site files in the File Inspector.

Figure 15.7 In the View palette, you can show or hide columns and paths.

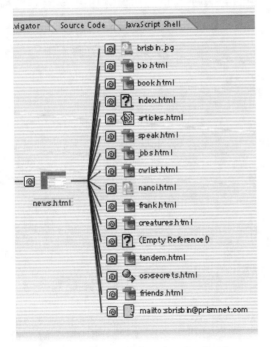

Figure 15.8 The In & Out Links palette is often the quickest way to spot a broken link. Here, the two links with question-mark icons (index.html and Empty Reference) are broken.

Site and contextual menus

Most of the commands in the Site menu duplicate options available elsewhere. Among other things, menu items allow you to add site elements or make global changes and verifications. You can reach the Navigation and Links views (introduced next) and connect to remote servers from the Site menu.

You'll find a variety of contextual menus in the Site window. Some of them mostly repeat toolbar and Objects palette options. There's also a contextual menu available from the column headings. This menu, like the Show Columns pop-up menu in the View Inspector, lets you choose which columns are visible in the Site window.

Navigation and Links views

The Navigation and Links views provide a graphical look at the contents of your site. Where the Site window displays the files and resources themselves, the Navigation view shows the relationships between HTML files. Those relationships are defined by links. The Links view takes the display one step further, showing all links coming to and from a selected page. I'll cover the Navigation and Links views in more detail in Chapter 16.

In & Out Links

There's no easier way to see what links to and from a particular site object than with the In & Out Links palette. Click on a site object and choose Window > In & Out Links. You'll see the selected object at the center of a diagram, with files that link to it on the left and files and resources to which it links on the right (**Figure 15.8**).

Diagram window

You can use the Diagram window (**Figure 15.9**) to "sketch" your ideas for site designs before putting them into effect. Like the Navigation and Links views, the Diagram window provides a graphical representation of the site, but it's not a view of the pages or hyperlinks you're currently using. It's a place to build prototypes that may (or may not) eventually become elements of your site. I cover site diagramming later, starting on page 319.

Workflow palette

You can use the Workflow palette to keep track of the status of items within your site as you build it. Information you enter in the Workflow palette appears in the Site window and is associated with the file whose status you've selected. Open the Workflow palette by choosing Window > Workflow. If you don't see the palette, choose Edit > Preferences and then click the Modules icon. Check the Workflow module and quit GoLive. When you launch GoLive again, the Workflow palette will appear on the Window menu. Tracking a site's workflow is especially useful when you're using the Adobe Web Workgroup Server to develop projects collaboratively. I'll have more to say about workflow in Chapter 18, "The Workgroup Server."

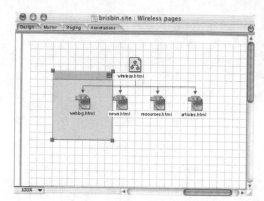

Figure 15.9 You can create a sketch of a new group of pages you would like to add to your site in the Diagram window.

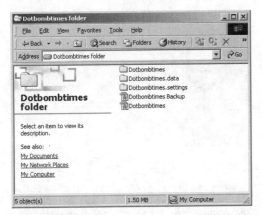

Figure 15.10 In Windows, the top-level site folder holds the site file and the three folders that contain the site's elements and settings.

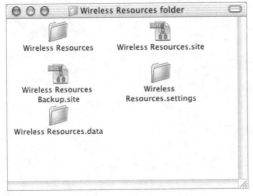

Figure 15.11 The Site folder has the same structure in Mac OS X.

Creating Sites

To begin a GoLive site, first create the site structure and then add HTML and media files to it.

Site structure in GoLive

A GoLive site is a collection of files, but it's also a folder structure that gives you access to tools and views that make building a site easier. When you create or import a site, GoLive creates a site file and three folders that store files, objects, and preferences. The *site file* is your site's master control: It knows where every site object is and whether the links between them actually work or not. The site file and the folders are all stored within a folder bearing the name of the site. **Figure 15.10** shows the contents of an overall site folder in Windows. **Figure 15.11** shows the Mac OS X equivalent. If a site is open when you view its folder, you will also see a temporary site backup file inside the folder. The site folder's subfolders are named after the site (`sitename.suffix`):

◆ `Site`, also called the root-level folder, contains the site's home page (`index.html`) and mirrors the hierarchy of the site. All of the HTML files, images, media files, and other files that are displayed on the Web are stored in this folder.

◆ `Site.data` contains items that support the site—site diagrams, stationery files, templates, components, and other files that you want to store with the site—but that you don't upload to a Web server.

◆ `Site.settings` contains the preferences associated with the site.

Start the site

There are four ways to begin a site:

◆ **Create a blank site:** Build a site from scratch.

◆ **Create a new site based on a site template:** GoLive includes several templates—sample sites with HTML pages, images, and a site structure—that you can use as the basis for your own site.

◆ **Import an existing site that is stored on a local hard disk:** If you have created pages in GoLive without building a site or have made HTML pages in another Web development application, you can migrate them to a GoLive site.

◆ **Import a site from a remote Web server:** You can download your existing site from a server and bring its contents into a GoLive site.

You can also create a workgroup site that can be uploaded to an Adobe Web Workgroup Server and edited by several developers or designers. I'll give you full details on workgroup sites in Chapter 18.

To create a blank site:

1. Choose File > New Site. The Site Wizard opens (**Figure 15.12**).

2. Choose Single User and click Next.

3. Select the Blank Site button and click Next.

4. Name the site and leave the "Create Site folder" box checked to store the site in a new folder. Click Next.

5. Choose a location for the site folder by browsing your hard drive.

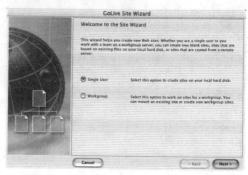

Figure 15.12 Use the Site Wizard to create a new GoLive site. The wizard walks you through the process and allows you to choose the type of site you want to build.

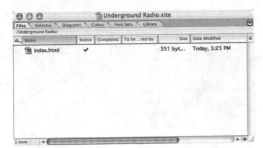

Figure 15.13 After GoLive creates a new site, the Site window displays the home page (index.html).

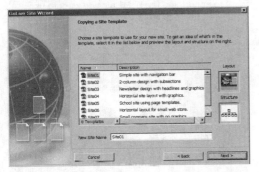

Figure 15.14 The Site Wizard shows a list of templates and their descriptions. Click a template name to see a preview of its layout and structure.

6. If you wish to choose options related to the case-sensitivity of URLs and the encoding format used on your site, click Advanced and select one or more options.

7. Click Finish.

GoLive displays the Site window, which contains a single file, index.html (**Figure 15.13**).

To create a site from a template:

1. Chose File > New Site, and click Single User in the Site Wizard. Click Next.

2. Select the Copy from Template button and click Next.

3. Choose a template from the list (**Figure 15.14**). Notice the description and the layout and structure previews. For more information about the specific templates included with GoLive, see "Using Site Templates" on page 318.

4. Type a name for the new site and click Next.

5. To choose a location for your site, click the Browse button and navigate to the location you want.

6. Click Finish to begin copying the template files to your new site folder. When the process is complete, the Site window opens. It contains the HTML files and objects associated with the template.

To import a local site:

1. In the Site Wizard, select Import from Folder and click Next.

2. Click Browse and locate the folder containing the files you want to bring into the new site.

(continues on next page)

3. Under the heading, "Please select the home page of the existing site," click Browse, and then choose the site's home page. If the imported folder contains a file called index.html, GoLive will choose that file for you. If you would like GoLive to create a home page for the site, click the "Create generic home page" check box instead. When you've chosen the folder and home page for the site, the window should look like **Figure 15.15**. Click Next.

4. Click Browse to choose a location for your site, and name the site in the Save dialog box.

5. Click Finish to exit the Site Wizard.

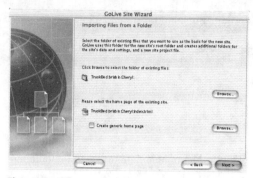

Figure 15.15 Choose the folder containing files you want to import and the HTML file you want to use as your site's home page.

To import a site from a server:

1. Choose File > New Site.

2. Click the Single User button in the Site Wizard and click Next.

3. Choose Import from Server and click Next.

4. Choose FTP or HTTP, depending on the server you want to use and the type of access you have. Click Next.

5. If you chose FTP, type the server name, your username, and your password. Type the directory path, or click the folder icon next to the Directory field to browse the server for the directory you want. **Figure 15.16** shows the FTP screen in the Site Wizard. Choose a home page for the site and click Next.

Figure 15.16 Enter information about the FTP server and choose a home page.

6. If you chose HTTP, type the URL of the site you want to import, overwriting the Adobe URL that appears by default. Choose whether to import the entire site or a limited number of hierarchy levels. Click Next.

7. Name your site and click Next; then choose a location for the site.

8. Click Finish to begin the import process.

Figure 15.17 To save a new file to your site's root folder, choose "Root folder" from the menu in the Save dialog box.

Adding Files and Objects

Once you've created or imported a site, you can add files and objects to it. Items you can add include files (HTML, images, multimedia, and scripts), URLs, and site objects such as font sets and color sets. These sets are GoLive-specific features that allow you to quickly add a color or font that has previously been defined within your site.

Adding files

You can create new files as you build the site, drag and drop files from your hard disk, or import files, as we did in the "Start the site" section of this chapter.

When you add files, GoLive checks to see whether they contain hyperlinks and tries to reconcile them with other files in the site. If you have instructed GoLive to check external URLs, it will connect to the Internet and attempt to verify that the links in your new files are good.

To create new files within a site:

1. Open a site.

2. Choose File > New Page to open a blank document.

   or

   Choose Site > New > Page.

3. Add content to your page.

4. Save the document to your site root folder—this folder is located inside the top-level folder that GoLive created to hold your site. To open the root folder in the Save dialog box, click the Folder icon at the bottom of the box and choose Root (Windows) or Root folder (Mac) (**Figure 15.17**). If you don't want to store the file in the root folder, you can store it elsewhere, though it may not link properly within your uploaded site. In the upper pane of the dialog box, you can open a different folder.

To add existing files to a site:

1. In the Files tab of the Site window, Control-click (Mac) or right-click (Windows) and choose Add Files from the contextual menu. A dual-pane Add to Site dialog box appears.

2. Browse to the first file or folder you want to add to the site.

3. Select the item and click Add (**Figure 15.18**). Items you add appear in the lower pane of the dialog box.

4. Add all the files you need and click Done.

5. If any files you've added need to be updated, GoLive will show you a dialog box that lists each file to be updated, and shows a checkmark for each (**Figure 15.19**). Uncheck any you don't want to update and then click OK to update all the files you added. GoLive copies your files and folders to the site root folder and updates the Site window.

To add files with drag-and-drop:

1. In the Site window, be sure that the Files tab is visible. If you need to add files to a subfolder below the root level, make sure that the folder is visible or open.

2. In the Finder (Mac) or in Windows Explorer (Windows), locate the folder containing the files you want to add to the site and open it.

3. Drag the files (or the whole folder, if you like) you want to add into the Site window (**Figure 15.20**). GoLive examines the files you've added and copies them to the site's folder.

✔ Tip

■ If you begin dragging to the Site window and realize that the Files tab is not the front tab, you can drag over the Files tab to bring it to the front. With that done, you can drop into the Files tab.

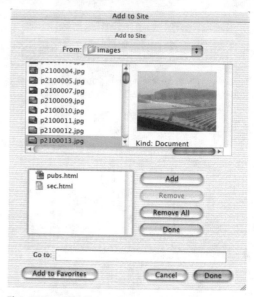

Figure 15.18 Add files or folders to your site by locating them in the upper pane. Double-clicking a selected item adds it to the list in the lower pane. To add a folder, select it and then click Add.

Figure 15.19 When you add files to your site, GoLive may present a dialog box listing the files and giving you the chance to check their links or to leave broken links unmarked.

Figure 15.20 You can add a file or folder to a GoLive site by dragging it from the Finder (Mac) or Windows Explorer (Windows) to the Site window.

✔ Tips

- No matter how you bring a URL into the External tab, if you edit that URL within the context of the External tab, GoLive will display the Change Reference dialog box so you can control which instances of the URL get updated. (In contrast, if you edit a URL on an individual Web page, the External tab will display the old and the new URL after you run the Get References Used command.)

- Anti-spam experts recommend that you do not include live email addresses on a Web site, since live addresses become easy pickings for spammers' Web robots. For a while, Web designers made graphic images of email addresses and linked those images to JavaScripts, but the robots are smarter now, and that trick doesn't work reliably.

Adding non-file objects

In addition to locally stored HTML files and graphics, GoLive sites can include pointers to external resources and references to custom colors and font sets. Once stored in the site, these resources can be added to pages with Point & Shoot.

You can import groups of external resources or add them one at a time. There are three ways to import multiple URLs: Add files that contain external links (and any URLs they contain), import resources from bookmark files, and import from address book files. You can also add external resources individually, much as you would a new file.

Adding referenced URLs

Adding HTML files that contain external URLs doesn't automatically bring the URLs into the site. To add them, click the External tab and choose Site > Get References Used. The links appear in the New Addresses and New URLs folders of the External tab.

Importing external resources

If you're creating a site from scratch using GoLive (rather than updating an existing site), there may be no external URLs associated with the site. However, you may have bookmark files from a Web browser for URLs that you'd like to link to from your site. If you'll be using a lot of email addresses you may also be able to import them from an email program. When you want to use the URLs to create links, you can use Point & Shoot to add them to a page within your site.

ADDING FILES AND OBJECTS

To import bookmarks:

1. In the Site window, click the External tab.

2. Choose File > Import > Favorites as Site Externals.

3. Browse your computer to locate a favorites (Internet Explorer) or bookmarks (Netscape Navigator) file and click Open. The URLs stored in the file are imported into the site and stored in a section called Favorites or Bookmarks, as appropriate.

4. Click the triangle (Mac) or plus sign (Windows) to the left of the new folder to display its contents. If your bookmark or favorites file contains folders, GoLive preserves the folder structure. (**Figure 15.21**).

To add a single URL:

1. Click the External tab of the Site window if it isn't already visible.

2. In the Site set of the Objects palette, double-click or drag the URL icon (**Figure 15.22**) into the Site window.

   or

   Control-click (Mac) or right-click (Windows) in the External tab and choose New URL from the contextual menu.

   or

   Choose Site > New > URL. An untitled URL appears in the Site window.

3. Click the URL to view the Reference Inspector (**Figure 15.23**).

4. In the Reference Inspector, type a name for the URL.

5. Type the full URL (including http://) in the URL field.

Figure 15.21 When you import a favorites file from Internet Explorer, its URLs appear in the External tab of the Site window.

Figure 15.22 Use the URL icon from the Site set of the Objects palette to add a new URL to the Site window.

Figure 15.23 Set up a new URL in the Reference Inspector.

✔ Tips

■ I could give you a likely path to the bookmarks/favorites files on your computer, but the easiest way to find them is to search for favorites.html or bookmarks.html using Sherlock (Mac) or the Start menu's Search command (Windows).

■ Another way to add a new URL to a site is to drag it from a Web browser. In the browser, select the link that goes to the URL and drag it into the External tab of the Site window. Then select the new URL and—if necessary—give it a name in the Reference Inspector.

Figure 15.24 Add an email address to a site with the Address icon.

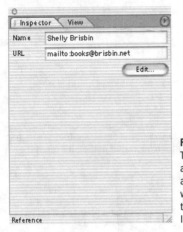

Figure 15.25 Type a name and the email address you want to add in the Reference Inspector.

To add an email address:

1. From the Site set of the Objects palette, double-click the Address icon (**Figure 15.24**) or drag the Address icon to the External tab of the Site window.

   or

   Control-click (Mac) or right-click (Windows) in the External tab and choose New Address from the contextual menu.

   or

   Choose Site > New > Address.

   An untitled address entry appears in the External tab.

2. With the Inspector open, click the untitled address entry to display the Reference Inspector.

3. Type a name for the address.

4. Type the email address in the URL field, as shown in **Figure 15.25**.

✔ Tip

- GoLive helps you enter email addresses by filling out a portion of the URL for you. When you add a new address using the Address icon or a menu, the URL field of the Reference Inspector includes the mailto: required to begin an email link. If you delete the mailto: accidentally and type info@adobe.com, GoLive will restore the leading mailto: to complete the URL.

Adding site colors

You can store colors within a site, much as you do files and external resources. You'll find this option useful if you have created a custom color in the Color palette or want to maintain a sitewide color scheme. Like other site objects, colors can be added to a Web page by drag-and-drop or Point & Shoot.

To add colors to a site:

1. In the Site window, click the Colors tab (**Figure 15.26**).

2. Double-click the Color icon (**Figure 15.27**) in the Site set of the Objects palette or drag the icon into the Colors tab of the Site window.

   or

   Control-click (Mac) or right-click (Windows) in the Site window, and choose New Color from the contextual menu.

   or

   Choose Site > New > Color.

   An untitled color appears in the Site window.

3. Click the color to select it.

4. In the Color Inspector, give the color a descriptive name and press Enter.

5. Click the Color field in the Inspector. The Color palette opens.

6. Choose a color from one of the Color palette sets. (For more information about customizing colors, see Chapter 5, "Working with Color.") The color may appear in the Color field and in the Color tab of the Site window.

7. If necessary, to finish setting the color, drag from the Preview pane at the left side of the Color palette into the Color field of the Color Inspector (**Figure 15.28**).

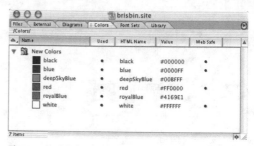

Figure 15.26 Colors associated with your site are listed in the Colors tab.

Figure 15.27 Add a new color to a site with the Color icon, found in the Site set of the Objects palette.

Figure 15.28 Drag a color into the Color Inspector's Color field to save it in the site.

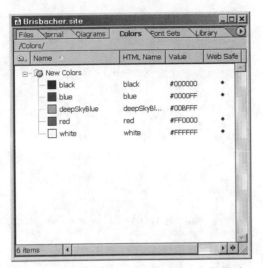

Figure 15.29 Colors that are Web safe have a bullet in the Web Safe column of the Site window's Colors tab.

✔ Tips

■ You can quickly add a site color by first selecting a color in the Color palette and then dragging it from the Preview pane (on the left side of the palette) to the Colors tab of the Site window.

■ When you add a new color, GoLive examines it to determine if it is Web safe—one of the 216 colors supported by all Web browsers and computer platforms. If it is Web safe, a bullet appears in the Web Safe column of the Colors tab (**Figure 15.29**). It's a good idea to choose a Web Safe color.

To make a site color Web safe:

1. In the Colors tab, select the color you want to change.

2. In the Color Inspector, click the Color field. The Color palette opens.

3. Choose a new color in the Web Safe set of the Color palette.

4. If necessary, drag the new color from the Preview pane to a color icon in the Site window. The color changes, and so do its HTML Name and Value. Look for the bullet in the Web Safe column in the Colors tab of the Site window to confirm that the new color is Web safe.

ADDING FILES AND OBJECTS

Adding font sets

Font sets allow you to save and use fonts with your Web site. You can store font sets as part of a site, just as you do custom colors.

To add a font set to a site:

1. In the Site window, click the Font Sets tab (**Figure 15.30**).

2. Double-click or drag the Font Set icon (**Figure 15.31**) from the Site set of the Objects palette into the Site window. An untitled font set item appears.

3. With the Inspector open, select the untitled font set to display the Font Set Inspector. Then, name the font set.

4. Click the New Item button. The field near the bottom of the Inspector becomes active, along with a menu to its right. Click and hold the menu to view a list of available fonts.

5. Choose a font from the list.

6. If you want to add more fonts to the set, repeat Steps 4 and 5. **Figure 15.32** shows a completed Font Set Inspector.

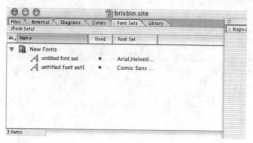

Figure 15.30 Store font sets in the Font Sets tab of the Site window.

Figure 15.31 Add a font set to the site using the Font Set icon.

Figure 15.32 The Font Set Inspector shows the fonts included in the selected font set.

To use a font from a document:

1. Open a GoLive document that contains custom fonts. The document need not be part of the site to which you will add the font.

2. If a site file is not already open, open it.

3. In the Site window, click the Font Sets tab.

4. In the Document window, select some text that uses the font you wish to add to the site.

5. Drag the text into the Site window. A new set appears in the Font Sets tab.

6. Click the new set to activate the Font Set Inspector.

7. The font used in this new set appears in the Font Set Inspector, in the Fontnames list. Enter a name for the font set.

✔ Tips

■ You can copy font sets or colors between sites. With two sites open, click a font set or color in the Site window and choose Edit > Copy. In the destination site, paste the font set or color into the Site window's Font Sets or Colors tab. You can also copy font sets or colors using drag and drop between Site windows.

■ For details about safely adding font sets that will be recognized by most browsers, see Chapter 3, "Working with Text."

■ Any time you create a new font set by copying or apply a font set to text within your site, a bullet will appear in the Used column of the Font Sets tab of the Site window. If you simply add a font from another site, it will not have the bullet because you haven't yet applied it within the current site.

ADDING FILES AND OBJECTS

Site Assets

GoLive supports a variety of site assets that make it possible for you to reuse code and HTML pages within a site. Library items, as GoLive calls them, or snippets, as Web developers generally call them, are chunks of code that you can store within the Site window, ready for use on any page of the site. Components are a lot like library items, except that you can link them to a page or pages, editing the component once to update all instances of it in the site.

Stationeries and page templates allow you to build a page framework and then use it to create new pages with common elements.

Library items (snippets)

Library items are sections of code, text, or objects that you save and apply when you need to reuse the item on several pages within the site. An obvious use for snippets is the creation of boilerplate text, logos, or navigation elements, but snippets are not the right choice for text or other HTML that will eventually need to be changed. Use stationery, a template, or a component (all described later in this section) instead. In either case, you can view snippets in the Library tab.

The sixth tab in the Site window is the Library tab (**Figure 15.33**). Like other sections of the Site window, you can store individual items here or use the New Folder button on the toolbar to create folders and store a group of items. Once you've stored a snippet with a site, you can add it to any page in the site by dragging it from the Library tab into the Document window.

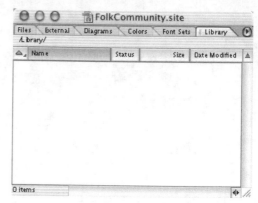

Figure 15.33 The Library tab of the Site window is empty until you add library items, a.k.a. snippets.

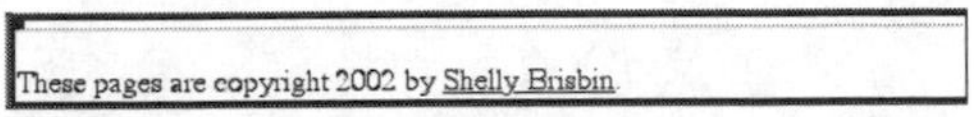

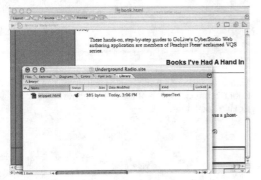

These pages are copyright 2002 by Shelly Brisbin

Figure 15.34 Select the items you want to turn into a snippet.

Figure 15.35 A new snippet appears in the Library tab as snippet.html.

Creating snippets

You can create a snippet by copying or dragging and dropping text (content or code) or objects from a GoLive document or another application. Snippets copied from within GoLive appear as HTML pages when you view them in the Library tab, while text copied from a word processor, for example, appears as text both in the Library tab and when you copy it into a GoLive document.

To create a snippet within GoLive:

1. Open a GoLive document containing code, text, or objects you would like to turn into a snippet—a navigation bar or boilerplate copyright notice is a good example.

2. Select the snippet content. If it is contained within a table, floating box, or layout grid, be sure to select the enclosing structural object if you want to include that as part of the snippet (**Figure 15.34**). All of its content will come along when you copy the container to the Clipboard.

3. Choose Edit > Copy.

4. If necessary, open the site into which you want to paste the snippet.

5. Click the Library tab in the Site window.

6. Choose Edit > Paste to paste the snippet into the library. An untitled snippet item called snippet.html appears (**Figure 15.35**).

7. Name the snippet in the File Inspector. Don't remove the .html extension.

To add a snippet from outside GoLive:

1. In the document containing the item you want to turn into a snippet, select the item.

2. Copy the item to the Clipboard.

3. Open the GoLive site to which you want to add the snippet, and select the Library tab in the Site window.

4. Paste the snippet content.

5. Using the Inspector, name the selected snippet.

To use a snippet in a document:

1. Select the Library tab in the Site window.

2. Open the document in which you would like to use the snippet. Move the Document window so that you can see the Site window and the snippet you want to use.

3. Drag the snippet from the Site window into the Document window.

✔ Tips

■ You can work with snippets in the Library tab of the Site window or in the Library folder in the Extras tab. You'll find the Extras tab in the right pane of the Site window (**Figure 15.36**).

■ You can also copy and paste or drag and drop snippets between two GoLive sites.

Figure 15.36 To use a snippet, drag it from the Library folder in the Extras tab of the Site window into a GoLive document.

Editing snippets

GoLive saves snippets as text files (though they are named like HTML files). They don't conform to the rules of HTML, meaning that they don't contain the requisite tags, but snippet pages do open as GoLive documents, and you can edit them just as you would any page. If you create a snippet using material from outside GoLive, you'll need to edit the snippet to associate HTML tags with it. Otherwise, snippet text will be unformatted.

To edit a snippet:

1. Select the Library tab in the Site window.

2. Double-click a snippet file. When you open a snippet for editing, GoLive will tell you that the snippet file has no encoding information. Click OK to choose the default encoding—the option selected in the Preferences dialog box.

If you would rather choose an encoding method, hold the Option key (Mac) or Alt key (Windows) while you double-click the snippet file. Then choose an encoding method from the pop-up menu in the Select Encoding dialog box and click Open.

3. Use GoLive editing tools to make changes or add formatting to the snippet.

✔ Tip

When you edit snippets, changes you make do not affect copies of the snippet that you have already placed. To save and use sections of code that will be updated when you edit them, use a component instead of a snippet.

Components

Say you have a site with hundreds of pages. At the bottom of each page is a footer containing a copyright notice and text links. On the left side is a navigation bar. With components, you can change the footer or navigation information once and have all your pages automatically updated.

Components can include any text or object that can be described with HTML. To create and use a component, you first build the source file, which contains the content you want to use on pages throughout your site. Then add a reference to the source file on each page where you want the component content to appear. The component content will become visible on each page containing a reference to it. When you double-click the area of a page containing a component, the component source file opens for editing.

To create a component source file:

1. Open a GoLive site.

2. Create a document containing the content you want to include in the component. **Figure 15.37** shows a footer I created.

3. Make certain you are in the Layout Editor and then open the Page Inspector by clicking the Page icon below the Layout tab. Then, in the Inspector, click the HTML tab (**Figure 15.38**).

4. If it is active, click the Component button. The Component button dims. (You can skip this step if the button is already dimmed.)

5. To save the file as a component, choose File > Save As.

6. Name the file and then select Components from the Site Folder pop-up (**Figure 15.39**) and click Save.

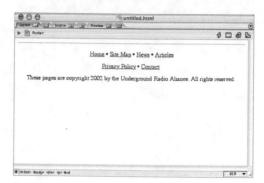

Figure 15.37 This new document contains a footer section for my site.

Figure 15.38 Click the Components button in the Page Inspector's HTML tab to identify the file as a component.

Figure 15.39 Choose Components from the Site Folder pop-up menu to store a new file in the Components folder.

✔ Tip

If you are comfortable with HTML, you may wish to work in the Source Editor to be certain that your component contains only the desired tags and text.

Figure 15.40 The Component icon appears in the Smart set of the Objects palette.

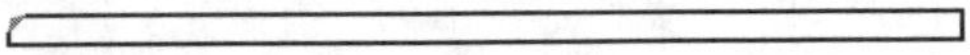

Figure 15.41 Adding a component to a document places a rectangular box in the Layout Editor.

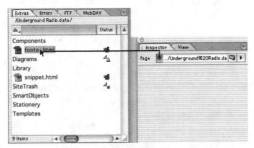

Figure 15.42 Point & Shoot from the Component Inspector to the Components folder.

To apply a component:

1. Open a document to which you want to add a component. Be sure that the site file is also open and that the Site window is visible.

2. Open the Smart set of the Objects palette.

3. Drag or double-click the Component icon (**Figure 15.40**) from the Smart set into the Document window. The placeholder for a component is a box with a rounded upper-left corner (**Figure 15.41**). The Component Inspector appears.

4. In the Inspector, Point & Shoot to the Components folder (under the Extras tab) in the right pane of the Site window (**Figure 15.42**). When the folder opens, choose the component you want to apply. The component's contents appear in the placeholder.

✔ Tips

- Components stored in the site's Components folder appear in the Site Extras set of the Objects palette. You can add a component directly by dragging its icon from the Site Extras set into the Document window.

- Although components may be any shape or size, they need to be the only object displayed on the horizontal line they occupy. They cannot share a horizontal space with another object, like an image or text block, unless the component is contained within a table cell or floating box, thus separating it from other items. Components are ideal for headers, footers, copyright notices, and other elements that occupy an entire horizontal unit of the page.

SITE ASSETS

To edit a component:

1. In a document containing a component, double-click inside the component. The component source file opens.

2. Make your changes to the component, and save the source file.

3. In the Updating Component dialog box (**Figure 15.43**), confirm that you want to update all of the files that contain this component. When you click OK, the component is updated everywhere.

Stationery Files

Stationery files are GoLive documents that you can use as the basis for new documents. Just as word -processing stationery documents let you create letters or reports based on standard elements and formatting, GoLive stationery files let you base new HTML pages on a document that contains standard items (navigation elements, fonts, and footers, for example).

For example, if every page on your site includes the same navigation bar and logo, you can build stationery that includes these elements and then build individual pages by adding content to the stationery file, which acts as a template.

You can access stationeries from the Stationery folder under the Extras tab of the Site window.

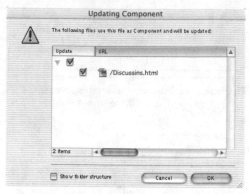

Figure 15.43 When you edit a component source file and save it, GoLive verifies that you want to update all files that use the component. Uncheck any files you don't want to update.

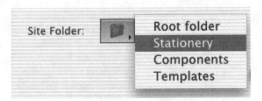

Figure 15.44 Choose Stationery from the pop-up menu to save your template to the Stationery folder within your GoLive site.

To create and save a stationery document:

1. With a site open, create a new document and add the items you want to appear in the stationery file.

2. Choose File > Save As.

3. In the dialog box, click the Site Folder pop-up menu (**Figure 15.44**) and choose Stationery. The Save dialog box displays the Stationery folder. Name the file.

4. Click Save. The new stationery appears in the Stationery folder of the Site window (look in the Extras tab).

To create a new document based on stationery:

1. Open the right pane of the Site window if it isn't already open and make sure the Extras tab is visible.

2. Open the Stationery folder.

3. Double-click the stationery you want to work with. A dialog box asks if you would like to modify the stationery file or create a new page based on it. If you create a new page, GoLive opens an untitled document containing all of the items in the stationery document.

4. Choose Create to open an untitled file. You can now add anything you like to the file, leaving the original stationery document unchanged.

5. Choose File > Save As and then click "Root folder" from the Site folder pop-up menu to reach the root folder of your site

6. To save somewhere other than the root folder, navigate to the folder within your site where you want to save the file.

7. Name the file (include the .html extension) and click Save.

✔ Tip

- You can also create a stationery document by dragging from the Files tab of the Site window into the Stationery folder of the Extras tab. When you do, the original file is moved, not copied. To copy the original, hold down the Option key (Mac) or Alt key (Windows) as you drag from the Files tab.

SITE ASSETS

Page Templates

Page templates are to stationery as components are to snippets. You can edit pages based on a stationery file, removing any or all elements that were built into the stationery. Templates, on the other hand, can be built with locked elements, allowing you to maintain consistency across all template-based pages that use particular elements. You can also edit the template later, updating all pages that are based on it when you do. When you design a page that you want to use as a template, you choose regions of the page that are locked—cannot be edited—and other regions that can be modified as needed to create new pages based on the template. When you edit the template source file, changes you make are applied to all documents associated with the template.

There are three types of editable regions you can create: objects, paragraphs, and inline. An object region can be a floating box, table, or layout grid, or even an image. Paragraph regions allow editing of a paragraph of text. Inline regions can include text blocks within a paragraph, but don't span paragraph tags.

To create a page template:

1. Be sure that a site file is open.

2. Design a page you want to use as a template for others in your site. Include a design for the portion of the page that will be customized. For example, if you design a template containing a navigation bar, a logo, and a page footer, you should also specify the container or format (a table, a floating box, placeholders for text blocks and images) for the portion of the page that will vary on each new page.

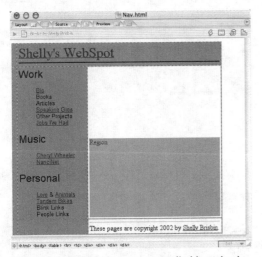

Figure 15.45 This page contains an editable region in the central portion.

3. Select the object or area you want to make editable in the template.

4. Choose Window > Template Regions.

5. Choose Special > Template > New Editable Region.

or

Control-click (Mac) or right-click (Windows) and choose Template > New Editable Region from the contextual menu.

or

In the Template Regions palette, click the New Editable Region button to make the selected object or text an editable region (**Figure 15.45**).

6. Select and name the new region by typing over the default name GoLive has given the new region.

7. Create additional editable regions as needed.

8. Choose File > Save As and select Templates from the Site Folder pop-up menu to open the site's Templates folder.

9. Name the template and choose Save. Be sure to retain the .html file extension.

To create a page using a template:

1. Create a page template and be sure that its parent site file is open.

2. Open the right pane of the Site window and then the Templates folder under the Extras tab.

3. Double-click the template you want to use.

   or

   Drag the template file into the Files tab of the Site window.

4. GoLive asks if you want to modify the template or use it to create a new file. Click Create.

5. Add content to the areas of the page that have been defined as editable regions.

6. When you are happy with the page, choose File > Save and choose "Root folder" from the Site Folder pop-up menu. Click Save to add the page to your site.

Using the Site Extras set

The site assets I've described in this section are all available both from the Site window and from the Site Extras set of the Objects palette. You can use a snippet, component, stationery, or page template by double-clicking its icon in the set. Depending on the type of object, double-clicking either opens a document or adds the object to the current document. To see a different kind of site asset, use the menu in the lower portion of the Site Extras set (**Figure 15.46**).

You can also save yourself a step when creating new documents based on a stationery file or a page template by dragging the appropriate Site Extras icon into the Files tab of the Site window. GoLive creates a new document for you, and when you save it, you'll find it already stored in the right place.

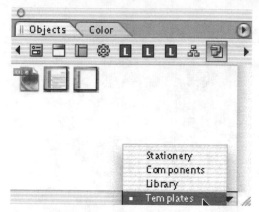

Figure 15.46 The Site Extras set shows site objects associated with the site.

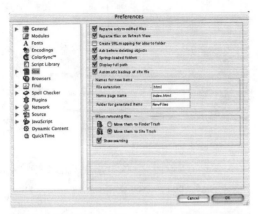

Figure 15.47 Set file-management and naming options that apply to all GoLive sites in the Site section of the Preferences window.

Fine-tuning Preferences

The Preferences and Site Settings windows include options that change the way you interact with sites. I've covered some of these options in the course of adding files and resources, and I'll cover more when I discuss publishing Web sites in Chapter 17. For now, though, there are a few settings you may find useful as you work on your site. These options apply globally to sites you create in GoLive. Use Site Settings (Site > Settings) to modify options for the current site.

To set site preferences:

1. Choose Edit > Preferences.

2. Open the Site section to display site-related options (**Figure 15.47**).

◆ To control how GoLive scans a site to verify that links are working, check "Reparse only modified files." You can also reparse files when the site is refreshed.

◆ Allow the use of aliases to files outside the site hierarchy by checking "Create URL mapping for alias to folder."

◆ "Ask before deleting objects" gives you a chance to change your mind.

◆ Spring-loaded folders in a site file behave just like folders on your desktop (except in Mac OS X, which does not support them). If you drag an item onto a folder while holding down the mouse button, the folder opens (this option works in all versions of GoLive, including OS X). This is handy when you need to Point & Shoot to an item deep within your site structure.

◆ "Display full path" shows the path from the root level to the selected item in the Site window.

◆ "Automatic backup of site file" creates a backup within the site folder. It's not a backup of the components of your site, but of the GoLive site file that keeps track of them.

◆ Use the fields under the "Names for new items" heading to specify default file and folder names used within sites.

◆ Choose options for deleting files under the "When removing files" heading.

Using Site Templates

I described site templates briefly in "Start the Site," earlier in this chapter. And in the "Site Assets" section, I introduced page templates. Despite the name similarity, the two are very different. Site templates are collections of pages and other files, along with a site hierarchy, that can be used to create a complete site. Page templates provide a framework for individual pages.

Let's take a look at the site templates included with GoLive, what they contain, and how to build your own.

Sample templates

The GoLive package includes eight sample site templates. Besides giving you a place to start when building a new site, these templates also provide great examples of how you can use GoLive tools like components, page templates, stationery, and smart objects to develop an advanced site. Even if you don't base your first GoLive site on a sample template, installing and exploring one or two is a great way to get to know what you can do with GoLive.

Poke around in the Site window. Open files. Double-click smart objects and components to view their sources. Open the Navigation or Links view to get a better look at the structure of the template site.

When you begin a site by choosing the Copy from Template option in the Site Wizard, GoLive shows you a description of each template, along with the layout of the site and its structure (**Figure 15.48**).

Figure 15.48 When you select a template, you see the layout of the home page and the navigation structure of the site.

GoLive's Sample Templates

◆ Site 1: A simple site with six pages and a common navigation bar.

◆ Site 2: A multi-column company Web site design with three levels of pages below the root and a number of components and smart objects.

◆ Site 3: A newsletter that features a text-heavy layout with just a few pages. Check this template to find a nice selection of CSS styles (in the style_03.css file).

◆ Site 4: This horizontally oriented company site is very basic, consisting of five pages.

◆ Site 5: A simple school site that features large blocks of text and a few images, organized within six pages.

◆ Site 6: A dense company site with a number of pages for product features and articles about the company. The site's hierarchy has three levels.

◆ Site 7: A cleanly designed site, ideal for a company that uses its site to provide information about what it does, rather than selling directly over the Web.

◆ Site 8: A company intranet that's another information-heavy site.

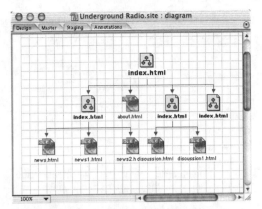

Figure 15.49 This site diagram includes several sections that represent groups of pages within a prototype site.

Site Diagramming

The best-organized Web sites are planned in advance. GoLive's site-diagramming feature gives you tools to lay out the structure of a whole site or a new section for an existing site. You can then quickly turn your design into a functioning site.

You can create as many diagrams for a single site as you like. Site diagrams are merely prototypes—their contents are not part of your live site—until you anchor the diagram to the site or to a page within the site. Once it is anchored, you can continue to work on the diagram, or submit it, turning its elements into real pages and making it part of the live site, which in turn adds its files for uploading to your Web server.

Site diagrams are stored with the rest of your site. Like the Navigation view, a site diagram is a graphical look at a site's contents (**Figure 15.49**). You can rearrange not only the contents of the diagram in the Diagram window, but also its layout, using the View palette. Diagrams are accessible from the Site window. Each diagram includes a Design tab, where you draw and arrange diagram elements; a Master view, where you can add elements that apply to every page in a multipage diagram; a Staging view, where you prepare a diagram to join the live site; and an Annotations view, where you can make notes about the diagram as you work.

Parts of a diagram

Diagrams can include these elements:

◆ Section: A group of pages within a diagram usually defined as a new branch of the site hierarchy.

◆ Page: Individual HTML pages can be added to sections or subsections as children.

◆ Link: A link defines a relationship between pages in the design.

◆ Group: Organize sections or pages into a group in order to move all items at once.

◆ Level: Use a level (a set of brackets) to indicate the position of an item within a diagram hierarchy.

◆ Annotation: Attach a text note to the diagram or to a part of it. Annotations appear only in the Annotations tab of the Diagram window.

◆ Box: Use a box to add formatted text or objects to a diagram at the presentation stages. A box is only a display tool, not an element of the diagram that will be uploaded.

You can also add pointers to a variety of objects to a diagram, including scripts, databases, and media files.

To create a diagram:

1. Begin or open a site.

2. Click the Diagrams tab (**Figure 15.50**).

3. Choose Diagram > New Design Diagram. An untitled diagram label appears in the Diagram folder and the Diagram view opens (**Figure 15.51**).

4. Switch back to the Site window and, with the diagram selected, rename the diagram, either in the Site window or in the Site Diagram Inspector (**Figure 15.52**).

Figure 15.50 Open the Diagrams tab in the Site window and choose New Design Diagram from the contextual menu. The diagram item will appear in the Diagrams tab and in the Diagrams folder on the right side of the window.

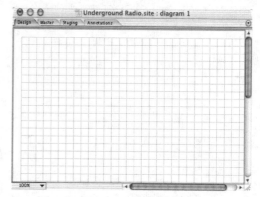

Figure 15.51 The Diagrams window has four tabs. You create and draw the diagram in the Design tab.

Figure 15.52 Name the diagram in the Site Diagram Inspector.

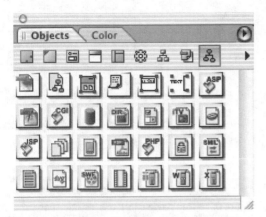

Figure 15.53 Choose objects to add to a diagram in the Diagram set of the Objects palette.

Figure 15.54 Choose the Section icon to add a new section.

Figure 15.55 Use the Inspector's Section tab to set options that affect the way new pages are added to the section.

Adding diagram elements

The best way to begin a site diagram is by adding a section. A section is actually an HTML page with links to other pages—its children. Pages and sections can also have families—parents, siblings, and children— based on links between them. The advantage of beginning a diagram with a section is that you can quickly create a group of children that share the section's characteristics, including its name. As an example, I'll start a site diagram with a section. This diagram represents a new subject, or category of information, I want to add to my existing site.

To add a section to the diagram:

1. With a diagram open in the Design tab, click the Diagram button to open the Diagram set in the Objects palette (**Figure 15.53**).

2. Drag (or double-click) the Section icon (**Figure 15.54**) from the Objects palette into the Design view. A new section object appears.

To configure a section:

1. Select the section in the Design view. The Section Inspector appears (**Figure 15.55**). You can now configure the section's page properties.

2. Use the New Filename field to set a base name for all pages in the section. When you add pages, they will be named with the prefix (news1.html, news2.html, and so on).

3. If you want child pages of this section to appear in their own folder, enter a name for the folder in the Folder field.

(continues on next pge)

4. To apply an existing stationery file to pages you add to the section, click the Stationery check box and choose a file from the menu. If your site contains no stationery files, you can add one for use with your diagram, but you must connect the section and the stationery here before you can create new pages that use it.

5. If you would rather associate a template with this section's pages, click the Template check box and choose a template from the menu.

6. Use the menus under Generate Links to establish links between the section's top-level page (the parent) and its children, or between the top-level page and other pages on the same level as siblings.

✔ Tips

■ The Section tab gives you a quick way to add child pages to the section. Enter a number in the Count field and click the Create New Pages button. **Figure 15.56** shows a diagram containing a section and four child pages. The pages all link in both directions.

■ The Page, Layout, and Graphics tabs of the Section Inspector are identical to the similarly named tabs in the Inspector for an individual page.

Diagram pages

You can add new pages to a diagram in a number of ways, making them children or siblings of existing pages. I described one way in the previous section—add a set of child pages as you configure a section in the Inspector. You can also create pages that are (or will become) sections with child pages of their own.

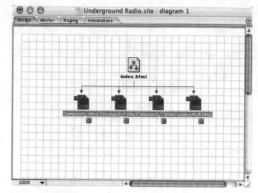

Figure 15.56 This diagram includes a section page and four child pages.

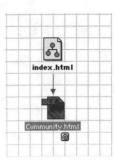

Figure 15.57 When you create a new child page, an arrow appears between parent and child.

Figure 15.58 Add multiple pages and configure them in the New Pages dialog box.

To add a child page to a section:

1. In the Diagram window's Design tab, click the icon of the section to which you want to add a child page.

2. Control-click (Mac) or right-click (Windows) and choose New > Child from the contextual menu (you can also choose Insert Object > Page).

   or

   Choose New Child from the toolbar.

   or

   Choose Diagram > New > Child Page. A child page appears below the section page, with an arrow pointing downward to the child (**Figure 15.57**). If you have configured the section page that is the parent of this page, the child may already have a file name, links, and template or stationery content.

3. GoLive automatically builds the new page using the stationery or template you've already chosen. To confirm this, double-click the new page.

To add multiple children:

1. Click the section page to select it.

2. Control-click (Mac) or right-click (Windows) and choose New Pages from the contextual menu.

   or

   Choose Diagram > New Pages.

3. The New Pages dialog box appears (**Figure 15.58**). Here you can configure all the same options as in the Section tab of the Section Inspector.

4. Enter the number of pages you want to add.

5. Leave the other options in the New Pages dialog unchanged if you want to retain those used for the section as a whole. To apply new settings only to the pages you are adding, adjust them here.

SITE DIAGRAMMING

To configure a diagram page:

1. Select a page within a diagram. The Inspector displays the Page tab (**Figure 15.59**).

2. Give the page a name, if you wish. The name is a label that appears only in the diagram, and only if you checked Design Name in the View palette (see "Customizing a diagram's display" on page 329).

3. Change the default page title. (This title will appear in Web browser title bars and bookmark lists when the page is displayed, and search engines may use it as well.)

4. Edit the file name, if you wish. If you gave the section a file name earlier, you will see it in the File Name field.

5. Click the check box if you want to apply stationery or a template to the page, and choose it from the menu.

6. If you want to base the selected page on an existing page that is not a template or stationery, click the Sample check box and Browse or Point & Shoot to the page you would like to use.

✔ Tip

■ The Stationery, Template, and Sample options will be available only if you have not previously selected a base page for child pages in the Section Inspector.

Adding to the page family

You can add parents or siblings to any page you create. When you add a sibling, you can choose to add Previous Page (which appears to the left of the selected page) or Next Page (which appears to the right). Like the options for adding children, commands to add parents and siblings appear in the contextual menu, on the toolbar, and in the Diagram menu.

Figure 15.59 Set up a page (a section page or any other page) in the Page tab of the Page or Inspector.

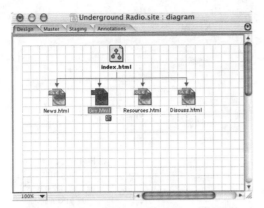

Figure 15.60 Click on a Page icon within a diagram to see the Fetch URL icon.

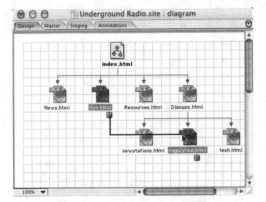

Figure 15.61 Create a new link between pages by dragging from the Fetch URL icon of the source page to the destination page.

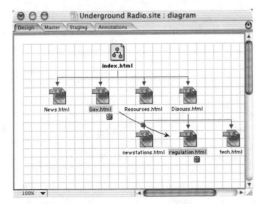

Figure 15.62 A link line appears between the two pages. The arrow indicates that the link is going to the regulation.html page.

Design diagrams can also include pages that don't yet have family relationships to existing elements in the diagram. To add an unrelated page, just click anywhere within the diagram and add a page using the contextual menu or Diagram set in the Objects palette. When you're ready, you can create a *pending link* between the new page and others within the diagram.

Pending links

As you build a diagram, you can add pending links between pages, whether or not the pages are members of the same family. Pending links help you manage the diagram as you move from design to presentation and publishing. When you work with pages with pending links in place, you will see warnings in the diagram interface and in the Site window.

You can add new pending links between pages that don't have them using the Link Inspector or by drawing the links (Point & Shoot) in the Design tab of the Diagram window. You can also use Point & Shoot to change the destination of existing links. In the Link Inspector, you can also alter a link's type.

To add a pending link:

1. Click on a page within a diagram (**Figure 15.60**).

2. Point & Shoot to another page in the Design tab (**Figure 15.61**). When the two pages are linked, the destination page's Fetch URL button becomes visible and a link line appears between the pages (**Figure 15.62**). The Link Inspector appears.

(continues on next page)

(continues on next page)

SITE DIAGRAMMING

3. Change the link type in the Link Type menu (**Figure 15.63**) if you want to use a tour link (a link between pages that are not in the same family). It's easier to create family links by adding pages, rather than by choosing them in the Link Inspector.

4. Type a value in the Deflection field or use the Deflection pop-up menu to change the angle of the link line in the Design tab.

5. From the Arrowhead menu, choose a square arrow or no arrow at all, if you wish.

✔ Tips

■ Simply dragging a new section page along-side an existing one does not create a sibling relationship. Using the preceding steps to link two visually parallel pages can make them siblings in reality, rather than simply siblings in appearance. After you link two pages, choose Next or Previous from the Link Type menu in the Link Inspector to link the two pages as siblings. If you want the pages to link in both directions—with links from each page to the other—make a second link. To do that, Point & Shoot from the page you just linked to back to the first page.

■ By default, pending links are red. You can change the color of an individual link, or all of them, in the Graphics tab of the Link Inspector (**Figure 15.64**).

To delete pending links:

1. Click on a link between two pages to select it.

2. Press Delete to remove the link.

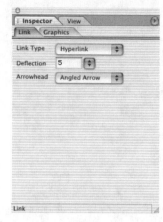

Figure 15.63 Use the Link Inspector to change a link's type and a link line's appearance.

Figure 15.64 The Graphics tab of the Link Inspector contains options for altering the appearance of pending links.

SITE DIAGRAMMING

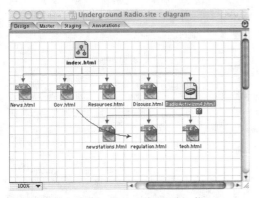

Figure 15.65 I added a Java applet to this diagram. I positioned it near a group of pages that will contain threaded discussions. The applet will manage and display the discussion forums.

Figure 15.66 Options in the Object Inspector are the same, regardless of the kind of object you're working with. The object's Type is chosen for you (and can be changed in the pop-up menu).

Custom objects

In addition to the pages and links that make up a site hierarchy, design diagrams can contain GIF images that represent portions of the site other than pages, such as databases, scripts, forms, and applets. You can add and manipulate these custom objects in the Design tab, just as you do pages and sections. When you present the design, either in print or electronically, the custom objects appear along with the page hierarchy.

Most of the icons in the Diagram set of the Objects palette represent custom objects.

To add an object to a diagram:

1. Choose an object from the Diagram set of the Objects palette, and drag or double-click to add it to a diagram.

   or

   Control-click (Mac) or right-click (Windows) in the Design tab and choose Insert Object > object name from the contextual menu.

2. If necessary, drag the new object to position it in the Design tab.

3. Click the object to select it. In **Figure 15.65**, I have added a Java applet to my diagram. The Object Inspector appears (**Figure 15.66**).

4. Name the object and specify a target directory, if you wish.

5. If you have added an object to an existing section, the object bears the section's name, as in the example in Figure 15.65, where the object is the fifth child of the RadioActivism section. Change the file name in the Inspector, if you wish.

(continues on next page)

SITE DIAGRAMMING

327

6. Just as in the Page Inspector, GoLive displays controls for basing an object on an existing template, stationery, or a sample file. To activate these settings, first click the Create From check box. These options are not applicable to most objects.

7. Choose layout and color options in the corresponding tabs, just as you would for a page or section.

Creating your own custom objects

If you need to represent a kind of content or code that GoLive doesn't include in the Diagram set, you can use a custom object of your own by adding to the Adobe GoLive 6.0 folder a GIF image to represent it. Your custom object then appears in the Diagram set of the Objects palette and in the contextual menu.

To add an object type to GoLive:

1. Quit GoLive.

2. Copy a GIF image file that will represent your object into the Adobe GoLive 6.0 > Modules > Diagram Objects folder on your hard drive.

3. Restart GoLive and verify that your new object appears in the Diagram set of the Objects palette.

Figure 15.67 Use the Display tab of the View palette to control which objects you see and how they look in the Design tab.

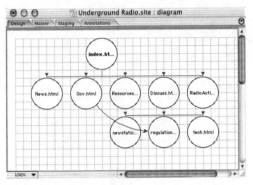

Figure 15.68 Choose Ovals in the Display tab of the View palette to get this look.

Customizing a diagram's display

The Diagram window's Design tab is a canvas on which you can organize pages, objects, and links in just about any way you like. You can change the way objects appear in the window, as well as which objects are visible while you work on the design. By default, the Design tab includes a 16 x 16 pixel grid, and objects you add to the diagram snap to the visible grid. You can change these settings, as well as others, in the View palette.

To change a diagram's display:

1. With the Design tab of the Diagram window visible, open the View palette by clicking the View tab in the Inspector window.

   or

   If the Inspector window is not visible, choose Window > View.

2. Click the Display tab in the View palette (**Figure 15.67**).

3. To change the look of pages, choose one of the Show Items As options. **Figure 15.68** shows a diagram whose objects are ovals.

4. Use the Item Label buttons to select how objects are identified. As I described earlier, you can set these name options in the Inspector for each page or object.

5. Use the Frame Size pop-up menu to make icons larger or smaller.

6. Click the Color field and choose a new color in the Color palette.

SITE DIAGRAMMING

To change the grid pattern:

1. Click the Grid tab in the View palette (**Figure 15.69**).

2. To change the density of the grid, choose new values in the Horizontal and Vertical fields.

3. Use the adjacent check boxes to control the grid's visibility and to choose whether items in the tab will snap to the grid when you move the objects.

4. Click the Collision Avoidance check box to activate options that allow you to set a minimum distance between objects and enter new values in the Horizontal and Vertical fields, if you wish.

5. To confine the diagram canvas to a single page, click the "Canvas as single page" check box. To control the number of pages a diagram can occupy, leave the box unchecked and enter values in the Page Rows and Columns fields.

To adjust your view of a diagram:

1. In the View palette, click the Design tab (**Figure 15.70**).

2. Change the Diagram window's orientation to Tall (the default is Wide) to make your view more vertical.

3. Click the Panorama check box to split the Diagram tab into two parts, showing a Panorama pane and a normal view. In the Panorama pane, you can move the rectangle to focus your attention on a portion of the normal view (**Figure 15.71**).

✔ Tip

■ The Panorama pane shows a reduced view of your diagram. You can also zoom the view in or out, whether you're working in Panorama or not. Use the Zoom menu in the lower-left corner of the Diagram window to enlarge or shrink your view.

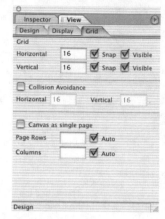

Figure 15.69 The Grid tab of the View palette gives you options for arranging diagram objects.

Figure 15.70 The View palette's Design tab gives you options for changing the way a diagram displays.

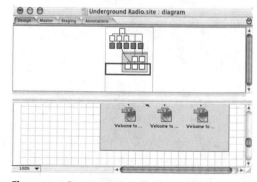

Figure 15.71 Panorama view allows you both to see all of a large diagram's objects and to focus on a portion that you want to work on.

SITE DIAGRAMMING

Figure 15.72 Use the Annotation icon to add a text note to a diagram.

Figure 15.73 Type a subject and text for your annotation in the Annotation Inspector.

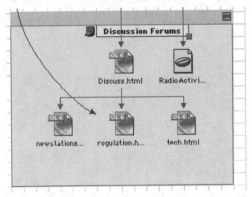

Figure 15.74 This subject-only annotation provides a short description for a diagram section.

Annotating a diagram

You can add annotations to a design diagram that will appear with it when you print or present it. Annotations can be simple captions or they can provide more detailed information.

To annotate a diagram:

1. Double-click or drag the Annotation icon (**Figure 15.72**) from the Diagram set of the Objects palette into the Design tab. An Annotation icon appears.

2. Click the Annotation icon to select it and to view the Annotation Inspector (**Figure 15.73**).

3. Type a subject and text for the annotation.

4. Use the alignment buttons to make the annotation flush left, flush right, or centered.

5. Click the Display Subject and Display Text check boxes to control text that appears on the diagram.

6. Choose a position for the annotation relative to its icon from the Position pop-up menu.

7. Choose colors for the annotation, its border, and its background in the Graphics tab of the Annotation Inspector. **Figure 15.74** shows an annotation (subject only) at the top of a section within a diagram.

Submitting a diagram

When you've completed a draft of your design diagram, you may want to begin filling it in with content in preparation for adding the diagram's pages to your live site. You may instead choose to present the diagram to others for their input before you convert diagram elements into live pages. You can, of course, go through both of these steps.

(continues on next page)

SITE DIAGRAMMING

Preparing your design diagram for presentation is called *staging*. Integrate the contents of a design diagram with a live site by *anchoring* the diagram to a page within the site.

Anchoring a diagram to a page

Until you anchor a diagram to a page within your site, the pages and objects you've added to it are only prototypes, even if you've added content and links to the pages. When you have anchored the design diagram, its contents will appear in the Navigation view along with the pages in the live site. To begin the process of adding a design diagram's components to the site and publishing them, you should first anchor the diagram to a page within the site. Doing so will also make the diagram's pages visible in the Navigation view. That's useful when diagnosing staging errors (covered in the next section).

To anchor a diagram to a page:

1. Choose a page within your site to which you want to anchor a diagram.

2. If it isn't already visible, open the diagram by double-clicking it in the Diagrams tab of the Site window

3. Click the Site window to bring it forward and click the Files tab.

4. Arrange the Diagram and Site windows so that both are visible on screen.

5. Drag the page's icon from the Files tab of the Site window into the Diagram window (**Figure 15.75**). The page appears in the Diagram window with an Anchor icon next to it (**Figure 15.76**).

6. Make links between the anchor page and a page within the diagram.

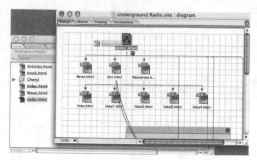

Figure 15.75 To anchor a diagram to a page, drag the page's icon from the Site window into the Diagram window.

Figure 15.76 When you anchor a page to a diagram, a Page icon with an anchor appears in the Diagram window.

✔ Tips

- You can anchor a diagram to a site, rather than a single page, anchoring the diagram to the home page (index.html, by default).

- If you've been working on a site for some time and already have a complex site structure, you might want to anchor a diagram to a page using the Navigation or Links view, rather than the Site window. The procedure is the same: Drag the Page icon from the Navigation or Links view into the Diagram window.

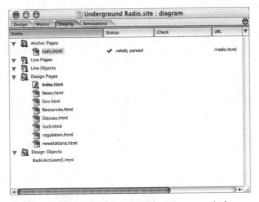

Figure 15.77 The Staging tab of the Diagram window lists the pages and objects in the diagram. If you have anchored the diagram to a page within your site, the page appears in the Anchor Pages folder.

 Figure 15.78 Use the Check Staging button to look for errors before you take a diagram live.

Figure 15.79 When you check staging, error icons may appear in the Staging tab of the Diagram window.

To stage a diagram:

1. In the Diagram window, click the Staging tab. The components of the diagram appear as a list (**Figure 15.77**).

2. Choose Diagram > Staging > Check Staging.

   or

   Click the Check Staging button on the toolbar (**Figure 15.78**).

3. Correct errors in the Staging tab of the Diagram window (**Figure 15.79**) as follows:

   ◆ Stage in Scratch errors occur when a page in the diagram is not linked to anything. Fix the error by making links in the Navigation view between the error page and others in your site. You must have anchored the diagram to a page in the site in order to fix the error. If you don't fix a Stage in Scratch error, the diagram page you save will not be staged to your site, but will be saved as a scratch page.

   ◆ Target Folder errors occur when you use the Section or Page Inspector to create a target folder for a diagram page, but have specified a folder that cannot be created. Make changes in the Section or Page Inspector to correct the error.

   ◆ Section Name errors occur if the index.html file that is associated with a section cannot be created in the folder you specified for the section because a file with the same name already exists. To correct this error, rename the file in the Section Inspector, or rename the index.html file that already exists.

4. Check staging again to verify that all errors have been eliminated. Error icons are replaced by checkmarks.

(continues on next page)

SITE DIAGRAMMING

5. To stage the diagram once it is error-free, choose Diagrams > Staging > Submit All.

or

Click the Submit All button on the toolbar. GoLive displays the diagram items in the Files tab of the Site window and shows them in Navigation and Links view as well.

✔ Tips

■ You can submit a portion of a diagram, rather than the whole thing, by selecting objects and then choosing Submit Items (instead of Submit All) from the Diagram > Staging menu.

■ You can "unsubmit" all or part of a diagram by recalling it. To do so, choose Recall All or Recall Items from the Staging submenu of the Diagram menu. The recalled items are removed from the site hierarchy.

VIEWING AND MANAGING SITES

The value of site-building tools lies not only in creating a well-organized site, but also in maintaining it. Large sites often become unmanageable because of their confusing hierarchical relationships and vast number of links. Adding, deleting, and moving files tends to introduce errors. Not to mention that things change on the Web, and over time, links get broken.

GoLive's site-management tools allow you to take a visual and logical look at your site and find and correct errors efficiently. You can also use these tools to diagram and report on the contents and condition of your site.

In this chapter, I'll cover

◆ Working with the Site window

◆ Working with site objects

◆ The Navigation view

◆ The Links view

◆ Peripheral panes

◆ Troubleshooting sites

◆ Site reports

A Closer Look at the Site Window

In this section, I'll introduce you to some Site window features you can use to manage your site and locate items that are part of it.

Changing your view of the Site window

When you open a new GoLive site, it appears in the Site window, which contains six tabs. You can expand the window to view four more tabs in the right pane. These four tabs give you access to several specialized types of GoLive site objects, and let you switch quickly to windows you can use to view errors and upload your site to a Web server. Items under each tab are sorted alphabetically by default, but you can change the sorting order of items and rearrange and resize columns. You can also resize the window and its two panes, and you can set preferences that control the appearance of the site.

To view the Site window's right pane:

◆ In the Site window, click the Split Pane button in the lower-right corner (**Figure 16.1**).

◆ Move the divider between the two panes to see more or less of each (**Figure 16.2**).

Figure 16.1 Click the Split Pane button to open the right pane of the Site window.

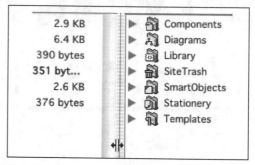

Figure 16.2 Change the size of the Site window's panes by dragging the bar between them.

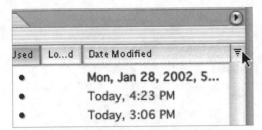

Figure 16.3 On the Mac, click the arrow to change the sort order for the chosen Site window column.

Figure 16.4 Choose a column to view from the View palette's Show Columns pop-up menu.

■ Like the Site window, the View palette is context-sensitive and shows different columns depending upon which Site window tab is visible. When you click the Colors tab, for example, the View palette shows columns for the HTML name of the color, value, Web-safe status, and whether or not the color is currently in use.

Sorting the Site window

You can sort items in the Site window by any column in the window. Click the column heading to sort by that column. On a Mac, you can also change the sorting order from ascending to descending by clicking the arrow to the right of the column labels (**Figure 16.3**).

To add or remove columns from view:

1. With a site open, choose Window > View.
   or
   Click the View tab in the Inspector window.

2. Click the Show Columns pop-up menu to view the list of columns you can display in the Site window. The currently displayed columns are checked (**Figure 16.4**).

3. To add or remove a column from your view, select it from the menu.

To resize a column in the Site window:

◆ In the column heading area, click the border of the column and drag to enlarge or shrink it.

To return to the default Site window configuration, choose Site > View > Default Configuration or choose Default Configuration from the flyout menu in the Site window.

✔ Tips

■ Choose Show All or Hide All from the pop-up menu in the View palette to view all available columns or hide all of them. If you hide all columns, only the file's name and icon appear in the primary pane of the Site window.

■ To rearrange columns, click a column heading and drag to the left or right, over the column whose position you want it to take.

Working with Site Objects

Files, URLs, email addresses, colors, and font sets are all objects within a GoLive site. Each type of object can be configured, renamed, and moved within the Site window using the Navigation and Links views discussed later in this chapter. Site objects, like objects on a GoLive page, can be configured using the Inspector. Options for different kinds of objects vary slightly, but the File Inspectors for HTML documents, images, style sheet documents, and other local files have very similar attributes.

Managing site files

You can use the Finder (Mac) or Windows Explorer (Windows) to manage files within your site. But using the Site window gives you access to file-and link-management tools that make it possible to move and rename files without breaking their connections to other parts of your site. Like the operating system-based file managers, the Site window is organized into files and folders. It also lets you view file attributes (file size and location relative to other items) and status within the site.

To view a file's properties:

◆ With a site open and the Files tab of the Site window visible, click a file to select it. The File Inspector appears (**Figure 16.5**).

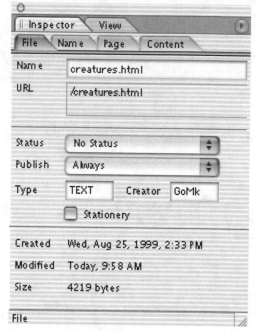

Figure 16.5 The File Inspector gives you options for viewing and changing file properties.

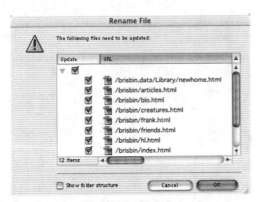

Figure 16.6 When you change a file's name or location within a site, the Rename File window appears, allowing you to choose whether to update references to that file that occur within other site files.

Figure 16.7 Change a page's title in the Page tab of the File Inspector.

To rename a site object:

1. Select a file, folder, or object in the Site window.

2. Type a new name in the Name field of the Inspector. Don't forget to preserve the file's extension (.html, .gif, etc.).

3. Press Tab to confirm the name. If the file is linked to others in your site, GoLive will search for URLs that need to be changed to preserve the link, and will display a window listing files that should be updated (**Figure 16.6**).

4. To change all URLs that refer to the file whose name you're changing, click OK. If you don't want to change a specific file reference, uncheck the box next to its name and then click OK to change the others.

✔ Tips

- You can also rename a file by clicking its name in the Site window and typing a new name over the old. You will be asked to update references, just as in the steps above.

- You can use the Inspector to change the title of an HTML page. With a file selected in the Site window, click the Page tab (**Figure 16.7**) of the File Inspector and update the Title field.

- To edit the name (but not the content) of a URL or email address, select the item in the External tab of the Site window and edit it in the Inspector. When you're done, GoLive will present the update window and give you the chance to correct references within your pages.

- If the External tab contains no URLs or email addresses, choose Site > Get References Used. GoLive will update the External tab with URLs and addresses it finds in the files that make up your site.

WORKING WITH SITE OBJECTS

339

File name constraints

Besides the constraints imposed by HTML when naming files, operating systems have their own character sets that impose more rules, depending on the OS used by your Web server. For example, Mac file names (and modern Windows ones) can contain spaces. Unix and old DOS/Windows names cannot. And since Unix uses the slash (/) in directory paths, you can't include one in a file name. DOS/Windows is quite picky, not only about which characters can appear in a file name, but how many there are.

File name constraints can be applied by file or folder. So if you plan to upload your site to servers on different platforms, you could apply different constraints for each server.

You can find out which platform's constraints you're using in the File Inspector, and you can choose them in the Preferences window. Once you've picked a constraint, GoLive will prevent you from choosing improper file names.

To view file name constraints:

1. Select a file or folder in the Site window.

2. In the File Inspector, click the Name tab. The default GoLive Standard constraints use a combination of Mac, Windows, and Unix rules (**Figure 16.8**).

To change file name constraints:

1. Choose Edit > Preferences and click the triangle (Mac) or plus sign (Windows) to open the Site section of the window.

2. Click Filename Constraints.

3. Choose an option from the Selected Constraints pop-up menu. A summary of the rules for the option you've chosen appears (**Figure 16.9**).

Figure 16.8 The Name tab of the File Inspector shows the file's naming constraints.

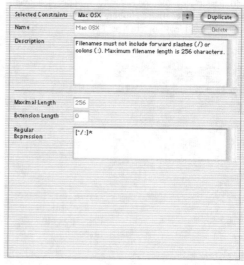

Figure 16.9 When you choose a new set of constraints, the rules appear in the Preferences window.

Figure 16.10 The Content tab of the File Inspector shows a thumbnail of GoLive-created HTML files and any image files that are in a Web-compatible format.

Figure 16.11 To view a thumbnail of the selected page, click the Update Thumbnail button.

Figure 16.12 Click this button to fit the selected image to the Inspector window.

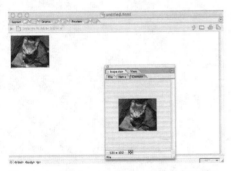

Figure 16.13 Drag an image thumbnail from the Content tab of the File Inspector into the Document window to add the image to a document.

Figure 16.14 You can play media files in the Content tab. This preview of a QuickTime movie includes playback controls.

More file properties

The File Inspector provides a lot of information about both HTML files and media files. In the File tab, you'll find the file's URL, size, and modification dates. Though this data is also available in the Site window, you may decide to hide the window's columns (as described earlier in this chapter) to make room for other columns.

To preview a file's contents:

1. With an HTML file selected in the Site window, click the Content tab of the File Inspector. A thumbnail representation of your HTML file or image appears (**Figure 16.10**).

2. If you don't see a thumbnail, click the Update Thumbnail button (**Figure 16.11**).

   or

   If you have selected an image file, the image appears at its original size in the Content tab. To make the image fit in the window, click the button below the image (**Figure 16.12**).

✔ Tips

- You can add an image or multimedia file (but not an HTML file) to a GoLive document by dragging the thumbnail from the Content tab into the Document window (**Figure 16.13**). The image is added at full size, even if you're viewing a reduced version in the Content tab.

- You can play a multimedia file in the Content tab just as you can in the Document window. If the appropriate plug-ins are present, GoLive will supply the needed controls in the Content tab (**Figure 16.14**). For a complete discussion of plug-ins, see Chapter 14, "Working with Rich Media."

Another nifty feature of the File Inspector, at least on the Macintosh, is the ability to change the file's creator code. This is useful if you've added an HTML file to your site that was not created with GoLive. If you try to open the file by double-clicking it in the Site window, it will open with the application that created it, rather than with GoLive.

To change a file's creator code to GoLive (Mac only):

1. In the Site window, select an HTML file that was created with an application other than GoLive.

2. In the File tab of the File Inspector, change the entry in the Creator field to GoMk.

3. If the Type field contains an entry other than TEXT, change it to TEXT.

4. Return to the Site window. The file's icon has changed to a GoLive icon.

Arranging files

You can make your site-folder hierarchy as simple or as complicated as you want. You can rearrange the site's files by moving them into different folders and adding new folders. In this section, I'll describe adding and using folders, as well as moving files and updating references to them.

To create a folder in the Site window:

1. With a site open, Control-click (Mac) or right-click (Windows) inside the Files tab and choose New > New Folder from the contextual menu.

   or

   Drag the Folder icon (**Figure 16.15**) from the Site set of the Objects palette into the Site window. A selected folder appears in the Site window.

Figure 16.15 Add a folder to the Site with the Folder icon.

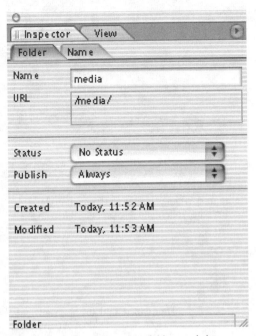

Figure 16.16 You can name site folders and view information about them in the Folder Inspector.

2. Type a new name for the selected folder and click outside the folder to confirm the name.

   or

   Type a name for the folder in the Name field of the Folder Inspector (**Figure 16.16**).

3. In the Site window, add files to your new folder by dragging them onto the folder's icon.

4. View the contents of the folder by clicking the triangle (Mac) or plus sign (Windows) to the left of the icon in the Site window.

To move a file within a site:

1. Locate a file you want to relocate. Drag the file into the folder where you want it to be. GoLive displays the Move Files dialog box and asks if you would like to update links that would otherwise be broken by the relocation.

2. Uncheck any files for which you don't want to update the links, then click OK to update the site.

WORKING WITH SITE OBJECTS

The Navigation View

Up to this point in the chapter, we've been working in the Site window, a file-hierarchy-oriented view of your GoLive site. You can also look at your site graphically, as a hierarchy of pages (Navigation view) or as a collection of links (Links view). In this section, I'll show you the Navigation view, and how you can use it to approach your site as a hierarchy of dependent pages.

Think of the Navigation view as a bird's-eye view of your Web site. Starting with your home page, the Navigation view displays miniature representations of each page in the site and their relationships to one another. The home page is the parent page for the entire site. Each page that links directly to the home page is a child of the home page and a sibling to other pages that also link directly to the home page. The Navigation view shows these relationships in graphical terms, just as the Design tab in the Diagram window does (see Chapter 15, "Building Sites").

To examine a site with the Navigation view:

1. With a site open, click the Navigation View button on the toolbar.

   or

   Choose Site > View > Navigation. The Navigation view appears (**Figure 16.17**). It shows an icon for the site's home page, `index.html`.

2. Click the plus sign below the page icon (**Figure 16.18**). The HTML pages at the root level of your site's folder hierarchy appear (**Figure 16.19**). Note that these pages are not necessarily linked to the home page. To expand the hierarchy further, click the plus sign below any Page icon in the Navigation view.

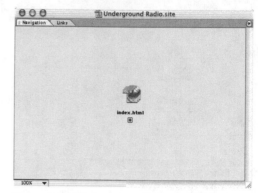

Figure 16.17 When you open the Navigation view for the first time, your home page appears alone in the window.

Figure 16.18 Click the plus sign below an icon to see children of that page.

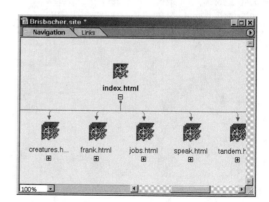

Figure 16.19 The Navigation view shows the site's folder hierarchy. Clicking a plus sign under a page reveals that page's children.

Figure 16.20 Click the Unfold All button to expand the view of the site.

Figure 16.21 Click the Toggle Orientation button to change the orientation on screen.

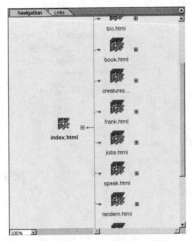

Figure 16.22 Rotate the Navigation view to see more of your site.

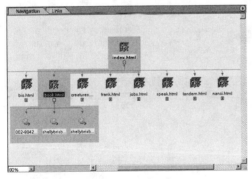

Figure 16.23 When Navigation view items are spotlighted, they appear in a colored box or circle.

✔ Tip

■ You can completely expand the Navigation view hierarchy by clicking the Unfold All button (**Figure 16.20**) on the toolbar. A page must be selected in the Navigation view to activate the button.

Navigation view display options

You can adjust how the site looks in the Navigation view in several ways. Changing the view's orientation is one of the most useful ways, especially if your site includes a lot of files on the same level. By default, the site appears in a horizontal (wide) orientation. Clicking the Toggle Orientation button (**Figure 16.21**) on the toolbar rotates the view (**Figure 16.22**).

You can also take a different look at your site by reducing or enlarging the Navigation view. To do that, choose a magnification percentage from the pop-up menu in the lower-left corner of the Navigation view, or Option-click (Mac) or Shift-click (Windows) to zoom in or out one level.

Spotlighting items in Navigation view

You can focus on a particular portion of your site—a single page or related elements in the page hierarchy—by spotlighting the area. When items in the Navigation view are spotlighted, they are distinguished from other items in the view by a colored box or circle (**Figure 16.23**).

There are several spotlight options available.

◆ **Family** spotlights a page, its children, and its parent.

◆ **Incoming** spotlights all pages with links to the selected page.

(continues on next page)

◆ **Outgoing** spotlights pages to which the selected page is linked.

◆ **Pending** spotlights pages with pending links to the selected page.

◆ **Collection** points to pages that are part of a collection containing the selected page.

To spotlight pages:

1. With the Navigation view visible, choose Window > View to activate the View palette and click the Navigation tab. If the Inspector is visible, you can simply click the View tab, then the Navigation tab (**Figure 16.24**).

2. Make sure the file you want to include as part of the spotlight is visible. Expand the Navigation view if necessary. Then select the file.

3. Choose a Spotlight option from the View palette.

   or

   Choose a Spotlight option from the fly-out menu (**Figure 16.25**) in the upper-right corner of the Navigation view window. The spotlighted page is highlighted in the Navigation view (**Figure 16.26**).

Figure 16.24 Choose a Spotlight option from the View palette's Naviation tab.

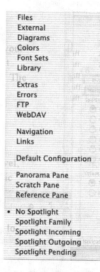

Figure 16.25 Or choose a Spotlight option from the Naviation view's fly-out menu.

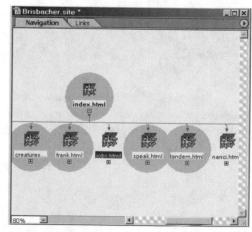

Figure 16.26 When you spotlight an incoming page, the spotlight is a circle.

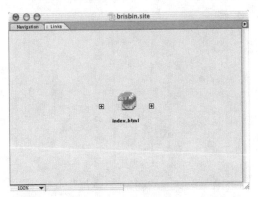

Figure 16.27 When you open the Links view for the first time, your home page appears and plus signs indicate links to (left) and from (right) it.

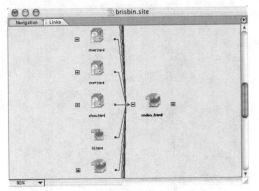

Figure 16.28 When you click a plus sign to the left of a Page icon in the Links view, you see all of the pages within your site that link to that page.

The Links View

When you're ready to move from a high-level, file-centric view of your site to a link-centric one, you'll go from the Navigation view to the Links view. The Links view presents your site in terms of the hyperlinks that exist between the pages, and also shows links to external items. This may or may not correspond to the file hierarchy you have built. In fact, the Links view is a great way to verify, for example, that all of the pages in your site's root directory have links back to the home page. If a page in the directory isn't linked to any other page, you won't see it in the Links view when you expand the site hierarchy out from the home page.

To view a page in the Links view:

◆ Choose Site > View > Links.

or

with the Navigation view open, click the Links tab. The Links view appears (**Figure 16.27**).

Viewing links

When you first open the Links view, an icon representing your home page appears. Just as in the Navigation view, plus signs let you expand the Links view hierarchy to see more of your site. But instead of displaying files that appear below the home page in the folder hierarchy, as the Navigation view does, the Links view displays links to (on the left) and from (on the right) your home page.

To view links to or from the current page:

1. With the Links view open, click the plus sign to the left of the index.html icon. The view expands to show all pages or files that link to the home page (**Figure 16.28**).

2. Click the plus sign to the right of the home page. Files your home page links to appear.

Notice that the pages that appear when you expand the view may also have plus signs next to them. Click one on the left of a page to see other pages that link to it. That's what I did in **Figure 16.29**.

If you view links from the current page (with the plus sign to the right of the source page), you will see not only files to which the page links, but also images and URLs. **Figure 16.30** shows a page that links to several files, email addresses, and a remote Web site.

The toolbar and the Links view itself give you several ways to alter the display of your site. You can also use the View palette to change Links view options.

✔ Tip

■ You can change the Links view's orientation or expand the hierarchy to view the entire site using the same toolbar and menu options I described in the "Navigation View" section.

To choose which links to view:

1. With the Links view visible, click the View tab in the Inspector.

   or

   Choose Window > View. The View palette appears, displaying the Links tab (**Figure 16.31**).

2. Under the Show heading, uncheck Incoming Links or Outgoing Links if you want to hide either kind of link.

3. Under the Explore heading, choose Single Link Path if you want to see only links that are part of the path you have expanded.

You'll learn about the options under the Show Panes heading in the "Peripheral Panes" section starting on page 351.

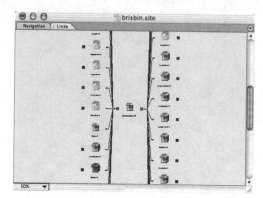

Figure 16.29 Here is a page, with pages containing links to it on the left and pages it links to on the right.

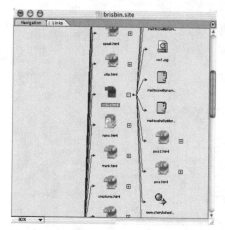

Figure 16.30 Clicking the right plus sign shows all items, including images, URLs, and email addresses that the source page links to.

Figure 16.31 Choose which items to view in the Links tab of the View palette.

Figure 16.32 The Display tab of the View palette allows you to change the look of the Navigation or Links view.

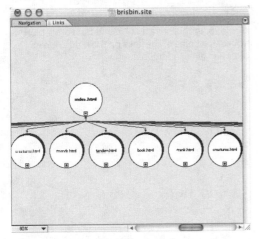

Figure 16.33 Here's the Links view when you choose to view items as ovals, rather than icons.

Figure 16.34 The Filter tab of the View palette allows you to exclude some items from the Navigation view or Links view.

To set display and filter options for the Navigation or Links view:

1. Open the Navigation or Links view and then the View palette.

2. Click the Display tab in the View palette (**Figure 16.32**).

3. Choose Outline to see the Navigation or Links view as a hierarchical list of objects. Note that if you choose Outline, the other options in the View palette's Display tab disappear, except for the Show Columns pop-up menu.

4. With the (default) Graphical view option selected, choose an option from among the "Show Items as" radio buttons. Your choices are Icons (the default), Thumbnails, Frames, or Ovals (**Figure 16.33**).

5. Under Item Label, choose Page Title to show the title of the page, rather than the file name.

6. Under the Cell Size and Frame Size headings, choose options for the size and color of objects in the Navigation or Links view. Cell Size (measured in pixels) controls the size of icons, while Frame Size ranges from Small to Large and controls the distance between icons.

7. Click the Filter tab in the View palette (**Figure 16.34**).

8. Uncheck file types that you do not want to see in the Navigation or Links view. Items that are checked will appear when you expand the views.

9. Click the Toggle Media button if you would rather see no media objects. Click again to view them all.

10. Uncheck boxes next to the types of links that you do not want to see in the Navigation or Links view. The Toggle Links button turns them all on or off.

✔ Tips

- Another way to view links—a way that works in all site views—is to use the In & Out Links palette. Choose Window > In & Out Links, and select an object in the Site, Navigation, or Links view. The In & Out Links palette shows the object with links to and from it (**Figure 16.35**). You'll probably want to enlarge it with the grow box. When you click a file within your site, the In & Out Links palette displays items that link to the selected page (left) and items that link from the page (right).

- Though the options for changing the display and filtering for the Navigation and Links views are the same, changing options for one view does not affect what you see in the other view.

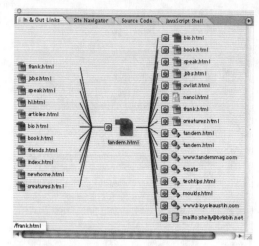

Figure 16.35 This page links to and from other pages. Notice that some of the links on the right are Web URLs and email addresses.

Peripheral Panes

In addition to the main graphical site views, GoLive includes three *peripheral panes*—alternative site views you can use while you also work in the Navigation, Links, or Diagram view (introduced in Chapter 15).

Peripheral panes have several uses: For example, you can get a wide-angle view of your site, looking at it as a whole while you work on smaller groups of pages and links in the Navigation, Links, or Diagram view. Peripheral panes (listed below) also allow you to focus on a particular portion or perspective of a large site, without forcing you to scroll endlessly through its contents in the main site views.

◆ **Panorama pane** shows the site "from 30,000 feet." You see the entire site, reduced in size and with simple boxes, rather than icons, representing pages or links. A movable frame within the pane lets you choose which portion of the site you want to focus on in the main view (Navigation, Links, or Diagram).

◆ **Scratch pane** displays HTML and media files that are stored within the root folder of the site, but are not linked to any other file in the site. You can only use the Scratch pane in the Navigation view.

◆ **Reference pane** shows images or other media files that are included within a selected HTML page. When you click the HTML file in the Navigation or Links view, all media files that are part of that page appear in the Reference pane.

To view a peripheral pane:

1. Open a site in the Navigation, Links or Diagram view.

2. Choose a peripheral pane from the flyout menu.

   or

   In the View palette,, click the check box in the Navigation tab for the peripheral pane(s) you want (**Figure 16.36**). (In the Diagram view, choose a peripheral pane in the Design tab.) The pane opens in the Navigation, Links, or Diagram view (**Figure 16.37**).

Tips

- To adjust the size of the panes you're viewing, drag the border between the panes.

- When you view a peripheral pane in the Navigation, Links, or Diagram view, the pane is attached to that view. If you switch views and then switch back, the peripheral pane settings are those that were in effect the last time you worked in that view.

- To remove a peripheral pane, click the menu item or check box in the View palette you used to add it. The pane disappears.

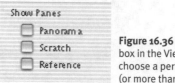

Figure 16.36 Click a check box in the View palette to choose a peripheral pane (or more than one) to view.

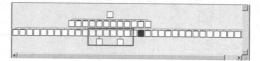

Figure 16.37 This Navigation view includes a Panorama pane. The frame indicates what portion of the site shows in the Navigation view.

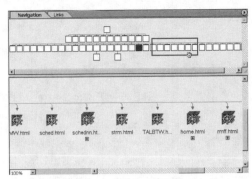

Figure 16.38 Drag the frame around in the Panorama pane to change the focus from one portion of your site to another.

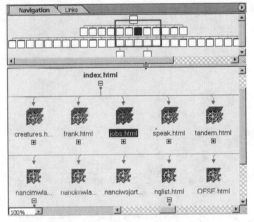

Figure 16.39 When you click a page in the Panorama pane, it is selected there and in the Navigation, Links, or Diagram view.

Figure 16.40 Use the Site Navigator to focus on a portion of your site.

Working with peripheral panes

Each peripheral pane gives you a different way to view and change your site.

To use the Panorama pane:

1. Open a site view (Navigation, Links, or Diagram) and display the Panorama pane.

2. Move the frame within the Panorama pane by dragging the border. The portion of the site you see in the main site view changes as you drag (**Figure 16.38**).

3. Click a page in the Panorama pane. Notice that it's selected both in the peripheral pane and in the main site view (**Figure 16.39**).

   When you select an object in the Panorama pane, it's just as if you had selected it in the main site view. You can view its Inspector, expand or collapse its relationship to other pages in the site, and work with the object in either pane.

✔ Tip

- The Site Navigator works just like the Panorama pane. You may prefer to use it if you just need to move the view of your site around. Unlike the Panorama pane, the Site Navigator (**Figure 16.40**) is simply a representation of the site: You can't select objects within it. To use the Site Navigator, choose Window > Site Navigator.

To use the Scratch pane:

1. Open a site to the Navigation view and display the Scratch pane. Note that you can't use the Scratch pane in Links or Diagram view.

2. Click a page in the main part of the Navigation view. Items in the same folder that are not linked to that page appear in the Scratch pane (**Figure 16.41**).

3. To move a page from the Scratch pane into the hierarchy of the site, drag it into the main Navigation view (watch for lines that indicate where you can drop the icon). The page is moved into the site's hierarchy, (**Figure 16.42**).

4. To create a link, open the selected page (double-click its icon in the Navigation view) and link to the parent page.

To use the Reference pane:

1. Display the Reference pane.

2. Click a Page icon in the Navigation, Links, or Diagram view. Icons for media files on that page appear in the Reference pane (**Figure 16.43**).

3. Click another page in the Navigation or Links view to see the media files linked to it.

✔ Tip

■ Just as the Site Navigator and Panorama pane have a lot in common, the Reference pane shares some capabilities with the In & Out Links palette (see "The Links View" section of this chapter). In fact, the In & Out Links palette is a bit more versatile because you can use it in any site view, and because you can Point & Shoot from the palette to an object within your site, should you need to change a link. You can get to the In & Out Links palette by choosing Window > In & Out Links.

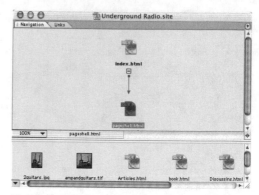

Figure 16.41 Here's the Scratch pane, showing files and other items that are stored in the same folder as the selected page but are not linked to it.

Figure 16.42 When you drag a page from the Scratch pane into the site hierarchy in the Navigation view, the page appears there.

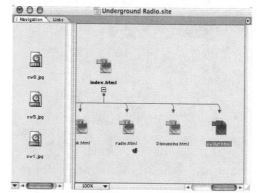

Figure 16.43 The Reference pane (left) shows all of the media files (JPEG images, in this case) that are embedded in the selected HTML page.

▲	Name	Status	Size	
	tandem.html	✔	4.5 KB	
	speak.html	✔	3.3 KB	
	sec.html	✔	918 bytes	
	pubs.html	✔	3.0 KB	
	officewarm.html	✔	1.6 KB	
	jobs.html	✔	5.3 KB	
	index.html	✔	5.5 KB	
▶	hl.html	✔	11.7 KB	
	friends.html	✔	3.4 KB	
	frank.html	✔	3.9 KB	
	creatures.html	✔	4.1 KB	
	book.html	✔	6.1 KB	
	bio.html	✔	3.7 KB	

20 items

Figure 16.44 Click the Status header to sort the objects in the Site window by their status within the site. Click again to reverse the sort order.

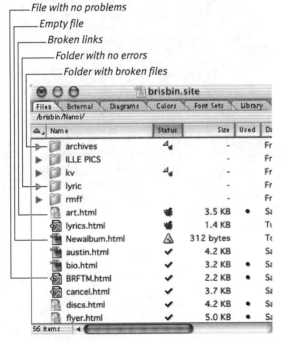

File with no problems
Empty file
Broken links
Folder with no errors
Folder with broken files

brisbin.site

Files | External | Diagrams | Colors | Font Sets | Library

/brisbin/Nanci/

▲	Name	Status	Size	Used	Da
▶	archives	⚠	-		Fr
▶	ILLE PICS		-		Fr
▶	kv	⚠	-		Fr
▶	lyric		-		Fr
▶	rmff		-		Fr
	art.html	🐛	3.5 KB	●	Sa
	lyrics.html	🐛	1.4 KB		Tu
	Newalbum.html	⚠	312 bytes		To
	austin.html	✔	4.2 KB		Sa
	bio.html	✔	3.2 KB	●	Sa
	BRFTM.html	✔	2.2 KB	●	Sa
	cancel.html	✔	3.7 KB		Sa
	discs.html	✔	4.2 KB	●	Sa
	flyer.html	✔	5.0 KB	●	Sa

56 items

Figure 16.45 This Site window includes files and folders whose links are in good shape and some with errors.

Troubleshooting Sites

Earlier in this chapter, I explained how to keep your site organized by examining it with the Navigation and Links views and how to update your site by changing file names. Changing things, though, can introduce errors. GoLive includes several tools for finding and fixing errors.

To identify errors in the Site window:

1. In the Files tab of the Site window, click the Status header (**Figure 16.44**) to sort files and folders by their status.

2. To reverse the sort order, click the Ascending/Descending arrow, located at the upper-right corner of the Site window (Mac only).

The Site window in **Figure 16.45** shows several possible Status indicators.

◆ A **checkmark** indicates that the file contains no errors and that all the links within it are valid.

◆ A **bug** indicates that the file contains broken links.

◆ A **stop sign** indicates that a file is missing.

◆ A **warning marker** (yellow triangle) indicates an empty file. You'll see empty files in your site if you dragged the generic Page icon from the Site set of the Objects palette into the Site window, but haven't yet edited the page.

◆ An **error indicator** next to a folder warns that files within it contain errors.

✔ Tips

■ The error icons you see in the Site window also appear next to files in the Navigation and Links views.

■ Email addresses do not display Status indicators because there's no way to verify them.

To fix broken links:

1. Locate an item in the Site window, Navigation view, or Links view with a bug icon.

2. Double-click the file to open it.

3. Look for any obvious problems, such as missing images. If you find a broken image link, click it to display the Inspector and try to fix the problem by locating the file that should be linked.

4. Choose View > Show Link Warnings.

5. Broken links are highlighted on the page. Click a broken link and use the Inspector to fix it (edit the broken link or Point & Shoot to the Site window). When you fix a link, its bug icon disappears.

6. When you've fixed all the links on the page, save and close the file. The Site window should now display a checkmark in the Status column for the file you've worked on.

To fix links with the In & Out Links palette:

1. In the Site window, Control-click (Mac) or right-click (Windows) a file with a bug icon, and choose Show In & Out Links from the contextual menu. You may want to enlarge the palette

2. In the In & Out Links palette, look for a linked object with a question mark (**Figure 16.46**).

3. To fix the link, click the Fetch URL button in the In & Out Links palette, then Point & Shoot to the correct file in the Site window (**Figure 16.47**).

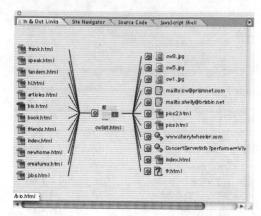

Figure 16.46 Notice the icon with a question mark near the bottom right of the In & Out Links palette. That's the source of the problem indicated by the bug icon next to the `cwlist.html` page in the Site window.

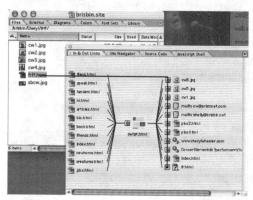

Figure 16.47 To fix a broken link in the In & Out Links palette, Point & Shoot from the problem link to the correct file in the Site window.

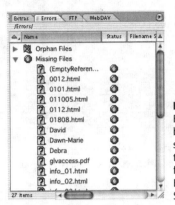

Figure 16.48
Files that can't
be found in the
site appear in
the Missing Files
folder within the
Errors tab of the
Site window.

Figure 16.49 The Error
Inspector shows the
URL for the missing
file—the broken link
that appears in the
source file.

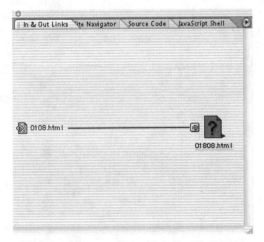

Figure 16.50 When you click a file in the Missing Files
folder, it appears in the In & Out Links palette, along
with the file or files that link to it.

To check a site for missing files:

1. Open the right pane of the Site window.

2. Click the Errors tab to display folders containing broken site items.

3. Open the Missing Files folder. It contains files that are linked to by other files, but can't be found in the site hierarchy (**Figure 16.48**). These files may have been deleted entirely, or their names may have been changed.

4. Click a missing file. The Error Inspector displays the URL for the missing file (**Figure 16.49**). This information may give you a clue to the file's actual whereabouts. You can Browse or Point & Shoot to fix the link.

5. If you can't resolve the broken link's URL, return to the In & Out Links palette. The missing file appears on the right and the file or files that link to it appear on the left (**Figure 16.50**). Now you can decide whether to solve the problem by eliminating the link, recreating the file, or finding the original.

To find a file if you think it has been misplaced within the site:

1. Click the Find Files in Site button (**Figure 16.51**) on the toolbar. The Find dialog box appears, displaying the In Site tab (**Figure 16.52**).

2. Type all or part of the name of the file you want to look for and use the pop-up menus next to "Find item whose" to narrow the search.

3. Click Find.

4. If GoLive finds the file, it will be highlighted in the Site window. If the file has been moved to the wrong folder, you can drag it back into its original location within the site. In that case, a Move Files dialog box will appear.

5. In the Move Files dialog box, click OK to update the site.

To update a link if you find the file:

1. With the folder containing the newly found file visible in the Site window, open the In & Out Links palette if it isn't already open.

2. Click the icon for the missing file in the Missing Files folder. The missing file and the item(s) to which it's linked appear in the In & Out Links palette.

3. Point & Shoot from the missing file in the In & Out Links palette to the file you found in the primary Site window pane. When you release the mouse button, the Change Reference dialog box appears.

4. Click OK to fix the link. The formerly missing file disappears from the Missing Files folder.

Figure 16.51 Click the Find Files in Site button to look for files you've lost.

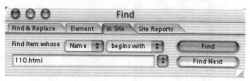

Figure 16.52 The Find dialog box appears, with the In Site tab selected, when you click Find Files in Site.

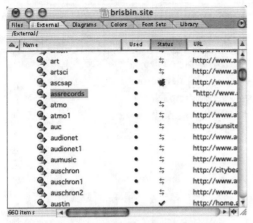

Figure 16.53 When you check external references, GoLive lets you know which URLs are valid and which ones it could not verify by connecting to them. A bug icon indicates a URL that GoLive couldn't find.

Figure 16.54 The Reference Inspector appears when you click a URL in the Site window.

✔ **Tip**

■ You can print a list of the items in the Missing Files folder. Just click within the window and choose File > Print. This list may help you identify any systemic problems with file naming in your site.

To find a file if you think it has been renamed:

1. In the In & Out Links palette, note the files to which the missing file should be connected. Write the file names down or print the In & Out Links palette. You can print the contents of the window by choosing Print from the flyout menu on the In & Out Links palette.

2. Search the site manually or using the Find command for the file.

3. When you locate the file you want, you can restore its original name (by typing it in the Site window or the Name field of the File Inspector), in which case all of the links will be repaired. Or you can open the file and add links according to the list you made from the In & Out Links palette.

To locate and repair external URLs:

1. If you don't have a continuous connection to the Internet, connect now.

2. Click the External tab of the Site window.

3. Choose Site > Get References Used. GoLive checks to see which URLs in the External tab are actually being used in your site and updates the Used column in the Site window.

4. Choose Site > Check External Links. GoLive checks URLs to see whether they are valid. The results appear in the Status column (**Figure 16.53**).

5. Click the Status label to sort URLs by their Status. If GoLive could not connect to a particular URL, the bug icon appears in its Status column.

6. If you find a bad URL, you can see it in the URL column or click it to open the Reference Inspector (**Figure 16.54**).

(continues on next page)

7. Open the In & Out Links palette to see which files within your site link to the URL. This step may help you determine what the URL is and whether it's likely to be in working order. Open the file containing the URL if you need more information.

8. Examine the URL for any obvious problems. If the full URL isn't visible, click the Edit button. The full URL appears in a new dialog box.

9. If all the information you've gathered leads you to believe that the URL should be valid, copy the URL from the Reference Inspector and paste it into your Web browser to check it.

10. If the URL doesn't work, delete it from your site and remove or replace any links to it. If it does work, try using the Check External Links command again to see if GoLive can now connect to the URL.

To find and fix orphan files:

1. In the Errors tab of the Site window, open the Orphan Files folder (**Figure 16.55**). The folder will not be present if there are no orphan files. An orphan file is one that is linked to a file within your site and is stored on your hard disk, but can't be found within your site's folder hierarchy.

2. Drag the orphan file into the Files tab of the Site window. The Copy Files dialog box appears, asking if you want to update references to the relocated file. If you click OK, files within your site that link to the file will be updated and the formerly orphaned file will be added to your site.

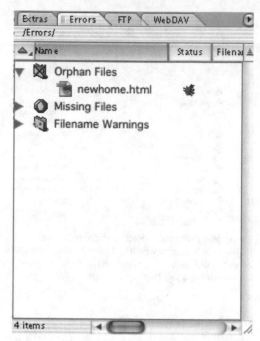

Figure 16.55 Drag an orphan file into the Files tab of the Site window to bring it back into the family and restore links to it.

Site Reports

Site reports provide extremely useful information about your site and its files that isn't available elsewhere. You can search for files by name and content using other tabs in the Find dialog box, but site reports are more analytical. They provide information about how your files work as a site, not simply as a collection of objects.

Site report options

You can search for five kinds of site information using the Site Reports tab.

- **File Info** includes options for file size, download time (based on file size and type), and date information.

- **Errors** lets you look for the kind of problems listed in the Errors tab of the Site window, as well as for image tags missing some attributes and HTML that is incompatible with specified Web browsers.

- **Site Objects** allows you to search for components, fonts, and colors (all stored as objects within a GoLive site) or pages that include a URL (Web site or email address) that appears in the site's External tab.

- **Links** gives you the option of searching for files with one of several protocols or with a particular file extension. You can also look for pages with external links.

- **Accessibility** allows you to analyze your site's accessibility to visitors with disabilities, based on the W3C accessibility guidelines.

- **Misc** lets you look for files that have a particular hierarchical relationship with other files. Specify a file and search for others that are within a set number of clicks of that item.

To create a site report:

1. Choose Site > Site Report. The Find dialog box appears, with the Site Reports tab selected (**Figure 16.56**).

2. In the File Info tab, click the check boxes to activate items you want to include in your report.

3. Choose an option from a pop-up menu and enter a value in the adjacent field. **Figure 16.57** shows a search for files that will take longer than 30 seconds to download at 56 Kbps.

4. Choose additional search criteria from the current tab or from one of the others. Site reports can be based on several search criteria.

5. Once you've selected all the criteria you want, click the Search button. When GoLive has finished searching your site, a Report Results window appears showing the files that match your criteria (**Figure 16.58**).

✔ Tip

■ Before you search, be sure that you have only the criteria you want to use selected. Click the Reset button to clear all criteria before beginning a new search.

The Report Results window contains three tabs, each of which displays your search results differently:

◆ **Files** lists files that match your search criteria.

◆ **Navigation** looks just like the Navigation view for your site. In a site report, the files that matched your search criteria are spotlighted. You cannot change or move items in this version of the Navigation view.

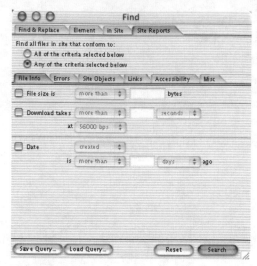

Figure 16.56 Create site report queries in the Site Reports tab of the Find dialog box.

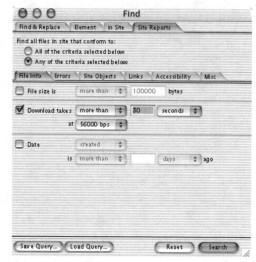

Figure 16.57 This search will locate all files that will take longer than 30 seconds to download using a 56 Kbps modem.

Figure 16.58 Site reports look like this. You see the name, modification date, and URL (among other things) associated with each file.

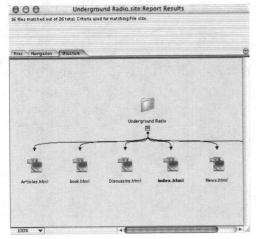

Figure 16.59 In the Structure view, you see all the files in your site report displayed in their positions within the site's file hierarchy.

◆ **Structure** displays the position of search results within the site hierarchy. The root folder and any folders that are part of the family of the result file(s) appear in the Structure tab (**Figure 16.59**).

✔ Tip

■ To work with items that come up as search results, Control-click (Mac) or right-click (Windows) on the object in the Files tab of the Report Results window. You'll see the usual file-opening options. You can also see where the file appears within the site by looking at the File Inspector or the URL column of the Files tab.

Reusing site report queries

The kind of information generated by a site report is often information that you want to access again and again. You might, for example, generate a new site report before each site update. You could design a report that looks for site trouble spots and helps maintain the integrity of your links and navigation hierarchy. GoLive allows you to save site report queries you may want to repeat; you'll find them in the Site Reports tab of the Find dialog box.

To save a site report query:

1. Create a query that you would like to save for future use. Include as many search criteria as you like.

2. Create a site report using the query to see how much information you're able to gather.

3. When you're satisfied with the query, click Save Query in the Site Reports tab and name the query.

To use a saved query:

1. In the Site Reports tab, click Load Query.

2. Locate a saved query and click Open.

3. In the Site Reports tab, click Search. Results appear in the Report Results window.

✔ Tips

■ Site report query files use the extension `.glqs`. Preserve this extension when you name saved queries.

■ You can store queries anywhere you like. The site data folder is a good place. If you use a lot of queries, you can create a folder for them within the site data folder.

■ If you decide to change a query you've already created and saved, there's no automatic way to update it. You'll have to resave it with the same name as the older version of the query, and in the same folder, overwriting the older version.

PUBLISHING SITES

After the text is typed, images placed, links connected, and errors checked, it's time to put your site on the Web. If your Web server is located in your own office, this may simply be a matter of copying folders to the server on your LAN. If you use an ISP, you'll need to use FTP to transfer your files to a remote server. You may even use WebDAV to develop and publish your site. (For more on using the Adobe Web Workgroup Server, see Chapter 18.)

Wherever your Web site lives, GoLive includes tools that can help you get everything in order for the big upload.

In this chapter, I'll cover

◆ Choices for publishing your site

◆ Two kinds of FTP

◆ Exporting a site

◆ Using WebDAV

Choices for Publishing Your Site

GoLive provides four ways to move a site or pages of a site from your computer to a Web server. You can use the following:

- FTP tab of the Site window
- FTP browser
- Site export
- WebDAV

The FTP browser and the FTP tab of the Site window are both FTP (File Transfer Protocol) clients. An FTP client gives you password-protected access to a Web server's files and allows you to add or remove items using Internet-standard commands. The Site export feature doesn't actually upload files to a Web server, it merely allows you to prepare your files for uploading. Finally, GoLive's WebDAV client tool gives you access to WebDAV servers for collaborative work.

We'll look more closely at each of these later in this chapter. For now, we'll focus on getting your files ready for whichever option you choose.

Getting ready to publish

Before you publish a site for the first time, make sure you're ready. The site organization, link checking, and error-correction steps I showed you in the previous chapter should all be completed before you publish. When you're ready to upload your site, be sure to clean up the site, removing all unused items and ensuring that everything is where you want it to be.

Next, configure access to a server (you can set up as many servers as you like) in GoLive.

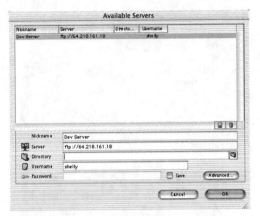

Figure 17.1 Add new FTP or WebDAV servers in the Available Servers dialog box.

Setting up server access

Before you connect to an FTP or WebDAV server, you must configure access to the server or servers from GoLive. Once these options are set, you can choose a server and connect to it from either of GoLive's two FTP clients or, if you're using a WebDAV server, from the WebDAV client within GoLive.

To configure access to a server:

1. Choose Edit > Servers. The Available Servers dialog box appears.

2. Click the New Item button to add a server.

3. Enter a nickname (the name the server will have in menus and dialog boxes).

4. Type the address of the server in the Server field, including the protocol (for example, `ftp://ftp.domain.com` or `http://www.domain.com`). **Figure 17.1** shows the server address entered in the correct format.

5. Type the path to your directory in the Directory field.

6. Enter your username.

7. To have GoLive remember your password, click the Save check box and enter your password. Otherwise, you will be asked for your password whenever you connect.

8. Click OK to finish configuring the server.

✔ Tips

■ You can locate the directory that will contain your Web site files by clicking the Browse icon (next to the Directory field). GoLive will connect to the server and ask for your password. Choose a directory and click OK (**Figure 17.2**).

■ GoLive supports the Mac OS keychain, a password-management tool that allows you to enter a single password for all keychain-supporting applications. If you've set up a keychain on your Mac, GoLive will ask whether you would like to manage server access with the keychain. If you do, the passwords for servers you add in GoLive are added to the keychain, and you no longer need to enter them each time you log on. If you don't want to use the keychain to manage access or you haven't set up the keychain, just choose not to add passwords to the keychain when prompted.

Using multiple servers

You can configure and use as many FTP or WebDAV servers as you like. Once configured, each new server appears on the FTP or WebDAV Server submenu, allowing you to choose it when working with your site. Choose the default server for each site in the Site Settings dialog box.

Figure 17.2 Choose the upload directory for your site files.

Two Kinds of FTP

Of GoLive's two FTP clients, the FTP tab of the Site window is the best choice for uploading a complete site. It's easy to use and nicely integrated with the rest of the Site window. If you want to upload just a few files, one at a time, or if you need to download files from your Web server, try the FTP browser.

Using the FTP tab

When you connect to an FTP server from the Site window, GoLive helps you determine which files to upload and does the work of copying files and folders for you. It's much easier to use than the FTP Browser when you're uploading a site for the first time or later on when you need to perform a major, complicated update.

You can make a variety of configuration choices for your server uploads in the Site Settings dialog box. You can choose to make these settings global or apply them only to the site that's currently open.

To configure FTP upload settings:

1. Open a site.

2. Choose Site > Settings.

   or

   In the Site window, Control-click (Mac) or right-click (Windows) and choose Settings from the contextual menu.

3. Click FTP & WebDAV Server.

4. Choose a server from the FTP Server pop-up menu. You'll see servers you've configured in the Available Servers dialog box. You can also reach the dialog box by choosing Edit Server.

5. Click Upload/Sync Times.

(continues on next page)

6. Click the "Site specific settings" check box. The fields in the window become active (**Figure 17.3**).

7. Choose whether to use the Publish status of folders or files to determine which files will be uploaded to the Web server. If you leave the boxes checked, only files that are labeled "Publish" in the File Inspector will be uploaded.

8. Leave the "Upload/Sync linked files only" option checked to instruct GoLive to ignore files that are not linked to anything within your site.

9. The "Show list of files to upload" and "Show options dialog" check boxes allow you to remove files from planned uploads individually.

10. Check the "Strip HTML code for" check boxes to remove GoLive-specific code, comments, or extra spaces.

11. Choose "Strip GoLive data from media files" to reduce the size of these files by eliminating smart object data added by GoLive.

12. If you're using the Script Library in support of GoLive actions in your site, select Flatten Script Library to compress this file before uploading. For more on the Script Library, see Chapter 19, "Using Actions."

13. Click OK to close the Site Settings window.

To connect to the FTP server:

1. With your site open, click FTP Server Connect/Disconnect on the toolbar.

   or

   Control-click (Mac) or right-click (Windows) in the Site window, and choose FTP Server > Connect from the contextual menu.

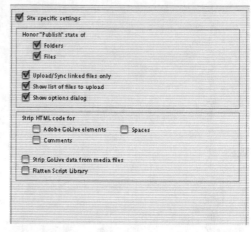

Figure 17.3 Upload settings become available when you click the "Site specific settings" check box in the Site Settings dialog box.

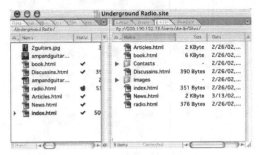

Figure 17.4 Connecting to the FTP server opens the right pane of the Site window to the FTP tab.

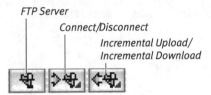

FTP Server

Connect/Disconnect

Incremental Upload/
Incremental Download

Figure 17.5 When you're connected to an FTP server, these options on the toolbar become active.

Figure 17.6 Use the Upload Options dialog box to eliminate files from a site upload. Click the Strip Options button to make special final changes in files before the upload.

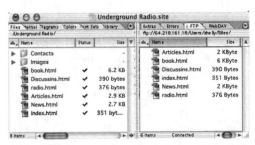

Figure 17.7 Files and folders that have been uploaded appear in the FTP tab of the Site window.

2. If you've set up GoLive to request a password each time you connect to the server, you will be asked for it now. Type your password. When GoLive has connected to the FTP server, the right pane of the Site window opens (if it's not already visible) and displays the directory for your site (**Figure 17.4**). The FTP options on the toolbar become active (**Figure 17.5**).

To upload a site for the first time:

1. Control-click (Mac) or right-click (Windows) in the Site window, and choose FTP Server > Upload All from the contextual menu.

or

Choose Site > FTP Server > Upload All.

2. The Upload Options dialog box appears (**Figure 17.6**). You have one more chance to globally limit the files that will be uploaded. These are the same as the Site Settings options described earlier in this chapter.

3. To make final adjustments to the files before uploading, click the Strip Options button. These options are the same ones found under the "Strip HTML code" area of the Site Settings window and described earlier in this chapter. When you finish choosing upload options, click OK.

4. In the Upload Site window, verify the list of files to be uploaded and uncheck any file you don't want to upload. Click OK. Your site's files will be uploaded to the server. When the upload is complete, the files and folders appear in the FTP tab (**Figure 17.7**).

Upload options

When you've successfully uploaded your site to an FTP server, you can update it by uploading new files or replacing changed ones. These are GoLive's upload options:

◆ **Upload All** copies all local site files to the server.

◆ **Incremental Upload** copies local files that have been created or changed since the last site upload (items whose modification dates are later on the local site than on the server).

◆ **Upload Modified Items** uploads only files that have been edited in GoLive since the last upload. Preference is always given to local files. If a file within your local site has changed since the last upload, but is older than its counterpart on the server, the local file will be uploaded anyway.

You can also select individual items to upload manually.

To upload items incrementally:

1. Connect to the FTP server containing your site.

2. Choose Incremental Upload from the toolbar or from the contextual menu.

3. Make selections in the Upload Options dialog box if you wish.

4. The Upload Site window displays files that meet your upload criteria and have been added or modified since your last upload (**Figure 17.8**). Uncheck any items you wish to exclude from the upload. When the upload is complete, GoLive updates your view of the server in the Site window.

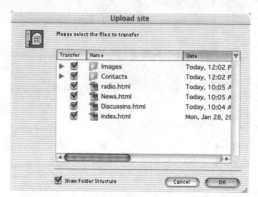

Figure 17.8 Files and folders that have changed since your last upload appear in the Upload Site window.

✔ Tip

■ The procedure for updating modified items is the same as described above. Choose Upload Modified Items from the contextual menu or from the FTP Server submenu of the Site menu.

Two Kinds of FTP

To upload selected items:

1. Connect to the FTP server.

2. In the Files tab of the Site window, select files or folders you want to upload.

3. Control-click (Mac) or right-click (Windows) and choose FTP Server > Upload Selection from the contextual menu.

4. Make any changes you wish in the Upload Options dialog box and click OK. In the Upload window, uncheck files to exclude then click OK to begin the upload.

✔ Tip

■ If you're thinking that it would be easier to drag selected files and folders from the Site window to the FTP tab, you're right, except that when you drag, GoLive doesn't offer any upload filtering options. Your files are simply copied, replacing previous versions or adding new files to the site without regard to their status. You can drag files to quickly add or update a file or two, if you wish.

Downloading sites

The FTP client's upload commands move files from the local site to an FTP server, but you can also download all or part of a site from the server to update your local copy. As with uploading, you can download the full site, download changed files, or select individual files to copy to the local site. Download commands appear on the Site menu and (when connected to a server) in the contextual menu.

TWO KINDS OF FTP

The FTP Browser

Just like any FTP client (such as Fetch, Interarchy, CuteFTP, or most Web browsers), GoLive's FTP Browser can upload and download files—from one file at a time to a whole site's worth. The FTP Browser is designed to give you a clear picture of the directory structure available on your FTP server and let you pick and choose files to copy. Like other FTP clients, it can also be used to grab any file stored on a remote server, whether it's a component of your Web site or not.

To use the FTP Browser:

1. Make sure that your computer can connect to the Internet before proceeding with these steps. If you can connect, but aren't already online, GoLive will connect you automatically.

2. With GoLive open (you can be working within a site or not), choose File > FTP Browser. The FTP Browser opens (**Figure 17.9**).

3. From the pop-up meu, choose a server or add a new server by choosing Edit Server (see "To configure access to a server" earlier in this chapter).

4. Click the Connect button. When the connection is complete, the server's directories and files appear (**Figure 17.10**).

5. Navigate through the directories as you would in the Finder or Windows Explorer.

6. To upload a file or folder, drag it from the Finder, Windows Explorer, or the Site window into the FTP Browser.

7. When you finish working with this server, click Disconnect.

8. You can download files by dragging them from the FTP Browser into the Files tab of the Site window or into the Finder or Windows Explorer.

Figure 17.9 The FTP Browser is empty until you choose and connect to a server.

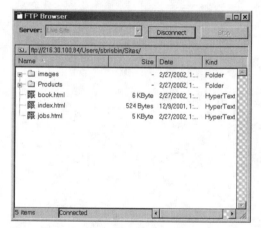

Figure 17.10 After you connect to an FTP server, files and directories appear. They look pretty much like Mac or Windows files and folders.

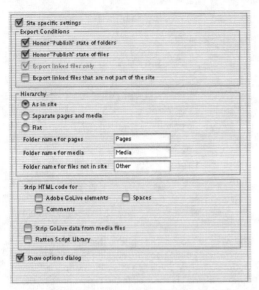

Figure 17.11 Choose export options in the Site Settings dialog box.

Exporting a Site

If you're not quite ready to upload your site, or if you need to prepare it according to a structure established by your Webmaster or ISP, you can use the Export Site command as the first step in publishing the site to a Web server.

Although most people will find FTP a better choice than exporting, there are a few circumstances in which it can be useful. For example, if your Web server is a computer on your network, you can export a site and drag it into the proper directory on the server using the familiar Finder or Windows Explorer interface and using your existing file-access privileges. You can also specify publishing options, like limiting an exported site to files that are being used within the site or files that include a Publish state ("flag").

Like FTP, GoLive's site export function has settings that govern which items in a site are affected. You can modify these settings in the Export area of the Preferences dialog box if you want them to apply to all of your sites or in the Site Settings dialog box if you want them to be used only for a particular site. In either dialog box, you can set options ahead of time or when you export the site. To do the latter, you'll need to click the "Show options dialog" check box at the bottom of the Export panel of the Site Settings dialog box.

To choose site export options:

1. Choose Edit > Preferences, then open the Site area and click Export.

   or

   Choose Site > Settings, then click Export and activate the Export pane by checking the "Site specific settings" box (**Figure 17.11**).

   (continues on next page)

2. Choose settings under the Export Conditions heading. If you want GoLive to export only folders and files marked Publish, be sure to select the appropriate check boxes. Also, note that if you turn off "Honor 'Publish' state of files," GoLive activates "Export linked files only," in case you want to select it.

3. If you want to export the site using a different folder hierarchy than it has now, choose "Separate pages and media" or Flat. The first option creates one folder for HTML pages and one for media files. The Flat option places all files in the same folder. A flat structure usually isn't the best way to set up a site, but you do have the option if you don't want to use folders.

4. Change the names of folders that will contain your exported HTML files, images, and graphics, if you wish.

5. Use the "Strip HTML Code for" options to indicate whether or not GoLive should remove GoLive-specific code, extra space, and comments before it exports site files. You can also flatten the Script Library, if necessary.

6. Leave "Show options dialog box" checked to view these options again at the time you export the site.

To export a site:

1. With a site open and the Site window visible, choose Site > Site Export.

or

Control-click (Mac) or right-click (Windows) and choose Export Site from the contextual menu. If you chose to show options when you export your site, the Export Site Options dialog box appears (**Figure 17.12**).

2. Click Export. In the Save dialog box, choose a location for the exported site, and click Save. GoLive exports the site.

Figure 17.12 Most of the options that appear in the Site Settings dialog box are also in the Export Site Options window. You'll see this window only if "Show options dialog" is checked in the Export pane of the Site Settings dialog box.

EXPORTING A SITE

Using WebDAV

WebDAV (Web-based Distributed Authoring and versioning) is a server-side technology that makes it possible for a group of people to work collaboratively on a single project, all from different, even remote, locations. Members of the group create files locally and upload them (check in) to a shared server. Members can also download (check out) and modify files and then return them to the server. The server manages group access and transmits information about who is working on which file. WebDAV is ideally suited for Web development, where several people often work together to develop a site.

GoLive supports uploading files to WebDAV-enabled servers. To use WebDAV with GoLive, WebDAV must be enabled on your development server. GoLive ships with its own WebDAV server, Adobe Web Workgroup Server, which you may decide to use for collaborative development. Whether you use the Adobe Web Workgroup Server or not, the information in this section will only apply to those who have access to a WebDAV server. I'll cover the Adobe server in Chapter 18. In this section, I'll approach WebDAV access from the client point of view.

✔ Tip

■ If you are currently unable to use it, but are interested in learning more about WebDAV, check out WebDAV Resources at www.webdav.org. If you're a Mac user, also see www.webdav.org/goliath/.

GoLive and WebDAV

GoLive's WebDAV interface looks and acts a lot like the FTP tab of the Site window. You configure and upload files to a WebDAV server the same way you do using GoLive's FTP tool.

You can work with WebDAV servers using one of GoLive's two WebDAV client interfaces—the WebDAV tab of the Site window or the WebDAV Browser.

First, set up global WebDAV access in GoLive, then connect to a specific server to transfer files.

To enable WebDAV server access in the Site window:

1. Configure a WebDAV server as described in the "Setting up server access" section earlier in this chapter. You may need to contact your Webmaster to obtain the precise URL for the server. Adobe Web Workgroup Server WebDAV URLs, for example, are in the format `http://server.domain:port/webdav/<<sitename>>`.

2. With a site open, choose Site > Settings.

3. Click FTP & WebDAV Server.

4. Choose a WebDAV server from the pop-up menu.

5. Click Upload/Sync Times and choose settings, as described in the "Using the FTP Tab" section of this chapter.

6. Click OK to finish configuring the WebDAV server.

Figure 17.13 Connect to a WebDAV Server from the toolbar.

Figure 17.14 You won't see files in the WebDAV tab unless you're connected to the server, as indicated here.

To connect to a WebDAV server for the first time:

1. Make sure that you have access to a site on a WebDAV server and that you know the exact URL and site name.

2. Create a new site in GoLive. Give it the name of the remote site you will connect to.

3. Configure access to the server in GoLive as described earlier, and associate the server with the open site by clicking FTP & WebDAV Server in the Site Settings dialog box, and choosing the server from the WebDAV pop-up menu.

4. Choose Site > WebDAV Server > Connect.

   or

   Click WebDAV Server Connect/Disconnect (**Figure 17.13**) on the toolbar.

   or

   Control-click (Mac) or right-click (Windows) in the left pane of the Site window and choose WebDAV Server > Connect from the contextual menu. GoLive connects to the server and the server's contents appear in the WebDAV tab of the Site window (**Figure 17.14**).

Uploading and downloading

The options available for uploading and downloading files to a WebDAV server are similar to those I described in the FTP sections of this chapter. You can transfer all files that have changed since the last site update (modified files), or you can select individual items to transfer. The WebDAV client also includes a synchronize feature that compares the local and remote site and makes them identical by copying the newest versions of files to and from each site.

(continues on next page)

To synchronize a site on a WebDAV server:

1. Open a site and connect to the server.

2. Control-click (Mac) or right-click (Windows) within the WebDAV tab of the Site window and choose Synchronize.

   or

   Click the WebDAV Synchronize All button on the toolbar. Files are copied from the server to the local site. If the local site contains files that are not on the server or files with the same name that are newer, those will be copied to the server.

To transfer modified files:

1. Open a site and connect to a WebDAV server containing a version of the site.

2. Click the WebDAV Upload Modified Items or WebDAV Download Modified Items button on the toolbar.

   or

   Control-click (Mac) or right-click (Windows) in the left pane of the Site window and choose WebDAV Server > Upload Modified or Download Modified. The Synchronize dialog box appears, showing which items will be moved (**Figure 17.15**). Arrows indicate files that will be copied to or from the server. Since this is an upload, files will only be copied to the server, not from it.

3. Examine the file list in the Synchronize dialog box. If you want to change what happens to a file, click the button in the column between the Site and Server columns to change the file's status (**Figure 17.16**).

   ◆ **Right-pointing arrow:** The file will be copied to the server.

   ◆ **Left-pointing arrow:** The file will be copied to the local site.

Figure 17.15 The Synchronize window shows files and folders on the local and server sites.

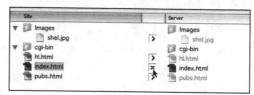

Figure 17.16 You can choose to add or skip files for synchronization by clicking on the status indicators in the middle column.

Site: BikeSite.site/pubs.html Modified: Today, 5:21 PM Action: This item will be uploaded to the server.	Server: This file does not exist. Action: This item will be created on the server.

Figure 17.17 Click a file's name or icon in the Synchronize window to see information about the file at the bottom of the window.

◆ **An X:** The file will be deleted from the local and remote sites.

◆ **A warning icon:** The file has been modified on both the local hard drive and the WebDAV server.

◆ **A slash:** The file is set to be skipped, even if it has been modified since the last upload.

◆ **No icon:** No action will be taken because the files are synchronized.

4. To see an explanation of the condition of a file, click the file name or icon. Information about the file and its status appear below the list of files to be synchronized (**Figure 17.17**).

5. When you're satisfied with the synchronization options you've chosen, click Synchronize.

To upload or download selected items:

◆ Drag items between the Files tab of the Site window and the WebDAV tab, while connected to the server. Verify your actions in the Synchronize dialog box.

To use the WebDAV Browser:

1. Choose File > WebDAV Browser. You don't need to have a GoLive site open. Choose a WebDAV server from the pop-up menu.

2. Click Connect. The contents of your Web directory appear in the WebDAV Browser.

✔ Tip

■ Frankly, the WebDAV Browser isn't particularly useful. Since the whole point of WebDAV is to compare your local site to the version on the server, it makes more sense to use the WebDAV tab of the Site window to upload and download files. You also won't have access to WebDAV synchronization features when you use the browser. If you're not managing your site with GoLive, however, using the browser is your only choice for adding files to a server using WebDAV.

THE
WORKGROUP SERVER

Web sites were once collections of HTML files and images that could easily be built and maintained by one Webmaster or designer. Many of today's sites are large, unwieldy things that, because they represent the organization's online presence, require the involvement of a group of people, perhaps even an entire corporate department. Sites are also typically larger, comprising scripts and databases, in addition to the familiar images and HTML docs.

GoLive's contribution to collaborative site development is the Adobe Web Workgroup Server, an application that lets you host a site on a server and allow a group of designers, developers, and users to access it locally as it is being built. This chapter describes the Workgroup Server and shows you how to build, develop, and manage a collaborative site using GoLive as the development environment and the Workgroup Server as the storage and management tool.

In this chapter, I'll cover

◆ Workgroup server architecture

◆ Setting up a workgroup server

◆ Collaborative authoring

Workgroup Server Architecture

The Adobe Web Workgroup Server is a collaborative authoring environment that consists of a Web-based Distributed Authority and Versioning (WebDAV) server with browser-based administration tools. WebDAV is a client-server technology that allows a group of users to share access to files stored on a server, checking individual files out for editing, and then checking them back into the server so that others may have access to them. Besides the obvious version control advantage of this structure, WebDAV makes it possible for managers to keep track of where files are and who has worked on them.

GoLive 5 introduced many users to WebDAV technology. Adobe didn't invent WebDAV, but GoLive was certainly among the pioneering applications that linked the Web development process with the management of workflow among a group of developers over a network. GoLive 5 supported uploading documents to an existing WebDAV server. The GoLive 6 bundle includes the free Adobe Web Workgroup Server software, taking the collaborative features of GoLive 5 a few leaps forward. As in the previous version, you can use the GoLive application as a WebDAV client, whether you're connecting to an Adobe workgroup server or another WebDAV server. And non-GoLive WebDAV clients (including Adobe Illustrator, by the way) can also connect to an Adobe workgroup server.

Though you can connect to an Adobe workgroup server with any WebDAV client application, using GoLive gives you much greater power to manage a workgroup site on the server. All of GoLive's advanced site-management tools are available to you, whether you're working exclusively on your own computer or sharing access to a site that is stored on a server.

✔ Tip

- An Adobe workgroup server can be hosted on Mac OS X and Windows 2000 or XP computers. You can connect to any Adobe workgroup server, regardless of platform, from any version of GoLive 5 or 6.

All about WebDAV

Simply put, WebDAV provides a means for a group of people to share access to files stored on a server. Those who have access can download (check out) a shared file to their local computer, view and edit it, and then return (check in) the file to the server so that others in the group have access to it. While a user works on a shared file, the copy of the file on the server is locked so that others cannot download and alter it. Once checked back in to the server, the file is available for check out by others. Users and administrators of WebDAV servers can view the list of files available on the server, including their current status (checked in or out, for example).

When GoLive is used as a WebDAV client, this client-server structure is applied to the GoLive Site window. When you log on to a WebDAV server and access a site for the first time, you download elements of the site to your computer. The site appears as a local site in the GoLive Site window. If you work on a file and then check it back in to the server, your version replaces the server version, and is downloaded to others' computers when they connect to the server.

WebDAV servers, like other file servers, can support access privileges that limit who can connect to the server and what they can access once there, though access control is not a part of the WebDAV protocol.

Workgroup server nuts and bolts

The Adobe Web Workgroup Server uses WebDAV and Simple Object Access Protocol (SOAP) to achieve a much higher level of collaboration management technology than was available in GoLive 5. Administrators set up sites, user accounts, and access privileges through a browser-based interface. Multiple administrators can manage a workgroup server, and users can be given access to individual sites on the server or to all sites.

Server hardware and network considerations

You will need a computer running Windows 2000, Windows XP, or Mac OS X to host your workgroup server. The server will also require a constant connection to the Internet (if you intend to give remote users access to the server) and to your local network. If people who work outside your office—not on your local network—will need access to the server, the server computer must also have a static IP address, providing it a permanent access URL.

If your network is a busy one, you can enhance the server's performance by giving it its own network segment or dedicating a high-speed, switched Ethernet point to it.

Although you can run other applications on the workgroup server computer, consider carefully what other tasks the machine must perform while running the workgroup server, especially if you need to give many users simultaneous access to the network. The server's primary tasks are to download and upload files and to maintain the integrity of the site's links.

✔ Tip

- Security is an important consideration for any networked computer, especially if the computer is a server containing valuable data—like your Web site. Before you implement a workgroup server, consider the security implications, especially if you will allow computers outside your network to access the server. Consider installing a firewall on your network so that unauthorized users outside your network can't get to it. To give trusted users access from the Internet, use the firewall's configuration options to allow specific addresses inside the firewall.

WORKGROUP SERVER ARCHITECTURE

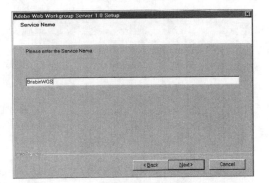

Figure 18.1 Name your Windows 2000 workgroup server.

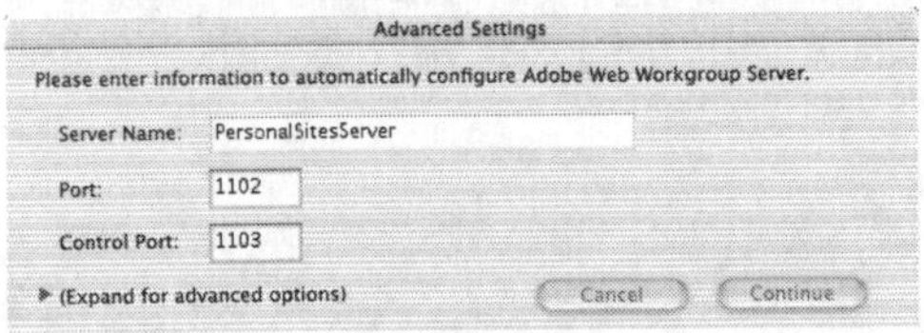

Figure 18.2 The Advanced Settings dialog box in the Mac OS X Workgroup Server installation program offers name and port settings, as well as some advanced options in the lower-left corner.

Setting up a Workgroup Server

Once you've chosen a computer to host your server and have connected it to your local network and/or the Internet, you're ready to install and set up the server. Adobe provides a wizard that helps you through the process of getting the software onto your computer and performing a very basic configuration. The next steps are to establish user accounts and create or import the site or sites you plan to build with your workgroup.

The names and locations of a few initial configuration settings are different for Mac OS X and Windows. I will describe the basic procedure and explain your options.

To install a workgroup server:

1. Run the Adobe Web Workgroup Server installer program and follow the screens that ask you to enter your serial number, choose a language, and accept the license agreement.

2. Windows: When you reach the Adobe Web Workgroup Server 1.0 setup screen (**Figure 18.1**), give your workgroup server a name and click Next.

   or

   Mac: Name the server in the Advanced Settings dialog box (**Figure 18.2**).

3. You can change the server's Working Port and Control Port (the defaults are 1102 and 1103, respectively), or leave these settings unchanged. You should leave the port settings alone unless you have a specific reason to change them, and you're sure that the port you want to use is not associated with another Internet application or protocol.

   (continues on next page)

4. When the installer has finished, it will launch a Web browser and show a one-time initial login screen (**Figure 18.3**). Read the instructions on the screen, replace the default login name, and type a password. After you click Save, the window shows your server's GoLive workgroup and WebDAV URLs.

5. On the Adobe Web Workgroup Server login screen (**Figure 18.4**), enter the master login name and password to connect to the server.

✔ Tips

■ Make a note of the URLs in the server administration window. Bookmarking the admin screen gives you quick access to the server's administrative interface from the server computer. Clients use the GoLive workgroup and WebDAV URLs to log in to the server.

■ To administer the server from a remote computer, use a URL with this format: `http://<server IP address>:1102`. If the server has a hostname (`myserver.company.com`), you can use the domain name, a colon, and the port number to administer the server.

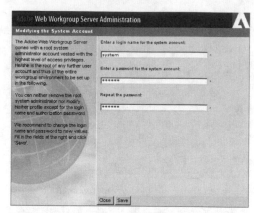

Figure 18.3 Type a master login name and password for the server. This account has all privileges required to manage the workgroup server.

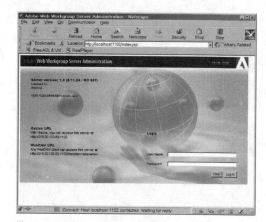

Figure 18.4 The Adobe Web Workgroup Server Administration screen appears in a Web browser. Here you'll find the server's GoLive and WebDAV URLs. You can also log in to the server to perform administrative tasks.

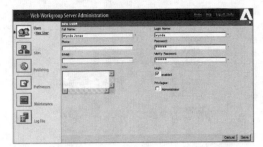

Figure 18.5 Create a user account by adding login and contact information.

Establishing administrative access

One or more administrators can manage a workgroup server. Adding users and creating sites are among the administrator's first tasks. The following steps apply to creating any user account. To begin, use the system account to create an administrative user account and then log in to add workgroup user accounts.

To add a user account to the server:

1. From a Web browser, connect to the workgroup server and log in using an Administrator account. (If this is the first account you've created, you will need to log in from the system account.)

2. Click the Users button on the left side of the window. A list of current server users appears.

3. Click the New User button to view a form where you can add a user account (**Figure 18.5**).

4. Enter contact and login information for the new user. By default, login is enabled, allowing the user to connect to the server from GoLive or a WebDAV client or, if the user is an administrator, from a browser.

5. If the user will be an administrator, click the Administrator check box. Click Save to complete the user's account.

Beginning workgroup sites

A single workgroup server can support any number of workgroup sites, assuming it has the disk space to accommodate them and can handle the number of users who need access to them. You can give any workgroup server user access to as many or as few sites as you wish. First, of course, you need to begin a site.

Starting a site from the server

There are several ways to start a site and add its files to a workgroup server. You can create a workgroup site using the workgroup server's Web interface, or you can use GoLive to start and upload the site to the server.

To create a new site on the server, you can begin the process from scratch or by building a site that's based on a template. You can also choose to import files from another server, whether they are contained in a GoLive site or not. Sound familiar? These are the same options that are available when you create a site in GoLive.

From the main server administration screen, you can begin a site with the Setup Wizard (**Figure 18.6**) or by clicking the Sites button.

To create a site with the Setup Wizard:

1. Log in to the workgroup server from an account with administrative access.

2. Click the New Site link.

3. Choose Blank Site and click Next.

4. Name the site and click Next.

5. On the next screen (**Figure 18.7**), name the site's publish server—the server where your site will be copied when you're finished developing it.

6. Choose whether you'll publish the site to a folder (File) or to an FTP server.

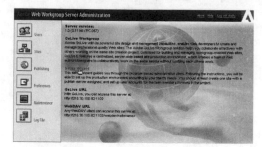

Figure 18.6 Click the Setup Wizard link or the Sites link to begin a new workgroup site.

Figure 18.7 Choose and set up a publish server for the new site.

✔ Tip

■ If you begin your site by clicking the Sites link (the next step is to click the New Site link), the server will take you through the same steps that appear in the Setup Wizard. There are two differences: the Setup Wizard offers more explanatory text at each step and prompts you to give users access to the site, and the New Site method conducts the site-creation process in its own browser window.

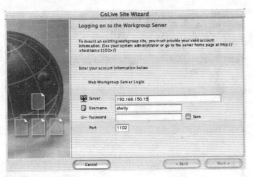

Figure 18.8 Enter server login information to begin a new workgroup site.

7. If you use a proxy server or a passive-mode FTP server, check the appropriate boxes and click Next.

8. When asked if you want to add another publish server, click Yes if you do and configure the server. Otherwise, click Finish.

Starting a workgroup site in GoLive

You can begin a workgroup site within GoLive, as long as you have network access to the server and have sufficient access privileges. The process is similar to creating a single-user site, but the site source options are a bit different. The Blank Site and Import Files from a Local Folder options available for single-user sites also appear in the workgroup version of the Site Wizard. But instead of the options for importing files from a server and creating a site from a template, the workgroup options allow you to mount an existing workgroup site from the server or to import from an existing single-user site.

To create a workgroup site in GoLive:

1. With GoLive open, choose File > New Site.

2. In the Site Wizard, choose Workgroup Site and click Next.

3. Choose Blank Site and click Next.

4. Enter the IP address or domain name of your workgroup server in the Server field. You can append the server's port number (1102 by default) to the server address, or you can enter it in the Port field.

5. Enter your user name and password. You must have administrative access to the server to create a site. **Figure 18.8** shows the completed screen. Click Next.

6. Enter a name for the new site and click Next.

✔ **Tip**

■ Use the workgroup server to start your site if you want to create a new site from a GoLive template or by importing files from an FTP or HTTP server.

(continues on next page)

7. Click the Browse button if you want to choose a different folder on your hard drive to hold a local copy of the site.

8. Click the Advanced button if you want to change URL formatting options. (For more on URL handling options, see Chapter 15, "Building Sites.") Click Next. GoLive creates the site on your computer and on the workgroup server. **Figure 18.9** shows the local copy.

Giving users access to workgroup sites

Once you have created a workgroup site—regardless of the method you used to do it—you must give users access to it. Until you do, the creator of the site is the only person who can mount the site locally.

To give users access to a site:

1. Be sure that you have created user accounts for each person who needs access to the site.

2. Log in to the workgroup server using a Web browser, as described earlier.

3. Click the Sites link.

4. Click the name of the site to which you want to provide user access. Information about the site and a list of server users appears. Checked boxes indicate users who can access the site (**Figure 18.10**).

5. Check the names of users you wish to give access to this site. If you need to add a user account, click the New User button, fill out information for the new user, and return to the screen for this site to add access for the user.

6. Click Save.

7. Give each user the workgroup server URL, along with his or her user name and password.

Figure 18.9 When you have created a blank workgroup site in GoLive, the local version opens in the Site window.

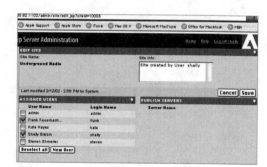

Figure 18.10 Grant access to a site by clicking the check box next to a user's name.

✔ Tip

■ You can also give a user access to a site by clicking the Users link on the left side of the screen, selecting a user, and clicking the check box for the site (all sites on the server are listed) on the user screen.

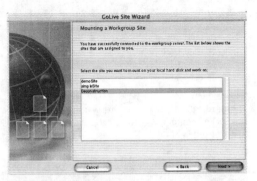

Figure 18.11 Choose the site you want to mount from the list of available sites.

Figure 18.12 Enter your password to mount a workgroup site you've previously worked on.

Connecting to the server

As described in the previous section, user accounts and sites must be in place before your team can begin collaborating. Next, each GoLive user should mount the workgroup site, to copy references to its resources to his or her local computer.

The easiest way to connect to a workgroup server is from the File menu. You can, as I mentioned in the previous section, use the Site Wizard to mount a workgroup site, but that method requires an extra step.

To mount a workgroup site in GoLive:

1. Launch GoLive and choose File > Mount Workgroup Site.

2. Enter the address of the server and your user name and password. Click Next.

3. A list of sites to which you have access appears (**Figure 8.11**). Click the one you want to mount and then click Next.

4. Click Browse to choose a folder for the local version of the workgroup site. Click Finish to create the local workgroup site on your computer.

✔ Tip

■ Once you've mounted a workgroup site on your computer, you can load it subsequently by double-clicking the site file. If you did not check off the Save Password option, GoLive will ask for your user name and password (**Figure 18.12**). To mount the site, you must have a network connection to the server, either on a LAN or the Internet.

Collaborative Authoring

Authoring a workgroup site in GoLive is a lot like authoring a single-user site in GoLive. As you've seen, workgroup sites look and act like single-user sites, right down to the Site window-based tools you use to manage and edit the site. You can do just about anything with a local copy of a workgroup site that you can with a single-user site. The catch is that others have access to the site and can make their own changes. The workgroup server and WebDAV protect the site from conflicting edits.

GoLive workgroup tools

Before I show you how to work with workgroup sites, let's take a look at the tools you'll use, and the workgroup-specific versions of tools you already know.

The Workgroup Site window. When displaying a workgroup site, the Locked column in the Site window is clearly visible, next to the Status column. The Locked column, which indicates whether a file is currently checked in or out in a workgroup site (**Figure 18.13**), is visible in single-user sites, but is out of view in most cases because it's located to the far right of the primary pane of the window. Two additional columns indicate whether the file is complete or still to be edited (**Figure 18.14**). These columns only become visible when you use the Workflow palette to note the page's status. (I'll describe the workflow feature later in this chapter.)

There's also a new tab in the Site window, called User Activity. Here, you'll find the names of users with access to the site and information about what files each has checked out (**Figure 18.15**). Finally, the Site window's secondary pane now includes the Publish Server tab, where you'll find the publish server assigned to this site.

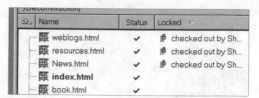

Figure 18.13 The Workgroup Site window includes the Locked column, which indicates whether files are checked in or out.

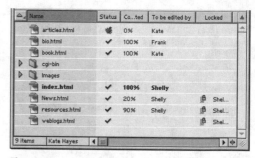

Figure 18.14 The Completed and To be edited by columns give you a way to track workflow within a workgroup site.

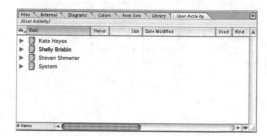

Figure 18.15 The Site window's User Activity tab shows users and the work they've done on the shared site.

COLLABORATIVE AUTHORING

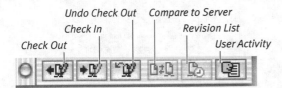

Figure 18.16 The Workgroup toolbar gives you quick access to some site management options.

The Workgroup toolbar. Tucked in the upper-right corner of the GoLive workspace (unless you've closed it) is the Workgroup toolbar (**Figure 18.16**).

Workgroup menu options. You'll find commands related to workgroup sites in the Site menu and in the contextual menus available in the Site window.

Checking documents out

With a workgroup site mounted on your computer, you're ready to begin editing files. First, you can check out a file, which locks the file, preventing other users from accessing it while you use it. You can then edit the file in GoLive as you would in single-user mode.

To check out a workgroup file:

1. Mount a workgroup site.

2. In the Files tab of the Site window, double-click a file to open it. When you try to make a change to the document, you are asked if you want to check out the file. Click Yes.

   or

   Control-click (Mac) or right-click (Windows) on a file and choose Check Out from the contextual menu.

3. Open the checked out file and edit it as you normally would.

✔ Tips

■ If you open your local version of a workgroup site while not connected to the workgroup server, you can work with any parts of the site that you have previously checked out. You will be able to see and link to read-only versions of other site elements. When you activate your network connection, launch the site again to update your copy and check in any files you have modified.

■ You can check out multiple files by selecting them all in the Site window and using the contextual menu or toolbar to check them out.

■ Use the Undo Check Out option (in the toolbar and contextual menu) to reverse any changes you've made to a checked-out file and revert to the previous version on the server.

COLLABORATIVE AUTHORING

To check out a folder

1. With a workgroup site mounted, click the folder in the Site window.

2. Check out the folder.

3. In the Check Out dialog box, click Check Out, or use the check boxes to exclude individual files from check out.

To check in a file:

1. When you're finished working with a checked-out file, save and close the file.

2. Select the file in the Site window and Control-click (Mac) or right-click (Windows) and choose Check In from the contextual menu.

3. In the Workgroup File Check In dialog box (**Figure 18.17**), enter a comment if you wish and click Check In.

Adding resources to a workgroup site

You add files, objects, URLs, and site assets to a workgroup site just as you do to a single-user site—by creating them in GoLive, dragging them into the Site window, or using the Add Files command. Items you add to your local copy of the site are uploaded to the workgroup server and are downloaded to other team members' computers when they check out the files.

To add a new item to a workgroup site:

1. Open a workgroup site in GoLive.

2. Create a new Web page in GoLive and save it to the site's root folder. You will be asked to check in the file.

   or

   Add a GoLive document, image, or other element to the site. The Copy Files dialog box appears. Click OK.

3. In the Workgroup File Check In dialog box, add a comment, and click OK. The server copy of the site is updated.

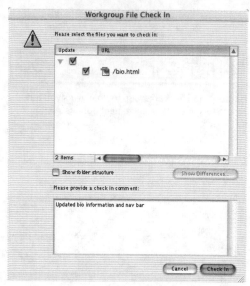

Figure 18.17 Add a comment to the file if you wish, then check it back in to the workgroup site, making it available to other users of the server.

✔ Tip

- Just as you can check out multiple files or folders all at once, you can check them in by selecting them all first.

Offline and read-only mode

To interact with the workgroup server, you must be connected to the server, and to make changes to workgroup site elements, you must check them out. But you can still work with a read-only file from the site, at least until you're able to connect again, or until the file you need is available for check-out. When you double-click a local copy of a checked-out file, you can view it but you can't change it. At least, you can't change the server copy. GoLive warns you that the file is a read-only copy and that it is already checked out. You have the option of editing your local copy anyway.

If you need to work on a file while you don't have Internet access, check out the items you need first. Though they won't be available to members of your team while you're away from the network, you can make all the changes you like and check the files in when you have access again.

To check out files for offline access:

1. Select the items you want to check out in the Site window.

2. Choose Download from the contextual menu to check out the most current version of the file and save it to the local site copy.

3. When you return to your Internet connection, select the items you downloaded and check them in.

File versioning

The workgroup server keeps track of the comings and goings of files within your shared site, which in turn makes it possible to resurrect the complete version history of everything that has been added to the site and all updates. You can use this information to roll a site back to a particular stage of development, or to remove changes that have been made to individual files. You can also track site activity by user in the User History tab of the Site window.

To view a file's version history:

1. In the Site window, select a file.

2. Choose Revisions > Revision List from the contextual menu

   or

   Click the Revision List button on the Workgroup toolbar. The Revision List appears (**Figure 18.18**).

3. Double-click a revision to open the file as it appeared when the revision was made.

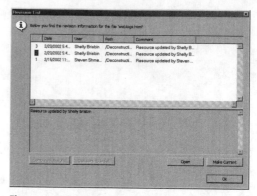

Figure 18.18 A file's revision history shows which users have made changes to the file and displays their comments.

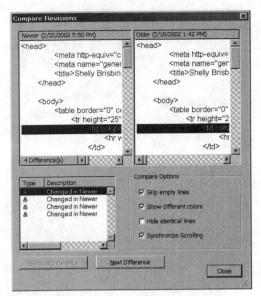

Figure 18.19 Comparing a revision to the current server version of the file shows both versions in the Source Editor.

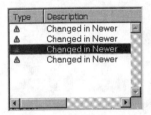

Figure 18.20 Select a revision in the lower pane of the Compare Revisions window. A selected difference is highlighted in the panes above.

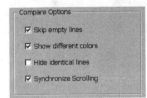

Figure 18.21 Comparing a revision to the current server version of the file shows both versions in the Source Editor.

To compare a revision to the server version:

1. Control-click (Mac) or right-click (Windows) on a revision from the list and choose Compare to Server. GoLive opens the revision you selected and the most recent server version of the file, showing each file in the Source Editor (**Figure 18.19**).

2. To locate a specific difference between the files, click on an item in the lower pane of the window (**Figure 18.20**).

3. You cannot edit the file here, but you can view all differences between the two versions of the file. To adjust your view of the two files, use the check boxes in the Compare Revisions window (**Figure 18.21**).

4. Click Close when you're finished looking at the two files.

✔ Tip

■ You can compare two non-current versions of a file in the Revision List. After selecting the first file, Shift-click (Mac) or Control-click (Windows) to select a second version. Click Compare Revisions.

To revert to an older version of a file:

1. In the Site window, select a file whose version you want to roll back, and view the revision list.

2. Click a non-current version of the file to select it.

3. Click the Make Current button.

COLLABORATIVE AUTHORING

Viewing user activity

The User Activity tab in the workgroup Site window lists all users who have access to the site and the files they currently have checked out. This list is the quickest way to find out who's using a particular checked-out file.

To find a checked-out file:

1. In the Site window, click the User Activity tab.

2. Click the triangle (Mac) or plus sign (Windows) next to a user's name. All files currently checked out by the user appear (**Figure 18.22**).

3. If you don't find the file you're looking for, open another user's list.

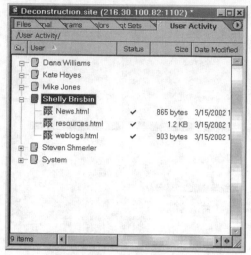

Figure 18.22 The User Activity tab shows all files currently checked out to each user.

USING ACTIONS

19

Actions are prepackaged collections of JavaScript and Cascading Style Sheets that allow you to add interactivity and automation to your pages by simply entering values in the Inspector. GoLive does all the coding for you, but if you know JavaScript, you can also create your own actions.

In this chapter, I'll cover

- ◆ Action tools
- ◆ Adding Action icons
- ◆ Configuring actions
- ◆ The external Script Library
- ◆ Types of actions
- ◆ Creating your own actions

Action Tools

You'll work with three sets of tools when using actions in GoLive.

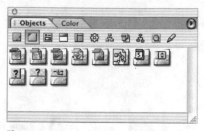

Figure 19.1 Open the Smart set of the Objects palette to work with actions.

◆ **Action icons**: GoLive includes several actions that you can use by dragging an icon from the Smart set of the Objects palette (**Figure 19.1**) onto the Document window.

◆ **Action Inspector**: When you've applied an action from the Objects palette, you configure it in the Action Inspector (**Figure 19.2**). Once you choose a particular action, the Inspector displays a set of options that are specific to that action.

Figure 19.2 The Action Inspector allows you to select an action, and has settings specific to each.

◆ **Actions palette**: When you've selected an image or other HTML element that can take an action, you can use the Actions palette to add and configure one. To activate the Actions palette (**Figure 19.3**), first select an item in the Document window and then choose Window > Actions. The Actions palette in GoLive 6 has two new features available from the flyout menu.

▲ **Highlight Actions in Document** makes it easy to find objects on your page that have actions applied to them by highlighting them with a color.

▲ **Action Filter** (**Figure 19.4**) gives you the ability to enable only actions that are supported by the browsers you choose. The default settings are for Netscape 6 and Explorer 6, so if you changed these settings to Netscape 4 and Explorer 4, you would not be able to apply actions that are only available to versions 5 and higher.

Figure 19.3 Set up actions in the Actions palette, available from the Window menu.

Figure 19.4 Use the Action Filter to set the browsers for which actions will be enabled.

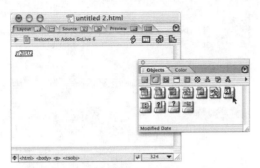

Figure 19.5 Use the Modified Date Inspector to select a date format by clicking a radio button next to a sample format.

Figure 19.6 This is how Modified Date looks on a page.

✔ Tips

■ You can use a Modified Date stamp just as though it were an HTML element: Drag it onto a layout grid, into a text box on a layout grid, or into a table.

■ Many Web authors create dynamic date and time stamps displaying the current date and time to a user visiting the page. See the instructions for the Clock Date (ID), Digital Clock, and World Clock actions later in this chapter for ways to add this feature.

Adding Action Icons

Let's start simply by adding Action icons to a document. In the next section, we'll move on to full-fledged actions.

Modified Date

The Modified Date icon adds a static date and time in one of several different formats, to your page. The date and time are derived from your computer's clock each time you save the page.

To add a Modified Date stamp:

1. Open a document in the Layout Editor and choose a location for the modification date or time.

2. Double-click or drag the Modified Date icon from the Smart set of the Objects palette onto the page (**Figure 19.5**). A date and time stamp appears.

3. To change the language or country that GoLive bases date and time conventions on, choose a different one from the Format pop-up menu in the Inspector.

4. Using the Modified Date Inspector (**Figure 19.6**), choose a display format by clicking one of the radio buttons. The first buttons will display time, the last will display the date.

5. In the Document window, select the stamp. You can edit the stamp's appearance, just as you would any text item, with the toolbar and the Text Inspector, which appears when you select the stamp (or double-click it if the Inspector isn't already open).

Rollovers

You can set a button image to change its appearance when a visitor moves the mouse over it or clicks on it. This interactive effect is commonly referred to as a *rollover*.

To create a rollover:

1. With a document open in the Layout Editor, double-click or drag the Rollover icon (**Figure 19.7**) from the Smart set of the Objects palette. The icon that appears in the Layout Editor looks like a standard image placeholder. The Rollover Inspector is activated.

2. In the Name field of the Rollover Inspector, name the button rollover (see the first tip on the next page).

3. In the Image pane, make certain that the Normal icon is selected.

4. Browse or Point & Shoot to locate the image that appears when the page loads. The image appears, both in the Document window and in the Normal area of the Inspector (**Figure 19.8**).

5. Click the Over box to select it. The URL box is now checked and the URL field is activated.

   or

   If you named your rollover images and set GoLive to find them automatically, you can skip to Step 8.

6. Browse or Point & Shoot to the image you want users to see when the mouse moves over the first image you linked. This new image will appear in the Over area.

Figure 19.7 Choose the Rollover icon from the Smart set of the Objects palette.

Figure 19.8 Assigning a Normal rollover image displays it both in the Inspector and the Document window.

Rollover Images

Before you can add a rollover to your page, you'll need to decide how the image should change. You'll probably want to use different iterations of a single image, though you can use two completely different images. If you decide to use one image, you'll need to create the variants using an image-editing tool, like Adobe Photoshop. Edit the original image, and save each version at the same size as the first image. When you have two or three images (the original, the rollover version, and possibly a final one that appears when the user clicks on the image), you're ready to hit the GoLive Rollover icon.

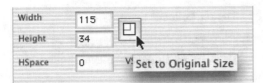

Figure 19.9 The Rollover Inspector's Set to Original Size button can be used to equalize sizing variations among a button set.

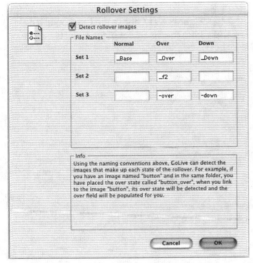

Figure 19.10 The Rollover Settings dialog box can be used to set which images will automatically be looked for when you add a rollover.

■ If the images you use for button elements aren't the same size when you create them, they may be stretched or shrunken to fit into the image placeholder in your document. If you want to try to reach a happy medium, you can experiment using the Set to Original Size button (**Figure 19.9**) in the Rollover Inspector. With your two or three images placed and configured, click the one whose size most closely matches the image size you have in mind in the Rollover Inspector. Then click the Set to Original Size button. The placeholder box changes to fit the image you've selected.

7. Select the Down box and repeat Step 6, placing an image that will replace the original when a visitor clicks on the button.

8. To use the image as a hyperlink, be sure to check the URL check box, and then Browse or Point & Shoot to a page you want to link to or type a complete URL. GoLive puts a # symbol in the field by default.

9. You can target the link to a new location (such as a window or frame) with the Target pop-up menu.

10. If you wish to display a message in the browser's Status area when a user mouses over the link, click the Message check box and type your text in the field next to it.

✔ Tips

■ If you use a consistent naming scheme for your rollover images, such as using short, descriptive names like name_Over.gif, name_Click.gif, and name_Down.gif, you can use a new feature in GoLive 6 to automatically find and set up your rollover images. You can change the names of the images that GoLive looks for in the Rollover Settings dialog box (**Figure 19.10**), available from the flyout menu in the Rollover Inspector.

■ To add rollover properties to an image already on your Web page, drag the Rollover icon onto the existing image. Then configure the button image as described in Steps 5–9.

Lean rollovers

With GoLive 6, Adobe introduced a rollover with easily understood and edited JavaScript: the lean rollover. The lean rollover may not always be a better choice than a smart rollover if your goal is to create less code on your pages. The code for the lean rollover is rewritten each time it is used. The code for smart rollovers, however, uses objects, reuses a lot of its own code, and places the information for the rollovers in arrays rather than rewriting it all for each rollover.

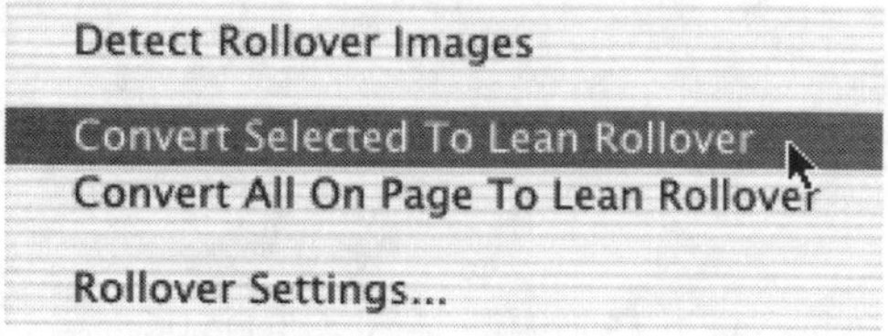

To change a rollover into a lean rollover:

1. Select your rollover in the Layout Editor.

2. From the flyout menu in the Rollover Inspector, choose Convert Selected to Lean Rollover (**Figure 19.11**).

✔ Tips

■ Both smart and lean rollovers can be called from the external Script Library.

■ You will need to use smart rollovers if you need your rollovers to interact with other actions.

URL pop-up menus

URL pop-up menus are used to add navigation elements to a page. For example, use one to provide a compact menu of destinations within your site or other sites.

To create a URL pop-up:

1. With a document open, double-click or drag the URL Popup icon (**Figure 19.12**) from the Smart set of the Objects palette into the Document window. A small pop-up box appears in the Document window. If necessary, double-click the URL Popup in the Document window to activate the URL Popup Inspector.

Detect Rollover Images

Convert Selected To Lean Rollover

Convert All On Page To Lean Rollover

Rollover Settings...

Figure 19.11 Choose Convert to Lean Rollover in the Rollover Inspector flyout to use a lean rollover.

Figure 19.12 Choose the URL Popup icon from the Smart set of the Objects palette.

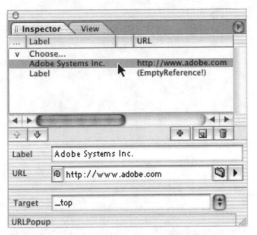

Figure 19.13 The URL Popup Inspector is where you add links that will appear within the menu.

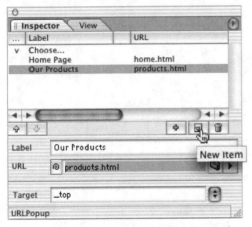

Figure 19.14 Click New Item to add a new item to the menu. Add a label and URL to complete it.

2. In the URL Popup Inspector (**Figure 19.13**), click the "Adobe Systems, Inc." label (assuming you don't plan to offer visitors a direct link to the makers of GoLive). Change the Label and URL fields to reflect the names and URLs of the page to be linked.

3. Click the New Item button (**Figure 19.14**) to add another item to the pop-up. Add a Label and URL for the new menu item.

4. Repeat Step 3 until your pop-up URL navigation system is complete.

5. Click the Preview tab in the Document window and click on your new pop-up menu to view your new pop-up items.

✔ Tips

- You can also use Point & Shoot to choose URLs for menu items.

- The Inspector allows you to specify locations within the page or frameset in the Target pop-up.

- Select an item and click "Remove selected items" to delete it from the list.

- Click "Duplicate selected items" to copy an item. It can save a lot of typing when you're entering long URLs!

- Use the "Move item upwards" and "Move item downwards" arrows to change the order of items in the list.

- The first item in the URL Popup Inspector is Choose. That's what visitors will see before they click the menu. You can change the label by clicking the item and editing the Label field.

Browser switching

Not all browsers are created equal. To begin with, they are designed by the software equivalents of the Hatfields and McCoys. Certain capabilities are possible only with certain browsers, at certain version levels.

A browser switch is useful if a page contains advanced features like style sheets and Java-Script that not all browsers support. You can use a browser switch either to redirect users to a different page (one without the advanced features) or to display a page telling the user to use a newer browser.

Browser switch is a head action, meaning its code sits in the head section of your HTML document. All head actions take place before the page loads, minimizing time wasted loading pages to browsers that don't fully support them.

To create a browser switch:

1. Open the current document's head section by clicking the triangle next to the page title, near the top of the Layout Editor.

2. Double-click or drag the Browser Switch icon (**Figure 19.15**) from the Smart set of the Objects palette into the head section of the document. A Browser Switch icon appears.

Figure 19.15 Choose the Browser Switch icon from the Smart set of the Objects palette.

Figure 19.16 Choose compatible browsers for your page with the Browser Switch Inspector.

3. If you don't already see the Browser Switch Inspector (**Figure 19.16**), double-click the icon to activate it.

4. If you want GoLive to determine which browsers your page is compatible with, leave Auto—the default setting—checked in the Inspector. To determine manually which browsers or platforms to support, uncheck Auto.

5. To choose specific browsers, click the browser versions that you think are compatible with your page's advanced features. (The infinity symbol means all versions.) Visitors using a browser version you did not check will be redirected to a different page.

6. Choose a preferred platform (Mac or Windows) from the Supported Platform pop-up menu, or simply leave it set to All to support both platforms. Visitors using the unsupported platform will be redirected.

7. Browse or Point & Shoot to the alternative page, using the Alternate Link field.

Configuring Actions

Actions are scripted events executed when a trigger is activated. Actions can be used to change the appearance of a page or its elements, open alert windows, play media files, and much more. GoLive's assortment of actions can be added to pages, using mouse- and keyboard-based triggers to make animations, text, and images interactive.

Triggers

Just as a sentence consists of a subject and a verb, an action consists of a trigger and an event. When the trigger is applied, the specified event occurs. GoLive provides nine event triggers that invoke actions. In addition to these mouse and keyboard triggers, there are four triggers specific to actions in the head section of a document. These head triggers are based on the behavior of the page rather than the users, so the events appear automatic. The head triggers are available from the Exec. pop-up menu in the Action Inspector. Finally, there are additional action triggers that apply to a form or form field.

Action placement

There are three locations within a GoLive document where you can add actions:

◆ **Head Actions** go in the head section and apply to the page as a whole.

◆ **Body Actions** can apply to hyperlinked text, images, or any other item within the body of the page.

◆ **Timeline Editor Actions** control animations based on floating boxes. These actions are configured with the Timeline Editor. I'll cover animation in Chapter 20, "Animation and QuickTime."

Figure 19.17 Select an image object, then add a link to it in the Image Inspector.

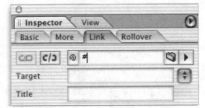

Figure 19.18 The Actions palette displays the options for the hyperlinked image.

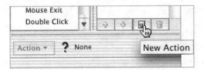

Figure 19.19 The New Action button adds an action to be associated with a trigger.

To add an action to the head or body section of a document, use the Head Action or Body Action tools in the Smart set of the Objects palette, respectively.

The process of adding actions is always similar, regardless of what the action does or what trigger you plan to use. I'll describe the general procedure, then move on to explanations of what the various actions are and how to use them.

To set up an action triggered by a mouse or keyboard event:

1. In the Layout Editor, select text or an image on the page. In **Figure 19.17**, I've placed an image of a left-pointing arrow onto a page that will return visitors to where they came from.

2. Create a link by clicking the New Link button on the toolbar.

   or

   Click the Link button in the Text or Image Inspector. The URL field (in the Link tab of the Text or Image Inspector) becomes active.

3. To associate an action with selected text or an image, type a number sign (#) in the URL field of the Inspector after deleting the text "(Empty Reference!)" from the field.

4. With the image still selected, choose Window > Actions to view the Actions palette (**Figure 19.18**).

5. Choose Mouse Click (or any one of the triggers from the Events pull-down menu on the left).

6. Click the New Action button, located below the Actions list (**Figure 19.19**). The Action pop-up menu is enabled.

(continues on next pgae)

7. Choose an event from the Action pop-up menu. I chose Link > Go Last Page (**Figure 19.20**). The action is complete: JavaScript has been added to the document and it will execute the event when the button is clicked.

✔ Tips

- To add multiple actions to a selected item, repeat Steps 5–7.

- Delete an action by selecting it in the Actions palette and clicking the "Remove selected items" (trash can) button.

- Not sure what an action does? Choose it in the Actions palette and read the explanation that appears at the bottom of the window (**Figure 19.21**). Not all actions have explanations, though.

- The Actions palette also indicates which browsers an action is likely to work with. Note in **Figure 19.22**, the ConfirmLink action works with Netscape 3 and higher and Internet Explorer 3 and higher.

Figure 19.20 Go Last Page is the event that will be associated with the image.

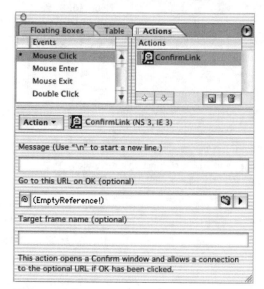

Figure 19.21 The Actions palette includes an explanation of what almost every action does, on which browsers, and what information it needs from you to do its job.

Figure 19.22 The ConfirmLink action can be used by version 3 and later of Netscape Navigator or Internet Explorer.

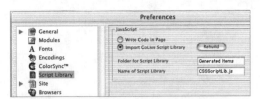

Figure 19.23 The application-wide Script Library preferences.

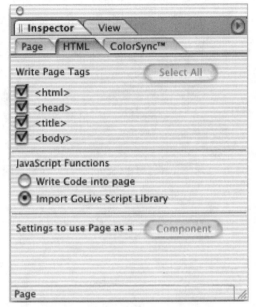

Figure 19.24 The Script Library settings in the HTML tab of the Page Inspector change library usage for individual pages.

The External Script Library

Adding actions to your site can greatly increase the amount of JavaScript code contained in it, especially when you add duplicate actions to many different pages (such as navigation rollovers). You can reduce the amount of code by using GoLive's external Script Library. Just write the repeated action into a single library file, instead of on each individual page in the site. This file is then loaded into the browser cache of site visitors, meaning each script has to be loaded once only.

Using the Script Library

GoLive can be set up to use the external Script Library for individual pages, for individual sites, or application-wide. If you choose to set it application-wide, existing pages and sites will retain their current settings, but all new pages and sites will be created with the new settings.

To set Script Library preferences:

1. To change the setting application-wide, choose Edit > Preferences, then select Script Library (**Figure 19.23**).

    or

    To change the setting sitewide, choose Site > Settings and select Script Library.

    or

    To change the setting for a single page, open the HTML tab of the Page Inspector (**Figure 19.24**).

2. Choose Import GoLive Script Library to have GoLive write the JavaScript code to the external Script Library. Choose Write Code in Page to have GoLive write the JavaScript code into individual pages.

3. By default, GoLive saves a file called CSScriptLib.js to the Generated Items folder in your site, but you can change both to whatever you would like, as long as the library name has the suffix .js.

413

Flattening the Script Library

GoLive's external Script Library contains all of the code from all of the actions that you have installed in GoLive, including ones that you aren't using in a site. You can flatten this file to remove the code from any actions that you aren't using, further reducing the size of this file and improving the download times of your pages. In GoLive 6, you can now set your sites to flatten the Script Library automatically upon uploading or exporting your site, and you can also do it manually as in GoLive 5.

To manually flatten the Script Library of an open site:

◆ Choose Site > Flatten Script Library, or choose Flatten Script Library from the contextual menu in the Files tab of the site.

To set a site to flatten the Script Library on upload or export:

1. Choose Site > Settings and select Upload/Sync Times from the left column.

   or

   Choose Site > Site Settings and select Export in the left column.

2. Select "Site specific settings."

3. Select Flatten Script Library (**Figure 19.25**) in the "Strip HTML code for" section, then click OK.

To set all sites to flatten the Script Library on upload or export:

1. Choose Edit > Preferences.

2. Expand Site in the left column and choose Upload/Sync Times.

   or

   Expand Site in the left column and choose Export.

3. Select Flatten Script Library in the "Strip HTML code for" section.

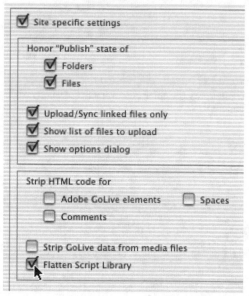

Figure 19.25 Flattening of the Script Library can be set to happen automatically on upload or export.

✔ Tip

■ If you've set site-specific preferences for some of your sites, they'll be unaffected by changes in the application-wide preferences. You'll need to update these sites individually to change the Flatten Script Library settings.

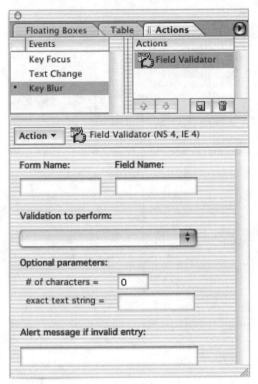

Figure 19.26 Assign a Field Validator action to a Key Blur event.

Types of Actions

GoLive includes 91 actions—events invoked by triggers—37 of which are new to GoLive 6. Some are beyond the scope of this book, but I will give you an overview of the types of actions available. (For more detail, go to www.peachpit.com/vqs/golive6.)

Actions are arranged in eight categories. Each category is a menu item in the Action Inspector. The Actions palette has a submenu of the actions in each category.

Getter actions

There are three types of Getter actions: Field Validator, Get Floating Box Position, and Get Form Value.

Field Validator checks that the data a user has entered into a form field matches a particular criterion or format. You can use this action to display an error message so that the user can correct the data before the form is submitted.

To create a Field Validator action:

1. Before creating this action, you must first add a form to your GoLive document. For more information about creating and using forms, see Chapter 10, "Working with Forms."

2. Select a text, text area, or password field in a document containing one of these form elements, and add a Key Blur or Text Change triggered action in the Actions palette. A Key Blur action is triggered when the user tabs out of the field, while a Text Change action is triggered when a user changes the data in a field and then leaves that field.

3. Select Getters > Field Validator from the Action pop-up menu (**Figure 19.26**).

(continues on next page)

TYPES OF ACTIONS

4. Enter the name of the form that the field is in, and the name of the chosen field.

5. From the "Validation to perform" pop-up menu, choose a method.

6. If you chose the "Field has this many characters" option, enter the number of characters the field must have in the "# of characters box."

or

If you chose the Field = Exact Text String option, type the text that the user must enter in the "exact text string" text box.

Get Floating Box Position is a head action that grabs the top-left coordinates of a floating box. You can use this data to invoke another action that acts upon this information. (To learn how to apply an action to an animation, see Chapter 20. For more on specific animation-related actions, go to www.peachpit.com/vqs/golive6.)

Get Form Value reads the data that a user inputs into a specified form field. The information can either be passed to another action or displayed.

To create a Get Form Value action:

1. Before creating this action, you must first add a form to your GoLive document. For more information about creating and using forms, see Chapter 10.

2. Add an action to the head section of a document.

3. In the Head Action Inspector, choose OnUnload from the Exec. pop-up menu.

4. Choose Getters > Get Form Value from the Action pop-up menu (**Figure 19.27**).

5. In the Form field, enter the name of the form from which you want to extract information.

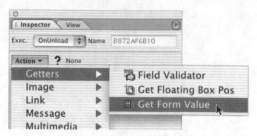

Figure 19.27 Add a connection to a form in the Inspector using the Get Form Value action.

Figure 19.28 Name your image in the More tab of the Image Inspector.

Figure 19.29 Daily Image URL changes the placeholder image to a different GIF for each day of the week.

6. Enter the name of the form element (the name you've assigned to the element itself, not the element type) in the Element field.

7. Add additional Get Form Value actions for each form field whose data you want to extract.

Image actions

GoLive 6 includes four different actions that affect images. Three of them—Daily Image URL, Random Image, and Set Image URL—swap images. The fourth, Preload Image, is a head action that affects image caching for the page.

Daily Image URL replaces the selected image with a different specified image, one for each day of the week. The day is determined according to the user's computer.

To add a Daily Image URL action:

1. Place an image on your page that you would like to swap daily. In the Image Inspector, click the More tab and give your image a name, but do not check the Is Form box (**Figure 19.28**).

2. Add an action to the head section of the document.

3. In the Head Action Inspector (**Figure 19.29**), choose Image > DailyImageURL from the Action pop-up menu.

4. Choose the image you just named from the Image pop-up.

5. Browse or Point & Shoot to an image that you would like displayed on Monday. A link to the image appears in the Inspector.

6. Repeat Step 5 for Tuesday through Sunday.

TYPES OF ACTIONS

Preload Image is a head action that caches images before the body of an HTML page loads. Caching a large graphic makes it possible for all images on a page to appear simultaneously. Preloading an image is commonly used with rollovers, which run more quickly if their component images are present when the page is loaded.

To preload an image:

1. Add an action to the head section of a document.

2. In the Action Inspector, choose Image > Preload Image from the Action pop-up menu (**Figure 19.30**).

3. Browse or Point & Shoot to an image for preloading. A link to the image appears in the Inspector.

Random Image replaces the image to which the action is attached with a random image from among several you specify. Set Image URL exchanges the current image for another, based on a trigger you specify.

To set an image URL:

1. Choose an image you want to exchange. If it doesn't already have a name, click the More tab of the Image Inspector and type a name in the Name field near the Is Form area. Don't check the Is Form check box.

2. Create a mouse- or keyboard-triggered event action, as described in the "To set up an action triggered by a mouse or key event" section of this chapter.

3. Choose Image > Set Image URL from the Action pop-up menu in the Actions palette.

4. Choose the named image from the Image pop-up menu in the Actions palette.

5. In the Link area of the Actions palette, Browse or Point & Shoot to an image to add its URL. The completed Actions palette looks like **Figure 19.31**.

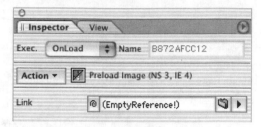

Figure 19.30 In the Link field, enter the link to the image you wish to preload.

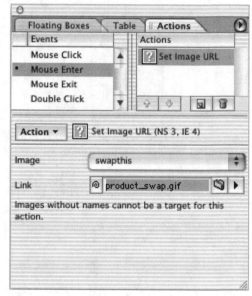

Figure 19.31 The Set Image URL action will exchange the currently displayed image for one you specify in this Link field.

Figure 19.32 Bring a page of your site back into your frameset with the ForceFrame action.

Link actions

These are some of the simplest and most useful actions GoLive offers. Despite the name, not all of them need links to work. Close Window, for example, closes the current browser window. Simply create a triggered action and choose Link > Close Window.

ConfirmLink, however does work in conjunction with a link. It brings up a dialog box asking the user to confirm the action before going to the linked page. It can be used to display a message or condition of entry, for example.

ForceFrame allows you to automatically load the entire frameset if someone directly visits a page that should be displayed in a frameset.

To add a Force Frame action:

1. Add a head action to the document.

2. Choose Link > ForceFrame in the Action pop-up menu in the Head Action Inspector (**Figure 19.32**).

3. Enter the link to the frameset in which you would like the page to appear in the Frameset field.

4. Enter the name of the frame in which you would like the page to appear in the Frame field.

✔ Tip

■ The Force Frame action can be applied to any page you wish to load only in your frameset, but cannot be applied to the frameset itself.

Go Last Page returns the visitor to the previously viewed page when he or she clicks on the link. Similarly, Navigate History uses browser history information—what pages a visitor has visited in what order—to take him or her forward or backward by a specific number of pages.

To add a Go Last Page or Navigate History action:

1. Create a mouse- or keyboard-triggered action.

2. Choose Link > Go Last Page, or Link > Navigate History from the Action pop-up menu in the Actions palette. The Navigate History action appears in **Figure 19.33**. If you're creating a Go Last Page action, you're done.

3. To complete a Navigate History action, in the Go Where field, type the number of history items to move when the action is triggered (negative numbers go backward, positive go forward).

Goto Link sends a visitor to a URL you select.

To create a Goto Link action:

1. Create a mouse- or keyboard-triggered action.

2. Choose Link > Goto Link from the Action pop-up menu. Goto Link options appear.

3. Type a remote URL or locate a URL within your site that you want to link to (**Figure 19.34**).

4. If you wish, use the Target field to choose a location for the new page.

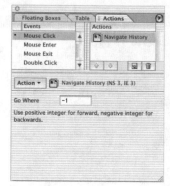

Figure 19.33 Configure the Navigate History action to direct users forward or backward to links they have visited.

Figure 19.34 In this example, the Goto Link action functions like a conventional hyperlink to a frame in a frameset.

✔ Tips

■ If it sounds like a Goto Link action does just what a normal hyperlink does, you're right—if you've chosen a mouse click trigger. Using another trigger, like Mouse Enter, makes things considerably more interesting. This isn't standard operating procedure on the Web, though, so be sure to give your visitors some kind of warning before you send them to another page or another site.

■ You can also use the Goto Link action as a browser- or timeline-triggered action, or in combination with other actions. For example, you could use it with a Timeout action to send the viewer to another location after a specific amount of time, or use the value set with one of the Variable actions.

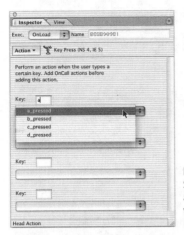

Figure 19.35
Select another action to call with the Key Press action.

Figure 19.36 The KillFrame action lets you break your page out of another site's frameset.

Key Press allows you to trigger other actions when the specified keys are pressed.

To create a Key Press action:

1. Create up to four head actions—one for each action you would like to call when the specific key is pressed.

2. Set these actions to OnCall (in the Exec. menu) and give them names that will be easy to identify.

3. Add another head action and choose OnLoad from the Exec. pop-up menu, then Choose Link > Key Press from the Action pop-up menu in the Head Action Inspector.

4. Type the key that you would like to trigger the first action into the first Key field, and choose the name of that action from the pop-up menu below it (**Figure 19.35**).

5. Repeat Step 4 for each different key that you would like to use as an action trigger (up to four keys).

KillFrame prevents another site from loading your pages inside their frameset. It's as easy as it is useful. Simply add a head action to the document, and in the Head Action Inspector, choose OnLoad from the Exec. pop-up menu and choose Link > KillFrame from the Action pop-up menu (**Figure 19.36**).

Slide New Window will open a browser window and slide it to the middle of the visitor's screen.

To add a Slide New Window action:

1. Create a mouse- or keyboard-triggered action.

   or

   Add a head action to your page, with Exec. set to OnLoad or OnUnload.

(continues on next page)

2. Choose Link > Slide New from the Action pop-up menu in the Actions palette (or in the Head Action Inspector).

3. Type a URL, Browse, or Point & Shoot to the linked page that will appear in the new window (**Figure 19.37**).

4. Type a name for the new window in the Window name field. This is especially useful if you're calling this action multiple times (for example, to display different pages in the same new window), as it will open each one in the existing named window rather than creating another window.

5. Enter a size in pixels for your window, and check the Resize box, if you wish. Leave any of the six browser display buttons checked to show scroll bars, menus, directory buttons, status indicators, toolbars, and location bars.

Target2Frames allows you to click a link in the menu frame and load both a new content page and a new menu page in the frameset.

To create a Target2Frames action:

1. Create a mouse- or keyboard-triggered action on a page that is used as a frame in a frameset.

2. Choose Link > Target2Frames from the Action pop-up menu in the Actions palette (**Figure 19.38**).

3. Type the name of the frame you would like to target with the first link in Frame 1.

4. In the Link field below Frame 1, type a URL, Browse, or Point & Shoot to the page that you would like to appear in Frame 1.

5. Repeat Steps 3 and 4 in the Frame 2 fields.

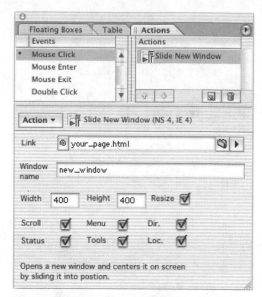

Figure 19.37 Open a new window and put it in the middle of the user's screen with the Slide New Window action.

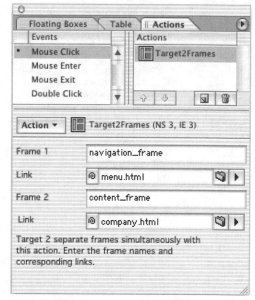

Figure 19.38 Load a new content page and a new menu page using Target2Frames.

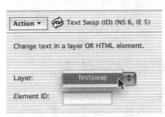

Figure 19.39
Choose a layer on your page to swap the text in and out of.

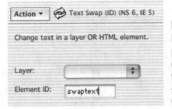

Figure 19.40
If you're using placeholder text or a table cell, type in the ID style you applied to it.

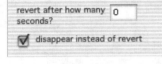

Figure 19.41
Enter the number of seconds you would like the text to appear.

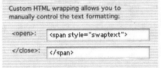

Figure 19.42
Add custom formatting to the text that appears on swap.

Text Swap enables you to change a block of text in either a floating box or a table cell.

To add a Text Swap (ID) action:

1. Create a mouse- or keyboard-triggered action.

2. Choose Link > Text Swap (ID) from the Action pop-up menu in the Actions palette.

3. From the Layer pop-up menu, choose the layer that contains the text you would like to swap when triggered (**Figure 19.39**).

   or

   Type the element ID of the text or table cell whose contents you would like to swap (**Figure 19.40**). For more information about setting the ID of an element see Chapter 13, "Working with Style Sheets."

4. Enter the new text that you would like to appear when the swap is triggered in the "New text" field.

5. Enter the number of seconds you would like the new text to appear for (**Figure 19.41**). Use 0 to have the text revert or disappear immediately after the trigger is stopped (for example, if triggered by OnMouseOver, the text will revert or disappear when the cursor is no longer over the link).

6. Check "disappear instead of revert" to change the behavior after the text swaps. Uncheck it to have your text revert to the original text rather than just disappear.

7. Optionally add opening and closing HTML tags in the <open> and </close> fields of the "Custom HTML wrapping" section to change the formatting of the text that appears on swap (**Figure 19.42**).

Redirect actions

As the name implies, all of these actions are used to send a site visitor to another page. CSS Redirect can be used to apply a different style sheet to your page depending on the browser or platform.

To add a CSS Redirect action:

1. Add a head action to your page.

2. Choose OnParse from the Exec. pop-up menu in the Head Action Inspector.

3. Choose Link > CSS Redirect from the Action pop-up menu in the Inspector.

4. Choose the platform and browser for which you would like to add a CSS Redirect from the Visitor's Platform and Browser pop-up menu (**Figure 19.43**).

5. Type the URL, Browse, or Point & Shoot to the style sheet you would like used if the specified browser and platform are detected.

6. Repeat Steps 1–4 to add redirects for another platform and browser combination.

Daily Redirect allows you to redirect to a different page depending on the day of the week.

To add a Daily Redirect action:

1. Add a head action to execute OnLoad to your page, to redirect when a page loads.
   or
   Create a mouse- or keyboard-triggered action, to redirect when the user does something.

2. Choose Link > DailyRedirect from the Action pop-up menu in the Actions palette (or in the Head Action Inspector).

3. Type the URL, Browse, or Point & Shoot to the page you would like to link to for each day of the week, based on the date set on the user's computer.

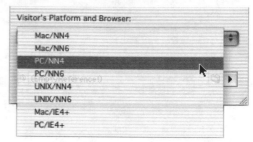

Figure 19.43 You can choose which browsers you would like to load a different CSS file for.

✔ Tip

■ If you want to redirect only on some days rather than every day (for example, only on Wednesdays and Fridays) you can enter the same URL for multiple days to redirect to a common page or enter # to remain on the current page.

TYPES OF ACTIONS

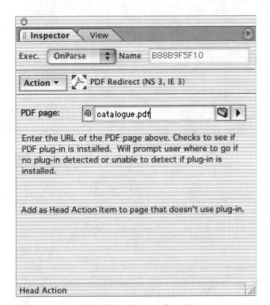

Figure 19.44 The PDF Redirect action gives you a fallback if the user doesn't have the PDF browser plug-in.

PDF Redirect, SVG Redirect, and SWF Redirect all detect whether the user's browser has the appropriate plug-in installed. They then redirect to a media file if the plug-in is loaded or to a Web page if it is not.

To add a PDF Redirect, SVG Redirect, or SWF Redirect action:

1. Create a page that will be shown to users who do not have the specified browser plug-in installed (the PDF, SVG, or SWF plug-in, depending on which you use).

2. Add a head action to your page and choose OnParse from the Exec. pop-up menu in the Head Action Inspector.

3. Choose Link > PDF Redirect, Link > SVG Redirect, or Link > SWF Redirect in the Action menu of the Inspector, as appropriate.

4. Type the URL, Browse, or Point & Shoot to the PDF, SVG, or SWF file that you would like users to see if they do have the plug-in installed (**Figure 19.44**).

5. The SVG and SWF Redirect actions also have the option to display a custom message if the user does not have the plug-in installed. Enter the message that should be displayed in the Alert field.

✔ Tip

- If you use any apostrophes in your alert message, you need to add a backslash (\) before them (like this: don\'t) so they don't break the JavaScript on the page. You can also add a line break to your message by typing \n (like this: This is on one line and\n this is on another).

Redirect Prompt allows you to ask the user a question and then redirect to one of up to five different places depending on the answer.

To add a Redirect Prompt action:

1. Add a head action to your page and set it to execute OnLoad to redirect when a page loads, or OnParse to redirect before the contents of the page load.

    or

    Create a mouse- or keyboard-triggered action, to let the user trigger the action.

2. Choose Link > Redirect Prompt from the Action pop-up menu in the Actions palette (or the Head Action Inspector).

3. Type your question in the Question field (**Figure 19.45**).

4. If you would like your choices to be shown in the user prompt (as in **Figure 19.46**), enter them in the "Display possible answers" field.

5. In the "Alert if invalid answer" field, enter the message you would like users to see if they answer incorrectly.

6. If you would like the user to have to enter this information only once, check the "Remember choice and auto-redirect next time" box. Enter a name for the cookie this will be stored in.

7. Enter the first answer to your question in the Answer 1 field.

8. In the link box, type the URL, Browse, or Point & Shoot to the page you would like to redirect to if Answer 1 is entered by the user.

9. Repeat Steps 7 and 8 for each answer and link.

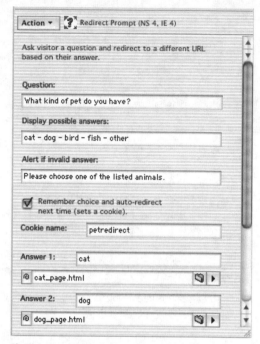

Figure 19.45 The Redirect Prompt allows you to ask users a question and send them to a different link depending on their answer.

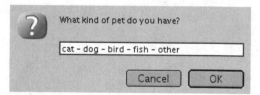

Figure 19.46 A prompt in the Mozilla browser displayed using the Redirect Prompt action.

Figure 19.47 A TimeRedirect prompt used to load a different page in the morning and the afternoon.

TimeRedirect allows you to redirect to a different page depending on whether the time on the user's computer is before or after the specified time. For example, you can use this to show one page for the morning and another page for the evening.

To add a TimeRedirect action:

1. Add a head action to your page and set it to execute OnLoad to redirect when a page loads or OnParse to redirect before the contents of the page load.

   or

   Create a mouse- or keyboard-triggered action to let the user trigger the action.

2. Choose Link > TimeRedirect from the Action pop-up menu in the Actions palette (or the Head Action Inspector).

3. Specify the hour you would like to redirect before or after. This must be an integer between 1 and 12 (**Figure 19.47**).

4. Select the PM check box to set the hour as PM, unselect it to set it to AM.

5. Type the URL, Browse, or Point & Shoot to the pages you would like to redirect to before and after your chosen time. If you want to redirect only before or after, you can set one and leave the other blank.

Message actions

Document Write fills an inline placeholder with text or with HTML. When used with a body action, it can replace the body action with text or HTML.

To create a Document Write action:

1. Add any mouse- or keyboard-triggered action to the body section of a document.

2. Add a second body action and choose Message > Document Write from the Action pop-up menu in the Actions palette.

(continues on next page)

TYPES OF ACTIONS

3. Type some HTML code or text into the HTML field to display text when the first action is triggered.

or

Click the button next to the HTML field twice. The button changes from a *c* to a question mark and you can choose the first action you created from the pop-up menu that now appears in the HTML field.

Last Modified (ID) adds the date that the page was last uploaded to the server. It can be displayed as text, in a floating box, or in a table cell.

To add a Last Modified (ID) action:

1. Add a floating box to your page, or assign an ID to an element on your page (see Chapter 13 for more information on using ID styles).

2. Add a head action to your page and set it to execute OnLoad in the Exec. pop-up menu.

3. Choose Message > Last Modified (ID) from the Action pop-up menu in the Head Action Inspector.

4. Choose your floating box from the Layer pop-up menu, or type the ID in the Element ID field (**Figure 19.48**).

5. Choose your display preference from the Date Format pop-up menu.

6. If you would like the day of the week shown before the date, check "Include day of week."

7. Optionally, in the "Lead in text" field, enter any text you would like shown before the date.

8. Optionally, enter opening and closing tags to add formatting to the date displayed. In Figure 19.48 for example, the tags will make the text size 2 and red.

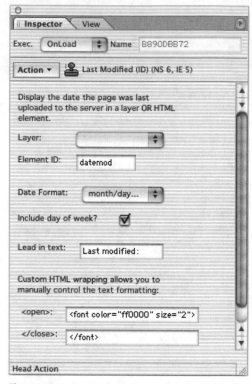

Figure 19.48 Let your users know when a page was updated using the Last Modified (ID) action.

Figure 19.49 Display the last-modified date for a page in a form field.

Figure 19.50 Alert your users by utilizing a browser alert window.

Last Modified (form) adds the date that the page was last uploaded to the server in a form field on the page.

To add a Last Modified (form) action:

1. Add a form with at least one text field to your page (see Chapter 10 for more information).

2. Add a head action to your page and set it to execute OnLoad in the Exec. pop-up menu.

3. Choose Message > Last Modified (form) from the Action pop-up menu in the Head Action Inspector.

4. Type the name of your form and the field in which you would like the modified date to appear in the appropriate fields (**Figure 19.49**).

5. Choose a date format from the pop-up menu.

6. If you would like the day of the week displayed in the form field as well as the date, check "Include day of week."

7. This action can display an alert box as well as the date. Uncheck the "Disable alert" box to have an alert box display when the page is loaded.

Open Alert Window displays a browser alert window onscreen when triggered. Simply create a mouse- or keyboard-triggered action, select Message > Open Alert Window from the Action pop-up menu, and type your alert text in the Message field (**Figure 19.50**).

Set Status displays a custom message in the status field at the bottom of the browser window. Create a mouse- or keyboard-triggered action, select Message > Set Status from the Action pop-up menu, and type your status message in the text field that appears.

Multimedia actions

Multimedia actions involve combinations of complicated techniques that are largely beyond the scope of this book. I'll give an overview of them here, but for more information, go to www.peachpit.com/vqs/golive6.

◆ Drag Floating Box allows a visitor to drag content (contained in a floating box) around in the browser window.

◆ Flip Move allows you to move a floating box from a starting point to another position on the page, and back again when triggered a second time.

◆ Float Layer locks the position of a floating box on your page so that even when a visitor scrolls the page, the floating box is shown in the same place in the window.

◆ Mouse Follow lets you set a floating box to follow the mouse cursor as it is moved around the browser window.

◆ Move By specifies the vertical and horizontal movement of a floating box. When triggered, the box moves according to the measurement in the Move By action and no further.

◆ Move To behaves just like Flip Move, except that the floating box does not return to the original position.

◆ Play Scene and Stop Scene actions control the start and stop points of animations created in the Timeline Editor.

◆ Play Sound and Stop Sound actions control the stopping and starting of sounds.

◆ ShowHide controls the visibility of a floating box on the page.

Figure 19.51 The Drag Floating Box action allows the visitor to drag a floating box and its contents around the browser window.

♦ SlideShow and SlideShowAuto let you display an image slideshow. The Slide-Show action lets the user control movement through the images, and the Slide-ShowAuto action automatically moves through the images after a specified time interval.

♦ SlideShowAutoStop is used with the SlideShowAuto action to allow the user to stop and restart an automatic slideshow.

♦ Stop Complete stops all animation, including visual and audio playback. It is useful to give visitors a trigger that allows them to stop animation if their Internet connections are slow, or if they simply don't want to bother with it.

♦ Wipe Transition creates a fading effect that applies to floating boxes as they enter and leave the visitor's view.

To add a Drag Floating Box action:

1. Choose or create a floating box. If the box is empty, add content to it.

2. If you like, rename the box in the Floating Box Inspector from the generic name assigned to it by GoLive. If you don't rename the box, note its default name. You'll be referring to it by name when you create the action.

3. Add a head action to your page.

4. Choose Multimedia > Drag Floating Box from the Action pop-up menu in the Head Action Inspector.

5. The Inspector now displays the Floating Box pop-up menu containing all floating boxes within the current document. Choose the box that you want visitors to be able to drag (**Figure 19.51**).

Other actions

- Clock Date (ID) can display the local date and time (according to the site visitor's computer) in a floating box or replace placeholder text on a page.

- Digital Clock lets you display a custom digital clock (the time gets set by the site visitor's computer) on your page. You create the images for the numbers 0–9 that the clock will use.

- Netscape CSS Fix works around a bug that causes some versions of Netscape 4.0 browsers to lose Cascading Style Sheet information when the page is resized.

- Print Document allows you to create a link that will open the browser's Print dialog box to print the current page or chosen frame.

- Resize Window changes the size of the browser window when triggered.

- Scroll Down, Left, Right, and Up move the browser display in the specified direction by the number of pixels you set, when it is triggered.

- Scroll Status shows a scrolling message along the Status bar in the browser.

- Search Engine lets you add a link to query one of the major search engines. You can set the query or choose a form field to use. The query results from your chosen search engine will open in a new window.

- Set BackColor changes the background color of the current window.

- World Clock shows the current time in a chosen world time zone.

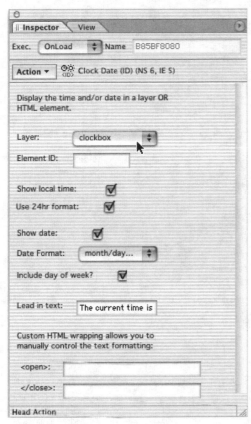

Figure 19.52 The Clock Date (ID) action allows you to place a clock on your page with the current time and date on the user's computer.

To create a Clock Date (ID) action:

1. Add a floating box to your page, or assign an ID to an element on your page (see Chapter 13 for more information on using ID styles).

2. Add a head action to your page, and set it to execute OnLoad in the Exec. pop-up menu.

3. Choose Others > Clock Date (ID) from the Action pop-up menu in the Head Action Inspector.

4. Choose your floating box from the Layer pop-up menu, or type your ID in the Element ID field (**Figure 19.52**).

5. If you would like the time displayed as well as the date, leave the "Show local time" box checked.

6. Choose your display preferences from the Date Format pop-up menu.

7. If you would like the day of the week shown before the date, select the "Include day of week" check box.

8. Optionally, in the "Lead in text" field, enter any text you would like shown before the time and date.

9. Optionally, enter opening and closing tags to add formatting to the date displayed.

To create a Digital Clock action:

1. Create 10 graphics depicting the numbers 0 through 9 and save them as GIFs or JPEGs in a directory of your site.

2. Add four placeholder images to a page, and give them unique names in the More tab of the Image Inspector (**Figure 19.53**). These are the base images of your digital clock.

3. Add a head action to your page, and set it to execute OnLoad in the Exec. pop-up menu.

4. Choose Others > Digital Clock from the Action pop-up menu in the Head Action Inspector.

5. Choose one of your placeholder images for each digit of the clock using the Digit pop-up menus (**Figure 19.54**).

6. Type, Browse, or Point & Shoot to one of the images you created in Step 1.

To add a Scroll action:

1. Create a mouse- or keyboard-triggered action.

   or

   Add an Action marker to the Action track of the Timeline Editor.

2. In the Actions palette, choose Others > Scroll Down, Scroll Left, Scroll Right, or Scroll Up from the Action pop-up menu.

3. Choose the number of pixels to scroll when the action is triggered.

4. Enter the speed from 1 to 100 (100 is fastest) at which the window will scroll (**Figure 19.55**).

Figure 19.53 Name your clock's placeholder images in the More tab of the Image Inspector.

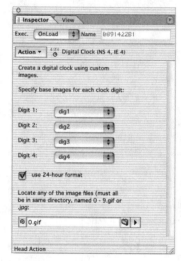

Figure 19.54 Add a custom-designed digital clock to your page with the Digital Clock action.

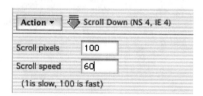

Figure 19.55 All of the Scroll actions—down, left, right, and up—are configured in the same way, allowing you to specify scroll movement and speed.

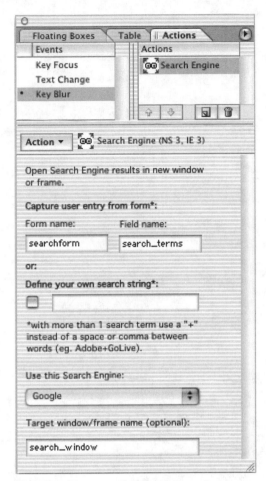

Figure 19.56 Let your users do a Web search at one or more of the major search engines with the Search Engine action.

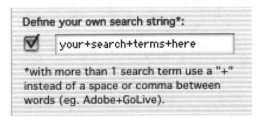

Figure 19.57 Preconfigure your search with the search terms of your choice.

To create a Search Engine action with user-defined search terms:

1. Add a form and form field to your page for users to enter their searches into.

2. In the Layout Editor, select the field you added to your page and assign a Key Blur-triggered action by selecting Key Blur in the Events column of the Actions palette. Then click the New Action button.

   or

   Add a head action to your page, and select OnLoad from the Exec. pop-up menu in the Head Action Inspector.

3. Choose Others > Search Engine from the Action pop-up menu in the Actions palette (or Head Action Inspector).

4. Enter the form and field names in the "Capture user entry from form" section (**Figure 19.56**).

5. Deselect the "Define your own search string" check box.

6. Select the search engine you wish to use from the "Use this search engine" pop-up menu.

7. Optionally, enter the name of the window or frame you wish to target.

8. In the "Define your own search string" field, enter the search terms you wish to search for, using the plus symbol (+) between words if you are using more than one search term (**Figure 19.57**).

✔ Tip

■ To show results from multiple search engines, add another Search Engine action for each search engine you want to use. They must all have the same trigger as the first action, if it is user-triggered rather than browser-triggered.

To add a Set BackColor action:

1. Create a mouse- or keyboard-triggered action.

   or

   Add an Action marker to the Action track of the Timeline Editor.

2. In the Actions palette, choose Others > Set BackColor from the Action pop-up menu.

3. Click the Background Color box to activate the Color palette, and choose a color.

4. If necessary, drag the color swatch into the Background Color box in the Actions palette.

Special actions

♦ Action Group gathers several actions together to be triggered at the same time.

♦ Call Action calls another action anywhere on the page. Use this to call an action stored in the head section of the page.

♦ Call Function calls any custom JavaScript function that you have added to the page. This action gives JavaScript programmers a special action with which to trigger their scripts.

♦ Condition actions are triggered based on whether defined conditions (such as other actions) occur. They use the Text Variable, Intersection, and Timeout actions.

♦ Idle actions periodically determine whether a condition has been met. They work with Intersection and Timeout actions, and yield a true/false result.

♦ Intersection actions can be used to trigger other actions when two floating boxes intersect in a browser window.

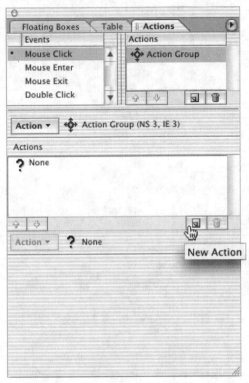

Figure 19.58 Add actions in the Actions palette to chain actions together.

◆ KeyCompare triggers another action when a specified key is pressed.

◆ Timeout allows you to either trigger another action or stop an action after a specified period.

To create an Action Group:

1. Create a mouse- or keyboard-triggered action.

or

Add an Action marker to the Action track of the Timeline Editor.

2. In the Actions palette, choose Specials > Action Group from the Action pop-up menu.

3. Click the New Action button to add the first action to your group (**Figure 19.58**), and configure the action.

4. Continue using the New Action button to add more actions, and configure these actions.

TYPES OF ACTIONS

Creating Your Own Actions

Learning the programming required to make an action is beyond the scope of this book. But if you know how to write JavaScript and are willing to learn a few conventions of action-building in GoLive, you can build your own actions or modify those that already exist.

Actions must contain a title, action tags, JavaScript, and a layout grid, which is used to create the fields that appear in the Actions palette and Action Inspector when you select the action. All actions must contain these basic elements in order to function properly.

Action files must have the file extension .action. Script files, which use the .scpt file extension, are made up of JavaScript code only.

Actions are stored in their own folder within the GoLive application folder. The Actions folder is located inside the JScripts folder, which in turn is in the Modules folder. Any action appearing in a folder within the Actions folder is available in the Actions palette and Action Inspector.

Starting with an existing action is a great way to get started building your own. It is a good idea to either duplicate an action you want to base your action on, or immediately save the action you open with a new name, so that you don't overwrite an existing action.

✔ Tip

- There are now quite a few resources on the Web where you can find out more information about actions, download or purchase third-party actions, or get support for using actions in GoLive 6. See www.peachpit.com/vqs/golive6 for a list of several good places to start

ANIMATION AND QUICKTIME

Animation and interactivity make your content more engaging and help you communicate more effectively with your audience. You already know how GoLive's DHTML tools allow you to control text and objects or add interactivity by incorporating actions. Now, I'll show you how to use some of these same tools to produce animation, video, audio, and advanced interactivity in your GoLive documents.

With GoLive, you can create the extremely complex sequences of JavaScript necessary for smooth animation without ever writing a single line of code. But the software's secret weapon is a robust and powerful QuickTime editor that offers even more options for creating and incorporating animated graphics, video, and audio into your documents.

In this chapter, I'll cover

- ◆ Animation basics
- ◆ QuickTime authoring and editing
- ◆ Working with QuickTime movies
- ◆ QuickTime tracks

Animation Basics

GoLive uses two main tools to create DHTML animation: floating boxes (covered in Chapter 9, "Floating Boxes and Positioning") and the DHTML Timeline Editor (**Figure 20.1**). Using these in combination, you can trigger animation automatically when a page loads, set a timer to delay it, run it once or as a loop, or have the viewer trigger the animation with a mouse click or a rollover.

The contents of an animated floating box can be anything that you can place directly into a GoLive document or static floating box. That includes images, text, form elements, even plug-ins and Java applets. There are certain media types you should avoid animating, however. Animating a QuickTime movie, SWF animation, or even an animated GIF file generally requires too much processing power for any but the newest and fastest computers to display smoothly. Animating layout grids and tables can also be problematic.

Before you can animate, you must first add and configure the objects that are to be animated, along with the floating box that will contain the animation. To prepare an object for animation, you can use your image editor or, if you have Photoshop installed, use GoLive's own "Save For Web" feature (see Chapter 4, "Working with Images"). If your animation will include multiple versions of the same image that change as you animate them, copy the original image and use the duplicate when you make the changes that will appear in the animation.

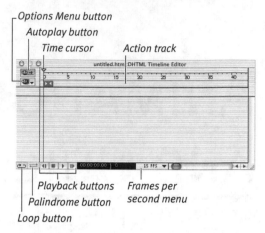

Options Menu button
Autoplay button
Time cursor   Action track

Playback buttons   Frames per
Palindrome button   second menu
Loop button

Figure 20.1 Use the DHTML Timeline Editor to trigger animations.

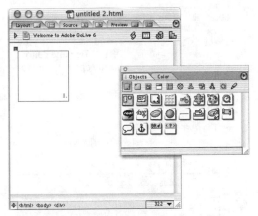

Figure 20.2 Drag a floating box into the layout window to begin building an element that will be animated.

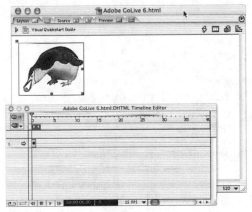

Figure 20.3 DHTML animation is based on using the GoLive floating box and the DHTML Timeline Editor.

To create a floating box for animation:

1. Add a floating box to a document by dragging or double-clicking the Floating Box icon from the Basic set of the Objects palette (**Figure 20.2**).

2. Drag the Image icon from the Basic set of the Objects palette into the floating box (**Figure 20.3**). If you double-click to add the image, it will appear in the document, but not inside the floating box.

3. Select the floating box and change its name in the Floating Box Inspector from "layer1" to something more descriptive. The name cannot include spaces or numbers.

4. Select the image placeholder and locate an image using the Image Inspector.

✔ Tips

■ If you drag an image file from the Finder or Windows Explorer directly into the floating box, it will become the background image for the floating box. If this is not your intention, link the graphic through the Image Inspector.

■ GIF and PNG files are perfectly suited for this type of animation since they can be set to have transparent backgrounds. PNG files have certain advantages: Their files sizes are, as a rule, smaller than comparable GIFs (up to 30 percent smaller) and they retain their color characteristics across platforms.

■ It is possible to animate text, so long as it's inside a floating box, but text has a tendency to reflow, disrupting your layout. You can ensure that animated text displays properly across platforms and browsers by applying a CSS style to text.

Beginning a Timeline

Once you've created your floating box, open the DHTML Timeline Editor by clicking its icon in the top-right corner of the Layout Editor (**Figure 20.4**). When you open the DHTML Timeline Editor, you'll see a list of all the floating boxes on your page. Each floating box has its own time track and can be animated independently. An arrow indicates the currently selected box, and the time slider (a vertical line) indicates the current time within the animation. In the time track, you should see a single keyframe (see sidebar below), indicated by a rectangular icon (**Figure 20.5**). This icon is solid for visible boxes and grayed out for invisible boxes.

Figure 20.4 Clicking the DHTML Timeline Editor button opens the editor.

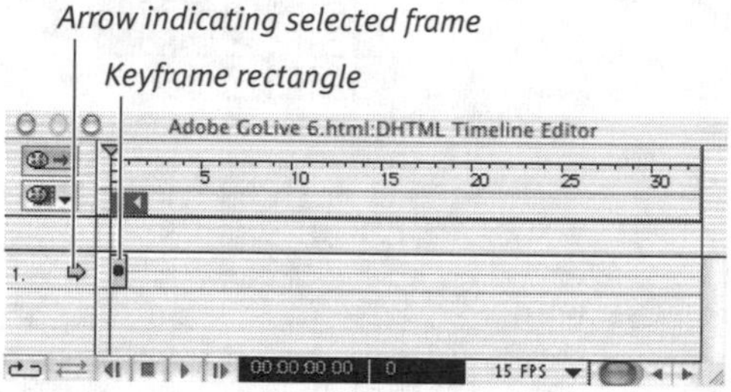

Arrow indicating selected frame

Keyframe rectangle

Adobe GoLive 6.html:DHTML Timeline Editor

Figure 20.5 When you first open the DHTML Timeline Editor, it shows one time track and a starting keyframe.

Animation 101

Here's a quick glossary of terms commonly applied to DHTML animations.

◆ **Actions** (see Chapter 19, "Using Actions") are prepackaged sets of JavaScripts and Cascading Style Sheet settings that can be used to control the behavior of a page or objects on a page. Animation-related actions are mostly in the Multimedia submenu of the Action Inspector or the Actions tab.

◆ **Animation frames** are the base time unit of animation. A frame is the single static image that represents a single state in an animation.

◆ **Frame rate** is the measure of how many frames are played in each second of animation; it's also called frames per second or FPS. GoLive defaults to 15 FPS. Slower frame rates result in jerkier animations, but require less processing power; faster frame rates create smoother animations, but might not play back on slower machines.

◆ **Keyframes** are markers within the animation that indicate the position or properties of an object at a given time.

◆ **Tweening** is what happens between keyframes in an animation. With GoLive, you set the keyframes indicating where you want the object to be at a given time; then GoLive automatically calculates the movement *between* those two points.

◆ **Time tracks** are viewed in the DHTML Timeline Editor and show the movement of an object in time. Time tracks are measured in frames.

◆ A **scene** is a single floating box, its contents, and its timeline, or a group of floating boxes you define. For any GoLive document, you can create as many scenes as you wish.

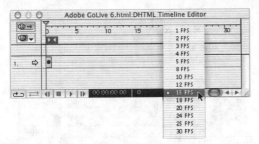

Figure 20.6 Choose the number of frames per second from the FPS pop-up menu at the bottom of the DHTML Timeline Editor.

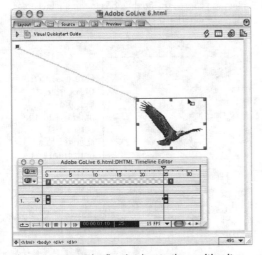

Figure 20.7 Drag the floating box to the position it should occupy for the selected keyframe. The gray line indicates the trajectory of the floating box from the starting point to the ending point.

Keyframes may seem intimidating at first, but remember, they just mark the position and properties of an object within the animation at a specific time. When you move your object and set another keyframe, GoLive will automatically figure out the motion required to get the object there smoothly and in the time allotted (called "tweening"). Naturally, the farther apart the keyframes are on the timeline, the more time the object has to move to its new position. Though you set the timing of movement in the DHTML Timeline Editor, you change the actual path of the box in the Layout Editor.

To create an animation:

1. At the bottom of the DHTML Timeline Editor you'll see a pop-up menu set to the default 15 FPS (**Figure 20.6**). Adjust this setting to achieve the desired effect, but remember that a high frame rate may not play (or may not play smoothly) on older machines.

2. Move the time slider to the position you'd like for your next keyframe.

3. With the floating box selected, Command-click (Mac) or Control-click (Windows) the timeline to set a new keyframe.

4. With the second keyframe selected, move the object to the position you'd like for this point in the animation. You should now see a faint gray line (**Figure 20.7**) between the two positions. This indicates the path along which the animation will travel.

5. To see the animation you just created, return to the DHTML Timeline Editor and select the first keyframe. The object will return to its original position.

(continues on next page)

6. Click the Play button (the right-pointing arrow) at the bottom of the DHTML Timeline Editor (**Figure 20.8**) to see your animation travel along its path and end at the last keyframe.

7. To play the animation in an endless loop, click the Loop button, and then click Play.

8. To make the animation play forward to the end, then backward to the beginning in a loop, with the Loop button clicked, click the Palindrome button, and then click Play.

✔ Tips

■ If you drag the first keyframe to the right, a grayed-out keyframe remains (**Figure 20.9**). Now when the animation is played, the object will not be visible until the "solid" keyframe is reached. You get the same effect if you set the floating boxes to invisible and use the GoLive Play Scene action, set to OnLoad so they start playing when the page is finished loading (see Chapter 19 for more on actions).

■ When selecting the floating box, be careful to select the box and not its contents. To do this, either select the floating box icon before dragging the box, or make sure the cursor changes to a horizontal hand (**Figure 20.10**) before you drag the box.

To add keyframes to an animation:

1. In the Document window, select the floating box.

2. In the DHTML Timeline Editor, Command-click (Mac) or Control-click (Windows) between two keyframes on the time track to insert a new keyframe.

3. With the keyframe selected, drag the floating box to a new position in the Document window (**Figure 20.11**). You'll see the animation path change as you move the keyframed position.

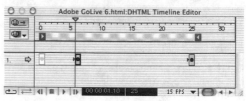

Figure 20.8 Click the right-pointing triangle (the Play button) to watch the animation.

Figure 20.9 Moving the first keyframe of the animation causes the floating box to remain invisible until the animation reaches the first "live" keyframe.

Figure 20.10 Grab the border of the box and drag, making sure the cursor first changes to a horizontal hand.

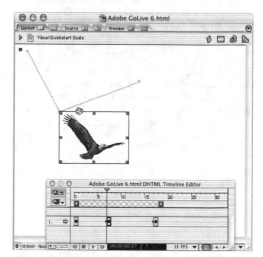

Figure 20.11 Adding a new keyframe between the first and last keyframes creates a point at which the animated object can change trajectory. Dragging the object away from the line between the start and end points changes the path.

Figure 20.12 Change the trajectory of an animation from the Floating Box Inspector's Animation pop-up menu.

Figure 20.13 Click the Record button in the Floating Box Inspector to record a complex animation path.

✔ Tip

■ GoLive errs on the side of creating too many keyframes rather than too few. Since extra keyframes can result in a needlessly complex animation, you should go back and carefully remove unnecessary ones from the time track. You can select multiple keyframes by Shift-clicking them or dragging over them, and then press Delete to remove them all at once.

Complex animation paths

To specify the shape of the path an animated floating box takes as it moves across the page, you can choose one of GoLive's several preset path shapes. You can also quickly and easily customize a path by moving the floating box while GoLive records its path and automatically generates keyframes, which you can edit later.

The preset path types are in the Animation menu of the Floating Box Inspector (**Figure 20.12**). None turns off GoLive's tweening function and causes the box to simply "appear" at each keyframe location at the appointed time; Linear, the default, moves the animation in a straight point-to-point line from one keyframe to the next; Curve moves the box along a curved path, creating a gentler, more organic type of movement; Random sends the floating box through a random series of gyrations as it moves from keyframe to keyframe.

To record a complex animation path:

1. Add a floating box to the Document window and place it at the starting point for the animation.

2. In the Floating Box Inspector, click the Record button (**Figure 20.13**).

3. Drag the floating box along the path you wish it to follow. As you drag, GoLive shows the path in the Document window. When you release the mouse button, GoLive stops recording and displays new keyframes in the DHTML Timeline Editor.

4. If you wish to adjust the timing of your animation, you can select a keyframe and drag it to a new position on the time track.

Animating multiple floating boxes

You can include multiple floating boxes in an animation. The Timeline Editor allows you to manage and set up each box on its own timeline.

To animate several objects:

1. Add three floating boxes to a new document and give them descriptive names.

2. Open the DHTML Timeline Editor and select box #2.

3. Position the box in the middle of the Document window. Note the arrow pointing to the time track for the selected box (**Figure 20.14**).

4. Without moving the box from its position in the Document window, add keyframes at frames 10, 20, 30, and 40. Notice that if you turn on looping by clicking the Loop button and then click Play, the timeline will move, but the floating box will not.

5. Select box #1 in the Document window. Note that the arrow in the DHTML Timeline Editor now points to the time track for box #1. In the Document window, move this box to a position to the left of and slightly above box #2 (**Figure 20.15**).

6. With box #1 still selected, add a keyframe at frame 10 in the DHTML Timeline Editor.

7. In the Document window, drag box #1 onto box #2 (**Figure 20.16**). Box #1 will appear to go behind box #2 because of its position in the stacking order. Add a keyframe at frame 20 in the time track for box #1.

Figure 20.14 Select the keyframe for floating box #2 in the DHTML Timeline Editor.

Figure 20.15 Floating box #1—containing the sports car image—is moved into position.

Figure 20.16 Drag box #1 to a position behind box #2. Stacking order determines which appears on top.

ANIMATION BASICS

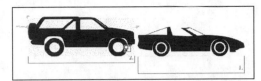

Figure 20.17 Continue dragging box #1 to a position below and to the right of box #2.

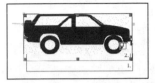

Figure 20.18 Change direction for the next keyframe, dragging box #1 once again behind box #2.

Figure 20.19 Returning to the approximate starting point completes a yo-yo-like relationship between boxes #1 and #2.

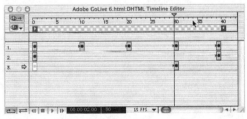

Figure 20.20 Drag the initial keyframe of box #3—the truck—so it lines up with the third keyframe of the other boxes. Now the box will not appear in the timeline until this point in the action.

8. Move box #1 to a position to the right of the box #2 (**Figure 20.17**) and insert another keyframe at frame 30. (If you have trouble selecting box #1 because it is stuck beneath box #2, select it from the Floating Boxes palette.)

9. Move box #1 back onto box #2 in the Document window (**Figure 20.18**) and insert a final keyframe for box #1 at frame 40.

10. Move box #1 back to its approximate starting point (**Figure 20.19**).

11. Click Play in the Timeline Editor to test the animation. Box #1 should slide "underneath" box #2 as it moves.

12. Select box #3. Drag its first keyframe to frame 30 (**Figure 20.20**) so that this object will be invisible until frame 30.

13. Drag box #3 over box #2 at frame 30. This will be its starting position when it becomes visible.

14. Without moving the box, add another keyframe at frame 40.

15. Click the Document window to deselect box #3. (If it is selected, it won't be invisible when you test the animation.)

16. Test the animation again. It should look the same, with box #1 sliding underneath box #2, until frame 30, when box #3 suddenly appears, hiding box #2.

✔ Tip

■ The DHTML Timeline Editor lists the boxes in the order they were added to the page, not their stacking order, or z-index (see Chapter 9). It's important to be aware of this third dimension when creating animations, as well as the fourth dimension of time.

Once you've established the movement for each object in your animation, you may wish to rearrange which items go "under" the others by changing the stacking order. Stacking order can be set at each individual animation position, so an object that was behind the others at one keyframe can appear in front of them at the next.

To change stacking order by keyframe:

1. Click the first keyframe of box #1 and type "1" in the Z-Index field of the Floating Box Inspector.

2. Move to the right in the time track, selecting the other keyframes in turn, and setting the z-index to 1 at frame 20, 2 at frame 20, 3 at frame 30, and 2 again at frame 40.

3. Select the keyframes for box #2, one by one, and set its z-index to 2, 2, 1, 1, and 1 at frame 40.

4. Select the keyframe for box #3 at frame 30 and set its z-index to 2. Select the keyframe at frame 40 and set it to 2 as well.

5. Click Play. Now box #1 crosses under box #2 and to the right. Returning, it crosses over box #2, which is seemingly replaced by box #3. When the animation is played, the relative positions between the floating boxes remain the same.

Figure 20.21 Click the Options menu in the DHTML Timeline Editor to rename a scene or add a new one.

Figure 20.22 A new set of tracks indicates the presence of a new scene in the DHTML Timeline Editor.

✔ Tips

- Do not attempt to control one floating box from two different scenes at the same time.

- The default method of playing back multiple scenes is to play them simultaneously after the page loads. Read the next section to learn how to use the Action track to control the timing of playback.

Working with multiple animations

Theoretically, there is no limit to the number of animated floating boxes you can include on a single Web page, but adding too many animated elements can cause instability and visual clutter.

GoLive lets you create and group multiple animations into *scenes*. With the DHTML Timeline Editor, you can build multiple animated scenes and run them concurrently sequentially, or control them with actions. (To learn about GoLive actions, see Chapter 19.)

To make a two-scene animation:

1. Create a complete animation.

2. Select Rename Scene from the Options menu in the upper-left corner of the Timeline Editor (**Figure 20.21**).

3. Name the new scene in the resulting dialog box and click OK.

4. Choose New Scene from the Options menu and name the scene. Three new time tracks appear in the DHTML Timeline Editor (**Figure 20.22**) and the new scene is displayed. Note that the set of floating boxes used in your first animation also appears in this set of time tracks.

5. Select the floating boxes to be used in the second scene and, by adding keyframes, build paths for the boxes' passage through the page. You may also choose to record the path of the floating box.

6. Preview the animation and edit the keyframes in the time track to make the animation as smooth as possible.

Controlling animation with the Action track

Just above the numbered time tracks in the Timeline Editor is the Action track (**Figure 20.23**). Actions inserted into this track are the same kinds of actions I showed you in Chapter 19, several of which are designed specifically to be used with and control animation—including playback. Actions occur when triggered in the timeline, or when an event such as a mouse click or keystroke occurs.

To control sequential playback with an action:

1. Click the Autoplay button in the DHTML Timeline Editor to deselect it on your second scene. Turn off looping and palindrome.

2. Select the first scene.

3. Command-click (Mac) or Control-click (Windows) in the Action track at a point near the end of the last keyframe. The Action Inspector opens and a question mark appears (**Figure 20.24**).

4. In the Action Inspector, choose Multimedia > Play Scene from the Action pop-up menu (**Figure 20.25**). The Scene pop-up menu appears; select the name of the second scene from it. The Play Scene icon (**Figure 20.26**) replaces the question mark in the Action track.

5. Use the playback controls to preview the animation.

✔ Tip

■ You can use other actions to further refine playback. For example, if you assign the Play Scene action to a button, visitors to your page will be able to start an animation with a click of their mouse.

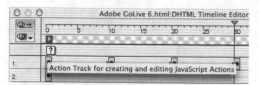

Figure 20.23 The Action track of the DHTML Timeline Editor is just above the area containing the keyframes.

Figure 20.24 An action placeholder appears when you Command-click (Mac) or Control-click (Windows) in the Action track of the DHTML Timeline Editor.

Figure 20.25 Select Play Scene as the controlling action from the Multimedia submenu in the Action Inspector.

Figure 20.26 The action's icon replaces the question mark.

QuickTime Authoring and Editing

Apple's QuickTime is a cross-platform, cross-browser, software package that delivers video, audio, and graphics using sprite animation, SWF files, and QuickTime VR. GoLive has a robust editor that taps into many of Quick-Time's interactive authoring functions, and also provides a fast and easy way to trim or combine video and audio clips. Even if you create and edit your video in another editor, GoLive's QuickTime Editor gives you the power to add such things as custom interactive controls and to incorporate disparate media types, such as linear video and Quick-Time VR in the same QuickTime movie. In this section you'll learn about GoLive's tools for creating and editing QuickTime, and its ability to add and manipulate these various media types.

QuickTime vs. Internet Explorer 5.5 and 6

Many people developing rich content in QuickTime were inconvenienced by Microsoft's decision to no longer support Netscape-style plug-ins, such as the QuickTime plug-in in Internet Explorer for Windows, beginning with version 5.5 SP2. At that time, GoLive's placeholder and default set-up for embedding QuickTime was no longer sufficient. Apple created an ActiveX control for QuickTime, but since most people didn't (and still don't) have it, you must include a "sniffer" that will install it if necessary. GoLive 6 now incorporates this by default when you drag the QuickTime icon from the Objects palette onto your page.

You should take a moment to prepare your files before beginning a QuickTime project with GoLive. Establish a media directory within your site. This will make working with and backing up these files much easier.

The primary tools within the GoLive QuickTime Editor are the Movie Viewer, the Timeline Editor (previously known as the Track Editor), and the QuickTime set of the Objects palette.

The Movie Viewer contains Preview and Layout tabs. The Layout tab lets you edit the visual movie components much the way you edit objects in a GoLive document's Layout Editor. You can position, resize, skew, and rotate the movie's visual tracks using the toolbar buttons, and transform and align tracks using the Transform and Align palettes.

The Timeline Editor serves as your primary editing work area, allowing you to edit samples, add and manipulate tracks, and control the sequence of events within the movie. Within the Timeline Editor you can edit, position, resize, rotate, skew, and lock tracks; make a movie streamable; and change the layering order of a track (**Figure 20.27**).

The QuickTime set of the Objects palette contains icons for all the track types that GoLive supports (**Figure 20.28**). To add a track to a movie, simply drag the appropriate icon to the Timeline Editor's track list.

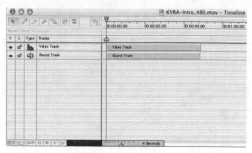

Figure 20.27 The Timeline Editor used to edit QuickTime movies looks something like the DHTML Timeline Editor used to build animations.

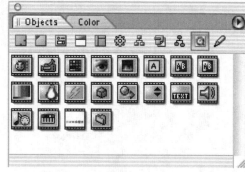

Figure 20.28 Add new tracks to a QuickTime movie with icons from the QuickTime set of the Objects palette.

Figure 20.29 Click this button on the toolbar to open the Timeline Editor.

Figure 20.30 If a movie is imported with video and sound tracks, they show up as separate tracks.

Figure 20.31 Name the movie in the New QuickTime Movie dialog box.

Figure 20.32 All size settings in the New QuickTime Movie dialog box are in pixels.

Figure 20.33 Choose a color for the background.

Working with QuickTime Movies

To begin using the QuickTime Editor you'll need to create a new QuickTime movie or open an existing one. If the movie you want to edit is already in a GoLive document, just double-click it in the Layout Editor and it will open directly in the QuickTime Editor. If the movie isn't yet in a document, choose File > Open and navigate to the movie file on your hard drive. Then either click the Show Timeline Window button on the toolbar (**Figure 20.29**) or choose Movie > Show Timeline Editor. The tracks contained within the open movie are displayed (**Figure 20.30**).

To create a new QuickTime movie:

1. Choose File > New Special > QuickTime Movie.

2. Type a name for the movie in the Name field of the New QuickTime Movie dialog box (**Figure 20.31**). The file name must end with the .mov extension.

3. Choose a size in pixels from the Sizes pop-up menu or type your own dimensions in the Width and Height fields (**Figure 20.32**). Because of the way QuickTime calculates images, it's best if both dimensions are divisible by 4. For example, 213 x 453 requires more processing power than 200 x 400.

4. Choose a background color for the track. The default is white. You can change it to any color you wish by clicking the Custom field and selecting a color (**Figure 20.33**).

5. Click OK. The Movie Viewer will open with the specified background color in place.

(continues on next page)

6. Open the Timeline Editor. The background color will be the only current track and it appears in the track list (**Figure 20.34**).

To annotate a movie:

1. Click in the Movie Viewer to activate it and open the Movie Inspector. (Make sure the whole movie is selected and not just one of its components.) You can choose a few options in the Basic tab of the Movie Inspector (**Figure 20.35**), which we'll cover later in this chapter.

2. Click the Annotation tab (**Figure 20.36**). This is where the information about the ownership and authorship of the movie is established and maintained. If a viewer opens the movie in the QuickTime Player and selects Movie Info, these fields become visible. Fill in the information you find useful.

✔ Tip

■ It's best to add your information to the annotations at the beginning of the process, since this is a step often overlooked. This is especially true if you are working on a number of movies.

Figure 20.34 Once you've chosen a color, GoLive will create a vector-based color track to act as a background. In a new movie, it will be the only active track.

Figure 20.35 Information about the movie appears in the Movie Inspector's Basic tab.

Figure 20.36 This type of information is called "metadata"; it helps identify the movie and its creators.

About Flattening

QuickTime movies are generally saved in one of two ways: with Allow Dependencies or as stand-alone or "flattened" movies. Like the graphics on a Web page, a QuickTime movie can be made up of references to external files (dependencies). Unlike a Web page, QuickTime gives you the option of storing most of these references internally. That is what is referred to as *flattening*—saving most or all of the external references within a single movie file. The two track types that always maintain their external links are movie and streaming tracks.

Figure 20.37 The Sample tools on the toolbar allow you to manipulate and edit the various track samples in the Timeline Editor.

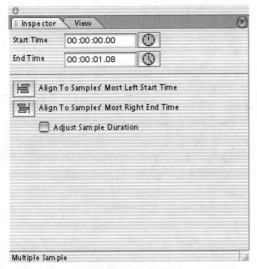

Figure 20.38 When you select multiple samples, the Multiple Sample Inspector appears.

Figure 20.39 You can also select multiple tracks, prompting the Multiple Track Inspector to appear.

QuickTime Tracks

Tracks are the source of QuickTime's authoring power and part of what sets it apart from other, similar technologies. In many ways QuickTime movies are like Russian nesting dolls. Each track type is a container for specific media content; within these containers, individual blocks of data are called *samples*. Many track types can have more than one sample (though only of one kind). For example, you could build a simple slide show by adding many picture samples into a single picture track along the timeline.

The Timeline Editor provides several tools for working with samples within a track, including Inspect/Move/Copy, Create, Divide, Glue, and Delete Sample (**Figure 20.37**). Each of these tools assigns certain characteristics to the sample, which can be manipulated in the Inspector. Selecting multiple samples opens the Multiple Sample Inspector (**Figure 20.38**), and selecting multiple tracks opens the Multiple Track Inspector (**Figure 20.39**).

Video tracks

QuickTime supports video in a wide variety of compressed formats. Most video editors (like Apple's Final Cut Pro or Adobe Premiere) are able to output to compressed or uncompressed video in a format that QuickTime understands.

While the list is too long to include here, its worth mentioning two of the most popular: DV (used by most digital video cameras) and Sorenson Video 2 and 3 (used to compress movie trailers for the Web).

QuickTime video is compressed because uncompressed video is too data intensive for even the fastest desktop computers to play back smoothly. For this reason, all video presented on the Web is compressed using a *codec* (compressor-decompressor).

To insert video tracks from another movie:

1. Open an existing movie or create a new one.

2. Open the Timeline Editor window (Movie > Show Timeline Editor)

3. Drag the Video Track icon (**Figure 20.40**) from the QuickTime set of the Objects palette into the track list in the left pane of the Timeline Editor (**Figure 20.41**). An Open dialog box appears.

4. Choose the QuickTime movie containing the video track you'd like to import. The first visible track of the selected movie will be added to the track list. If the movie has an audio track, that will also be added.

5. Rename the track if you wish by double-clicking its name in the track list or by selecting it in the Timeline Editor and editing the name in the Track Inspector.

To copy an individual track from another movie:

1. Open the source movie and the destination movie in GoLive.

2. Select the source movie.

3. Open the Timeline Editor.

4. Select the track you wish to copy from the source movie.

5. Choose Edit > Copy.

6. Switch to the destination movie and make sure it's selected in the Timeline Editor.

7. Choose Edit > Paste. The track copied from the source file appears in the Timeline Editor track list.

8. Rename the pasted track.

Figure 20.40 The Video Track icon appears in the QuickTime set of the Objects palette.

Figure 20.41 Drag the Video Track icon from the Quick-Time set of the Objects palette into the track list of the Timeline Editor.

✔ Tip

- You can also import animated GIF images into a QuickTime movie. Drag the Video Track icon into the Timeline Editor to set up an empty track. Then choose the animated GIF file, which will be converted into a video track.

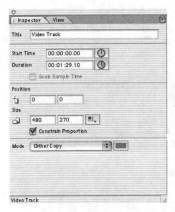

Figure 20.42
Like the other inspectors, the Video Track Inspector is used to name the track, as well as set its dimensions and position on the page.

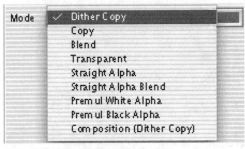

Figure 20.43 The Mode menu offers overlay modes for video tracks.

To set the properties of a video track:

1. Click a video track in the Timeline Editor to view the Video Track Inspector (**Figure 20.42**).

2. Enter the time at which you want the video track to start during the movie in the Start Time field.

3. Use the Duration box to set the length of the video track.

4. To shorten the time scale of a video sample (or any other sample for that matter), set the time slider to the new time, select the sample and click the clock button next to the Duration field in the Sample Inspector.

5. Set the horizontal and vertical coordinates for the video in the Position fields. QuickTime calculates the 0,0 coordinates as the top-left corner.

6. Change the track width and height in pixels. To scale the size of the track in relation to the other tracks, click the button to the right of the Size fields and choose Normalize Track/Set Track Dimensions.

7. Use the Mode menu to choose how the video track overlays other tracks (**Figure 20.43**). Dither Copy overlays the selected track by combining colors in the existing palette. Copy does this without dithering, making the track less color-rich. Blend makes the selected track translucent. Transparent defines a single Op color that will be transparent in the visual track. Alpha Channel creates complex masking effects that knock out a section of the image. Straight Alpha and Straight Alpha Blend combine the color qualities of each pixel at the same location in the movie. Premul White Alpha supports images with a white background and a premultiplied alpha channel. Premul Black Alpha supports images created on a black background with a premultiplied alpha channel.

Picture tracks

Picture tracks can either contain a single image or a series of static image samples in any graphics format that QuickTime can read. Some of the most commonly used are BMP, GIF, JPEG/JFIF, SWF (Flash 4), native Photoshop, PNG, TIFF, and QuickTime Virtual Reality (QTVR or Cubic VR).

To add a picture track:

1. With the Movie Viewer and the Timeline Editor open and active, drag the Picture Track icon (**Figure 20.44**) from the QuickTime set of the Objects palette into the track list in the Timeline Editor. The Picture Sample Inspector opens (**Figure 20.45**).

2. In the Picture Track Inspector (**Figure 20.46**), name the track and choose start time, duration, position, and size, just as you did for the video and movie tracks in the previous sections.

3. Click the Inspector's Images tab.

4. Choose whether the images will be inserted at the current time marker position (Insert Images) or if they will be a part of a slideshow, replacing previous images (Replace Images).

5. Click Import and in the Open dialog box, select an image (or images) to add.

6. Click Done to finish adding images.

Figure 20.44 Use the Picture Track icon from the QuickTime set of the Objects palette to add tracks for still images.

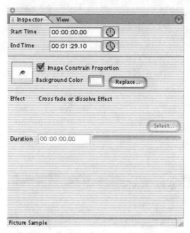

Figure 20.45 Add images to the track by clicking the somewhat-misnamed Replace button in the Picture Sample Inspector.

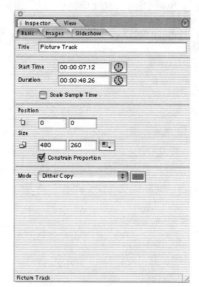

Figure 20.46 Configure a picture track in the Basic tab of the Picture Track Inspector.

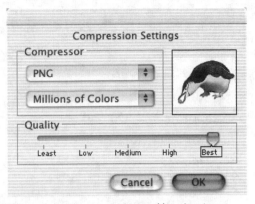

Figure 20.47 After you add image(s) to the picture track, you will see a Compression Settings dialog box where you can choose the type and quality of compression you want to apply to the image.

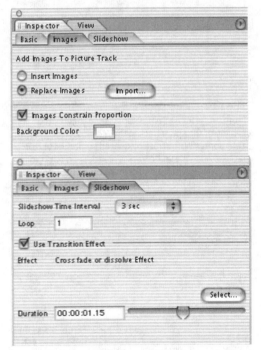

Figure 20.48 In the Picture Track Inspector, you can set the picture track properties using the Images and Slideshow tabs.

Figure 20.49 Click Play to preview a movie and the new picture track.

7. When the Compression Settings dialog box appears (**Figure 20.47**), change the compression, bit depth, and quality settings if you wish, then click OK to return to the Picture Sample Inspector. I favor the PNG compression method.

8. Working in the Images and Slideshow tabs, set the other properties for the image or images (**Figure 20.48**).

9. In the Movie Viewer, click the Play button (**Figure 20.49**) to preview the movie, including the new picture track.

Sprite tracks

Sprites are graphics files, in any media format that QuickTime understands, that can be interactive or animated. Sprites can have specific GoLive actions that occur at the events Mouse Click, Mouse Enter, Mouse Exit, Mouse Down, and Mouse Up. For example, a sprite can be used to play sounds on a mouse click, jump to another point in the movie, or start and stop video playback. These actions make use of interactive components built into the QuickTime architecture. These components are called "wired atoms," so interactive QuickTime movies are often referred to as "wired" movies by QuickTime authors.

To add a sprite track:

1. Drag the Sprite icon from the QuickTime set of the Objects palette into the left-hand pane of the Timeline Editor. A new sprite track will appear in the track list and the Sprite Track Inspector opens.

2. Name the sprite and set its options in the Basic set as you would for other kinds of QuickTime tracks.

(continues on next page)

3. Next, click the Sprites tab in the Sprite Track Inspector and set preferences related to the appearance and activity of sprites (**Figure 20.50**).

4. In the Add New Sprites box, enter the desired number of sprites.

To add images to a sprite track's image pool:

1. Select the sprite track in the track list. Click the Images tab of the Sprite Track Inspector and select a still image to use as the first sprite (**Figure 20.51**).

2. Follow step 7 in "To add a picture track" (**Figure 20.52**).

3. Return to the Images tab and click the Import button.

4. Navigate to the folder containing your images, select each one, and click Add. When all the images are added, click Done.

5. In the Compression Settings dialog box, select a compression scheme for your images. Once again, I've selected PNG, rather than the default JPEG setting.

6. Select a color depth from the pop-up menu. Unless your images are black-and-white or file size is of special concern, leave it set to Millions.

7. Select a level with the Quality slider. Again, unless there's a pressing need to do otherwise, leave it set to Best.

8. Click OK to close the Compression Settings dialog box. The sprite images appear in the subtracks below the sprite track (**Figure 20.53**), each assigned a name (Sprite 1, Sprite 2, etc.) and a keyframe on each track.

9. Click one of the new sprite keyframes to open the Sprite Object Inspector.

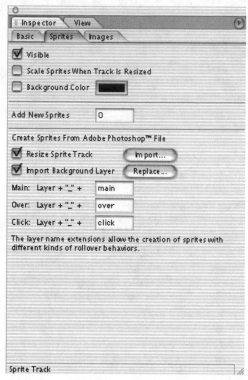

Figure 20.50 In the Sprites tab, Visible toggles the visibility of the sprite track in the Movie Viewer window; Scale Sprites When Track Is Resized smoothes vector graphics when the sprite track is resized; and Background Color sets the background color of the sprite track (the default is black).

Figure 20.51 In the Images tab of the Sprite Track Inspector, add to the image pool of the sprite track.

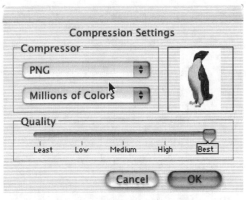

Figure 20.52 When you add images as sprites, the Compression Settings dialog box opens.

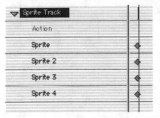

Figure 20.53 Each sprite is assigned its own subtrack beneath the sprite track.

Interactive Buttons

GoLive makes it easy to create custom wired buttons using graphics from Photoshop. Design an interface using Photoshop's layers. Build your button rollovers in three states: the main (neutral) state, the over state, and the click (down) state. Put each state in a separate layer with whatever effects, such as glows and color changes, flattened into the layer. Don't use layer styles, because the GoLive QuickTime Editor won't recognize them. Create a single Photoshop file with buttons laid out together, instead of separate files. Name each layer using this convention:

◆ Main state: `layername_main`

◆ Mouse over state: `layername_over`

◆ Mouse click state: `layername_click`

For example, `Button1_main`, `Button1_over`, and `Button1_click` create a single sequence.

10. Rename the sprite so that you can easily identify it.

11. Click the sprite track, and open the Basic tab of the Sprite Track Inspector. Use the settings to position the selected sprite in the Movie Viewer.

Adding behaviors to sprites

In the same way you can attach actions to events (such as a mouse click, or rollover) you can attach actions to sprites. Sprites have a unique set of actions that act on the various track types. Using the Sprite Sample Inspector with the individual sprite's keyframe selected, you can do things like change the movie's playback speed, or switch child movies in a movie track at the click of a sprite.

Adding an action to a sprite is basically like adding an action to any other element. Choose the individual sprite by selecting its keyframe, and from the Sprite Sample Inspector, choose the event that will trigger the action. Then, from the Action pop-up menu, select an action. A description of the selected action appears, along with a dialog box that allows you to fill in the action's parameters.

GoLive includes a number of QuickTime-specific actions. There are many actions available to sprites, so check out www.peachpit.com/vqs/golive6 for a more complete list.

✔ Tip

■ You can't target the QuickTime player to open and play a movie from an HTML page. If you want to launch a movie into the QuickTime player, create a sprite and use the GoTo URL action with the target `_quicktimeplayer`.

Filter tracks

QuickTime supports built-in effects, known as *transitions* and *filters*. Effects tracks are used to apply these to other visual tracks in the movie. GoLive provides for four types of filter tracks: one-source filter, two source filter, three-source filter, and generic filter.

One source filter tracks are actually image filters that can be applied to any visual track.

Generic filter tracks provide access to three special visual filters: cloud, fire, and ripple.

Two- and three-source filter tracks are actually misnamed and are not filters at all. In fact, they provide various transitions from one visual track to another. For this example, we'll use a two-source filter track. Adding a three-source filter is much the same—except, of course, you have three sources instead of two.

To create a transition using a two- or three-source filter track:

1. Create a movie containing multiple visual tracks. These can be video or picture tracks.

2. Drag the Two Source Filter Track icon from the QuickTime set of the Objects palette into the Timeline Editor's track list. Make sure the filter track appears below the track you want to add your transition to (setting it closer to the viewer).

3. Use the Two Source Filter Track Inspector (**Figure 20.54**) to set the properties of the track.

4. Choose a visual track from the Source A pop-up menu and another from the Source B menu.

5. In the Timeline Editor, click the triangle to the left of the track to expand it so you can edit the sample.

Figure 20.54 Set properties in the Two Source Filter Track Inspector.

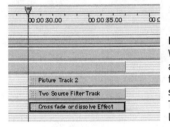

Figure 20.55
Set effects in the Two Source Filter Sample Inspector.

Figure 20.56
When you have added and configured a two-source track, the Timeline Editor looks like this.

6. Use the Create Sample tool to create a sample bar and sample content area by drawing the sample into the sample track. For this type of transition, you should set your visual tracks to overlap, then set your filter track the length and in the position of the overlap. The Two Source Filter Sample Inspector now opens (**Figure 20.55**).

7. Click the Select button to open the Select Effect dialog box.

8. Choose an effect from the list.

9. Click OK. The Sample Content bar now contains the name of the effect (**Figure 20.56**).

10. Choose whether you want the effect to transition from Source A to B or Source B to A.

11. Preview the movie in the Movie Viewer to see the filter. You can adjust the filter in the Timeline Editor or in the Layout tab of the Movie Viewer.

SWF tracks

Macromedia Flash and Adobe LiveMotion can create interactive animations and vector artwork in the Shockwave/Flash (SWF) format. QuickTime allows you to import files created in this format. One of the main advantages of presenting SWF files this way is that it eliminates the need for multiple plug-ins, since both the QuickTime and SWF content are presented within the Quick-Time container. SWF files retain their own interactivity and animation within QuickTime and can interact with QuickTime sprites.

To add a SWF track to a QuickTime movie, simply drag the SWF Track icon from the QuickTime set of the Objects palette into the Timeline Editor. A new track appears and you can use the SWF Track Inspector to configure it further.

✔ Tips

■ The Two and Three Source Filter Sample Inspectors allow you to save filters for later use in another movie. Open a saved filter by clicking Load (in the Select Effect dialog box) via the same Inspector that originally generated it.

■ This is one of those times when "can" doesn't mean "should." Since QuickTime renders these filters and transitions "on-the-fly," they may not play back well, particularly on older machines or where bandwidth is limited. It's better to do your filtering and transitions in your original editing program or an encoding program.

Sound, MIDI, and instrument tracks

QuickTime supports a wide variety of sound formats (such as AIFF, AVI, MP3, MIDI, and Wave) and sound compression Some of the most commonly used are: IMA 4:1, MACE 6:1, Q-Design Music, and Qualcomm PureVoice).

Sound tracks must be generated in a separate sound-editing application (which may be the same one used for video) and are often linked to a video file.

MIDI tracks play back sounds created in an external application that uses MIDI (Musical Instrument Digital Interface) as its format.

Instrument tracks allow you to create music and sound effects right inside QuickTime. They're a great way to add sounds for events like button clicks and mouse rollovers without adding much to the file size. The only drawback is that the end user must have installed the QuickTime Musical Instruments component, which is not part of the minimal QuickTime install.

To add music and sound tracks:

1. Open a movie containing at least one visual track and open the Timeline Editor.

2. Drag the MIDI Track or Sound Track icon (**Figure 20.57**) from the QuickTime set of the Objects palette into the Timeline Editor's track list. Since this isn't a visual track, it doesn't matter what layer it sits on.

3. When you drop the Sound Track icon into the Timeline Editor, you'll see an Open dialog box. Choose a sound file and it will be inserted at the current position of the play head.

Figure 20.57 The Sound Track icon is in the QuickTime set of the Objects palette.

4. Click Play in the Timeline Editor to see how well the sound file synchronizes with the existing tracks.

5. To change the duration of the sound or music track, enter a new value in the Duration field of the Sound Track Inspector, or change the track's start and end points on the track. Note that this will affect the sound of the track, speeding it up or slowing it down.

Chapter, HREF, and text tracks

Text tracks display either static or animated text within the movie. They may also contain specialized text data—chapter and HREF tracks are really just specialized text tracks modified to perform a specific function.

Text tracks can be used to add captions and even subtitles to a movie, while chapter tracks act much the same as the chapter tracks on a DVD, allowing you to navigate instantly to a predefined place within the movie. Text tracks and HREF tracks can also contain links, just like text links in a GoLive document.

Let's start with HREF tracks, since they're one of the most powerful implementations of text tracks. You can use HREF tracks to create links that remain active for a specific period of time or an action that automatically launches a URL in time with the movie. This is called *integrated synchronous media*, and it can be an impressive presentation form. For example, you could use it with a speech to make graphical information (such as slides) pop up in time with the video in another frame.

To add an HREF track:

1. Open a movie file and the Timeline Editor.

2. Drag the HREF Track icon (**Figure 20.58**) from the QuickTime set of the Objects palette to the track list in the Timeline Editor.

3. To make the HREF track visible, click the eye icon in the track list (**Figure 20.59**).

4. Configure the options for the HREF track in the HREF Track Inspector, as necessary.

5. In the Timeline Editor, click the triangle next to the name of the HREF track to display the sample (**Figure 20.60**).

6. Click the Create Sample button (**Figure 20.61**) to create the sample content bar for this sample (**Figure 20.62**).

7. With the sample selected, Browse, Point & Shoot, or type the URL in the Link field of the URL Sample Inspector.

8. From the Target pop-up menu, choose where the link should open. As I stated earlier, if the target is another QuickTime movie and you'd like to open it in the QuickTime player, target _quicktime-player.

9. If you want the link to open automatically, check the Autoload URL box. If the box is not checked, the link can be activated only by the viewer clicking on the movie at the appropriate time.

Figure 20.58 The HREF Track icon appears in the QuickTime set of the Objects palette.

Figure 20.59 Click the eye icon to make the new HREF track's name display in the sample.

Figure 20.60 Click the triangle next to the HREF track name.

Figure 20.61 To activate the Create Sample tool, click the Create Sample icon.

Figure 20.62 The Create Sample tool is used to draw the sample content bar, which represents the sample in the Timeline Editor.

Chapter tracks are a simple way to give a movie navigation features like the chapter or scene selections often found on DVDs. Since they're really just text tracks, they're a great way to add some interactivity to a movie without a significant increase in processing demand.

To create a chapter track:

1. Drag the Chapter Track icon from the QuickTime set of the Objects palette into the Timeline Editor to create a Chapter Track. The Chapter Track Inspector opens.

2. Name the chapter track in the Title field of the Chapter Track Inspector. The name is important, as it will display in the movie's control bar and allow viewers to jump to the named chapter.

3. Use the "Act as Chapter Track for" pop-up menu to set the track that this will act as the chapter track for. For most movies this is the video track.

4. Click the sample and use the Duration field to set the duration for this Chapter sample.

5. As previously mentioned, some tracks can have multiple samples. Chapter tracks are among these. Use the Create Sample tool (the pencil) to add additional chapter samples and set their titles and durations.

6. Preview your movie in the Movie Viewer. You should see your chapter titles visible in the chapter pop-up.

7. If necessary, resize the movie to accommodate the new pop-up menu, and choose a chapter from the list.

Text in a QuickTime movie has all the advantages and disadvantages of text in any GoLive document. For example, you have access to your complete list of fonts, but your text may appear in strange and unpredictable ways to a viewer who doesn't have the same fonts. Size is also an issue, since text displays larger on a PC than it does on a Mac. On the plus side, if you want to add links to your movie, using QuickTime text to do it demands much less processing power than using other track types.

To add a text track:

1. Drag the Text icon from the QuickTime set of the Objects palette into the Timeline Editor.

2. Set the track's properties in the Text Track Inspector (**Figure 20.63**).

3. In the Timeline Editor, click the triangle to the left of the new text track's name and open the sample. Set the duration of the sample using the Samples tools.

4. With the sample selected, open the Text Sample Inspector (**Figure 20.64**). Select the Text tab and enter your text in the text box. Click Apply to have the text appear in the movie.

5. Using the Align pop-up menu, choose the text alignment.

6. Click the Layout tab of the Text Sample Inspector and set any other options you choose (margin settings, background color, and so forth).

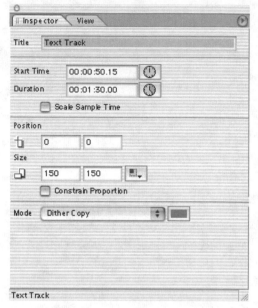

Figure 20.63 Configure text tracks is the Text Track Inspector.

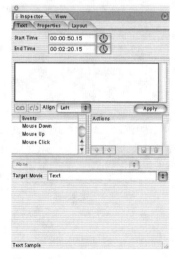

Figure 20.64 Enter text in the Text Sample Inspector.

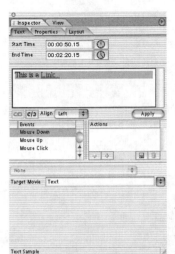

Figure 20.65
Text chosen for
a link changes
to blue with an
underline.

Figure 20.66 A movie multiplayer uses a video window created from a movie track, just like switching channels on a TV set.

To add a link to a text track:

1. In the Text tab of the Text Sample Inspector, select the text that you want to make a link.

2. Click the Link button. The linked text will turn blue and be underlined (**Figure 20.65**).

3. From the Events list in the Text Sample Inspector, select the event that will trigger the link action.

4. Click the New Item button, and then select an action from the Action pop-up menu. Typically this would be GoTo URL.

5. If you chose GoTo URL, use the Link field to set a destination URL and click Apply.

Movie tracks

A movie track isn't a real track at all; it's a container that can include externally referenced movies—even a movie sitting on a Web server. These can be in any form that QuickTime understands: graphics, video, audio, even movies with other movie tracks. The main movie that holds the movie track as well as any other sort of track is called the "root" or "parent" movie. The external movies are usually called "child" movies, though if a child movie has its own movie track (a "grandchild"), it takes on its own child and parent relationship.

Movie tracks allow you to tap into one of QuickTime's most powerful features, Movie-in-a-Movie, or MIAM. One common application for movie tracks is creating multiplayer parent movies that use sprites (discussed earlier in this chapter) and attached actions as controls to load several different child movies into a single video window within the parent movie. Think of it like television, with different channels offering different content within the same container. (**Figure 20.66**).

Unlike video tracks, movie tracks don't store their information within the movie, even when flattened. As with graphics in a Web page, it's important to make sure that the child movie file is where the parent movie expects to find it.

To add a movie track:

1. Open an existing movie or create a new one.

2. Open the Timeline Editor (Movie > Show Timeline Editor).

3. Drag the Movie Track icon (**Figure 20.67**) from the QuickTime set of the Objects palette into the track list in the left pane of the Timeline Editor.

4. In the Movie Viewer, you'll now see "Failed to Load" in the movie track you've just added. You must now add a URL for the child movie. Click the URL tab in the Inspector and enter the URL of the child movie (**Figure 20.68**). As with Web pages, URLs can be relative or absolute, local or on a Web server.

✔ Tip

■ If the URL entered in the Link field identifies a streaming video—that is, it points to a movie located on a QuickTime streaming server using RTSP (Real-Time Streaming Protocol)—click the Get Movie Properties button. This opens a connection to the RTSP URL to obtain attributes of the streaming movie, including dimensions and duration. Use the Timeout popup menu to determine when the connection attempt is deemed unsuccessful. This option applies only to working within GoLive and does not apply to a browser.

To edit a movie track:

1. Click the movie track in the Timeline Editor to open the Movie Track Inspector (**Figure 20.69**).

Figure 20.67 The Movie Track icon is the first track icon in the QuickTime set of the Objects palette.

Figure 20.68 Add the URL of the child movie in the URL tab of the Movie Track Inspector.

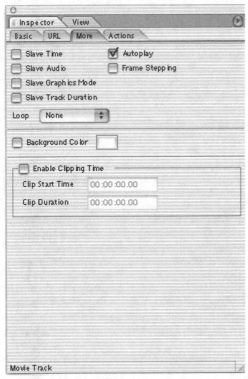

Figure 20.69 The Move tab of the Movie Track Inspector allows you to select the slave settings.

2. Enter the time at which you want the movie track to begin during the movie in the Start Time field.

3. Enter the length of the movie track in the Duration field. The track length doesn't have to match the length of the child movie. A movie with a length of 1 second can play a child movie of any length, as long as it's properly configured.

4. Set the size (in pixels) and position for the movie track. To scale the size of the track relative to other tracks, click the button to the right of the Size fields and choose Normalize Track or Set Track Dimension.

5. Use the Mode menu to set the drawing mode for the track. This determines how the track displays relative to the tracks behind it.

6. Use the Type pop-up menu to set how the child movie will display in the movie track window.

There are several display options that control how the child movie displays in the video window. The most commonly used are these: None displays the movie within the window, but makes no change in the size or proportion of the child movie. Fill Movie will display the entire child movie within the track by scaling it to match the dimension of the track exactly. If the child movie is not proportional to the track, it will cause the movie to be stretched or squashed. Meet Movie reduces or enlarges the child movie to fit the smallest dimension of the track, but maintains the aspect ration of the original. Slice Movie reduces or enlarges the file's dimensions to fit the smaller dimension of the track. It doesn't change the aspect ration, but does clip the larger dimension of the image.

In the More tab of the Movie Track Inspector, choose the appropriate slave settings for the movie. When a child is "slaved" to its parent, it takes on settings from the parent (see Figure 20.69). Slave Time restricts the embedded file from playing until the parent movie time reaches the file's start time; Slave Audio discards audio in the embedded file and uses the parent movie's audio; Slave Graphics Mode uses the parent movie's graphics mode instead of the embedded file's; Slave Track Duration sets the movie track's duration to the full length of the embedded file; Enable Clipping Time lets you specify what portion of the embedded file's clip will play.

In the Actions tab of the Movie Track Inspector, select the Movie Loaded event, then click the New Item button to add an action for the child movie to perform as soon as it is loaded. (For more on adding actions, see the section on sprites.) Choose an action from the pop-up menu, set its properties, and click Apply.

Streaming content tracks

A streaming track is a reference to an RTSP stream. RTSP streams can be audio, video, or both. Other track types cannot be streamed, but it is possible to combine streaming (RTSP) and non-streaming (HTTP or Progressive) components in the same movie. For example, you can have complex media skins that include sprites or SWF tracks and a streaming track. The streaming content streams and the rest is downloaded by progressive download to the viewer.

To add a streaming track to a QuickTime movie, simply drag the Streaming Track icon from the QuickTime set of the Objects palette into the Timeline Editor. A new track appears, and you can use the Streaming Track Inspector to configure the track further.

Media Skins

With the addition of several new track types in GoLive 6, Adobe has managed to include most, though not all, of Quick-Time's native track types. The most notable exception is the QuickTime 5 "skin" track, which allows you to completely customize the look and functionality of the QuickTime player by creating a *custom media skin*. A more detailed discussion of media skins is beyond the scope of this book, but advanced readers can find more information at www.peachpit.com/vqs/golive6.

QUICKTIME TRACKS

DYNAMIC CONTENT

All kinds of Web sites depend on databases to supply their content. Commerce sites, search engines, and portals are obvious examples of sites that query a database to deliver information requested by users. Any large site, though, where information must be continually updated can benefit from a data-driven approach. GoLive's Dynamic Content module and other tools included with the software can help you develop data-driven Web sites and connect their pages to databases or other data source. Though a full explanation of dynamic content is beyond the scope of this book, I will give you an overview of how it works and the choices and tasks required to implement it, so that you can decide whether and how to use it.

If you do not currently have a data-driven Web site, chances are very high that you will need to hire or acquire expertise to build and maintain the site, and even to choose the combination of tools.

In this chapter, I'll cover

◆ Dynamic content basics

◆ Dynamic content resources

Dynamic Content Basics

Dynamic Web sites work by connecting a database or other data source to a Web server and, ultimately, to site visitors' browsers. To build a dynamic site, you must extract information from a data source and create pages that can display the information in a browser. GoLive provides the tools to do both.

Known as Dynamic Link in version 5, Dynamic Content is a GoLive module and a collection of tools that you can use to build data-driven Web sites. The dynamic content package on the GoLive CD now includes two Web servers (Apache and Tomcat), along with scripting languages (ASP, JSP, and PHP), sample databases, and sample sites. GoLive itself supports dynamic content with the dynamic content module. It is enabled by default, and activates the Dynamic Content set in the Objects palette and the Dynamic Content toolbar.

Elements of a dynamic site

Dynamic Web sites (whether created in GoLive or not) include these basic elements:

◆ **Databases** provide the content in dynamic sites. Most often, these are relational databases that consist of tables, records, and fields representing everything from product catalogs to indexes of searchable documents. GoLive supports several databases, including Microsoft Access and SQL Server; Oracle and other ADO-compliant (ActiveX Data Objects) databases; and databases accessed through Open Database Connectivity (ODBC), such as FileMaker Pro.

◆ **Data sources** define the way information is requested from a database. Data sources serve as pointers—containing the name and location of the database. A data source may itself be a database, or it may be an XML file or a form. A data source may also control the way permissions are applied when accessing a database.

◆ The **Web server** (hardware) stores the static elements of the Web site and the scripts that communicate with the database and result in dynamic pages. It's also the Web server's (software) job to combine dynamic content with static pages and deliver the results to site visitors' browsers. The GoLive Dynamic Content package includes versions of the Apache, PHP, and Tomcat Web servers, giving you a choice of staging platform for dynamic sites. You can build or deploy your site using your choice of Web server software, so long as it is compatible with the scripts and databases you'll be working with.

◆ **Server scripts** contain instructions to the Web server and the database for delivering and displaying dynamic content in a browser. GoLive's dynamic content supports the three most widely used Web scripting languages: Microsoft ASP (Active Server Pages), Sun JSP (Java Server Pages), and PHP (hypertext preprocessor). Server scripts are embedded in the dynamic template pages you create using GoLive's dynamic content tools.

◆ **Template pages** provide a shell into which dynamic content is poured. These pages are not GoLive templates, but standard HTML pages. They can include the navigation and other design elements of your site, along with placeholders for dynamic content.

GoLive's Dynamic Content module and the supplied server software can take you from site planning and building to dynamic site implementation—at least in a testing environment. In order to mount a fully functional dynamic site on the Web, you'll need database software and content, as well as the server hardware to support it. These things may exist within your organization. Having access to them, especially a database, during the development of your site, will be extremely helpful as you debug it and add dynamic capabilities.

If you don't have full access to databases and Web servers, the tools included with GoLive will allow you to build a functioning dynamic site for testing purposes.

Dynamic Content Resources

Building dynamic sites requires more than
an understanding of GoLive's dynamic content interface, however. You'll need to learn
something about configuring Web server
software, preparing data sources, and using
the scripting language that will make your
site dynamic. Your first stop should be the
GoLive documentation, which explains many
of the configuration and development tasks
you'll do within GoLive. You'll also find an
overview of the server-side tools supplied
with GoLive, allowing you to choose the
right combination of database, data source,
Web server software and scripts. For more
general information on these topics, check
out online resources that provide documentation, software, and links to even more
resources (**Table 21.1**).

Table 21.1

Scripting and Web Server Resources
Check out these Web sites for details about the server-side software used with dynamic content.

ASP Data Access for Beginners	www.15seconds.com/Issue/001025.htm
Sun Chili!Soft ASP	www.chilisoft.net
JSP	www.apl.jhu.edu/~hall/java/Servlet-Tutorial
PHP	www.php.net
PHP Documentation	www.fokus.gmd.de/linux/httpd-help/php/manual/manual.html
Apache	http://httpd.apache.org/
IIS	www.microsoft.com/windows2000/technologies/web/default.asp

INDEX

INDEX

WWW.PEACHPIT.COM

Quality How-to Computer Books

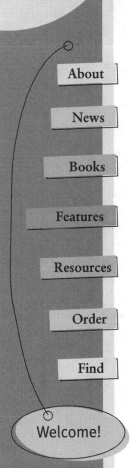

- About
- News
- Books
- Features
- Resources
- Order
- Find
- Welcome!

Visit Peachpit Press on the Web at www.peachpit.com

- Check out new feature articles each Monday: excerpts, interviews, tips, and plenty of how-tos

- Find any Peachpit book by title, series, author, or topic on the Books page

- See what our authors are up to on the News page: signings, chats, appearances, and more

- Meet the Peachpit staff and authors in the About section: bios, profiles, and candid shots

- Use Resources to reach our academic, sales, customer service, and tech support areas and find out how to become a Peachpit author

Peachpit.com is also the place to:

- Chat with our authors online
- Take advantage of special Web-only offers
- Get the latest info on new books